THE JEW

ESSAYS FROM
MARTIN BUBER'S JOURNAL
𝕯𝖊𝖗 𝕵𝖚𝖉𝖊, 1916–1928

Selected, edited, and introduced by
Arthur A. Cohen

Translated from the German by
Joachim Neugroschel

The University of Alabama Press
University, Alabama

Library of Congress Cataloging in Publication Data

Main entry under title:

The Jew, essays, from Martin Buber's journal Der
    Jude, 1916–1928.

  (Judaic studies   ;   )

   1. Judaism—Addresses, essays, lectures.
 2.   Zionism—Addresses, essays, lectures.
 3.   Judaism—Germany—Addresses, essays, lectures.
 I.   Cohen, Arthur Allen, 1928–   II.   Der Jude.
 III.   Series.
 BM40.J39   296'.08   79-10610
 ISBN 0-8173-6908-2

CONTENTS

ACKNOWLEDGMENTS

The suggestion to undertake this selection and presentation from the pages of Der Jude first arose in conversation with Morgan L. Walters, then director of The University of Alabama Press. I welcomed the opportunity of such a difficult task, principally because I had in my library two complete runs of the periodical and the various special issues with which it concluded its precarious existence. It seemed to me an admirable means of enforcing study. I do not regret the undertaking, although I wish that so much time had not elapsed between my commitment to the project and my ability to fulfill it. Many other projects intervened, claiming my time; moreover, the difficulties of rendering the often infelicitous syntax of the original made for problems that not even the splendid Joachim Neugroschel could always overcome. I have been fortunate, therefore, in having the assistance of my friend, Laurance Wieder, who worked closely with me in the editing of the translations and the reconstruction of often impenetrable passages.

My old friends in scholarship, Professors Nahum N. Glatzer, Steven S. Schwarzschild, and Ernst Simon offered suggestions, comments, and elucidations that assisted my pursuit of the somewhat elusive history of this remarkable periodical.

My particular thanks to Professor Leon J. Weinberger, who contributed revisions of many of the notes in David Baumgardt's essay, bringing it more into consonance with recent studies on the development of the Hebrew liturgy. His notes to this essay are signed L.J.W.

I am most grateful to Professor Robert Rosen of Baruch College, who helped me with the translation of some of the Yiddish poems in Moses Calvary's essay and for his scholarship about Yiddish and plattdeutsch.

I should like as well to acknowledge the warm cooperation of Rafael Buber and Rafael Rosenzweig, who were gracious in permitting me to have translated essays by Martin Buber and Franz Rosenzweig. Martinus Nijhoff, publisher of the Franz Rosenzweig Gesammelte Schriften, has granted permission for the publication of an English translation of "Apologetic Thinking."

In addition to those aforementioned I should like to thank Hilde Kaufmann, Gertrude Hallo, and Professor Jacob Taubes for responding to various appeals for help. The library of the Leo Baeck Institute was also a source of much valuable information.

ARTHUR A. COHEN

For Martin Buber (1878–1965)
on the centenary of his birth,
and to the Jews of Germany,
living and dead, for whom
Der Jude was published

THE JEW

INTRODUCTION

How astonishing it is that a monthly magazine published in the German language during and after World War I should call itself, quite simply, *The Jew*. That a periodical should regard itself as having sufficient breadth and sensitivity to speak, if not for all Jews, than at least to all Jews, that it should be *The Jew* that spoke, that it is the encompassing Jew (not simply the Jewish ingredient in everyone or the German or professional man or city dweller or artist and betimes Jew) who is straightforwardly and unabashedly addressed—all this is even more remarkable. That it was a personal journal, a periodical founded by one man and printed and distributed in its final years by the publishing house he had helped to establish, explains something of the forthrightness that its masthead claimed. Even so, calling the periodical *The Jew* (not merely a vehicle of Jewish opinion or Jewish religion or Jewish *Wissenschaft*) says something about its audience as well as about its auspices. It would be hard to imagine the postman dropping such a periodical into the mailboxes of American Jews. Yet in Berlin, Vienna, Prague, and all the countries of the European Jewish dispersion there arrived with relative punctuality each month between April 1916 and 1923 (and irregularly thereafter), wrapped but not concealed, this periodical called *The Jew*.

Martin Buber (1878–1965), the most prodigious figure among modern European Jewish intellectuals, founded his periodical *Der Jude* in 1916. Though still a relatively young man, Buber was regarded as one of the most significant modern littérateurs and German stylists; several careers, each one sufficient to have established the reputations of less ambitious talents, were already behind him. By 1916 he had published numerous translations and commentaries on the Hasidic mystics, including *Die Geschichten des Rabbi Nachman (The Tales of Rabbi Nachman)* (1905); *Die Legende des Baal Schem (The Legend of the Baal Shem)* (1908); an edition of the Kalevala, the national epic of the Finns; selections from Tschuang-Tse; and a thematic anthology of the mystic tradition, *Ekstatische Konfessionen (Ecstatic Confessions)* (1909). A mystic, anthologizer of mystics, and gatherer of mystical events and personae, Buber brought this particular aspect of his spiritual life to consummation in his book of mystical concentration and elevation, *Daniel* (1913), which described the progress of the single man to self-realization and numinal awareness. It was a work born of Buber's solitude and retirement, seriously sustained although periodically suspended for raids upon the world—lectures in the capital cities of Europe and throughout Germany. At the same time, while withdrawn, preoccupied by questions of aesthetics and mysticism, literature and aesthetics, Buber was undoubtedly an amazingly persuasive and indeed charismatic figure, a man quite capable of persuading by his mere presence, a presence invested by language, that others should commit themselves, if not to the same views, then at least to modes of shared action by which the renewal of spiritual community might be achieved. Buber, never a contemplative mystic—that is, one who regarded the self-absorptive procedures of the mystic as being not only spiritually edifying but morally sufficient—was throughout his growth to maturity a forthright Jew.

Born in Vienna in 1878, Martin Buber was raised by his Galician grandparent, Salomon Buber, to whose home in Lemberg he came, after his parents' divorce, when he was still a child. One of the last great figures of the Haskalah, Salomon Buber was rich, influential, and learned, a banker and a scholar of major importance, whose editions of the Midrashic literature are standard works to this day. At the instance of Salomon Buber, the young grandchild mastered Bible, Jewish literature, and the Hebrew language, and encountered the living presence of the Hasidic communities in nearby Sadagora and Czortkov. There followed the requisite years in a Polish gymnasium, which undoubtedly moved him to undertake a translation into Polish of Nietzsche, Buber's earliest great influence, and studies at the University of Vienna, which began in 1896.

Those early student years in Vienna marked, not an alienation from Judaism (saturated as he had become with his grandfather's learning) but rather a distancing for the sake of general learning. Not Jewish subjects at all, but classical literature and philology, philosophy and psychology, art history, literature, economics—indeed, a range and intellectual cosmopolitanism that might seem frivolous were it not so evident that everything was ultimately put to use. Buber acquired the humanist orientation, moving from Nietzsche and Bergson, both of whom made a profound impression on his early thought, to Jacob Boehme, Nicolas of Cusa, Paracelsus, the German pietists, all of whom were eventually to enable him to describe the analogues and comparisons that rendered the Hasidic mystics less exotic and estranging. Although that *fin de siècle* generation frequently gave way to intellectual delicacy, picking the bones of nineteenth-century culture with a fastidiousness that slid easily off into preciosity, Buber was saved from this undoubted temptation by the anxiety of his precarious childhood and his strenuous Galician education. His early books, filled with predictable vagueness and the imprecisions of a mystagogue, were nonetheless moving towards a social relevance and realism that his early training in the Scriptures and the Midrash had abundantly supplied. The young man, Martin Buber, German stylist of excellence, cultivated son of German internationalism, immensely learned student of German literature and Protestant religion, was yet profoundly a Jew.

A curious and untypical Jew, it should be stressed! Jewishly learned, sensitive to Jewish disability and aspiration, but a nonobserver, indifferent to Jewish *minhagim* (custom) and *halakhah* (law and observance), Buber was assimilated. Assimilated, but not assimilationist; removed, but not estranged. As a distinction it is crucial, for many, indeed, were not only distant from Jewish substance but were willfully alienated and ultimately pathological in their self-hatred (one has only to recall Otto Weininger, a contemporary of Buber's in Vienna[1]). Certainly this was not the case with Buber. Buber's estrangement was at the most temporary, an enterprise of self-discovery, seeking out the ground on which he would sink his Jewish foundations.

Buber's Jewish foundations became Zionist, although his first biographer (led, one fears, by Buber's careful orchestration of the manuscript, to stress and modulate) states that during his Viennese days Buber was threatened by assimilation.[2] One doubts Kohn's dramatization, but one is no less certain that Buber's meeting with Theodor Herzl in Berlin in 1898, the year after the first Zionist Congress, marked a process of crystallization. What had been unfocused and without center, diffuse and unstructured, acquired a Jewish raison d'être. As Buber notes in a letter to Herzl in 1902,[3] describing a meeting he and an associate had with the painter Max Liebermann to persuade him to join in their publishing enterprise, Liebermann regarded Zionism as a utopian dream, whereas Buber—despite the fact that he was irreligious—regarded Zionism as an authentic centerpoint in which Palestine is not an issue of return, but an advance, not a slinking from the stage of history or a mode of retreat (as later Hermann Cohen would regard it), but as a stepping out into history. Zionism was, at the same time, a method of securing generational continuity, a binding of Buber to the sources of his past and the ransom of the future. In these early years of the Zionist movement, it was a Western European movement of Jewish self-liberation; religious meeting, Messianic trust, the modalities of encounter between the I and its divine Thou were yet far from Buber's thought. What figures like Herzl and later Chaim Weizmann were to demonstrate to Buber were the styles of leadership—the interior transposition of the requirements of the self and the demands of history.

It is no wonder that in 1902 Buber should have joined with Berthold Feiwel, Ephraim Lilien, and Chaim Weizmann in the establishment of the Jüdischer Verlag, which responded to Herzl's ideological challenge: "If you will it, it is no fairy tale."[4] The Jüdischer Verlag and its collateral project, the Jüdische Hochschule, had as their principal activities the formation of the moral and political leadership of the nascent Zionist movement, the development of intellectuals who could teach, lecture, train, and agitate the Jewish conscience of Western Europe. The publishing program of the Jüdischer Verlag included the famous Herlitz-Kirschner Jüdische Enzyklopädie, Dubnow's ten-volume Weltgeschichte des jüdischen Volkes, Hebrew dictionaries, and Biblical, historical and literary atlases, as well as works of Jewish history and literature in which Jewish life and thought were presented as objective disciplines that needed no artificial religious rationalization to command the attention of serious Jews.

Buber's concern was not that Judaism be made respectable but that Jewish life and destiny be taken seriously. His Zionism, already in the process of articulate unfolding, pits the pride of human beings who determine their own destiny (Zionists) against those who allow the forces of otherhood to determine their lot, the aspiration to difference and ultimate self-realization against the oppression of *galut*. What Buber sought in these early days was the recovery of the primal Jew *(der Urjude)* who would, by his instructed will—regnant in his ancient homeland—regain self-sway and self-mastery, and be able to will the deed of which Kant and all idealists had dreamed, that man always be an end and never an instrument. Buber's Zionism, from the very beginning different from both Herzl's and Weizmann's, was not a strategy of ideology but an ideology that entailed strategies as a dimension of its reality. It is for this reason that in its earliest phase, with hope of a regenerated Zion still distant and perhaps unrealistic, Zionism was an agitation for Jewish maturity in the Exile, and therefore a mode of *Kulturpolitik*.

Even in these early years Buber had conceived of a Jewish periodical that would serve as a form of "Zionistica"—one that would define the concerns and prescribe the dialectics of Zionist discourse. Buber had apparently planned a periodical (with Weizmann and Feiwel) as an extension of the activities of the Jüdischer Verlag[5] and had even commissioned an essay from Ahad Haam, whom he greatly admired, for its first issue.[6] However, *Der Jude*, as the periodical was named early on, did not appear in 1903, when it was conceived, and it would not appear for more than a decade. During this period Buber edited (for the firm of Rütten & Loening) *Die Gesellschaft (Society)*, a series of forty books to which many of the most prestigious representatives of the German-speaking intellectual world contributed.[7] While conducting these and other editorial activities, Buber lectured and wrote, acquiring for his enterprise and energy a reputation throughout the European intellectual community. It was, however, his acquaintance with Gustav Landauer, the anarchist intellectual who became his closest friend and political mentor during these years, that marked Buber's transition from the fictive polarity of the world's busyness and the privacy of mystical self-realization to a mode of integration that would in the early 1920s find its fruition in the development of the dialogic principle and the publication of his most important work, *I and Thou* (1923).

Gustav Landauer, although an older contemporary of Buber's and in that respect a child, no less than Buber, of the *fin de siècle*, came from entirely different circumstances. Born in 1870 in Karlsruhe into a home quite similar to Buber's in intellectual style and minimal Jewish observance, Landauer, unlike Buber, early associated himself with the anarchist extreme of the socialist movement and during his twenties was imprisoned three times for political and journalistic offenses. Buber and Landauer presumably met in connection with the so-called Neue Gemeinschaft founded by Heinrich and Julius Hart, which undertook, through social and cultural means, to reconstitute society.[8] From the Neue Gemeinschaft, their collaboration extended to the Sozalis-ticher Bund, a movement of anarchist stripe that Landauer established on the basis of small, communal units. It was very much the period of intimate confederations, *Bünde,* in which like-minded intellectuals or proletarians or

Zionists gathered to establish, through essentially social and political empathy, the model of which the reconstruction of the whole of society would be but a magnification.

Landauer, by this time a celebrated littérateur, critic, Shakespeare scholar, and philosopher, as well as an anarchist-socialist organizer, and undoubtedly better known through a wider circle than Buber, engaged Buber's attention with undertakings to establish small communities in German-speaking Europe, where the alienation and loneliness of industrial urban technocracy might be modified or, indeed, overcome. These utopian aspirations, which one senses were projected by Landauer, clearly established his moral leadership in their friendship. A charismatic speaker and organizer, Landauer kept his distance from the Jewish world, although he was outspokenly and sincerely Jewish; he cared to extend the promise of revolution to a world beyond the Jews, turning outward the formulation that Buber addressed to the interior Jewish world. When Buber asserted, "We do not seek Revolution. We are Revolution,"[9] he was addressing a gathering of *Hapo'el Hasa 'ir* (The Young Workers), a Zionist group he had helped to found. This "revolution" was not Landauer's revolution. Buber never tired of seeking the revolution of the spirit, whereas Landauer, while loathing the violence of the streets, knew that one day the revolution would mount the barricades.

Buber and Landauer's friendship was profoundly strained by the outbreak of war in 1914. Landauer was convinced that the violence of nations was ultimately a means employed by advanced capitalist and military societies to send the proletariat to their death. The workers fought the wars; the owners made them profitable—a simple analysis, but one that remains essentially true. It is remarkable, given the intensity of their friendship and the presumable breadth of their intellectual itinerary, that Landauer and Buber had not, until the outbreak of war, articulated their disagreement over the question of violence and pacifism, German imperialism and German humanism. And yet, despite their joining in the formation of the strangely elitist Forte Kreis, which was to have assembled in Forte, Italy, a hundred of Europe's most distinguished spiritual and intellectual leaders in order to agitate for, if not the war's end, then at least the humanist community that transcends national boundary, Buber and Landauer had not, apparently, confronted each other on the issue of their personal attitudes towards the war. It proved immensely disquieting, therefore, when Buber greeted the outbreak of war with unforeseen enthusiasm. Writing to Hans Kohn, whom he had met in the Prague Bar Kochba Zionist circle that Kohn had helped to establish, Buber wrote:

> Never has the concept *Volk* been such a reality for me as during the last weeks. A sincere and great feeling also prevails among the Jews. Among the millions who have volunteered were Karl Wolfskehl and Friedrich Gundolf . . . I myself, alas, have no prospect of being accepted; but in my own way I shall try to contribute. . . . Addressed to anyone willing to accommodate himself to these times are

the words of John: "He that loveth his life shall lose it." If we Jews really felt,
thoroughly felt what this means for us then we would no longer need our ancient
motto: "Not by might, but spirit"—might [*Kraft*] and spirit [*Geist*] would become one. *Incipit vita nova.*[10]

This passage from Buber's letter, although interpreted and reinterpreted by
other forms of his *Erlebnis*-mysticism, remains typical of Buber's mood during
the early years of the war. What is curious about this extract, indeed about
other passages that culminate in his disagreement with Gustav Landauer over
the war, is Buber's willingness to draw ever finer distinctions in order to
separate out from mass psychology, from jingoism and war hysteria, all the
fine points of the "nameless spark . . . through which the deed from being the
Erlebnis [experience] of an individual becomes an event given to all."[11] This is
the language of sparks, which ignites the "kinesis" of which Buber speaks
often in *Daniel* to describe the movement of man and society from potentiality
to realization, from potency to act, from the wish to transform to the reality of
transformation. Buber felt obliged—persuaded as he was by the notions of his
Daniel—to regard the outbreak of war as a species of eschatological fulfillment, a *kairos* bringing together possibilities whose language and historic
nexus he had only charted.

This metaphysical excursus on the war, set forth with patriotic fervor in the
opening issue of *Der Jude*, drew Landauer's fury. That opening essay, *"Die
Losung"* (*The Watchword*), describes the Jewish resonation of the war. Despite the fact that "Jewish troops are fighting one another, they are nonetheless
fighting for their Jewishness." This essay, which had been delivered initially in
1914 as a talk to Berlin Zionists celebrating the feast of Chanukah, was
regarded by Buber as so accurate a summary of his views that it was repub-
lished in altered form more than a year later as the first essay in *Der Jude*. The
way of war, even though Jew is pitted against Jew, is a means of deepening
self-awareness. The war, by some curious reasoning, becomes the instrument
of gaining a more profound grasp of Jewish reality, of drawing together
the community in blood and tears to a new beginning. Buber attests that in all
the letters he has received from the front, his correspondents witness to the
strengthening of their relations with Judaism through "a clarification of vision
and a strengthening of will."[12]

This position, anticipated by Buber's description of the Jewish warrior of the
Great War as if he were the reconstituted Maccabee struggling against the
pagan Hellenists, was attacked by Landauer as early as October 18, 1914, as
the expression of sheer "aestheticism," in which Buber's *Erlebnis* doctrine is
treated as a species of hortatory rhetoric, serving only to rationalize the
unconscionable. Buber was annoyed by Landauer's charge and sought to
clarify his views viva voce. Apparently they managed some patching up, even
joining in late November, 1914, to address a joint appeal to the men of letters
they had sought to bring together in Forte. But the entente did not last; only a

month later Buber gave his Berlin Chanukah address and later incorporated its thrust and elaborated it further in his essay, "The Watchword."

It was at the time of the inaugural issue of *Der Jude* that Buber left Berlin and established residence in Heppenheim. For more than a decade Buber and Landauer had been virtually daily intimates, but Heppenheim, a town near Frankfurt-am-Main, was not as readily accessible to Landauer. It was approximately two months after the appearance of *"Die Losung"* and Buber's renewed elaboration of his "Jewish" vindication of the war that Landauer visited him. After he departed he wrote Buber as follows:

> This time, just as at our meeting in Berlin, our companionship was confirmed through meeting. This companionship was established before the war and should, I trust, survive it. I cannot emphasize sufficiently that the issues which I shall presently broach were especially disturbing to me at our last meeting: I had not been in the company of the *Kriegsbuber* [the war Buber] and had nearly forgotten him.[13]

This was only the beginning of Landauer's reply. The letter continues, reviewing his bitter disappointment not only with Buber's *"Die Losung"* but also with the argument of the first lecture on "Judaism and the Spirit of the East." (*Der Geist des Orients und das Judentum* was published in *Vom Geist des Judentums* [*Concerning the Spirit of Judaism*], published in Leipzig at approximately the same time.) Landauer's lengthy letter criticized point by point Buber's flagrantly nationalistic analogies between the classical world and the contemporary German, taking Buber to task for arrant generalizing, aesthetic emotionalism, historicism, racialism, and more.[14] There is no evidence to contravene Paul Flohr's conclusion that Landauer's letter to Buber produced an about-face.

The letter was not included in the two volumes of Landauer's correspondence that Buber edited, and Buber's controversy with Landauer was not recorded in Hans Kohn's authorized biography; even so, there can be little doubt that Landauer's critique of May 12, 1916, was, in Flohr's words, "of major significance in Buber's personal and intellectual biography."[15] It marked Buber's passage from the *Erlebnis*-mysticism, with all its attendant dangers of subjectivism, privacy, and intellectual confusion, to that focusing of the world out of which a philosophy of dialogue was to emerge. The fact remains that Buber retreated from the exposed salient of his position. The second edition of *Vom Geist des Judentums*, published in 1919, carried a note by Buber explaining deletions from the objectionable essay on the role of Germany in the transmission of the culture of the East; and his various writings in *Der Jude* and *Die Jüdische Bewegung* signal a repudiation of precisely the chauvinistic nationalism that he was earlier only too willing to endorse with cosmic enthusiasm. It is well that the *volte-face* occurred. Not only did it remove from Buber's reputation a dubious mark and reinstate Landauer in the role of exemplary moral clarity that was shortly to press him to his own ineluctable destiny, but it in fact saved *Der Jude.*

It is of course difficult to prove that *Der Jude* was "saved." Indeed, *saved* is undoubtedly too strong a word, since the periodical was never threatened by the extremity of Buber's prowar sympathies (quite to the contrary, Buber's nationalistic defense was undoubtedly welcomed by many German Jews). Rather, one speaks of moral credibility. The fact that *Der Jude* spanned the years of war and peace, addressing Jews embattled and Jews released from uniform, but addressing them always with the same questions. How do you live in *galut?* How do you prepare the way for your own redemption? Do you make ready the conditions for your own liberation and fulfillment? These primary questions would surely have been compromised had Buber naïvely persisted in supplying rationalizations to the war machine of either Imperial Germany or the Allies. The issue of religious self-maturity—Jewish or otherwise—cannot be tied to the celebration of any flag, any nation, any terrestrial cause. The fact that Buber came to see this clearly enabled *Der Jude* to acquire a moral correctness, a species of Jewish internationalism, a breadth and solicitude toward the realities of worldwide Jewish life, and a focus upon Zion that made it unique and remarkable.

Buber, at the conclusion of his initiatory essay, "The Watchword,"[16] observes that Gabriel Riesser, the early enthusiast of German-Jewish emancipation, had founded in 1832 a periodical called *Der Jude.* Riesser, however, as Buber comments, "had intended his periodical for the individual Jew for whom he sought equal civic status before the law." "We give our organ the same name, but we are not concerned with the individual, but with the Jew as the bearer and beginning of nationhood." And it is nationhood that Buber seeks—nationhood struggling to be born out of the raging conflict of war. The Jew, then, had in Buber's eyes a secret battle to conduct—to prove himself capable of struggle not for freedom of conscience but "for the freedom of life and work for a hitherto repressed national community."[17]

Der Jude carried on its masthead, beneath the name and address of its editor, a simple statement of purpose: "The monthly, *Der Jude,* is an independent organ for the knowledge and advancement of living Jewishness [*lebendigen Judentums*]. Its contributions are not the proclamations of any group but rather expressions of the personal opinion of the editor."[18] Even after *Der Jude* had passed to the editorial direction of Buber's colleagues, its scope and intellectual direction were set by him.

Der Jude was Martin Buber, but it also drew particular strength from the Prague circle around Robert and Felix Weltsch, Hans Kohn, and Max Brod. They comprised an editorial subgroup that undoubtedly fed many editorial ideas to Buber, as is clear both from their own contributions and from the letters that passed between Brod and his friend Franz Kafka and between Kafka and Buber. Kafka, in addition to publishing several stories in *Der Jude* during 1917, also suggested a Viennese friend—a Yiddish actor—to supply a memoir of the Jewish theater. It was, however, Max Brod who had first proposed to Buber that he invite Kafka to contribute, a curious inversion, since by that time it was more usual for writers to be importuning Buber than the other way around; however, Brod had asked as early as November 17, 1915, that Buber invite Kafka to contribute, and it was in response to his solicitation that the stories "Jackals and Arabs" and "A Report to an Academy" appeared in successive issues under the general heading of "Two Animal Stories."[19] The sorts of intricacies by which Kafka came to contribute to Der Jude are no less roundabout in the cases of other famous and celebrated Jews who needed persuasion and cajoling to appear, not least Hermann Cohen, who was honored but not admired by Der Jude, and Franz Werfel, about whom harsh words were written even though he was a sometime contributor.

Buber in fact knew everyone, Jew and non-Jew, assimilationist and anti-Zionist, regarding all as reasonable sources for contribution and collaboration. It was not that Buber was interested in editorial feu d'artifice; he had none of the obvious preoccupations that have come to dominate contemporary journalism—the wish to impose a single style and voice, the need to maintain control and an editorial uniformity that reduces all discursive argument to a single tonal register, making everyone sound the same, bowed as they are under the tyranny of a single red pencil. Quite the contrary. Buber's wish was that all be dissimilar, articulating from different vantage points, speaking from different disciplines and perspectives, and yet all joining together to speak out from Zion to Zion.

As Max Brod early suggested to Buber,[20] each issue of Der Jude should have a focus, a specialty of concentration and clarification that might facilitate the development of informed opinion on the various issues of the day. And indeed, mutatis mutandis, Buber concurred with Brod's suggestion, devoting entire issues to the situation of Jewish refugees from Eastern Europe, whose case by the middle of the war was in dispute among both Jews and non-Jews in Germany as to their admissibility into the country. Many German Jews wanted the borders closed to the admission of Eastern European Jews, regarding them as impoverished, unclean, and worse, religiously and culturally recidivist. Although Hermann Cohen would contribute an essay in favor of the admission of Polish Jews, Buber would take exception to the reasons Cohen gave. It was a burning issue, which opened for the first time in many years the whole issue of the relation between West European Jews (namely, German Jews) and the Jews of the East in whom both tradition and the Zionism of the Hoveve Zion (Lovers of Zion) had taken hold alongside labor Zionism, socialism, and revolutionary Marxism.

Der Jude served at the very least to transmit information. There were long articles describing the economic structure of the Jews of Galicia, Great Russia, and the Ukraine; the educational institutions of the East; the religious customs of shtetl orthodoxy, as well as novellas by S. Y. Agnon, initially translated by then Gerhard (Gershom) Scholem, stories by Mendele, Sholem Aleichem, and Peretz, and a superb series of essays by Arno Nadel on Jewish folk music, the hymnody of love and worship, profane and sacred. Such concerns—this particular one for example—were sustained throughout the life of *Der Jude*, the refugee question being resolved by the war's end only to be replaced by others emerging from the peace conference at Versailles and the efforts of the Council of the Four Lands to define the internal autonomy of East European Jewry.

Der Jude's editorial structure was essentially lean and instinctively focused. Not more than a hundred contributors reached its pages during its life, which is to suggest that Buber, unlike most present-day editors, was interested not so much in cultivating the new, acquiring the fresh or eccentric or current, as he was in maintaining a tone of voice without having to edit it. One suspects— records of the periodical are not available—that Buber edited little, although he reacted strenuously to his contributors, with letters of appreciation and criticism, while reserving the right, exercised from time to time, to comment upon a given essay at its conclusion in a little riposte (signed only "The Editor"), or in an explanatory note to the title page, or as was more often the case, introducing little notes of timeliness and intensity in the section of the periodical called "Observations," in which he commented on books, on the political situation in Germany, on anti-Semitism, signing his contributions with a simple "B." Buber dominated the periodical, but—and this should be underscored—he did not appear in many issues. He wrote editorials only occasionally, and he commented only from time to time. He translated Hasidic tales and sermons for use essentially as filler to the editorial matter that preceded the "back of the book."

Each issue was dominated by a theme or continuing the serialization of a lengthy essay (some being carried through seven or eight issues until completed[21]). Frequent offerings were translations of hitherto unavailable materials (Bialik's great essay on "Halakhah and Aggadah" was translated into German by Scholem), discussions of unfamiliar Jewish literatures (Müller and Scholem on the Zohar and the Kabbalah), comments on the history of Jewish philosophy, literature, and historiography; but principally, repetitively, and consistently *Der Jude* underscored and elaborated the ideology of Zionism, publishing texts by A. D. Gordon, Nahum Goldmann, Arthur Ruppin, Bin-Gorion (Micha Joseph Berdyczewski), Berl Katznelson, Yitzhak ben-Zvi, commentary on Nordau, Herzl, Moses Hess, documents from the early *kibbutzim*, essays on the role of women in the Zionist work movement, as well as early and informed discussion of the problems that would affect both Arabs and Jews in the process of buying a whole country from the Turks.[22] These essays, rarely more than five to an issue, were followed by a progressively larger number of editorial features, which were to become of immense importance to the life and longevity of *Der Jude*.

The first "back-of-the-book" feature was the *Bemerkungen (Observations)*, a loose catch-all for short, tendentious editorializing, to which Felix and

Robert Weltsch, Max Brod, Joseph Meisl, Leo Strauss, and Buber himself often contributed, and to which Franz Rosenzweig's prose contributions were assigned,[23] as were controversial exchanges between Gustav Landauer and Max Brod. To the section of "Observations" was added a fascinating documentary feature that supplied the raw materials for a new sociology and demography of the Jews. Called *Daten und Materialien,* it contained detailed statistical discussion of the economic life of Palestine, the productivity of the *kibbutzim,* the participation of Jews in the American proletariat, the numeration of Jewish population (which opens with the provocative assertion of Arthur Ruppin, that with the exception of the Chinese, the Jews are the only people who have been counting themselves since ancient times[24]), the statistical breakdown of Jewish immigration to the United States, among others. This feature gave way by the end of the third year to a broader-based feature, *Umschau,* a review of events in politics, Zionism and the national movement, letters from abroad, religion, *Frauenfragen,* education and pedagogy, philosophy, Jewish culture, music and the arts, incorporating in a more general fashion the best aspects of *Daten und Materialien.* Lastly, each issue carried a number of book reviews by Franz Rosenzweig, Romain Rolland, Elias Auerbach, Meir Wiener, Hans Kohn, Benno Jacob, Josef Meisl, Arieh Tartakover, Hugo Bergmann, and Margarete Susman, among others.

Clearly it is unnecessary to describe the contents and substance of *Der Jude.* It was regarded with considerable hostility by the extremely orthodox, whom Buber persistently criticized for allowing themselves to be co-opted by German nationalists into criticism of secular and Zionist Jews, while at the same time being regarded with suspicion by assimilationist and literary Jews who thought Buber a dangerously seductive influence, capable of making Jewish life and culture both well-educated and palatable. *Der Jude* was clearly one of the most influential and formative organs of cultural Zionism and proud Jewishness, a model achievement of Buber as cultural publicist. It conducted its career with clear-headedness and passion, recognizing that the Jew was in Exile, but curiously acclimated to a humanist tradition reflecting the best in the European tradition; openhearted and capacious to new winds of doctrine and persuasion; strong in support of the Hebrew language, while maintaining a stylist's eloquence in German and an affection for Yiddish; continuously examining new modes of Jewish education in both the *galut* and in Palestine; militant in its conviction that the Jewish poor had to achieve economic independence through cooperative enterprise and socialist collaboration; sensitive to the literary and poetic achievement of Diaspora Judaism while dodging the question of Biblical doctrine and teaching, which figures only marginally in its pages (undoubtedly because the issue of Scripture and the rabbinic tradition did not bear directly on the Zionist question and were too visibly tied to religious and theological *parti-pris* positions in which Buber had no interest).

Der Jude was, in sum, a heroic enterprise, a free journal, independent of party or movement and committed only to the highest intellectual discussion and commentary concerning issues principally and primarily Jewish. The other world—the world of nations and movements—entered its domain only rarely and on occasion, scarring the Jewish world with its wars and revolutions, addressing the particularity and vulnerability of the Jew only when it threatened to ruin or kill him. That other world, the world of gentile principalities and powers, defined the perimeter of the Jewish question, while Christianity pressed to the heart of Israel the salient of its particular Messianic dialectic. To both, *Der Jude* turned not a stone face of indifference, but the countenance of composure, regarding the nations and their beliefs as what they are—immensely powerful, often murderous, but finally nugatory in their ability to withstand the energy and truthfulness of the Zionist idea. *Der Jude* was based upon a moral optimism that was both destroyed and vindicated: the humanism withered, socialism turned both nationalist and genocidal, but from the ashes of Europe's Jews, the remnant endured and Zionism established a homeland for the Jewish people.

ARTHUR A. COHEN

A NOTE ABOUT SELECTION

In selecting material for this anthology I have made no effort to be representative. Being "representative" is a species of editorial formaldehyde, and I have no interest in preserving specimen examples of all the modes of intellection and passion to which *Der Jude* opened its pages. Many of the issues that exercised Martin Buber and his collaborators are no longer alive—the people to whom they *were* alive are dead; the lands to whose concern they were addressed are now empty of Jews; and the Land to whose upbuilding much of the argument of *Der Jude* was devoted is now Israel.

My principle of selection was the vitality and endurance of issues. As my brief introductory comments to the essays make clear, they deal with issues that are alive and speak even now. This is what makes a magazine memorable, that it can echo to hearing long after the speech has ended. Such a simple application of one of Buber's fundamental insights into the nature of living address is certainly appropriate to this anthology.

It should be noted, however, that many, many other essays drawn from any monthly issue of *Der Jude* and its various supplementary sections could have been offered in place of or in addition to those I have selected. My selections, although obviously subject to vagary, personal preference, or sheer caprice, were also influenced by factors that should be clarified. Much of the material published by *Der Jude* for the first time in the German language had been published previously in Yiddish or Hebrew or is now available in English and other languages (for example, virtually all of the essays by Ahad Haam, Sholem Aleichem, S. Y. Agnon, Franz Kafka, and Martin Buber). Many of the best essays on Zionist ideology and politics would have little interest to the general reader, although they deserve collection as documentation of the development from Zionism as *Kulturpolitik* to real community. Lastly, a number of essays ran through many issues of *Der Jude* and are of themselves whole books. Among these are Samuel Rapoport's *From the Religious Life of Eastern European Jewry,* which traced the custom and practice of *shtetl* Jewry through its *minhagim* and folk traditions; S. A. Horodetsky's *The Community Life of the Hasidim;* Arno Nadel's extraordinary series on Jewish folk music; S. L. Zitron's *Toward a History of the "Love of Zion,"* and Arnold Zweig's prophetic suite of essays, *Contemporary German Anti-Semitism.* Lastly, the omission of all the contributions of Gershom Scholem to *Der Jude* is out of respect for his wishes.

The essays that do appear reflect a conspectus of intellectual and spiritual preoccupations that dominated German Jewry during its last productive generation. *Der Jude* was not the only periodical of German Jews, and it was not a representative periodical. It was the journal of Martin Buber, for the *"Buberschen Juden"* (as Franz Rosenzweig wittily refers to it, for by 1919 Rosenzweig counted himself among its fraternity, although in 1916, when he compared *Der Jude* to Hermann Cohen's periodical *Neue Jüdische Monatshefte,* he was far closer to his teacher) and the *Buberschen Juden* were not vast in number, although their influence was immense. *Der Jude* constellated a covenant of Jewish intellectuals and professional men, precisely those who made up the *Geistesaristokratie* of pre-World War I Germany. That war, Buber's *volte face* on the issue of Germany and the war, the expanded horizon of Jewish spirituality, tied *Der Jude* to Jews everywhere, but most particularly to German-speaking Jews, to the Jews of Palestine and East Europe.

Der Jude is to be celebrated by this record. Martin Buber, in another aspect—as editor and Zionist publicist—is to be celebrated by *Der Jude.* But more than Buber or his periodical, the achievement in vigor, intellectual passion, essential generosity and toleration of the Jews of Germany is most to be honored. *Der Jude* was not a very successful periodical; its subscription list diminished towards the end, and its publisher curtailed format and regularity of appearance while raising its price per issue. Nonetheless, although Buber was disappointed by its only modest success, he had made a signal and unique contribution. In great measure it might be said that those German Jews who found their way to Palestine during the thirties, saved by their own imagination and desperation, were in no small measure given ideological nourishment during the publication years of *Der Jude.*   [A.A.C.]

PART ONE

THE JEWS AMID THE NATIONS

1. NATIONALISM
HANS KOHN

EDITOR'S INTRODUCTION

HANS KOHN (1891–1971) was born into the German-Jewish Czechoslovakian community where he was associated early on with the Bar Kokhba group within the Zionist movement. The author of numerous books both before and after his emigration to the United States in 1933, he is best known for his studies of the history of nationalism and for his early biography of Martin Buber, which was first published in 1930 and revised and expanded in 1961. One of his last works was a study of *Karl Kraus, Arthur Schnitzler, Otto Weininger* (Tübingen, 1962). Kohn was a frequent contributor to *Der Jude*. The present essay appeared during Jahrgang VI (1921–1922), pp. 674–86.

Hans Kohn, like his era, was young when he wrote this hopeful, impassioned, almost romantic essay on the rise and fall of traditional nationalism and the emergence, in the aftermath of World War I, of a nationalism of sensibility, quintessentially embodied in the Zionist movement. The supererogatory domination of religion that imposed unity upon Europe until the Reformation was shattered first by the historical critique of faith—the recognition that "common faith" was but another mask for tyrannizing the nonconformist conscience (most terribly signified for Kohn by the massacre of St. Bartholomew's Night, when Catholic moved against Huguenot). Following the decline of faith, the source of unification shifted from religion to nationalism, bonds of unity being sought henceforth in peoplehood, language, cultural community, and territory rather than in divine fiat. The integrity of the nation was in due course subsumed to a doctrine of state that became, in the logic of the Hegelians, an ordering reason superior to the vital bonds of nationality. The state became the ordering principle of nation, its rule and law. The triumph of the state became the tyranny of the nation, draining from its corpus vitality and ethical immediacy, forcing down upon the living people an identity derived as much from sheer abstractness and generality as from its self-conception as the principle of law and order. The achievement of the national state, its consummation and victory (in Kohn's ironic formulation), but also its witch's orgy, was the Great War.

"The myth of nationalism as the ultimate ordering principle of history is dead," Kohn asserts, and the times await a new faith. The Jews, Kohn continues in his peroration, know this truth more cruelly than any other people, for the Jews know how desperately the nineteenth-century ideologies have

failed, and how miserably dispirited is the generation that sought the immola-
tion and transfiguration of death for the German principle, or European unity,
or the humanism of the West. Whatever the premises of the 1914–18 war, its
brutality was the only one to be confirmed and, prophetically, Kohn sees
down the road a future of continental wars, wars that will be not for nation or
state, but will engulf whole worlds, presumably for the sake of some ideological deformation. We have seen it!

Kohn, whose Zionist concern centered upon its ethical content, its generation of moral principles for the revivification of the Jewish people, took the
apocalypsis of the war as an almost messianic marker of a new beginning, an
almost eschatological forerunner of a new possibility for human community
in which individuals would reassert their claim upon history and nationalism,
no longer "a deadly drug or a hypocritical camouflage," would aid the free
growth of the human essence.

It is tempting here—and elsewhere, indeed, throughout this anthology—to
lay upon the essayist the thorny crown of the Holocaust. But it is—indeed
remarkably—too easy, and it will be foreborne. The Holocaust *is,* and although with the arrogance of hindsight it can be foreseen, *it was not foreseen,
and that, too, must be remembered.* This registration of the history of the
German-Jewish experience, its origins, vectors, and polemics, is grounded in
the conviction not that we will find the answer to the Holocaust, or its
explanation, but rather a sense of how an intellectually creative community
conducted an astonishing career with its back to the wall of Armageddon.

[A.A.C.]

NATIONALISM

Dedicated to Martin Buber

Great and far-reaching events of the outer world, determined as
they are by the level of consciousness of contemporaries and their forerunners, always have long-range effects upon reshaping and refashioning human
thought and opinion. Such shifts in consciousness are accompanied by deep
shocks; they create a time of disquiet, tension, isolation, and disassociation.
For many years the essence of this process is barely to be sensed, yet it is
obscure and ambivalent in its results, and uncertain as to what new world-
image it will produce. These are times of increased emergency; nothing
thrives well, a seeming regression joins dying or dead things in an indis-
criminate struggle with newness and growth. Such times of transition and
disjointed systems are profuse and peculiar; the old tarries with senile stubbornness and the new is announced in its birth-pangs.

Georg Simmel,[1] in his latest writings, has shown that the generation of
independently meaningful content from the materials of the spirit is immanent
to life. The bond structure of life, its organic dynamics, and its more-or-less

teleological, all-entwining necessities, generate out of themselves certain existential contents. These, originally pulsing and imbued with the stream of life, form the totality of the given (by dint of its uniform and consistent meaning) into an autonomous closure and thereby become themselves shapers of life and the material of life. The guiding idea of these spiritual world-forms appears each time as the goal of all life. Georg Simmel has applied this formative principle of shaping life-contents into a closed world subject as a general rule in the most diverse spheres: in the world of art and the world of religion, in the world of law and the world of cognition. But he has not applied it in the most comprehensive area of all, the sphere that controls the mass behavior of people of a specific age in all these spiritual worlds. Its lower manifestation we call politics. Its higher manifestation we call the mysticism or faith of an era. The stream of life creates this faith. The elements of tradition contribute to a formative guiding principle of all spiritual comprehension, until faith, which has constructed its own world—a world transcending life—becomes the *telos* of all life.

The faith of the nineteenth century was its nationalism; more precisely, its state-nationalism, the attachment of a sovereign people to a specific territory that it owned and possessed. The dominant principle of the age, nationalism ruled from the French Revolution to the World War; it made history, and, as its goal, it subordinated human strivings. Nationalism was the principle that separated and attached.

A few centuries earlier, religion had been the dominant principle. It separated and attached; it made history and, as its goal, it guided human strivings. The differences between races and nations consisted in their variety of temperaments, aptitudes, traditions; but the highest ordering principle was religion, which constituted an inner experience and set of traditions, and an outer bond of custom, way of life, and connecting politics. This epoch lasted until the Thirty Years' War. To us, but not to those who lived through it, that war appears as the end of an era, a turning point. And here we see a strange phenomenon: a conclusion, an end that seems more like an ultimate culmination than a dying fall, as though the previously dominant principle, in its enormous external concentration, intended once more to stamp its intense formative will upon a world that was already internally slightly alienated. The Thirty Years' War, with its religious motives, signifies a high point of religion as a formative political principle. The sentence *cuius regio illius religio* aims at an insurmountable power-gain of religious politics.

The Thirty Years' War marked a high point and, simultaneously, the end of an era. The principle ordering the world lost its universal validity. Deism, stemming from England and subsequently dressed in the skepticism of the French Encyclopedists, introduced the Enlightenment. At the same time, the feudal hierarchy with its distant decentralized freedoms of provinces, towns, and trades, which prevented the political—and cultural—unification of the future nation, dissolved. In its place arose the centralized state, the nation, of

myth of religion, yet he simultaneously prepared nationalistic romanticism. The Schlegel brothers, however, distinctly rejected the patriotic bards. In his Berlin lectures, Wilhelm Schlegel made fun of Klopstock's disciples for their "fanatical patriotism devoid of any historical knowledge as to the character of the Germans, their present situation, and their past deeds." Yet in *Atheneum Fragments* [*Athenäumsidee*] he went on to say: "The German artist has no character, not that of an Albrecht Dürer, Keppler, Hans Sachs, a Luther and a Jakob Boehme"—no glorious transfiguration, but a guide to the future. "In the model of Germanness, which a few great patriotic inventors have set up, there is nothing to criticize except for the false position. This Germanness lies before us and not behind us."[6]

For Fichte, nationalism is a duty and mission, just as religion used to be; and being a German is as much of a mission as being a disciple of Christ. Soon people were "Germans," as their ancestors had been "Christians." In *Addresses to the German Nation* [*Reden an die deutsche Nation*], Fichte himself ascribes to nationalism a task that once belonged to religion: to be a carrying faith, a myth, a principle unifying the world-image, "to weld the everlasting to earthly work, to plant and nurture the permanent in the ephemeral, connected with the Eternal, not merely in an incomprehensible manner and through an abyss that mortal eyes cannot penetrate, but in a fashion visible even to the mortal eye."

Here, in the discovery of the most intimate and eternal in national cohesiveness, there also arose the danger of a connection with the external phenomenon of power interest and the ephemeral phenomenon of momentary benefit. The nation turned into the state, an equation that still prevails in Western European languages. The nation is something natural, that binds together national sentiment. The state is a practical artifice and, in its essence, it separates not only outwardly but inwardly as well. According to Fichte's *Handwörterbuch der Staatswissenschaften* [*Pocket Dictionary of Political Science*], the state emerges and exists through a distinction between a ruling and a ruled class. "What makes the State the State are the legal norms connecting the ruling power and the people in terms of superordination and subordination. In every State there are rulers and ruled. Without rule there is no State."

Connection with the state once meant the fall of religion, and the same was now true of the nation. Wilhem von Humboldt, who in his feeling for folk language and mores encouraged the meaning of nation, recognized the danger. Schiller, in his poem *German Greatness* [*Deutsche Grosse*], known only through drafts recently discovered, said a few pertinent things. "German *Reich* and German nation are two distinct things. . . . Apart from the political, the German established his own value, and even if the imperium were to collapse, German validity would remain unchallenged. It is an ethical greatness, it resides in the culture and in the character of the nation, and its character is independent of its political destiny." Messianic thoughts are introduced. The German "is chosen by the world-spirit, to labor on the eternal construction of shaping man during the struggle of time and to preserve what time brings. That is why, until now, he has acquired alien things and preserved them within himself. He has preserved everything of value that emerged in other times and nations, that came into being and vanished; it remained alive for him, the treasure of centuries. . . . Not to shine for a moment and play his role, but to win the great trial of his age. Every nation has its day in history, but the day of the Germans is the harvest of all time. When the circle of time draws to a close and the Day of the Germans shall appear, when the Scha. . . . [sic] unite in the beautiful image of mankind."

Fichte wrote in *The Learned Vocation* [*Bestimmung des Gelehrten*] "The State, exactly like all human institutions that are merely means, aims at its own annihilation; it is the purpose of any government to make governing unnecessary . . . Until that time arrives we are not yet true human beings." The State "aims at self-cancellation, for its ultimate goal is ethicalness."[7] And ethicalness cancels out the State. But only a few years later, the decisive step was taken spiritually. The national state became absolute; it became an idol. "The territorial body politic set up with original ruling power" (Jellinke) became a "self-conscious ethical substance," a "rational, organized divine will" (Hegel), "the total will of a people" (Treitschke). At the same time, the very same step was taken in political life! The goal of the political aspirations became the national state. Germans and Scandinavians, Italians and Balkans, Slavs and Magyars strove for independence. The national state became the subject and object of all wars; it dominated the century.

The rule of nationalism, uncontested politically until the coming of Bolshevism, was never uncontested intellectually. The ever-growing impossibility of economic and geographic isolation, the reduction and disappearance of all great distances through the perfected exploitation of natural energy, the common ownership of most cultural elements, the steadily increasing complication and connection of all life, slowly and imperceptibly began undermining state borders. The feeling of a joint property came to the fore in several outstanding personalities, even in critical times of tribulation. The words of Gaston Pâris, a professor at the Collège de France, deserve to be noted. He spoke them in a lecture on the *Song of Roland* delivered on December 8, 1870, during the German siege of Paris:

> I fully and unreservedly acknowledge the doctrine that scholarship has no other object than truth and truth for its own sake, with no consideration of the good or bad, the regrettable or fortunate consequences that this truth might have in practice. The man who, out of a patriotic, religious, or even moral motive, permits himself the slightest concealment of the facts he is investigating, the least modification of the conclusion he draws, is not worthy of having a place in the great laboratory where honesty is a more indispensable title of admission than propriety. In this way, the common studies, undertaken in the same spirit in all civilized countries, form a vast fatherland over and above narrow nations, which

are various and often hostile, a fatherland that no wars can soil, and no conqueror threaten, and in which souls may find the refuge and unity once offered in former times by the *civitas Dei.*

And among the uprisings of the alert and enlightening conscience against the suggestiveness of nationalistic faith, the movement of the intellectuals in the Dreyfus Affair deserves special mention.

With the end of the nineteenth century, there began a time of disintegration as the myth that bore society continued to weaken. The enormous suffering of existence, the enigma of life, staring at us eternally, the plethora of all things and connections assaulting us with a destructive gesticulation, the dark beast that inexplicably threatens, keeps arising within us—all these things would be unendurable if a faith, a sustaining world-principle, did not bind them into a unity and give them meaning and purpose, making the remote and the unsure more familiar through the threads of myth. At the end of the nineteenth century, life seemed to be losing its meaning; society disintegrated into individuals; the enigmas of existence gaped unconcealed; everything began to be questionable. People called their era cold and soul-less; no great goals unified life, imbuing it with the fire of enthusiasm. Being was replaced by having. People tried to disguise their nakedness in the rags of faith while the worst romanticism of state and nation celebrated their victories.

The World War began [1914], apparently the loftiest triumph of the national principle. New national states came into being; even an awakening Asia, in which, until recently, the still vital principle of a religious world-order ruled exclusively (as in Europe five hundred years ago), and the drowsiest nations were affected by the myth of nationalism. Nevertheless, this era marked the end of a politics of minor, national states; mankind outgrew it economically and politically. Future wars will involve whole continents. We cannot say, however, what new faith will carry and unite the coming age. Just as we cannot say what economic system will replace the capitalism peculiar to the passing era. All we know is that through all these epochs mankind is growing, that the Kingdom of Freedom is blossoming ever more richly, and that its unity is becoming more and more obvious. The Age of Nationalism will maintain its extraordinary significance in the development of mankind: our possibilities have multiplied a thousandfold, every individuality has gained more than we realize in personal dignity and freedom, our coming solidarity was anchored more and more deeply. But we can travel further along our road only if we rid ourselves of the remnants of the political national myth, with its ghostly adornment of a romantic youth. The national war will then appear as impossible as the religious fanaticism of St. Bartholomew's Night or as blood vendettas within the nation. The sacred rights of the nation, which both parties are always convinced of representing, will be as incomprehensible as the military and murderous fury released by a disputed interpretation of a Biblical word or form of the sign of the cross.

Today, national pseudo-values are still influencing minds as their religious counterparts used to do. The time will come when "national sovereign independence," the goal of the age of political nationalism, will vanish because mankind will have realized that, just as individual men can never be fully sovereign and must be bound by myriad dependencies and obligations and, for the sake of solidarity, must put up with restrictions and temporary suppressions, so national independence, the nonintervention of the "foreigner" in "our" affairs, is a dangerous phantom that, under the suggestiveness of the myth of the nineteenth century, has become an article of faith. Enthusiastic and soul-felt and fervent as any article of faith at its inception, through its attachment to politics and violence and rights, this one has become emptier and emptier, more and more deathlike.

But before it publicly stripped off its final adorning vestments, nationalism was granted one more unique elevation and purification, a second youth, no longer with the consumingly stormy fire of its first youth, but full of the sweetness and melancholy given by experience and wisdom and premonition of the end. This new level also announced the future road, the new, purified, primally human value of the nation, its release from politics and from suggestiveness, and its elevation into clarity. Nationalism no longer dominates the life of man as a carrying faith transcending any moral valuation because it is more fundamental. It struggles away from the naïve and self-limited egoism of sacred faith, which, because of its suggestiveness, is unconsciously mendacious and hypocritical. It knuckles under to moral laws, eternal valuations; it dares to look into its own eyes with ultimate clarity, thereby salvaging its justice and truth beyond the deception of the moment and the interest of selfishness.

The age of religious myth in Europe, just before its end, also knew such a deepening and inwardness, a purification and ferment; the eternal in religion had let this inspiration, stripped of all its contemporary trappings, shine forth, and preserved it for the future. The fire of the Reformation (which affected the later Luther, the fear-ridden servant of princes, least of all), the Anabaptists and the Bohemian Brethren, Pascal and the Jansenists, all lived before and during the Thirty Years' War. The similarities are tangible: "the enormously increasing vital urge" in an era when the old seems unshakably powerful, is already feeding from new sources.

At the beginning of the twenties in our century, one can see this reformation of nationalism almost everywhere. It is the sense of a new, powerful, connected life, the certainty of standing in tradition and yet being touched by totally new winds, the yearning for a new strong faith, that holds all these movements together.[8] At the same time there is a conscious seeking for an ethical anchoring of nationalism. People are going back to its idealistic beginnings, to Fichte and the French Revolution. They are lifting it from its narrow confines into worldwide light, trying to shift it from its involvement in the realm of being to the moral level of duty, from the present to the future.

They are giving it Messianic hues. Nationalism is becoming a question of personal ethics, personal shaping of life; it is becoming questionable. It is faced with new problems. Things close to it are now remote. Certitudes are questionable, and people are trying to interpret uncertainties from the breadth and depth of solitude.

In Germany, it is the time of the Free German movement, of the youth convention on the Hohen Meissner. In France, it is the time of Charles Péguy, who could so keenly distinguish between the *mystique* and the *politique* of a faith, and who fought for the *mystique* of nationalism against its *politique*. It is the time of youth: to them the last volume of [Rolland's] *Jean Christophe* is dedicated. It is a patriotism "avec caractère universaliste: il aime la France particulièrement en tant que répandant sur le monde les idées qu'il aime, en tant qu'illuminant l'Univers" ["with a universalist character; it loves France in particular while spreading the ideas it loves throughout the world, thereby illuminating the Universe"].[9] Everywhere people feel the desperation of a time without faith or myth, the fatigue of termination, but people are trying to get away from these things. A new song of life affirmation and powerful courage is to begin. Nietzsche, the unique genius, as lonesome as a gigantic figure, who overshadows the decline of an era of faith, is the father of this desperate temerity, this endless hope for a new heaven. A lyricism, likewise Nietzsche's heritage, characterizes this movement, and constitutes its danger; it lacked the cruel awareness that it so badly needed.

Among the Jews, Martin Buber gave form and expression to this movement. With the deep awareness and the painful isolation of the Jew, this movement found a clearer and more powerful utterance. Jewish fervor and Messianic responsibility imbued the concept of nationalism. "Official" nationalism was countered by an "underground" nationalism, just as Péguy had separated *mystique* and *politique*. Jewish nationalism was brought before the tribunal of moral words, of eternity; it found its justification as a link in world redemption. It was not a camouflage for state needs and collective power aspirations; spiritual necessity alone drove it: the thing that the loneliest man of any race [*Mensch einer Rasse*] feels and suffers and yearns for on a desert island is the national question. A relentless slash cuts away everything that is politics, state, or economy. All that counts is the "question that we find in ourselves, that we clarify in ourselves, and that we have to resolve in ourselves." And this utterly personal is no longer the opposite of the human; the dignity, the ethical stature of a nation is independent of the play of interest conflicts, of the vain delusion of political independence. Nationalism reaches for the stars here. It redeems the world, and a redemption of the world is possible only by way of self-sacrifice. The greatest, the most grandiose poetry of redemption that ever sprang from the human brain and heart, the Jewish notion of the servant of God, the 'Ebed Yahweh, is imitated in the "today still ineffable human world-feeling" of a modern Jew.

This movement contains both an elevation and a dissolution. It could not hold up the end. The St. Bartholomew's Eve of national-independence politics began and has still not ended. In the face of its most absurd consequences, people are thinking up palliative devices, such as national-minority rights. They are gradually starting to realize that nation and state are distinct, and that the nation in its vital utterances, in its culture and development, must be protected even without national independence, without the national state. The principle of the national state has been applied to the point of absurdity. Europe has created economically unviable, mutually threatening minor states, thereby prolonging national warfare and the delusion of national states, until mankind, having grown weary of such politics, will find it as incomprehensible as religious wars and witch trials. The solidarity of men will bring them together in larger and larger state alliances, which will be able to give greater and greater freedoms to communities and groups, federations and parishes. The national sentiment, detached from its territorial state-faith, enriched and deepened by the era in which it was the carrying faith, will help determine the destiny of mankind through the power of the traditions of blood, will make their souls tremble at the dark attachment to past powers, will give their thinking the fervor of profound experience. The common ancestry and similar mentality of groups and alliances will come to the fore in characteristic forms and contents of art and views of life, in characteristic behaviors and social institutions. The same dreams and premonitions that arise in their quiet hours from the depths of the blood shall magically wind about them, the same attitude towards all problems and the same response to the pressure of the world around them will bind them together more closely and keep them seeking one another. But the myth of nationalism as the ultimate ordering principle of history is dead, and in these times of transition, when the new faith is announcing itself, at first intangible and unintelligible, the world must still face a great deal of wildness and confusion, uncertainty and despair.

To live in this chaos is the task of today's mankind. A time of uncertainty, of change and beginning, produces a generation that has maintained the sensitivity of youth to crises, that is building in uncertainty and homelessness, that is still capable of change and beginning. People of today feel younger than people in the past: big with destiny, and richer in potential, though at the cost of being poorer in achievement. Contentment and prudent adjustment are alien to them; nihilism hovers as a danger.

The yearning of the prewar era for faith, for community and elevation, had made it overlook reality, had darkened its awareness, had failed to sharpen its conscience. It awaited a new era, and failed to recognize that it was fated to live in a dying era towards a future that would dearly touch it. The uniform meaning of events, the myth of the era, is lost. This generation had to live through the lamentable collapse of the principle of faith, its watchwords and pseudovalues; they were turned into lonesome seekers. Each man sees himself alone in his increased sensitivity, each man feels too weak to help or to act; each man is sobered, and bleeds from incurable internal wounds. Every common goal seems to have disappeared, chaos seems to have broken in.

To a greater degree among us Jews. Our tensions are stronger, our sensitivity stronger, our homelessness deeper than among others. The nation of crises since time immemorial, we feel them, torn along and announcing the storm, twice as much as anyone else. Scattered throughout the world, we carry the suffering of all mankind. Millennia of intense ethical sensibilities are active within us, whereas others still preserve the seed of unconscious peasantry that was scattered only very recently. We, who for centuries have been living only in the past and the future, but never in the present, are bleeding from wounds that have healed in others or have not yet broken open.

In this chaos of the era, we have no choice but to be cruelly aware. A new enlightenment will come. Nietzsche also introduced it in his twilight, manifold interpretations. A certain sadness, but a warlike sadness, a humility, but full of calm restraint, are seemly in the face of the Demonic of the supraindividual fate of our era. A severe discipline full of distrust toward affects and drives is necessary in the full freedom of conscience. The heir, in our time, to the best traditions of Europe, Romain Rolland, and his contemporary Refoel Posner, the author of the novel *Heim und Welt* [*Home and World*], which derives from opposite assumptions, have come to a similar position from totally different backgrounds. The nation bound up with territorial and economic politics and its forced formation will be replaced by the freedom and personal responsibility of national tradition and life. Instead of the suggestiveness of national faith, which permits and excuses everything, the utterances of national life will be ruled by the standard of universality and the feeling of solidarity that has already started to gain power over the utterances of individual life. Nationalism will then stop being a deadly drug or a hypocritical camouflage. In a new day of mankind, the early dawn of which we believe we have already perceived, nationalism will become more loving and more attached to the life of individuals, will fashion it more richly and freely, will be the most private and most hidden essence of mankind.

2. YIDDISH
MOSES CALVARY

EDITOR'S INTRODUCTION

MOSES CALVARY (1883–1942), teacher, writer, Zionist, visited Palestine for the first time in 1914 but at the outbreak of World War I returned to Germany, where he became, in 1916, secretary to Salman Schocken and with Buber founded the Hauptausschuss für Jüdische Kulturarbeit. He lived again in Palestine, then again Germany, and spent the last period of his life as a teacher in Lithuania. Calvary's essay in *Der Jude* appeared during Jahrgang I (1916–1917), pp. 25–32.

Moses Calvary's essay on Yiddish, written during the first year of *Der Jude,* was prompted in great measure by the increasing interest among Germans in general and German Jews in particular (those of neuresthenia and Jewish affection at the same time) in the woeful economic deprivation of Polish Jewry, which first became apparent as the German army drove through Poland toward Russia. Franz Rosenzweig had his first contact with Polish Hasidism when he returned to Germany from Macedonia by way of Warsaw, but he was not alone. The background to Calvary's essay and its timeliness arose from the concern that the settled and smug Jewish burghers manifested to the specter of an influx of poor Jews from the East in the event of economic disaster and the ravages of war.

Moses Calvary undertakes to save, not the Jews of the East, but only their language, with its vitality, independence, and authenticity. It would have been easy were it demonstrable to make the *Ost-Jude* merely a factotum of German Jewry, a servile member dependent upon the generosity of the more settled, assimilated, and correct German Jew. The argument for the servility of Eastern European Judaism had been going on for some time, since it was a prejudice already lodged in the psyche of Wissenschaft des Judentums, which willy-nilly associated arid Talmudism and ecstatic Hasidism, proletarian poverty and the prideless capitalism of the Jewish estate overseer with the east, and most audibly and immediately, the voice of the Jewish east, the gutturality, gesticulation, intimacy, sentiment, and toughness of the Yiddish language.

Apparently in 1916 the argument was already being advanced that Yiddish did not deserve the status of a language. Regarded as a mere bowdlerization of German, it occupied a relation to the parent tongue, no different than the ward of the household, allowed to take tea with the foster parent only on special occasions. Yiddish was acceptable for vulgar communication (some would

say profane)—street talk and table talk—but not for business and the voca-
tions (hence the debate about the use of Yiddish in predominantly Jewish
schools, rather than as Martin P. Philippson had urged, Polish) and certainly
not for that prize of assimilation, literature. The fact that in great measure even
the Jewishly educated among Eastern European Jews regarded Yiddish as the
secular twin of Hebrew and Polish or Russian to be a *koine,* a distinctly
inferior concession to the gentiles, was overlooked. Calvary has his assumptions and they draw from the unconscious of the German-Jewish *Weltschau,*
but there lives in this essay a fierce courage, an insistence that Yiddish is not
dialect, but language, that it began in closer dependence upon the vocabulary, cadence, syntax of German speech, but drawing as it has upon Hebrew
and Slavic tongues, it acquired by the end of the nineteenth century a style and
with style a grammarian's precision. Yiddish is no longer a ward of German; it
is fully matured and independent and deserves to be regarded as such.

The conflict between Yiddish and German was only one part of the contention. The other part, the tension with Hebrew, we will see in Yehezkel
Kaufmann's "The Hebrew Language and Our National Future."   [A.A.C.]

YIDDISH

One of the most important questions confronting the future
development of a Jewish way of life in Eastern Europe is the issue of a language
in schools. The struggles for Yiddish in the school have already begun.
Professor Philippson[1] prefers Polish, partially because it is natural (he claims)
for Jews to attach themselves to the culture of their host-nation. It is almost
painful to see the way a man—certainly inspired by good intentions, the
author of historical works—can so totally misunderstand the essence of
Judaism as a movement. He takes an admittedly inevitable condition of our
people and turns it into an ideal, a demand. On the other hand, the opinion of
a Jewish weekly is more comprehensible, at least to anyone who has no
illusions about the psyche of German Jews and their devotion to practical
motives. To wit:

> No matter how highly one may esteem the cultural value of the Yiddish lan-
> guage, it is certainly not a Western European language, and it has no crucial
> significance for the economic growth of the economically disadvantaged Jews
> in Eastern Europe.

This is the utilitarian viewpoint in its purest form. It would be just as advantageous for the economic growth of the Bulgarians and their participation in
world commerce if they consigned their language and their poetry to the

rubbish heap in exchange for German, or at least Turkish. Ultimately, our author might permit them, as he allowed the Jews, to speak the domestic tongue at home, in fairy tales, and in lullabies, so long as they conceal it in public and use an international European language to make better business.

If such peculiar attitudes are assumed towards Yiddish, the cause lies in a very specific impression uninterruptedly articulated in various ways.

Yiddish, so we hear, is not an educated, national language. It is termed a German dialect on the same level as Low German [*Plattdeutsch*].

Not an educated language. Yiddish is supposedly unattractive, and then (we hear this from Hebraists as well), it is allegedly impossible to use it for science and scholarship. The gutturals are reproached as unattractive—they probably came from the Hebrew,[2] but have also developed in other, non-Semitic languages, e.g., Dutch or Swiss German. Mainly, however, it seems that the Yiddish intonation is unattractive. Well, we know next to nothing about the laws that shape an intonation in a specific climate, or in a specific nation; however, I doubt that High German, for example, would essentially modify the accent. Not even the Hebrew language could be an antidote: in Palestine, I have often encountered an ardent opponent of Yiddish retorting with a *"madua lo"* (why not?) in the loveliest Yiddish accent. It is a risky business to condemn any language as being unattractive. Romance speakers regard the dynamic accent of Teutonic as extremely unattractive. In any case, I must confess that I have often enough listened with sheer delight to women and children chattering in Yiddish.

There may be more to the objection that Yiddish does not allow for scientific precision. Certainly Yiddish entices one into chatty garrulousness; it just happens to be very young as a literary language. If we compare it with the Greek language, which has had an unusually pure development, scarcely troubled by any foreign influences, we can say that Yiddish prose is more or less on the same level as Greek in the early fifth century before it was polished by the Sophists. It wasn't so long ago that Russian went through this stage. A living people, with its own academy, will also create its own scientific style.

However, the constantly repeated opinion that Yiddish is a German dialect is completely superficial.

The argument goes that Yiddish should no more be the language of Yiddish schools than *Low German* should be the language of *Low German* schools. Yet it is no foregone conclusion that the introduction of literary German, i.e., the High German language, in Low German elementary schools has been absolutely useful to Low German culture. Low Germans more and more are coming to realize how much native Low German culture has been murdered through this forced acceptance of literary German. On the other hand, one advantage is certain: the possibility of understanding classical German literature (which is simply not Low German) and consequently the possibility of achieving a uniform German literary culture. Only the person striving for the integration of Eastern European Jews into German culture and rejection of their own culture, has the right to use such an argument. But then he should not conceal this fundamental premise.

Is Yiddish, however, really a German dialect, which would greatly facilitate such assimilation? This is not so easy to decide. Just what is a "dialect"? What distinguishes a "dialect" from a "language"? Why is, say, Dutch, which is extremely close to the Rhenish-Westphalian dialect of German and easily understood by its neighbors, an independent language? It cannot be due to the independent political status of Holland, since Swiss German is similarly part of a separate state and yet is felt to be a German dialect, whereas Flemish, even without a Flemish state, possesses the independent situation of a language. A first determining factor is the existence of a separate literature. The intellectual stage that the European nations have reached requires an independent and separate cultivation of literary form virtually as a proof of qualification. The Swiss in their literature are attached to literary High German, whereas the Dutch have fashioned a literature of their own. From this point of view, we must acknowledge Yiddish as an independent language, at least since the 1880s.

To be sure, Low German has a literature too. In fact, Low Germans, for instance Klaus Groth,[3] have claimed that Low German is really a language divided into various dialects: Prussian, Mecklenburgian, Holsteinian, etc. General opinion has not gone along with him, due to the peculiar dependency of Low German writing on High German, a relationship totally different from that between Yiddish and German literature. We shall demonstrate this with a few examples.

> Oever de stillen straten
> Geit klar de Klokkenslag;
> God' Nacht! Din Hart will slapen
> Und morgen is ok en Dag.
>
> Noch eenmal lat uns spräken
> Goden Abend, gode Nacht!
> De Maand schient ob de Däken,
> Uns' Herrgott hölt de Wacht.
>
> Over the silent streets
> The bells toll clear;
> Good night! Your heart wants to sleep
> And tomorrow's another day.
>
> Let's say it once again,
> Good evening, good night!
> The moon shines on the rooftops,
> Our Lord keeps watch.

The feeling throughout is High German, and the poem can be readily translated into High German. This immediacy, however, is not based on the relationship between Low and High German oral speech, which are vastly different in tempo, rhythm, syntax, and feeling. (Theodor) Storm simply did not develop these Low German elements, he is totally dependent on High German artistic form.[4]

This dependency is not due to his having generally written in High German. The same dependency is equally evident in Klaus Groth:

Min Modersprak, wa klingst du schön!
Wa büst du mi vertrut!
Weer ok min Hart ut Stahl un Steen,
Du dreevst den Stolt herut.

Du bögst min stive Nack so licht,
As Moder mit ern Arm.
Du fiechelst mi umt Angesicht
Un still is alle Larm.

My mother-tongue, how fine you sound!
How intimate you are!
If my heart were made of steel and stone,
You'd drive the pride right out.

You lightly bend my rigid neck,
Like mother with her arm,
You wave around my face and then
Still my alarm.

This poem, too, shows no peculiarly Low German feeling developing into an independent art form. The words are Low German but the artistic form is lifted directly from literary High German, which has spent centuries developing forms through its own aesthetic. (Here, too, only the rhyme prevents us from translating word for word into High German with no aesthetic reduction, just as Hebel [1813–1863] did with many of his own Swiss German verses.)

This immediate influence of High German aesthetic may be even clearer, although in a different way, in Fritz Reuter:[5]

'Ik lid dat nich, Gevadder Dreier'
Seggt de Stadtspreker Snider Meier,
'Wenn hüt de Burgemeister Lisch
Will wedder pachten unse Bullenwisch:
Ik slag ganz patzig vör em up den Tisch,
Dat geiht j'e rein ut Rand und Band!
Fiw Daler!—Un dat man Kurant?'

'I won't have it, neighbor Dreier'
Says the townspeaker tailor Meier
'If today Mayor Lisch

Again wants to lease our *Bullenwisch* (bull pasture?)
I'll bang the table with my fist.
That's going beyond all bounds!
Five dollars!—and that in cash?'

If we were to translate this poem verbatim into High German, the new version
would clearly reveal that the original lines had a Low German feel to them.
Not because Reuter may have been the greater poet, but simply because his
verses directly take over the rhythm of living Low German speech, with no
elevation into poetic style. Yet whenever Reuter attempts such elevation, as in
Eikboom, in parts of *Hanne Nüte,* we once again sense the immediate
borrowing of High German forms.

There are, of course, beginnings of a poetic style in Low German, for
example Groth's *Matten Has.* Oddly enough, such a style emerges particularly in humorous poems, but such poems are the exception.

Prose is another matter. In Fritz Reuter's *Ut mine Stromtid,*[6] there are
enough passages in authentic Low German form that do have style. I once
read a Pomeranian translation of Homer in prose, which, though prose, may
have come closer to the mood of the original than any German translations
because, like the original, it was drawn from a living, spoken idiom. But the
few exceptions cannot eradicate the impression that no independent Low
German literary style has arisen side by side with the High German style.

Now, for comparison's sake, let us look at Peretz, who in many of his earlier
poems is certainly influenced by High German style. However, his Yiddish
translation of Frug's poem *The Cup*[7] surely evinces an independent language:

Der Koss
Sog mir, Mameschi, ich bet dich,
Is dos Emess, wos es hot
Mir verzählt der alte Seide,
As in Himmel dort vor Gott

Steht, kabjochel—steht a Becher,
Un wenn mir quälen sich do schwer,
Hot der grosser Gott Rachmones,
Lost in Koss arein a Thrär?

—Emess, Kind meins!—Sog noch, Mame,
Is dos auchet Emess secher,
As kummen demelt wet Meschiach,
Wenn vervüllt wet sein der Becher?

—Emess! Un dos Kind verklert sich,
Wart a Rega traurig still,
Fregt dernochten: Wennse, Mame,
Wet der Becher sein schäun vüll?

Un er hebt die blaue Augen
Träurig zu der Mutter auf:
Zü is ohn a Kno der Becher,
Wos mir leiden ohn a Ssoff?

Wos mir leiden aus in Goles,
Un der Koss will vull nischt weren!
Efscher tricknen durch die Johren
In 'm Becher aus die Thrären?

Un zerudert bleibt die Mutter,
Auf'n frummen Kind gebogen,
Un es zittern die Bremen
Über traurig-feuchte Augen

Un es fallen zwei Brillanten
Aufn Kinds verklerten Stern!

Gott in Himmel, hob Rachmones,
Nehm in Koss arein die Thrären.

The Cup
Tell me, mama, I beg you
Is it true, that there exists
As my old grandpa told me
That in Heaven before God

Stands, as it were—stands a cup
And if we have a hard time here
Does the Great God have mercy
And drops a tear in the cup?

—True, my child!—Say now, mama
Is it also real truth
That the Messiah will come
Only when the cup is full up?

—True! And the child ponders,
Waits a moment in sad silence
Then asks: When, mama
Will the cup at last be full?

And he lifted his blue eyes
Up sadly to his mother:
Is it because the cup has no bottom
That we suffer no end?

What we have to endure in exile
Without the cup ever getting full
Is perhaps due to the drying up
Of the tears in the cup in all the years?

And the mother remained uneasy
Leaning upon the pious child
Her brows tremble
Over her sad and wet eyes

And there dropped two brilliant tears
Over the child's pensive forehead

God in heaven, have pity,
Put the tears into the cup.

Here there are a few points, for example the word *troirik* (sad) in the fifth stanza, or the end of the seventh stanza, which I feel are not so much Yiddish as borrowings from literary German—but all in all, the tempo, the brevity of thought and phrasing, the coordination and emphasis of clauses, make for a strongly Yiddish character totally independent of literary German.

Or take the beginning of *Monisch:*[8]

Ihr weisst—min hasstam—
Die Welt is a Jam,
Mir sennen Fisch;
Teil sennen Hecht,
Schlingen nisch' schlect—
Sogt, efscher nisch?

Die Welt is a Jam,
Breit ohn a Schier;
Die Fisch sennen mir
Der Fischer is Ssam.

You know—quite certain—
The world is a sea
We are the fish;
Some of us are pike,
Not hard to swallow—
Say, perhaps so?

The world is a sea,
Broad without end;
We are the fish,
The fisher is Satan.

Who can deny that here Yiddish has developed an immediate, living completely un-German aesthetic of its own.

The issue becomes more complicated in regard to folk songs, especially because we have no truly authentic texts. Originally, the Yiddish folksong was certainly a rendering of the German folksong. The effects can still be perceived:

Mir heben die Hend gegen Misroch und schwören
Bei Zion ihr Fahn, bei ihr heiliger Erd,
Bei alls, wos mir lieben, wos heilig mir ehren,
Bei unsere Heldens zerbrochene Schwert.

I raise my hand against the East and swear
By the flag of Zion, by her holy earth,
By all that I love, by all I hold sacred,
By our hero's broken sword.[9]

There is no independent form here. The songs about nature also evince a strong dependence on literary German:

Kinder, kummt, der Friling ruft,
Bloh der Himmel, klor die Luft,
Schmekken süss die frische Blumen
Un die Tejchlach freilach brummen,
Leift in freien Feld.

Children, come, spring calls
Blue sky, clear air,
The fresh flowers taste sweet
And the Little Latkes murmur gaily,
Run in open fields.[9]

In comparison, let us look at the Yiddish version of a humorous song, known in German as the song about the ten little Negroes.[10]

Zehn Brider sennen mir gewesen,
Hoben gehandelt mit Lain,
Is einer gestorben,
Is blieben nein.

Oi—Jossel mit dem Fiedel,
Tewje mit dem Bass,
Spielt sche mir a Liedel,
Chotsch afm mitten Gass.

Ten brothers were we,
Who traded in linen,
One died,
Nine remained.

Oi—Yossel with the fiddle,
Tevje with the bass
Play me a song
Although it's the middle of the street.

Not only the change of contents, but the syntax, rhythm, intonation, and mood as well, are decidedly Yiddish. It indicates that the Yiddish folksong has a character of its own, particularly in humorous poems.

And now for prose. Such disparate writers as Mendel Mocher Sforim and Sholem Aleichem have taken the Yiddish sense of life and the Yiddish language and created a form that cannot be confused with any High German art. In fact, if there is any relationship here with European literature, it would tend to be with a Russian atmosphere: the same predilection for sketches, for abrupt utterance of emotions, for mellow absorption in moods.

The difference becomes quite clear when we compare the original text of a poem of Rosenfeld's[11] with Feiwel's translation into German. Feiwel was simply forced to restylize the poem, just as Schlegel did with Shakespeare and Fulda with Molière:

Ich bet euch, wie lang wet noch jagen
Der Schwacher dem blutigen Rad?
O, wer kann sein Ende mir sagen,
Wer weiss jenem schricklichen Ssod?

O schwer, seher schwer, dos zu sogen,
Doch eins is bewusst und beschedt:
Wenn ihm wet die Arbeit derschlagen
Sitzt teekef a Zweter un näht.

I ask you, how much longer will
The weak man pant (chase) behind the wheel?
Who can tell me when it will come to an end,
Who knows this terrible secret?

O hard, very hard, it is to tell;
Though one thing is known and certain:
When the work will kill him (grind him down)
Another will take his place and sew.

Feiwel's version:

Wer kündet grause Zukunft mir.
Wie lange der bleiche Mann
Noch jagen mag das furchtbare Rad?
Wer weiss das Ende, sagt an?

Ich weiss es nicht. Doch weiss ich wohl:
Wenn den,—ob früh, ob spät—
Die Arbeit erschlägt—sitzt ein anderer da
Und näht und näht und näht . . .

Who can predict the terrible future?
How long shall the pale man
Run behind the terrible wheel?
Who knows the end, pray tell?

I know it not. Yet I know this:
When—whether early, or late—
Work kills him—another will sit there
Sewing, sewing, sewing.

I don't mean to imply that these hazy, gentle half-tones cannot be recaptured in German, but they *are* characteristic of Yiddish, a Yiddish raised to a form of its own. A title like *Ois Yontev* (Holiday's over) is simply untranslatable in its painful melancholy that can instantly be understood by anyone who feels Yiddish, and Feiwel's lovely *Laubhüttenfest vorbei* [Sukkot is over] is simply not as full of immediate emotion. Nathan Birnbaum [1864–1937] is right: as great as the linguistic relationship may be between Yiddish and German, their spiritual relationship is insignificant.

A style that has developed on its own: that is the mark of an independent literature. When Birnbaum maintains that Yiddish, deriving from Middle High German, Hebrew-Aramaic, and Slavic, is a mongrel language like English, we must certainly protest. If we are to categorize a language in terms of its vocabulary and the main structure of its syntax, then Yiddish must be a Germanic language. But as soon as a people creates a literature, the question arises: can the writer take the language of life itself and raise it to an artistic form on its own terms? Yiddish has succeeded in doing so, Low German has not. Whereas the Low German writers, with a few exceptions, have been faced with the choice of either remaining trivial or borrowing from High German, the Yiddish writers, both in poetry and prose, have created something from the elements of colloquial speech, something that is no longer colloquial speech but style. Yiddish style, however, means autonomy of Yiddish. Not a dialect, but a language. This linguistic relationship does not involve a judgment, merely a statement of individuality.

This certainly does not exhaust the issue. I have already said that Yiddish does not yet have a scientific style. Not even German has one (although, granted, in German it is a matter of nonstyle due to abundance and not, as in Yiddish, lack of style due to poverty or immaturity), at least to the extent that French and English do, and if the generation of Ranke (1795–1886) and Freytag (1816–1895) once created such a style, it has meanwhile been long since overgrown with all kinds of subjectivism. The growth of style is essentially contingent on the possibilities of intellectual development in the people. At the moment, the Yiddish-speaking nation is experiencing a peculiar antagonism, the hostilities and encounters of Hebrew and Yiddish. Jewish youth in the Orient, from Aleppo and Teheran to Cairo, are passionate speakers of Hebrew; in Poland, Yiddish is growing into a literature. Contradictory developments. Hebrew, all style—and therefore, as Berdichevky (1865–1921) once explained, the language of young Jewish science and scholarship—in the process of becoming softer, subtler, more alive; Yiddish, once only a spoken, malleable language, has been moving towards style for several generations now. This essay is not meant to decide the issue, but merely to demonstrate the right of Yiddish to exist as a separate and independent language alongside German.

3. GRAETZ AND NATIONAL JUDAISM
JOSEF MEISL

EDITOR'S INTRODUCTION

JOSEF MEISL (1883–1958), historian and archivist, although born in Brno, became an official of the Berlin Jewish Community and in 1908 its librarian. He is the author of several important works including *Haskalah, Geschichte der Aufklärungsbewegung unter der Juden in Russland* (Berlin, 1919) and *Geschichte der Juden in Polen und Russland* (Berlin, 1925). After his emigration to Jerusalem, Meisl directed the General Archives for the History of the Jewish People. The present essay was published in *Der Jude,* Jahrgang II (1917–1918), pp. 471–78.

One aspect of the editorial energy of *Der Jude* was its simple preoccupation with pedagogy, its concern to compass the range of Jewish events, bibliography, and personae. These come together with particular felicity in Josef Meisl's essay on Heinrich (Hirsch) Graetz. Graetz, of course, has come under a cloud in recent decades; he has been cast as a mere raconteur of history who would rather select and highlight than report the Jewish past in its entirety, and as one who, in Salo Baron's epithetical characterization, was principally interested in "the story of Jewish sufferings and scholars."

In a certain sense the strength, and deficiency, of Graetz's reading of the history of the Jews may be accounted for by the times in which his ambition matured. Graetz was born on the cusp, so to speak, between two worlds, the one that concludes the enforced separation and isolation of the Jews of Western Europe and the other, marked by Mendelssohn's translation of the Hebrew Bible into German, the beginning of the *Aufklärung,* the emergence of the Science of Judaism, the rise of Reform Judaism, and the acceleration of Jewish acculturation. Graetz's decision to avoid dealing in his *History* with the personages of his day did not preclude his being one of the remarkable partisans and polemicists not only of Jewish traditionalism, but a very specific kind of traditionalism, one informed by notions of divine reasonableness and an almost architectural providence. The past of the Jew—its grandeur and misery—is the consequence of an enterprise that God sets in motion but leaves to human freedom to work out. Reason and freedom, twin motifs of

Graetz's intelligence, were not themselves the subject matter of any theological scrutiny for however much he regarded theology and theologians to be proper subject matters of history, he was not a theologian and, unlike Nahman Krochmal, his contemporaneous predecessor, he did not devise a collateral metahistorical schema to accompany the drama of events. The Hegel that Graetz had learned in Breslau from Christian Julius Braniss (1792–1873) and earlier from his association with Samson Raphael Hirsch proved sufficient to afford him principles at once rational, conservative, Western European, German, and with only modest wrenching and extension, Jewish.

Indeed, *avant le fait,* Graetz had been a German nationalist, seeking the unification of Germany and the realization of *ein Reich* well before 1870. There was, for Graetz, a natural affinity between the styles and rectitudes of Jewish tradition and the positive law and tradition of the German people, between the spirit of German humanism and that of the Jews, and German was the appropriate secular language of Jews, not Yiddish. Graetz considered Yiddish vulgar and of a piece with Polish and Russian Jewry, which he hardly understood, and the vagaries of Hasidism, which he reviled.

As Graetz has written in his essay, *Die Konstruktion der jüdischen Geschichte (The Construction of Jewish History),* "God is at one and the same time Lawgiver and King of the Nation; the civil is at the same time religious and holy, in like manner the religious has civic obligation. The civil servant is a servant of God." It is only now, considerably later, that one can read beneath the lines of Graetz's historiography to the recognition of a fundamental confusion that blocked not only his interpretation of the irrational and the mystical dimensions of Jewish history, but cajoled him to a view of an enlightened civility in European culture that has all but collapsed in our century. Before continuing it should be made clear that he was quick (much quicker, for example, than Hermann Cohen, a younger contemporary) to recognize the dangerous proclivities of German nationalism to embrace anti-Semitism, but he was unable to realize that Judaism as civil religion—however it may be grounded in an intellectualization of the role of *halakhah* in Jewish civic identity—did not convert the Jew as Jew into a civil servant. He did not see that the natural panoply of the Jew as citizen and worker in a secular society was citizen and worker in a society fallen from grace (that is to say, a society that, even if it abandons Christianity, is still in flight from Christian impulse and is in no sense secular in its origins), that the Jew amid the nations is always a Jew amid recidivist Christians, that the supernatural Jew—whose vocation is elsewhere—has still to guard the natural Jew with more than a post-Kantian, quasi-Hegelian shield and buckler.   [A.A.C.]

GRAETZ AND NATIONAL JUDAISM

(On the centennial of his birth, October 31, 1917)[1]

A whole gamut of praise and criticism has been showered upon this historian (Heinrich) Graetz. His partisans extol his learning, his thorough knowledge, his intuition and his inventiveness, which particularly equipped him to set about his great task of erecting that gigantic structure of his Jewish history with the small amount of raw material at his disposal. His opponents cavil at innumerable gaps, inaccuracies, biased distortion of facts, stylistic blunders, etc., labeling him a phrase-monger who told stories instead of history, accusing him of gross plagiarism, and so on. Which side is right? Both or neither. If we overlook doctrinaire condemnation of Graetz by the extreme orthodox because of his allegedly over-liberal and reckless attitude to the supposed dogmas of Judaism, and if we refrain from measuring Graetz's history by the standards of modern methodology and historiography we will be more or less in a position to justly appreciate the stature of the *oeuvre* of this man, who single-handedly produced it in the most difficult circumstances and with no significant outside help.

Graetz's *Geschichte der Juden (History of the Jews)*[2] remains, despite everything, a standard work, a peerless achievement, a national feat. This opus is precious not so much for its scholarly merit (which even the harshest critics, who have at least learned from its mistakes, both in detail and in the overall structure, cannot simply shrug off), as for being a truly popular book, which, unsurpassed in its genre, has exerted a tremendous influence on our life. Whole generations have been nourished by crumbs from the master's table. Particularly in Eastern Europe, this work, especially in its Hebrew translation, has deeply affected the enlightenment that has developed into the national movement. The key to this profound influence is to be found in Graetz's unique personality, in his thoroughly Jewish being, in his knack for living, rather than writing, history. This faculty, although naturally detrimental to scholarship, is the source of the undeniable virtues of his opus, which cannot be regarded as a mere bookish work, a herbarium, like, say, Jost's *History*.[3] This, more than any other emphasis, must be underscored by nationally oriented Jews, and if, hitherto, attention was generally focused on Graetz the historian, it is now time to say a word about Graetz the Jew.

Brought up traditionally in a pious home, Graetz rigorously stressed throughout his life the unalterable and basic religious character of Judaism, never deviating by so much as a jot from the ceremonial law. Even in his boyhood, while he may have been afflicted by doubts and aberrations, they never had a permanent effect upon his soul, nor could they lead him from the path of faith and deep religious feeling.[4] Ben Uziel's (Samson Raphael Hirsch's) *Nineteen Letters on Judaism (Neunzehn Briefe über das Judentum)* became his gospel, revealing a new understanding and immunizing his soul against all shallow enlightenment.[5] His profound study of profane subjects did not lead to apostasy, as was the case with most of the Enlighteners, and he remained a sworn enemy of the self-styled "modern" humbug and blind parroting that sought to force Judaism into the procrustean bed of a church. In his university days, he openly and unequivocally sided with the anti-Reformers in the quarrel between Geiger and Tiktin,[6] and in countless letters he poured his biting sarcasm over the "Reading and Teaching Association" created by a "respectable Jewish cleric, whose lectures are more and more richly seasoned with malicious remarks against celebrities of different opinions, who can't be slaughtered as effectively from the pulpit."

Graetz's sarcasm was also aimed at the "stubborn neologists," his caricature of the reform service with its "beadle-supervised system of silence," the "new agenda," the behavior of the rabbinate in the "Kasualfrage" and similar gains of the modern spirit.[7]

Hoping thus to bring fertile seeds to Judaism, he had joined forces with Zacharias Frankel, the ranking rabbi of Dresden,[8] in an abortive attempt at organizing the "more moderate" elements in the German rabbinate as a counterpoise to the destructive spirit of reform. But the full wrath of his fiery temper was leveled at the Mendelssohn school,[9] on which he heaped reproach and abuse, for which no invective was too strong. The entire eleventh volume of his *History* is one long protest against Reform Judaism and its followers: David Friedländer, that "ape of Mendelssohn"; Herz Homberg, " a producer of religious books on behalf of the Austrian police"; Israel Jakobson, who had no sense of "how shameful and ridiculous it was to bedizen the grey-haired mother in her daughter's shimmering gewgaws, which disfigured rather than adorned her"; all the Euchels, Löwes, Herzs, Kleys, Holdheims, et al. In short, all those whom Heine maliciously referred to as the "corn-removers of Judaism," who no longer "had the strength to wear a beard, to fast, to hate, and to suffer."

A whole world separated Graetz from Reformism, yet neither had he anything good to say about a Hirsch type of orthodoxy, or, otherwise expressed, the latter movement was completely unresponsive to him and the Breslau trend. It forgave neither him nor Frankel for the fact that so many seminary students left the "golden middle road" preached by their teachers and sold their souls to "Liberalism," and that Graetz had ventured into Biblical criticism, "running astray in the labyrinth of these airy hypotheses and hazardous conjectures" questioning the divinity of the Torah, and in *Israelit* (1891, no. 74), taking an objectionable stand on post-Biblical literature and the development of Judaism.

The journalistic trial waged against Wertheimer's essay "The Rejuvenation of the Jewish Tribe" (in *Jahrbuch für Israeliten,* 1863–64),[10] gave clearest expression to this antagonism, even though Graetz had nothing to do with the whole business. The imputation that the prophecies of Deuteroisaiah couldn't possibly pertain to a personal Messiah, but referred only to the entire people, had, in the opinion not only of the Viennese district attorney, but also of the rabbinical guardians of Zion, "defamed, ridiculed, and debased the Messianic doctrine of the orthodox Jewish church."[11] One can understand the fury of these "Jewish Tartuffes" at seeing their circles disturbed by such teachings, and their wish to suppress such an uncomfortable trend with all the petty means that seemed permissible to them in their feeling of powerlessness.

Thus one can easily refrain from reckoning Graetz as either purely orthodox or purely liberal. His Jewish sensibilities were beyond the conventional party clichés or, as he himself put it, "the patchwork of Jewish creeds." He regarded Judaism as a religion, but in a very wide sense, far surpassing the limits of the average conception.[12] He was imbued with the Jewish ideal of that ethic which prevented culture from becoming the gravedigger of Judaism and enabled it to keep its racial strength pure for thirty centuries of tenacious existence. Preventing the gap that would appear in the world if Jews and Judaism were to vanish must be regarded by every single Jewish man and woman as a sacred mission, so that the "thread may not tear which connects them with the ancestral line of millennia, not out of defiance or aristocratic pride, but out of an overwhelming sense of duty, in order to continue and make visible the miracle of the further existence of our national tribe."[13]

Such theses as these only seemingly overlap with the substance of apologetic sermons. After all, they were based on a completely different attitude and led to far greater consequences. Graetz certainly conceived Judaism as a national unity, which, of course, requires some explanation in order not to be confused with modern concepts.

Judaism, strictly speaking, is not a religion, if by this we mean the relationship between the earthly son to his Creator and his hopes for a direction of life here below. Judaism, in this sense, is a state law. The Torah, the Israelite nation, and the Holy Land are (if I may put it this way) in a magic relationship to one another. They are indissolubly linked by an invisible bond. Judaism, without the solid ground of state life, is like an inwardly hollowed, half-uprooted tree, shooting leaves only in its crown, but no longer capable of growing twigs and branches. You can put Judaism through a process of sublimation, extract modern thoughts from its copious contents, and blare out this extract with self-important, pompous phraseology, brilliant catchwords, as being the true essence of Judaism; you can erect a church for this sublimated, idealized Judaism and pass a profession of faith, but you will have embraced merely a shadow and mistaken the dry shell for the succulent fruit. You possess neither the Judaism that the Scriptures teach in unambiguous letters, nor the Judaism of three thousand years of history, nor the Judaism that lives unshaken in the conviction of most of its followers.[14]

Graetz lays claim to the national character of Judaism not only for the Biblical era but also for the Exile. His *History* is by no means a mere history of religion or church, because its subject is not just the development of doctrine but also an independent nation, which may have lived without soil, fatherland, geographical borders, or a political organism, but which managed to replace these material conditions through spiritual potencies. Scattered over the cultivated parts of the earth and holding to the host's ground, the members of the Jewish tribe have never stopped regarding themselves as a unified being in religious creed, historical memory, custom, and hope. . . . The Jewish tribe felt, thought, spoke, and sang in all the tongues of the nations that offered it cordial or cautious hospitality, but it has never forgotten its own language; it has always loved, enriched, and ennobled it in accordance with the cultural level that it has reached with all humanity. [*History*, Vol. V, Introduction]

No modern Zionist could more clearly emphasize the national being of Judaism.

Nonetheless, there is still a wide gap between ourselves and Graetz. He didn't go so far,as to acknowledge an inviolable solidarity of Judaism. We can occasionally infer a quiet premonition of a sense of community, for example, when he welcomes the July Revolution for striking a blow at "boundary-post patriotism, which demands that the German Jew be a German and the French Jew a Frenchman before everything else, and so on throughout Europe and the rest of the earth" [*History*, Vol. XI, p. 457]. But, a true son of his era, he could not abandon the various Jewries, and he felt an insuperable wall between himself and Russian and Polish Jews. Indeed, he did appreciate some of their virtues, their intellect and wit, and returned very enthusiastic from a journey to Galicia undertaken to publicize the orphan asylum in Jerusalem; but ultimately he saw them through the eyes of the German Jew, who imagines he has a monopoly on culture. In addition, so much of the life of the Eastern European Jew is so far from the line of official German Rabbinism that it could all too easily arouse a sense of strangeness and essential difference, which even such a warm-natured Jew as Graetz could not bridge.

Thus, he saw Hasidism as nothing but a "system of cretinization," mocked the "wily, joking method" of the Polish Talmud-teachers, called their thinking "perverse," their language an "ugly bastard tongue," "a repulsive stuttering and stammering," a "gibberish,"[15] accused them of having lost the sense of all that's "simple and true," of having "brought a new Middle Ages upon European Jewry in the era of Descartes and Spinoza, when the three civilized nations, the French, English, and Dutch, had dealt the Middle Ages a mortal blow," and of prolonging this new Middle Age in part well into the nineteenth century [*History*, vol. X, pp. 74–75]. And Graetz didn't even take notice of contemporary cultural trends among the Russian Jews, although he occasionally claimed to be familiar with them. Thus, in regard to J. B. Levinsohn, he felt: "If writing does not stimulate large groups of people, it has no historical momentum."[16] But that was as far as he went, and he became a partisan, who, like certain modern world-reformers in our midst, sat in judgment above Polish and Russian Jewry.

And there is one more essential difference between Graetz and Zionist theory. Despite his deep sense of Jewishness, he felt himself to be not just a Jew but also a national German. With some qualifications, one can apply the modern party formula to him: in Jewish matters Jewish(-national), in German matters German(-national). He acutely criticized the Germans and their anti-Semitism, thereby reaping a good deal of animosity.[17] And he did not shrink from vehemently attacking the anti-Semitic milieu and Christianity, "the arch-enemy." But this did not prevent him from feeling inviolable loyalty to the German nation. As a student, he had taken an active part in the German-National movement, and dreamed of a *Reich* long before 1870. When Treitschke suspected his German patriotism, Graetz took it as a harsh blow.[18]

Emancipation and civil egalitarianism, even at the price of Jewish solidarity, were idols riveting his gaze and not infrequently dimming his sense of Jewishness.

And yet it was more than an omen when large numbers of German Jews, who felt impelled to counter Treitschke's attacks, were nevertheless reluctant to identify with Graetz. Despite all the respect paid him, he remained basically alone and isolated, and too full of love for his tribe to find any refuge in the partisan politics of his age. This elemental love had created within him a great faith in the indestructibility and resurrection of his nation, the Messiah-people, who were to be faced with an even greater mission than spreading a higher morality. After all, throughout its history Israel has often enough proved capable of awaking from deathlike slumber, and destined for immortality. As evidence of this "slumbering vitality," which the Jewish nation has "kept as an inextinguishable spark," Graetz recalls the Talmudic legend of the resurrection of the body. "When death and decay have scattered the atoms of human organism to the four corners of the earth, there still remains a tiny bone that resists all destruction, that cannot even be demolished on an anvil. And it is from this indestructible essence that resurrection proceeds. If a nation has such a diamond core, then iron and fire are as naught against it, and corrosive acid even less; it actually spreads out again though the weight of pressure may have caused it to shrink to a tiny point."[19]

And Graetz believed in such a regeneration of Jews spiritually through science and scholarship,[20] as well as politically in Palestine. He knew Moses Hess personally,[21] would meet with him in Breslau, and got him to write for the *Monatsschrift;* he was influenced by George Eliot's and Oliphant's writings; he knew about the nationalistic currents in Russia, and about the beginnings of the campaign (in England, Russia, and other countries) for colonizing Palestine. On his own, he formed the conviction that the Jews as a cultural nation must come into their own politically. They would convey European culture to the Orientals, and could obtain the help of France, which had taken over the patronage of the Catholic Christians in the Orient, and the help of Louis Napoleon, who might be won over with the thought of strengthening his influence in the Orient, and possibly even the assistance of America, too.[22] Graetz, who never felt it necessary to mention these thoughts beyond an intimate circle of friends, never campaigned for them either. Yet everyone knew of his quiet love, and Hermann Cohen was not so far off when he accused him of being the very prototype of the "Palestinian," i.e., the national-minded Jew.[23]

In March 1872 the great desire of Graetz's life, the wish to see the land of his fathers with his own eyes, came true. He had long wanted to carry out this plan (once with Moses Hess), but had to keep postponing it. Not so much the alleged necessity of the scholarly "autopsy" for finishing the first two volumes of his *History,* as the desire for the experience of seeing the land in which his tribe had originated, induced him to go on this journey with two friends. And no less than the conviction of the "truthfulness" of the Biblical accounts, as a result of his observations he brought home a wealth of profound impressions left by the splendid natural surroundings of the land and the conditions of its inhabitants.

In a memorandum on the conditions of the Palestinian communities, he and his friends wrote all these impressions down.[24] He was horrified at the poverty, the terrible beggary, the deceitful organization of the *halukah* [distribution of charity], the physical misery of the population. He demanded a campaign against early marriage, as well as the building of schools, orphan asylums, and similar useful institutions. No wonder he and his comrades provoked the most vehement anger of Palestinian and German Orthodoxy, who were up in arms at his vilification of the *Talmide-hahamim* (Talmud scholars) as idlers and beggars. The orthodox spared no anathemas against these bold critics. After his return, Graetz began a lively agitation for a Jewish orphan asylum in Jerusalem. He undertook countless trips, lectured in various cities, cofounded the "Association for Educating Jewish Orphans in Palestine," told Baron Rothschild of his interest in promoting the agricultural school *Mikveh Israel,* and recommended Rabbi Samuel Mohilewer and several pioneers of the Palestine colonization to Rothschild.[25] The orphan asylum was founded and eventually combined with the Lämel School; its first director was Dr. Wilhelm Herzberg, the author of *Jewish Family Papers* [*Jüdische Familienpapiere*]. Graetz, until his death, devoted himself lovingly to that institution. For a short while he was on friendly terms with the *Hoveve Zion* [Lovers of Zion] movement. Dr. Leon Pinsker visited him on the way back from the Kattowitz Conference (autumn 1884), and Graetz was then elected a member of the committee through a circular vote. He didn't remain long, however, for he was repelled by the hypernationalistic propaganda, especially the kind expressed at the celebration of the millennial issue of *Ha-Melis* (*hag ha'elef*), early 1885. It was impossible for him to go along with such a nationalism, and he wrote a letter of resignation to the Committee of the

Friends of Zion. Thus ended Graetz's activity for the Palestine idea. In regard to Jewish political matters, he stepped forward only once more, at the meeting of the *Alliance Israélite Universelle* for Rumanian Jews.

Graetz loved the language of his ancestors as much as their land. He was no master of Hebrew style, however, and he knew the most recent Hebrew literature only through hearsay. He was much more interested in reviving the Hebrew works of Jehuda Halevi and others, hoping that this revival would have a great effect on arousing a Jewish tribal feeling, and so in 1862 he published *Blumenlese neuhebräischer Dichtungen/"Leket shoshanim"* (an anthology of modern Hebrew poetry from the second to thirteenth centuries). He felt greatly honored that his *History* was translated into Hebrew, and, as his letters reveal, he followed the translation of the first few volumes with great interest, until his death.

Love for everything Jewish permeates every line of Graetz's *History*. This love of his, not the scholarly worth or worthlessness, assures its immortality in the literature of our people. For Graetz, his *History* was not so much an object of research as an experience. Once, in Michael Sachs' home, Leopold Zunz, upon learning of Graetz's plans, commented: "Another Jewish history!"; Graetz replied: "But this time a *Jewish* history!" And he faithfully kept his word. He had a fine instinct for feeling his way into the past; he himself was the Jewish people, the wandering Jew, "who speaks all languages, has been in all countries, escaping all dangers and terrors in a way that must be considered a miracle, the youngest brother of time" [*Historic Parallels* . . .]. Thus Graetz, the national Jew, put up a prodigious monument to his people, a monument that may have cracks and flaws, and yet one that, as a whole, remains standing in incomparable splendor.

4. THE POLISH JEW
HERMANN COHEN
With an Afterword by Martin Buber

EDITOR'S INTRODUCTION

HERMANN COHEN (1842–1918), founder of the Marburg School of Neo-Kantianism, announced his renewed interest in and commitment to Judaism after the Jews were publicly attacked by the German historian Heinrich von Treitschke in 1880. Thereafter, Cohen's work took him to the Lehranstalt für die Wissenschaft des Judentums in Berlin. Among his important works dealing specifically with Jewish questions are *Religion und Sittlichkeit (Religion and Ethics)* and *Die Religion der Vernunft aus den Quellen des Judentums (The Religion of Reason from the Sources of Judaism)*, and the posthumously published *Jüdische Schriften,* edited by Bruno Strauss, with an introduction by Franz Rosenzweig. Cohen was a frequent contributor to *Der Jude;* the present essay appeared in Jahrgang I (1916–1917), pp. 149–56.

In the wake of World War II and the Holocaust, there is something particularly sad, even melancholic, in Hermann Cohen's anachronistic essay *The Polish Jew,* which might well have been omitted from this anthology, as an element of *Galgenhumor* obtruding upon the process of selection. It is precisely this paradox that is arresting.

It is not simply that the Jews of Poland are no more, but even more that when they lived—then, flourishing in those days during World War I—they were perceived by Hermann Cohen, the most distinguished and influential German-Jewish philosopher of his day, as somehow a stunted flower, put forth amid poverty, superstition, foolishness, to be rescued by the higher *Kultur* of German Jewry. Nearly a century after Heinrich Graetz, German-Jewish intellectuals continued to regard the Jews of Eastern Europe as essentially benighted. Although the view was not shared by many of the most important religious thinkers of German Judaism—certainly not by Martin Buber or his younger contemporary Franz Rosenzweig, whose own experience of Polish Jewry was diametrically opposed to that of his teacher Hermann Cohen—the attitude of Cohen was lamentably prevalent.

At the very heart of Cohen's thesis regarding the Jews of the East, his concern that they be raised up to the Idea, washed clean of their superstitions and bad manners, is the deepest order of embarrassment. The Jew who had to be presented to Treitschke "for approval" was one unencumbered by anything that might be taken for provinciality, rudeness, or narrow-mindedness. The Jew, whom Hermann Cohen had espoused before the intellectual anti-Semites and of whom in fact Cohen was proud, was not merely the equal of the German Christian, nor even *primus inter pares,* but one essentially superior. The splendid Jew of Hermann Cohen was a Jew pared of flesh—a man of prophetic spirit, ethical expansiveness, and metaphysical clarity. Such a purified Jew, stripped of vulgarity, a man of reason and spirituality, could stand beside the ordinary Christian, his visible peer, as his essential superior. Cohen's moral doctrine, it has always appeared to us, was grounded in a supernal *ressentiment,* a *ressentiment* that reversed the palpable signatures of alienation, making of the virtuous and civil Jew an order of excellence containing at best an extraordinary rage. The Polish Jew—Cohen is speaking in this essay not of the secular Jew (whose impetus he misunderstands) or the Marxist Jew (whose ethic he romanticizes), but of the poor Jew whom he thinks of as willy-nilly orthodox and Hasidic (drawing no distinction between the *mitnagdim* and the *ḥasidim).* It is an essay of tragic sentimentality, from which much cautionary wisdom may be gleaned.   [A.A.C.]

THE POLISH JEW

The Jew is a problem everywhere. The more his presence is felt as a fact, the more of a problem he becomes. But the Polish Jew, having been always a sensitive fact for German Jews, has been constantly more than a theoretical problem because he has been an ongoing object of their charity and a running entry in community budgets. At the same time, however, as the Polish Jew has remained a continuous source of sorrow, claimant as he is upon charity, he has aroused a deeper sympathy with the undeserved misfortune of a fellow Jew. Long before Whitechapel and New York became populated with Polish Jews, the Polish-Jewish wanderer burdened German Jews with the anxious question as to how to maintain such a huge number of people who were quite capable of living but were always exposed to the threat of extermination. And this political problem was connected, obviously enough, with concern about preserving Judaism in the face of a most serious threat to this major portion of Jewry. But such worries were not all: a more intimate problem became apparent. These hybrid people were certainly Jews in body and soul, and yet at the same time Poles or Russians as well. And since they had reached those countries only after migrating from Germany and had preserved in their popular speech, with Jewish loyalty for home, the German language, they have always constituted, especially through their constant migrations, a dynamic panorama of Jewish wandering.

Each and every Jew can learn an enormous amount from these wanderings, and personal experience is a fine substitute for the ever-increasing sums spent by the community administration. Every Friday morning my pious mother would follow the morning service with a prayer that such a Polish wanderer ('oraḥ) would appear as a guest at the Sabbath table. And when the guest in his rags turned out to be a rabbinical scholar, then Talmudic conversation between him and my pious father would spice our Sabbath meal. I am sure that many German Jews have had similar experiences in their childhood. How deeply such incidents have helped a genuine social attitude take root in us. Poverty was thereby associated in our minds with spiritual dignity. Charity was not so much a sacrifice to indigence as a forfeit to spiritual and moral virtue. No trace of disdain or uneasiness could remain in us; instead we felt a great surge of emotion for the fellow Jew who wore the crown of Torah upon his head. Such an experience, recurring from week to week, became not only a source of Jewish enthusiasm but at the same time a primary force of social idealism.

Gradually, however, the political conditions in these countries worsened, very much so in Galicia and to an atrocious degree in Russia. At the same time, national assimilation had reached Jews in all these countries, and had been a fact for some time in Poland. In the middle of the last century, Rabbi Meisels of Warsaw,[1] had been an enthusiastic advocate of Polonism in the Galician Diet without really giving up his national Jewishness. And we all know about the great part the younger generation of Jews have played in the Russian Revolution. We could not help being amazed at this Russian patriotism, for the Jewish intelligentsia should have seen the great danger in the mystical writings of the Greek-Byzantine orthodoxy. These artistically powerful writings are certainly a wellspring of Pan-Slavism, and they form the human, the moral rationale for the inhumanities of Russianism in its direct and indirect pogroms.

Despite these atrocities, which have been shaking the world for generations and have sparked protest meetings in England—despite all these devastations, the Jewish people has not been wiped out nor debilitated. Today, as during those past years, new spiritual energy is emerging from the jaws of hell. In all fields of knowledge and scholarship, music and fine arts, as well as industry and commerce, Polish and Russian Jews are astonishing the world, though such amazement may be tacit and discreet. The *parvenu,* after all, doesn't boast about his origins when he is permitted to bask in the radiance of Europe, nor does Europe honor the ghetto as the stable from which more than one hero of the mind has arisen. But the Jew, who loves his one God and recognizes in this single jewel the letter of safe-conduct for his eternal wanderings, recognizes it in the full depths of his being and therefore loves it with all his heart and soul.

Such a firm believer asks himself: where does this almost inexhaustible energy come from, surging from poverty, arising from the worst misery? Did Slavic poetry enchant the heart and mind of Jews, or did the Russian élan of intellect and judgment (which, despite the Slavs' weakness of will, cannot be denied) give the Jewish mind such an energy that it can not only compete with those nations in art and science, but even fecundate the West with its specific genius? How can we explain this enormous vitality, which gainsays the general reciprocal effect between well-being and spiritual culture?

My experiences at home with my parents offer what I believe to be the only correct answer. The spiritual energy of the Jews has its ultimate source in the literary treasures of the Jewish religion. The more familiar a Jewish generation becomes with these millennially ancient and eternally youthful treasures, and the more vital the contact of the Jewish essence with these basic mainsprings, the more alive and the more universally appealing its religious strength will be, along with an ethical and aesthetic self-esteem for its own right to live and for the historical future of the religion of the one God.

From these basic considerations there issues a conclusion that suddenly makes the Polish-Russian Jew a problem in an entirely new sense. The combination of poverty and strength, degradation and martyrdom, is no longer a problem; it is sufficiently clear in terms of Judaism's strength of faith and power of knowledge. And whatever the Polish Jew has accomplished for science and culture in general depends solely or mainly, in the deepest sense, upon this source. But meanwhile a new difficulty has arisen through which he becomes a problem—not merely as a Jew, but specifically as a Polish-Russian Jew—for both Jews and Judaism, and thereby for civilization in general.

Plehve[2] supposedly told a Russian Jew who had argued from the example of Western European Jews in their advantageous political situation that if [the Russian Jew] had the morality and religiosity of European Jews, "we would be able to deal with you in a completely different way." Yet long before I heard this alleged comment of Plehve's, I had, following my numerous encounters with these people, become preoccupied with much the same thought. I was often constrained to perceive the spiritual gap in the intelligentsia of Eastern European Jews: the absence of reconcilation between orthodoxy and religious indifferentism. When I told Zionists that I believed in God, some of them would reply with a skeptical or pitying shrug. And among many thoroughly noble members of orthodox circles, who after all are completely impregnated with habits of rabbinical scholarliness, I was horrified to discover a total ignorance of and therefore alienation from Jewish ideas and hopes. Since cultural historians tend to discern some kind of rationale for all the horrors of history, I was able to translate the familiar reproach about the participation of the Jews in Russian nihilism into that of their religious nihilism, and thus once again the imponderables that enter into pogrom policy had been located with dismal satisfaction.

The East European Jew does constitute a special problem in this connection. For no matter how great that same gap may be in cultured Jews, it has nevertheless been bridged to some extent by a much-decried religious liberalism. Moses Mendelssohn not only taught us the German language, thereby providing us with a maternal right to German citizenship; he also erected in our religion the great bulwark against modern civilization's war of aggression. All concomitant phenomena that appear to contradict this are impotent in the face of the historical fact that, in our alleged disbelief and after the actual disposal of a number of (though not all) ritual accessories, we German Jews, nearly alone, have created the *Science of Judaism*. This discipline is the greatest product of the spirit of Mendelssohn and the incontestable proof of his historical significance for the preservation of Judaism itself. In this creation of our discipline, he has become a second Johanan ben Zakkai.[3] The ritual, ultimately connected with sacrifice, was not abolished after all, but insofar as it has perished under our hands, we have continued our religious life all the same, and we reveal ourselves as an authentic people of culture through the revelation of the science of, and by, our religion.

This is the great example, the paradigmatic importance, of the German Jew for the future of Judaism, and even for Judaism in its religious development throughout the world. Even orthodoxy, as wholesome as its survival may be for us all, has been greatly helped—and not only in its own development—by our example. We free Jews, with the earnestness and the rapture of our monotheism, evince a sufficient vitality for modern religiosity. We offer this proof not only against all miscreance and all ethical skepticism but also against the Christological doctrine of redemption. And with the strength of these ideas, we defy and resist all the challenges, misinterpretations, and blandishments that have continued to diffuse their poison even today. We have managed to harmonize our history, as the continuance of our cult, with the innermost powers of both our religious tradition and our culture in general. No reasonable observer can doubt that our free religiosity is a vital energy of our cultural attitude and, particularly, of our general programs.

This unity, which the German Jew generally manifests in himself, has been lost—or, rather, was never attained—by the Eastern European Jew. This perception prompted me to visit Russia two years ago, and it was the correctness of this perception that was responsible for the immediate and enormously great success of my lecture tour through Saint Petersburg, Moscow, Riga, Vilna, and Warsaw. I can boast about it only because all credit is due to the issue and to the people themselves. In those countries there can still be found the old respect for scholarship that is a prime force in Jewish existence. I am better known there—which I admit quite sadly—than even in my own country, I daresay in Christian scholarly circles as well, not only in regard to my religious writings, but also my philosophical works. And with the directness that characterizes true intelligence, a personal rapport instantly developed during my long lectures between the speaker and the audience, and banquets and constant meetings solidified and deepened it. During these four weeks of May 1914 I had detailed conversations with more than a thousand of these people. It is therefore no idle fancy, but an insight into and a conviction about the possibility of success for the plan that gave rise to my desire and decision to take the trip in the first place: *My plan is to vitalize in those countries the foundation of a free, energetic religiosity in keeping with their cultural capabilities and to work toward the establishment of seminaries for the Science of Judaism.* A true life of religiosity for a cultured man is contingent on the living connection with religious science and religious education. It is from this coherent relationship that the social institution of worship draws its vitality and its true norms.

I am exhilarated by the hope that I will be able to continue and repeat my interrupted journey as planned. After all, old age has the right to speak personally. So permit me to say that I can wish for no higher conclusion to my life than such, albeit temporary, influence among these fellow Jews, whose spiritual and emotional energy, whose patient equanimity, whose simplicity and naturalness will be honored and loved by anyone whose sense of the natural has not been deadened. And if I am not destined to work personally on this necessary project for the future, nevertheless I have no doubt that the plan will succeed gradually and I feel that it must not be allowed to fall by the wayside. It is not enough that a vast spiritual and ethical energy abounds there in full vigor. We must also provide for those who are close to apostasy, for they are almost dead to this eternal life of ours. The cradle of European Jewry must be preserved as such in all its strength and unequivocalness. This is the only way to keep alive and enhance the cultural energy of the Jew for the sake of those countries themselves and for their own culture and politics.

Few of us realize what a vast amount of social energy is being generated there by the Jews themselves. We are overly prone to fancy that the Western European Jews are doing a great deal more simply because they accomplish much in their praiseworthy zeal. But anyone who has viewed the training institutions for handicrafts and applied arts in all these cities is filled with great admiration both for the social efforts of these people and for the talents of Jewish youth throughout East Europe in the minor arts and not just, as we know, in fine art and scholarship. I was deeply moved as well by my visits to exemplary orphan asylums, especially the one directed with ineffable love and modern understanding by Dr. Goldschmidt in Warsaw. And thus in the schools we have to admire the various ways with which Jewish leadership is trying to elude the cruel regulations of the authorities.

On the other hand, it is more than well known that Russian youth has been courageously and with self-sacrifice participating in the political and social efforts at elevating the Russian proletariat.

Despite all these manifestations of political maturity in Eastern European Jews, we should nevertheless not scorn the model of the German Jew in terms of politics. Here, too, German Jewry, by founding the Science of Judaism, has acquired and maintained ideal preeminence among all the Jews of Western Europe. From the mineshaft of specific scholarship, the living wellspring comes to flow through all the currents of Jewish culture. Historical facts are supported by the circumstance that the truly great men among us in all domains of the mind are inwardly associated with, and have sprung forth from, Jewish life and knowledge. The Jew anywhere is a Jew first, and this because of *Jewish religiosity,* not simply Jewish nationality. Wherever that religiosity is deadened, no genuine life can be produced by any modern magic. Jewish intelligence, like Jewish ethics, is not rooted in Moses and the Prophets and the Psalms alone; it is no less rooted in the oral teachings in the Talmud and the Midrash, as well as in the religious philosophers of the Middle Ages.

The East European Jew was a problem for us at first in a way that was injurious to him, because his living cultural Jewishness had been put in question. In the meantime, a look at not only his martyrdom but also at the social energy conserved within his suffering should console us that a great deal of genuine Judaism is still alive within him. On account of this, we must not despair that he will himself bring us salvation if he continues in even larger numbers than before to return to our lands, from which many of his number once migrated. With an almost superhuman endurance, which he has tried and tested, he will add a new impetus to our ideal ethics, our willingness to make sacrifices for spiritual tasks. And his acute intelligence and intuitive capacity makes him the right person to sharpen us, temper us, and spur us on to intellectual trials of skill. For, among us, the effects of Talmudic dialectics are unfortunately lapsing. But in Eastern Europe, they are as fresh as ever. Anyone who has experienced even a smattering of the intellectual nature of the Talmud will understand the great inner value that is to be had in accustoming oneself to gymnastics with vastly intricate mental concatenations, not just for research but also for social communication. The old heritage of intellectual elasticity will inspire emulation among us, and the natural intellectual gift of the Jew will find new strengthening.

However, all richness in cultural life depends on reciprocity. So the Polish Jew will not merely learn German scholarliness and German ways, plainness, uprightness, and rigorous conscientiousness, traits that have been weakened in him by the tricks and intrigues of despotism and persecution; he will acquire a deep empathy with the religiosity of the German Jew, which is annexed for his own personal life and that of his community, independently and in accordance with his own way of life. He will learn to understand that only true, scientific philosophy, which does not cultivate the dilletantism of imagination but is methodically integrated with the sciences, can justify the one God. This faith is therefore a matter of ethical cognition. German philosophy calls it "rational faith." *And this ethical rationale of religious morality will also become the basis of the political principles of the Eastern European Jew; out of it he will subjectively derive his right of citizenship.* He will confront not only Dostoevsky, but Tolstoy as well, with the banner of the one God, the intellectual doctrine of pure monotheism, without a trace of pantheism and in full scientific precision and unequivocalness.

It is with such an idealization that I view the future of Eastern European Judaism. On the old and venerable sites of the *Yeshiva,* there shall be erected faculties of Jewish scholarship. The creative energy of the Jewish mind and heart are inexhaustible. Jews of all countries shall unite against the persecution of the Jewish spirit just as previously they have united for political and social assistance. And the greatest triumph of the German Jew will take place when his Fatherland is permitted to bring about this true liberation, this inward rejuvenation of East European Jews through a gradual progress. How it would overshadow the piecemeal emancipation hitherto granted to the Jews! The higher meaning of this liberation would derive not alone from the greater number of people enjoying it. It is the true achievement of the historical meaning of Jewish emancipation that will ripen fully in the self-awareness of the Jew.

When, in the towns and villages of the East, the synagogue service is no longer performed with the drama and gesticulation of lamentation and immediate woefulness, but instead with a solemnity derived from a sense of the present, a solemnity of an intellectually objective cult of religious consciousness, when the Idea gains priority over the compulsive power of traditional sentiment with the magical paraphernalia of superstition, and when, accordingly, the spirit of genuine criticism enters science and scholarship so that studying doesn't turn into praying, and finally into skepticism and error because it is a confident persistence on the trail of scientific truth, when all these things come about, the house of prayer and the house of study will be unified into true places of culture. Then, in that day, the idealism of deep-rooted endurance, as well as the equanimity and mischief of the humor it nourishes and the indestructible sense of life and world inherent in these still-natural people, will become a blessing for Jews the world over.

Their suffering has granted the Jews of East Europe an historical privilege. It has preserved, with wit and humor, a naturalness that has a kind of aboriginal quality. We should not therefore scorn the virtue of assimilation. But its cultural value is coupled with an ineradicable vestige of aboriginality. If assimilation occurs without this combination there will be something wrong with it. The primal energy of aboriginality is the natural, the irreplaceable world-power inherent in all nations yet able to preserve its heritage and its property, until—as the Jew says—the Messiah comes, or as Ethics says: until the Idea of humanity comes closer and closer to its realization.

Afterword by the Editor [Martin Buber]

In a time like this, when leading German politicians are defending a border blockade [against Jews from Eastern Europe—J.N.], supposedly in accordance with "the general wish of their coreligionists," i.e., German Jews, we are more than glad to welcome the dispassionate and open statement by their spiritual leader that the free immigration of Polish Jews to Germany is in the best internal interests of German Jewry. In the light of these words, we can momentarily overlook the fact that we feel so differently about many other matters, that, especially in regard to the essence of a living Judaism and the means of maintaining it, we have entirely different ideas than does Hermann Cohen, we are at one with him in recognizing the enormous reservoir of spiritual, ethical, and social energy of Eastern European Jewry.

PART TWO

ZIONISM, JUDAISM, AND GERMANY

5. GERMANISM AND JUDAISM: A CRITIQUE

JACOB KLATZKIN

EDITOR'S INTRODUCTION

JACOB KLATZKIN (1882–1948), Hebrew editor and philosopher, was born in Poland, but pursued his education in Germany, where he was actively associated with the Zionist movement. After World War I he joined with Nahum Goldmann in founding the Eshkol publishing house, which published, among other works, the *Encyclopedia Judaica* under Klatzkin's editorship. After the accession of the Nazis to power, Klatzkin settled in Switzerland, where he died. He was a frequent contributor to *Der Jude;* the present essay was published in two parts in Jahrgang II (1917–1918), pp. 245–52, pp. 358–70.

It is immediately unacceptable that a great philosopher such as Hermann Cohen (and let there be no mistake, Hermann Cohen was a great, late, perhaps final, expression of the tradition of Kantian idealism) should describe a connection, an intimacy, a moral bond between a national spirit and a religious vision, between something called "Germanism" and Judaism. It is palpably unacceptable: who could tolerate a thinker—other than a pseudointelligence—who would write of Americanism and Judaism, except to satirize the former and exalt (or belittle) the latter. It is a juxtaposition of rhetoric, a polemical stance that means nothing, illuminates nothing, and finally condemns and exalts nothing. There could be no connection, nothing that would rationalize the influence of Judaism on Americanism or the spiritual roots of Americanism in Judaism. One remembers many essays of earlier decades when Jewish thinkers—I would call them quasi thinkers (thinkers, that is, who could manipulate the screens of intellection, working a mode of spectacle and presentation)—defined the interconnection between the Jewish rage for equity and justice and the tradition of English common law and toleration that lie at the roots of the democratic ethos described by Locke, Mill, Bentham, and the egalitarian philosophes. But Americanism—an essence of America, a spiritual condensation that can be called America (blue or beautiful no matter)—conjoined to Judaism is anathema to my mind.

And yet, before us, is Hermann Cohen's essay "Germanism and Judaism," written admittedly under the patriotic impulse of World War I, at a time when German Jews (but not Gustav Landauer, Gershom Scholem, and other rank-and-file members of the pacifist Socialists) were virtually solid in their support of the Kaiser's war. The essay, much of whose argument is quoted by Jacob Klatzkin in his fierce rebuttal (and available as well in abridgment in *Reason and Hope: Selections from the Jewish Writings of Hermann Cohen,* translated by Eva Jospe [New York: Viking Press, 1973], pp. 176–89) presents an argument that may be reduced to an essential trinity of notions: the intimacy, bond, cultural compatibility of the German and the Jewish national spirits rests upon a consideration of the moral resources and roots of the former in the latter, which Cohen purports to document as being the creative alignment of Judaism and Hellenism (and hence in Cohen's argument, given the roots of Christianity in Hellenism, the continuity of Jew and Christian); the *analogia realitatis* of Christianity and Judaism, the former supplying the roots of Germanism, the latter supplying the roots of Christianity, and by palpable syllogism, Judaism supplying the primordial roots of Germanism (albeit in its Protestant manifestation, Catholicism being hopeless for purposes of this argument); and lastly given, the Jewish resource of all that is excellent in the moral vision of a perfected and saved humanity (the ethical ideal of the Messianic), Judaism, Jewishness, and by implication, the Jew is the alter ego of the German.

Klatzkin's argument is devastating. He disposes of each phase of Cohen's analogy, demonstrating the selectivity of sources, the *petitio principii* on which much of the reasoning depends, the misreading and purposeful suppression of obviously contradictory evidence (Cohen's celebration of Luther's emphasis on internality and the transformed will, for example, which Cohen reads as Luther's indisputable dependence upon Jewish sources, despite the equally obvious fact that Luther despised Jews and preached their conversion or destruction), until the argument disintegrates.

Cohen's essay, which in its day was immensely influential and hence had earned the full weight of Klatzkin's attack (and another by Martin Buber) is an antique and need no longer be taken seriously in its details, but the form of the argument still obtains. It is structurally the argument from the purified absolute to the mundane embodiments of culture, from the exaltation of the Idea (whether of God, the Prophets, the Messianic vision) to the lists of concretion, where Jews of this or that nation and Christians of this or that society continue to confront each other. As Gershom Scholem has documented in his essay "Jews and Germans" (in *On Jews and Judaism in Crisis* [New York: Schocken, 1976], pp. 71–92), the argument between them was never really joined (much less dissolved into the moral harmonies and compatibilities Cohen envisaged). The German admired the energy and talent of the Jew, Scholem avers, precisely to the extent that the Jew gave over to the national culture the energies it could employ, while shucking the particularism that gave him identity as Jew. The Jew, for his part, was only too willing to shed the marks of ethnic particularity in return for being regarded as a fit German to interpret Goethe and Kant, admire the humanity of Schiller, and dream the dream of consummated assimilation. The Scholem argument is that Jews and Germans never met; Germans never celebrated the talents of Jews until long after Jews had struggled to their own fulfillment (Kafka, Benjamin, Freud), and then never acknowledged in their situation what was distinctively Jewish. Jews besought German culture and Germans condescended to grant it to them, but to imagine that there was symbiosis, dialogue, continuity between the Germans and the Jews is, in Scholem's view, to misread the facts.

But what of America? In the absence of the same insecurity, the same threat to civil rights, the end of the great fights for social justice and equity in which Jews were allied with the working classes (as fellow workers, not as Jews), the threat to Jews is not assimilation as the price that America demands for their liberation, but rather the ennui and desuetude of affluence. What will hold the Jews as Jews if America does not persecute them and the Israelis make peace with the Arabs? This question Klatzkin could not have foretold in his critique of Hermann Cohen, but it is here perhaps that Cohen, as a thinker who said of himself that "abstraction is my fate," has some proposals that may oblige us to think beyond particularities and to raise once again the most interesting theological question: why did God choose to create something rather than nothing, and among the entities of the world, why did He elect the Jews?

[A.A.C.]

GERMANISM AND JUDAISM: A CRITIQUE

The uncommonly inventive but not very fruitful literature on "Judaism and . . ." or ". . . and Judaism" has been enriched with a new work. This work demands special attention not simply because of the author's personal distinction, but also because of its new, young theme. It deals with a problem that was born in the first hours of the world conflagration and the ravaging turmoil of the spirit. It is a part of the war literature, which, ethically, particularly in terms of scholarly discipline and truthfulness, bears the mark of these dismal times. The literary location of this work and the newness of its theme make its subject of inquiry dubious from the very outset. We have instantly to ask: Why is it that the spiritual relationship between Germanism and Judaism has been discovered only now, in this time of war? How was it possible that, hitherto, we had no knowledge and no sense of the many ties that are said to exist between German and Jewish culture?

Rootless, ideological Judaism, which is not self-defining and is therefore constantly and arbitrarily forced into new relationships by an "and" placed fore or aft, has always been a convenient and pliable material for all possible theories, its adjustability making it just right for the role of intermediary that is extolled as its mission. The elasticity of abstract Judaism enables it to enter reciprocal relations suitable to the conditions of time or place; its methodological sophistry makes it constantly ready to couple, in accordance with its respective needs, with an alien national spirit and to ferret out a new relationship according to its respective requirement. No wonder that Judaism, in this age of chaos in concepts and law, is exposed, as a derelict, to all playful and serious undertakings that comment upon its ideas in various ways and in different countries, according to the demand of the hour, and force them into the alien ideology of the host nation. Thus Germanism and Judaism have suddenly been related because of events of war.

Let us turn now to Hermann Cohen's essay, *Deutschtum und Judentum*.[1] First and foremost, we have to say that it is rather difficult to subject it to a scholarly critique. The author formulates theses without proving them. Although they provoke contradiction, he offers them as established axioms. Loosely, desultorily, abruptly, he casts about the most astonishing thoughts that form the essence of his ideas on Germanism and Judaism, and when we set out to test them, we fail to find anything concrete to go by. We miss a legitimate construction of reasons. Before the postulates have even been sufficiently demonstrated, we encounter weighty conclusions that are forced, unchecked, upon the reader. The methodological carelessness with which Cohen treats his subject this time, actually forces the critic to limit himself to a few marginal remarks. Nevertheless, I will try to eke out this essay of Cohen's on the basis of his fundamental works and occasional articles and use the comparisons gained thereby to find a concrete frame of reference for investigating the philosopher's new doctrine in terms of its consistency and truth.

I. Judaism and Hellenism

"The third term of the comparison (alongside Germanism and Judaism) is Hellenism, to which both Judaism and Germanism were allied creatively so that the specific qualities of each acquired a new energy and physiognomy."[2]

Cohen uses this thesis to introduce his theory of Germanism and Judaism.

We have always thought of Judaism and Hellenism as opposites, as two spiritual sources and roots of life, two ways of thinking and feeling, two great world-conceptions and cultural directions, which, in their essence and their manifold shapes, were set off from one another and still have not reached a point of reconciliation. Despite all this, Cohen takes an alliance between Judaism and Hellenism, indeed, a creative alliance, for granted. He goes so far as to equate the Judeo-Hellenic relationship to that of Judaism with Germanism, since "both Judaism and Germanism were allied creatively" with

Hellenism. But we fail to find any evidence for this completely new teaching. To counter it, we need only cite all of Cohen's works, in none of which, whenever he speaks about Judaism and Hellenism, does he ever deny the deep gap between their world-views. Never does he express the peculiar idea of a creative alliance between them.

To be sure, there was an era in our history in which a part of the nation was under the sway of Greek culture. But if we wanted to view Judaism—which in its wanderings from land to land came into contact with various cultures—in terms of the geographic and chronological influences of its environment, we could find all sorts of spiritual relationships. But temporary influence and nonorganic mixing are not so much as essential kinship and essential fusion decisive for judging the spiritual dynamics of a culture. Such a seminal relationship may exist between Judaism and the culture of Babylon, Assyria, and Arabia, but in nowise between Judaism and Hellenism. "The opposites are harshly mated here, Greek frivolity and Judaea's idea of God" (Heine).

Philo the Jew, to whom Cohen ascribes the role of intermediary between Moses and Plato,[3] may have paved the way for Christianity, but was unable to reconcile Hellenism and Judaism. After all, Cohen himself calls Philo's Logos "the greatest conceivable deviation on the horizon of prophetism: the question as to an intermediary between God and Man. A profanation of God's transcendence, which cannot be conceived more abruptly within prophetic Monotheism."[4]

Philo's gnosis could not take root in Judaism, and, like the offshoots of the logos idea, had to lead to Christianity. In general, Alexandrine Jewish theosophy had no profound effect on the development of Judaism. Not because many works of this literature were lost: they were lost because they were forgotten, and they were forgotten because they had an apologetic and therefore purely temporal character. This genre is a patchwork, the abortive efforts of artificial interpretations, meant to justify Judaism before the forum of Hellenism. It was a momentary demand, unable to create any permanent values. The allegorical and sibylline books, with their manipulated and forced comments and interpretations (interpretation is the instrument of apologetics), never found any entry into Judaism, and proved impotent in their syncretic efforts to clothe Jewish contents in Greek garments.

The influence of Plato and Aristotle on our religious philosophy is not to be underestimated, but the influence of Islam on Jewish thought is far more important. Cohen himself certifies Islam for its "spiritual leadership in Jewish philosophy."[5] Can we see a creative alliance between Judaism and Hellenism in the fact that the Greek sciences were introduced into the vestibule of our Law "as female cooks and makers of spiced sauces" (Maimonides) in order to explain rationally and give sanction, when necessary, to our religious laws? Even for the author of *Guide of the Perplexed* the influence of Greek philosophy didn't get as far as the Mishnah Torah; he uses it only in the introduction; his great life's work, which acquired an authoritative power for our community, was untouched by Greek ideas in its foundations and its doctrinal contents.[6]

And one more thing. One can talk about a specific trend in Greek philosophy as affecting Judaism, but not about an alliance of Judaism and Hellenism per se. After all, the spirit of Greece does not consist of Plato's doctrine alone. Plato is merely one of its representatives. Many scholars of Hellenism, including Nietzsche, see in Plato and his moral philosophy premonitory signs of the decadence of later Hellenism. Whatever one may make of this, Greek philosophy is not exhausted by Plato's idealism and the "idea of the good." Can we simply ignore Heraclitus, the doctrine of opposites, and the fundamental thought that "War is the father of all things?" Or is the picture of Greek philosophy complete without the doctrine of the laughing philosopher and without the schools of the Cynics and the Skeptics? Did any of these philosophies exert even the slightest influence on Judaism?

Now Judaism has certainly been profoundly influenced by Neo-Platonism ever since Solomon ibn Gabirol (Avicebron). The effect of pantheism is unmistakable in all creations of the Kabbalah. Yet Cohen describes pantheism as the sharpest contrast to Judaism.[7] So he cannot base his theory on this relationship between Judaism and Greek thought. In what, then, does the creative alliance between Judaism and Hellenism consist?

We find even less of an answer to this question when we look at Hermann Cohen's own teaching of the spirit of Judaism!

He has probed deeply into the essence of Judaism and focused correctly on the contrast with all cultures deriving from myth. Cohen teaches that myth lacks the ethical knowledge that separates man from nature. It cannot, therefore, erect any standards for the relationship between man and man. It is aimed at what is and not at what should be; it is limited to the relationship between man and God, seeking to fathom the nature of God, the essence of the Creator and the universe. The gods of myth proclaim the good fortune or misfortune of men, victory or destruction, but not what is good and what is bad.

On the other hand, the prophetic notion of God is based on the relationship between man and man. It is only from this level that the relationship ascends to God. The Jewish religion is animated not by a metaphysical interest in the nature of the essence of God, but by the knowledge of God. God tells man what is good. He does not proclaim anything about Himself. God tells us not what God is but what man is. "He has told you, o Man, what is good." God teaches ethics. This teaching is his office. And only here does God reveal Himself to man. When the God of the prophets requires man to recognize and love Him, He is asking man to recognize and love ethics. Recognizing God does not mean recognizing His nature and essence. The prophets resist the extraethical interest of myth in the being of God. God knows the ways of man and the thoughts of his heart; but God's ways and God's thought are not the ways of man. "Would you want to find the secret of the Godhead?" Hence the rebellion against God's attributes. Maimonides even dares to abstract the attribute of life from the notion of God, completing the negation by arguing that ignorance of the attributes is ignorance of God's essence. He denies all attributes of divine being and essence and limits the cognition of God to the attributes of action, to the qualities that can serve as model concepts for human behavior. "Be merciful the way God is merciful. Be forgiving the way God is forgiving." God's essence is defined as the ideal of the virtues, as the prototype of the ethical in whose image man is made. Beyond this cognition of divine ethicalness, the essence of God is unfathomable, that is to say, God is not an object of religious knowledge and belief. God, however, does not signify the power from which man can draw his ethics. Cosmically, and no less ethically, every kind of emanation is proscribed. Ethics cannot overflow from the essence of God to the essence of man. Monotheism does not know of any union of man with God. God is the exemplar, the ideal by which man gauges his actions. The commands "shall" and "shall not" are merely a different expression for the essence of God as prototype and ideal, as the ultimate law and pattern of human ethics.

The problem of the Jewish religion is man, not God. Man is the crown of creation. "From the very beginning You separated Man and chose him to stand before You." Man does not merge into the being of nature; his realm is the being of ethics. He has to perform and realize the ethical. God can assist him. But this is already an expression bordering on popularization. The Talmud puts it more precisely: the fear of God lies outside the sphere of divine omnipotence. While myth sets up and holds fast to an immediate relation between man and God, the prophets oppose such a relationship and direct the eyes of man to his fellow man. The idea of humanity is not a product of Greek philosophy which, even in its Platonic depth, is still bound up with the myth of the local gods. Myth has nothing in common with humanity; its interest is at best in the family, the tribe, the nation: no pagan myth has ever focused upon humanity. The idea of humanity is the fruit of the idea of the oneness of God. The oneness of God simply means nothing but the oneness of mankind. The one God makes mankind a unity. The one and single God is the opposite of both the multiplicity of gods and the multiplicity of men and nations. It is only in the uncritical view customarily associated with the books of the Old Covenant that the prophets come later than the five books of Moses. The prophets discovered the One God. And they discovered Him in the Messianic idea of the eventual unification of mankind. By defying the mythical correlation between man and God and replacing it with the correlation between man and man in the matrix of the Jewish religion they were able to discover the oneness of the human race, the highest and ultimate notion of ethics: the Messianic idea.

It was only in the Messianic idea that the Jewish notion of God became meaningful and perfect: the idea of the future. *God signifies the guarantee of the reality of ethics.* Nature is not ethics nor is ethics nature; however, that which should be is not denied the being of nature. Ethics is not a given. It is a mission, an ideal rather than a reality. Ethics becomes reality; it is not invented, fabricated, or fantasied. There is a correspondence between the two modes of being, between the being of ethics and the being of nature. The Jewish God is the God of truth: ethics is truth because it is the future of all reality. Perhaps even more characteristic of monotheism (in opposition to the gods of myth) than oneness is *truth*.

The Messianic idea of God, with its concepts of truth and the future, does not say that it is good, but that it *will* be good. For the Greeks, hope is merely a vain affect and no more valid than fear. Myth remains trapped in this relationship to the future. It shifts ethics back into the past. For myth, ethics becomes a lost paradise. The will does not soar up to the future in positive activity. It slackens into the desire for a golden age, the age of a lost ethics; it has no image of the future. The prophets project the ideal of ethics into a faraway future, the end of days. They are not content to say that this is how it should be. They also say that this is how it *will* be. They are the creators of a new kind of thinking, which we call religion.

Once we understand fully the scope of the Jewish concept of God it will be seen that there is no basis for the argument of priority between Israel and Babylon respecting the notion of monotheism. For Judaism, monotheism signifies not only the oneness of God, His indivisibility, but also, and even more so, the uniqueness of divine being. The uniqueness of God means that His being is not the being of nature, but rather the being of the ethical. God's being is one: His mode of being differs from all modes of being in nature. This means that the reality of the ethical differs from the reality of nature. It is the reality of the ideal, of the future, of eternity.

Jewish monotheism is an unconditional denial of pantheism, which ultimately derives from myth and which recognizes and levels God in nature. Pantheism is naturalism; it reabsorbs ethics into nature. There is thus no compromise possible between monotheism and pantheism. The *pan* of nature is the absolute contradiction of God's uniqueness. Xenophanes' concept of oneness does not share the sense of monotheism because it does not have a sense of uniqueness. Xenophanes binds God and the world; the world is one and God is one. Such an analogy means finally that God is one with the world. Clearly the Eleatics were the founders of pantheism. Not even Anaxagoras, with his *nous,* inaugurated a monotheism of metaphysics. In contrast to all myth and pantheism, monotheism teaches the transcendence of God. "Transcendence, however, does not come from this catchword of Plato's, but from the God of the prophets."[8]

Cohen sees, in sum, an irreconcilable antithesis between Jewish religion and all pantheism, an insuperable gap between the spirit of Judaism and any cultural spirit rooted in myth. There is a consequent gap, in Cohen's view, between Judaism and Hellenism as well. He stresses that the concept of oneness in Greek cosmology never overlaps with Jewish monotheism. He asserts that hope, as an ethical anticipation of the future and the basic motive of Messianism ("a new way of thinking"), was alien to the Greeks. He emphatically and resolutely maintains that the idea of humanity, which he makes the fundamental notion of Judaism, was never a part of Greek philosophy, which "even in the Platonic depth remained bound up with the myth of fatherland gods."

How are we to take Cohen's sudden discovery, in 1915, of a creative alliance between Judaism and Hellenism?

If Cohen had followed up his theory of Judaism in contradistinction to all cultures anchored in myth, he would never have been tempted to connect Judaism with Germanism, and, as an intermediary link in the comparison— Judaism and Hellenism.

It is not enough to grasp Judaism as an ethical doctrine. There are other ethical doctrines, but their source is mythic. One has to determine the specific characteristic of the Jewish ethical doctrine. To understand the two ways of being and the separation between divine and natural being does not yet constitute the essence of Jewish religion.

The peculiarity of Jewish religion is the Law, the Constitution of the Law. Many other mythical religions are permeated with ethical tendencies, but in none of these does myth have a legislative function; none of them is a code of rites, ethical rules, and political laws. The opposition to myth did away with the metaphysical as well as the cosmological motive and shifted the focus of the spirit from the universe to man, from theoretical interest to the practical knowledge of good and bad. Jewish religion, basically, has no metaphysics. Its religious philosophy developed very late and under foreign influences. Our religion has norms, "shalls" and "shall nots," but no ideology, no doctrinal axioms, no dogmas; they did not appear until the Middle Ages, and then only as systematic guidelines. In short, the Jewish religion is a teaching of laws and not of ideas.

Spinoza and Mendelssohn recognized this peculiar feature and distinguishing mark, the essential trait of the Jewish religion as legal constitution. Cohen cannot forgive them for this, especially since Kant, led astray by them, asserted that Judaism was not really a religion, for "the Jewish faith, in its original structure, is an epitome of merely statutory laws, on which a state constitution was founded."[9]

In their alleged apologetics, the so-called liberal Jews are eager to demonstrate that our religion has the character of an ideology rather than a church. This opinion, which has become a common property of modern Western European Jews, distorts, in its correct opposition, the relationship of the two concepts and, thereby, the unique physiognomy of the Jewish religion. Because it is a legal constitution rather than a metaphysical doctrine, our religion is not a church. *Torah* doesn't mean simply teaching but rather teaching of the Law; it is described as a command, a set of regulations, a legal system. No other religion has the normative power of obligation and validity; no other religion determines and encloses every last detail of human activity; no other religion is as full of works. The Jewish religion encompasses all existence in its full diversity, regulates all actions, rivets the life of the individual and the community in legal forms, from the most intimate and most chaste to the most external and most profane. Our princes in exile, our geniuses and rabbis, were not clerics and pastors; they were leaders and administrators of our communal life; they were judges, but they never had the aspect of saints.

All the magic of pantheism, which not even the Jewish religion could withstand, was therefore unable to shake it to its very foundations. The Kabbalah did not manage to effect a schism in Judaism since it wanted to be only a theoretical renewal and not a practical reform; it never assailed the Law at all. The only disputes detrimental to the unity of Judaism were those striving for a reform of the Law, e.g., the sects of the Essenes, Sadducees, Karaites. Christianity had to leave Judaism only when the Pauline struggle against the "curse of the Law" gained primacy.[10]

Thus, the ideas of Hellenism could never penetrate to the core of legislative Judaism. They always remained on the periphery of our knowledge, on the edges of our religious philosophy, at best acting as "cooks and makers of spiced sauces" to render some assistance to the doctrine of the Law; they never influenced the legal constitution itself. It is significant that Maimonides, although using the teachings of Greek philosophy in his apologetic Arabic work *Moreh Nebukhim,* refused to let them influence his Hebrew codex Mishnah Torah; the alien laws did not in any way weaken the "Strong Hand" (*Yad ha-ḥazakah*). It is for this reason that this codex could become a cornerstone of our religious edifice.

Judaism simply could not unite creatively with Hellenism. If Judaism had entered such a relationship, it would have had to abandon the spirit of the Law and thus its ultimate source and basis. Nor could Christianity have united with Hellenism had not its teachings killed the vital nerve of Jewish doctrine, rejecting the supremacy of the Law and adopting a position irreconcilably contrary to that of Judaism.

II. Judaism and Christianity

Christianity is a principal prop for Cohen's bridge between Germanism and Judaism. He apparently argues to the following conclusions: Judaism is the source of Christianity, Christianity the source of Germanism, hence Judaism is also a source of Germanism.

By this analogy, however, Judaism would have to be seen as the source of the spiritual culture of all Christian nations. Why does Cohen claim the advantage of a connection with Judaism for Germanism alone? Why does he exclude the Christians of all other countries? Because, he says, the original Jewish power of Christianity became alive and effective only in Protestantism, and it was only in Protestantism that the spirit of Germanism found its true expressive form. But what of the millions of German Catholics? Perhaps they will forgive Hermann Cohen for not finding them worthy of an alliance with Judaism, but they will assuredly protest his denying them their Germanism and their participation in the German *Volksgeist*.

Cohen regards the most intimate bond between Germanism and Judaism to be the idealism common to them.

1. "German philosophy is idealism."[11] Cohen never proves this statement. Nor does he prove that idealism, the "conscience of philosophy and science," is peculiar to German philosophy alone and absent in any other, e.g., French philosophy. He refers to the teachings of Nicholas of Cusa, Leibniz, and Kant. But here we come upon a simple, but crucial question: what about Hegel? Why is this great thinker not reckoned among the German philosophers? The answer is simple: since Hegel is not an idealist (in Cohen's sense), he cannot be regarded as a representative of German philosophy, which is posited as being founded upon idealism. This is the purest *petitio principii*. Cohen condemns Hegel because of the precept "What is rational is real," and says

Here we see the enormous difference between Hegel and Kant, for Kant would say: What is rational is not real, but should become real. The difference generally between what is and what should be not only distinguishes two worlds, but also distinguishes the world-view of pantheistic metaphysics from that of ethical idealism because it is theoretical idealism.[12]

This is the basis and root of materialism, in which the materialism of the historical view, which, to their great detriment, rules all Socialistic groups, is grounded.[13]

The materialism of the historical view is in sharpest opposition to ethical idealism.[14]

But does Cohen have the right to read someone like Hegel out of German philosophy? Can he deny the powerful influence of the materialistic-historical view on German thinking?

And what about the historical-legal school headed by Savigny[15] (the State is "the physical form of the spiritual *Volksgemeinschaft* or national community . . . the organic manifestation of the *Volk*")? How can Cohen omit this school from German scholarship? Or can he insert it in German idealism as he defines it? After all, he does say: "The historical-legal school is rooted in a naturalism which, according to the customary way of spiritualism, establishes itself and presents itself as such."[16]

And Schopenhauer? Doesn't he belong to German philosophy? Cohen says openly that "the fact that Schopenhauer could actually call optimism nefarious—that one word reveals the ethical emptiness in that man's political attitude."[17] But does Cohen have the right to ban great German thinkers from German philosophy because they are not idealists in his sense?

And Nietzsche, with his doctrine of the ego and the will to power? Quite a number of people find in him the authentic expression of the German spirit free of any foreign paraphernalia. In any event, one cannot simply leave Nietzsche out of German philosophy.

And as well Spinoza ("who likewise was not offended by the formula identifying law and power"),[18] the father of philosophical pantheism, who, Cohen repeatedly says, fashioned the greatest contrast to ethical idealism (note the chapters on "The Ideal" and "The Idea of God" in the *Ethics of Pure Will*)?[19] How vast and deep was the influence of Spinoza's world-view especially on the German spirit, on German philosophy, scholarship, and poetry? Cohen himself does not underestimate this factor, but he painfully regrets it: "And so it came to pass that according to Kant, Spinoza took over the inner leadership of the spirit" (*The Religious Movements of the Present*, p. 20).[20]

Cohen emphasizes a further feature of German idealism: humanity. He thereby posits a further inner relationship between the German spirit and Judaism. And French humanity? Cohen replies: "The thing that distinguishes the German concept of *Menschheit* from the *humanité* of the French revolution is the ethical foundation. German *Menschheit* alone is based on ethics."[21] Yet elsewhere he says: "But in the connection and agreement with the model ethics of the new age that began with the French revolution, we can find solace and hope alike for both (law and cultural power)."[22]

2. Cohen locates the idealism of Judaism in singularity, pureness of soul ("My God, the soul that you have given me is pure"), and the reconciliation of man with God as the redemption of man from sin.

On the other hand, Cohen regards these same concepts as the basis of the contrast between Judaism and Christianity. But if they separate Judaism from Christianity, then they would have to separate Judaism from Germanism as well. After all, according to Cohen, Christianity is the source of Germanism. Isn't there an obvious contradiction here?

Cohen regards the Jewish concept of the pure soul as the opposite of the Christian doctrine of sin. He says:

> And we should certainly not be surprised that the hatred of the cynics and self-idolaters is aimed at the Jews in particular: for we have never recognized original sin, and in our daily morning prayer we thank God for the purity of the soul. . . . Man is not holy. The holiness of a human being is a blasphemy. But man *is* pure, his soul is pure.[23]

And again:

> Purity of heart is the foundation of conviction, and this is claimed to be a particular virtue of Christianity. Experience is supposed to contain the deepest basis of conviction. However, we again see the sharp difference. Blessed are the

pure in heart, for they shall look upon God. A pure heart is connected with blessedness. In contrast, the Psalm asks for a pure heart as a renewal of life. "Create a pure heart for me, God, and renew a firm spirit within me." The pure heart and the firm spirit are thus the task of creation and its constant renewal, but not a possession, either in this world or the next. . . . Also as Paraclete the idea of Man, and therefore Christ, cannot be offered as our model. The power to struggle unceasingly for pure conviction is rooted in God alone, and therefore in our faith in Him.[24]

With regard to salvation and atonement, Cohen says:

Here, however, is where Judaism and Christianity differ in their conception of religion. For in the pure monotheism of Judaism, the God of mercy and forgiveness has only this meaning: to guarantee the goal, the success, the victory of the ethical work of man. . . . God's transcendence signifies the sufficiency of man for the assertion of humanity. Christianity, in contrast, participates in the ambivalence of pantheism and allows God to participate with man in ethical work. . . .[25]

Whereas Judaism sets up the relationship between man and man, and has God recede into the background of the ideal, Christianity resumes the immediate relationship between man and God. . . . The immediacy is meant to include the mediator. God must therefore become a mediator so that the relationship between God and man may become immediate. This is how it differs from Judaism.[26]

And once again, as regards salvation and the Messiah:

We have thus come to the outwardly sharpest difference between Judaism and Christianity. . . . For Christ is the redeemer of the individual, and that is the only way that he can or will be the redeemer of mankind. The Messiah, however, is the redeemer of mankind, and that is the only way he can or will be the redeemer of the individual as well.[27]

It appears therefore that the same factors distinguish Judaism and Germanism insofar as the latter is joined to Idealism, which ultimately derives from Christianity. I do not want to investigate the correctness of Cohen's distinctions between Judaism and Christianity. I am merely citing Cohen against Cohen, his major works against his most recent piece of writing.

We simply cannot understand how Cohen can say in his afterword to the second edition of Deutschtum und Judentum: "My striving, throughout my life and particularly in this work, has been to teach Christians and Jews that the contradiction between these two historical manifestations has been a deceptive one." It is not "particularly in this work" but only in this work that Cohen has sought to reconcile the contrast between Judaism and Christianity. We must, however, defend Cohen against himself and assert that "throughout his life" he has tried not to gloss over this contrast.

Aside from this internal contradiction, aside from these distinguishing factors to which Cohen has always referred as the deepest contrasts between Judaism and Christianity (and on which he now builds the bridge between Judaism and Germanism through the intermediary of Christianity), the connecting link must appear dubious per se. Can we judge and appraise the culture of the Christian nations, and especially of the German people, as Christian in a scholarly sense? Isn't the term "Christian culture" merely a popular expression of external appearance and not an adequate expression of the essence of this culture? It is Roman, Greek, anything but Christian. Jean Paul Richter asks: "We have a wandering Jew, but where is the wandering Christian?" He could state it more simply: We have Jews, but where are the Christians? Judaism is a reality, Germanism is a reality, but Christianity is a fiction or an anticipation, a thin patina on deeply non-Christian cultural stratum. There is a Christian doctrine, but no Christian life. After all, is the Christian state Christian? Is the notion of Christianity consistent with the notion of power? "A Christian state, a Christian politics is an impudence, a lie, somewhat like a Christian army command" (Nietzsche). Are the uninterrupted Christian persecutions of Jews Christian? If there ever was such a thing as true Christians, they could only have been the first Jewish Christians, and if there are any Christians today, one may have to seek them among the Christianizing Jews. . . . But the culture of the Christian nations remains, despite all churchly power, basically non-Christian. Or are we to take the present world war as proof of an existing Christian culture? Israel Zangwill feels that this war signifies the bankruptcy of Christianity. His judgment is unfair, since his assumption is false—as if Christianity ever had a cultural reality that could have gone bankrupt.

We have the right to demand that a great thinker like Hermann Cohen refrain from judging the spirit of culture in terms of its usurped name, and instead look upon it in terms of its roots, in terms of the living forces that also animate it unconsciously.

Germanism has a special right to boast that Christianity was unable to wipe away the national physiognomy of the German cultural spirit, that is, of Germanism. It is not Christian humility but Germanic courage that constitutes the peculiar characteristic of the German spirit. Not Christian asceticism, but Hellenic *joie de vivre*. There were good reasons competent representatives of Germanism proudly called themselves anti-Christians. They were fighting for the purity of Germanism, for the liberation of the Siegfried soul, which was starving in the dearth created by the alien dogma.

Is not pantheism—which Cohen assesses and rejects as the greatest contradiction to monotheism—a basic element of the German spirit? Cohen admits at one point that "despite the seeming recognition and rejuvenation of Christianity, pantheism actually took its place."[28] It was no accident that

Spinozism had such a powerful impact upon Germany, creatively influencing writers and thinkers such as Goethe, Herder, Schelling, Schleiermacher. And it was not mere chance that anti-Semitism found such a fine fostering soil in Germany and Germanism: Judaism and Germanism are two very profound world-views, two great cultural systems confronting one another.

Cohen insults and belittles the national quality of the German cultural spirit by denying its Germanic character and generalizing it under the rubric of so-called Christian culture in order to deduce a kinship of Germanism and Judaism.

III. Judaism and Germanism

German culture has certainly been repeatedly influenced by the Jewish spirit, whether through the Psalms, which primarily fecundated German poetry (although it is totally wrong to call the Old Testament or the Prophets a source of Germanism) or through the participation of Jews in German literature, art, science, and scholarship. But these aesthetic dynamics can no more be considered an essential connection of Judaism with Germanism than can the participation of Jews in German intellectual life be considered decisive or crucial for the Germans. These and similar influences have also appeared in France, Spain, and Italy.

We have, to be sure, taken over a few things from our German environment, but we have also received a good deal from Spain, France, and Italy. These influences never penetrated to the soul of the Jewish people. They formed a thin silt that settled over our life without essentially determining its contents or forms. True, we were never isolated. We had cultural exchange with many nations and traded spiritual values with them. But our national individuality has never suffered any permanent damage from all these contacts. It could never tolerate alien elements and had constantly to expel them. Were it feasible to trace the temporary foreign influences on Judaism, such an analytical dismemberment might reveal that the Jewish spirit entered into an alliance with the spirit of the Slavs. Many synagogal chants in Eastern Europe are permeated with motifs from Slavic melodies; many Jewish folkways (e.g., our Polish costume, the Purim plays, etc.) are of foreign origin, which we once resisted, but which, over generations, became sacred national customs, of which our sages say: "The custom of Israel is its law." The alien coat on the national body in the diaspora remained an outer thing, a stray mark, and never resulted in a union. The gap between Israel and the other nations is too great to permit Judaism to mate with an alien spirit, even after centuries of exile amid alien nations. If a part of the Jews (the Jews, not Judaism) united with the alien culture, those Jews were fully absorbed and withdrew eo ipso from Judaism. Assimilation as a national conversion is tantamount to religious baptism, although it is a less visible withdrawal. At best, our assimilants could destroy their subjective Jewishness, but not affect Judaism's objective content. Such inner union of the Jews with a foreign culture as took place constituted a merging of the Jews in their host nation, the extinction of their Judaism, and not a blend between Judaism and the spirit of the host nation. We cannot speak of a creative alliance between Judaism and French culture on the basis of our French exile. Likewise, we cannot speak of a creative alliance between Judaism and Germanism on the basis of our German exile. And like the French *galut,* the German *galut* will leave no deep traces upon the Jewish spirit.

Consider the following. Most Jews speak a German dialect: the jargon. Language is one of the most important national-cultural factors of assimilation. Thus, the jargon ought to have had an assimilatory, that is, a Germanizing effect on the Jews. Yet the jargon-speaking Jews, despite centuries of linguistic propinquity, have not been culturally assimilated to Germanism. And Jewish consciousness, too, remained nationally intact; not the slightest sense of belonging to German culture or to even a spiritual community with German ways is to be found in Jewish consciousness. We have Judaized the foreign tongue; its name, in fact, is: "Jewish" (i.e., *Jüdisch, Yiddish*).

Many people, like Cohen, claim they have uncovered a link between Judaism and Germanism in the jargon. But the very destiny of this German dialect speaks against them. It testifies to the impossibility of an identity of Judaism and Germanism, since not even the powerful influence of language was able to Germanize us in thought or feeling.

In short: Germanism was not Judaized, nor was Judaism Germanized through the jargon.

Bakunin remarked that the Jews appropriated the German tongue as their national language, so that the Cossacks believed the Germans were merely baptized Jews. Does Cohen intend to go even further and discover not only Judaism in Germanism, but also Germanism in Judaism?

Certainly, there is a cultural alliance between Germans and German Jewry—as between the French and the Jews of France, etc.—but not between Germanism and Judaism in general. Or does Cohen wish to judge the essence of Judaism not by the solid roots of Jewish peoplehood in Eastern Europe but by its enfeebled branches in Western Europe? Does he wish to regard as the exclusively valid representative and model of the Jewish spirit the Jewish assimilatory type, and yet not assimilants generally, but only the assimilated German Jews? Indeed, that is exactly what Cohen does.

One can certainly find a number of similarities and bases of comparison between the Jewish people and the German people. And not just in their common thirst for knowledge, in the Jewish obligation to study the Torah and the German obligation to go to school; or in their common features of ethical seriousness and ethical respect for all that is spiritual and human (Treitschke: "The human respect for anything human became second nature for the German"—which also means, as the context makes obvious, everything spiritual).[29] One can point out deeper analogies, e.g., the commitment to truthfulness innate in both nations. Truth, as our sages put it, is not just the stamp of the Jewish God and not just the driving force of prophetic *pathos;* it is the enduring and fundamental feature of our national character in all our transformations, even when, distorted by assimilation, it began to smack of an arrogance that our enemies harshly misinterpreted. Ethical, active love of truth—and not merely psychologically passive straightforwardness—is also a basic feature of the German national character, as we have found to be adequately confirmed in the present war, where lies have been presented as the cheapest and most successful weapons. Truthfulness makes the German nation unreceptive to current cultural claptrap, robbing it of a valuable military weapon.

But such similarities and connecting lines between national characters do not prove any essential similitude. Many identical features are shared by the Jews and the French, e.g., wit, a sense of humor, etc. On the other hand, there are such deep contrasts between Jewish and German mentality that Nietzsche could say: "What a boon a Jew is among Germans! How much dullness, how flaxen the hair, how blue the eye; the lack of wit in face, word, posture . . ."

One might even ascertain a certain parallelism between the historical situation of our people and the present-day situation of Germany. Just as the Jewish nation has been surrounded for two thousand years by a world of enemies striving to annihilate it, so the German nation is heroically fighting for its very existence against a world of foes, like little David against the giant Goliath. Generally speaking, the present position of the German is virtually a miniature of the special historical position of the Jewish people. Who is the most hated nation in the world? We Jews. Presently, however, we share this lot of *odium generis humani* with the German people. And perhaps this new harvest of venomous anti-Germanism will take some power from the old anti-Semitism; after all, *one* scapegoat is enough . . .

The Jews are hated not for real or imagined failings and vices, but specifically for their qualities and virtues: their intellectual ability, which enabled them, despite all persecutions, to assert themselves in economic and cultural life, and, not least, the rigorous ethics that our people gave to mankind. We would not have been hated had we sunk socially and morally to the level of the gypsies. Likewise, fierce hatred is now leveled at the Germans' good, not their bad, qualities: their industriousness, their capabilities, their accomplishments and successes, their strong individuality and their spiritual and intellectual power, and last but not least, their robust and blunt truthfulness, which makes them appear barbarians in the eyes of a coy and wishy-washy civilization. They are accused, like us Jews, of world domination, which is after all only an honest cultural expansion. The other nations want to weaken and humiliate them, like us. They want to discipline and reform them, like us. They pretend to be moral preceptors and yet they have the gall to say in all seriousness that the war has no other aim than to bring culture to the German people—the nation of Goethe, Humboldt, Herder, and Kant. All the persecutions and tortures of Jews were for our benefit; either because the

Christians were doing their utmost to bring the blessings of the true religion to us, the people of the Bible; or because, in modern times, they wanted to beat civilization into us and morally reform us, the proclaimers and bearers of the ideals of liberty and justice.

The German people have become our companions in misfortune to an even greater degree. The slanders being spread today against the German people confront them with the same ethnopsychological enigma as those traditional slanders that confound the Jews. We Jews always stand discomfited before the legend of the ritual-blood sacrifice: how could anyone devise such a charge, which has never, anywhere or at any time, had the faintest glimmer of truth? One can imagine a lie taking root if it is an enormous exaggeration and generalization; yet it has to possess some jot of the concrete. Yet how could the universal lie of the ritual-blood libel, a classic example of an absolute lie, maintain itself for centuries on end? Had people claimed that our laws command us not only to salt the flesh of an animal but to immerse our own bodies in a mass of salt for part or the whole of a day so that not a drop of blood might remain in a Jew's body—we might be able to understand such foolishness, which at least has a seed in the prescription of the ritual salting of meat. But the historical accusation of the ritual enjoyment of human blood by a nation that forbids eating even an egg containing a drop of blood is a psychological mystery.

We are amazed: for hundreds of years now, we have lived among Christians, and still they invent the most extraordinary cock-and-bull stories about us, and tell of things as if they had never seen a Jew, as if we were inhabitants of hell. This ethnopsychological phenomenon can now be observed in another nation. The very closest neighbors of Germany, who have myriad relations to her and draw their spiritual sustenance from her, act as if they had never seen a German person, as if this nation were some wild nomadic tribe of the desert.

Ahad Haam extracts as instructive observation from the enigma of the ritual-blood legend: Might we be wrong? If the whole world believes we are guilty, should we not, as a minority, accede to the judgment of the majority? How can we assume that the whole world consists of liars, villains, and fools? Should we not eventually believe the accusations ourselves? And is it not all too natural for an intelligent and honest Christian to say to himself: "I'm in no position to do any research in the matter, but since the whole world has been asserting it for so many centuries, it simply has to be true, or at least there must be something to it." Do not all the laws of logic stand against us? And now the German people are confronted with this very question, enough to drive a sane man mad. From now on, logic will always be speaking against the German nation: if the whole world believes it, there must be something to it.

A characteristic of slander is that all the refutations in the world cannot completely erase it: *Calomniez, calomniez, il en reste toujours quelque chose*. And this, too, is typical of slander: Defend yourself against the accusation, and you merely strengthen it. The slanderers know this *perpetuum mobile* of their diabolical work: *Qui s'excuse, s'accuse*. These psychological factors contain the strength of slander and the secret of its tenaciousness.

Only we Jews, who could fathom most deeply the nature of slander, are immune to its contagion. Only we Jews can defy the universal belief in the insane denigrations of a great cultural nation, and assert against the right of the many and despite all logic: yes, it *is* possible that a whole world lies and is lied to.

Our sympathy with this slandered nation is mixed with the sense of comfort offered by the community of companions in suffering. And it also gives satisfaction when we think of German anti-Semitism, which played a major part in the Christian slanders against us. Now the Germans experience the brunt of accusations by many against few, by all nations against one nation. They are now personally coming to know the value of the proof: "After all, the whole world says so. . . ."

Cohen may have been led astray by this parallelism between the historical situation of the Jews and the present-day situation of the Germans to seek a spiritual kinship between these two nations.

IV. Dual Loyalty

Cohen says:

> I only think that, in regard to the Jews throughout the world, even the Jew in France, England, and Russia owes reverence to Germany, for she is the mother-land of his soul, if his religion is his soul.

And later:

> We also have to expose the defamations of the French philosopher, who with all the means of virtuosity and publicity, which unfortunately have also been successful in Germany, has been playing the original philosopher: he is the son of a Polish Jew who spoke the *jargon*. What can possibly go on in the soul of this Mr. Bergson when he thinks of his father and denies Germany's ideas?[30]

I do not want to say anything about the form of Cohen's polemics against "this Mr. Bergson," but if I may say so, these gibes at a Jewish colleague are out of place even in these times, i.e., against an "enemy." The Talmud has already revealed that the bite of a Jewish scholar can be very sharp and painful. One might add that it is all the sharper and more painful when aimed at a fellow Jew. Here we see revealed the deep irony of our tragic situation: the two greatest Jewish philosophers feel called upon to stand for alien national cultures and, in patriotic zealousness, carry the antagonism over to the field of philosophy. If they were intimately bound up with the Jewish people, they would not confront one another as enemies but would instead stand together as great sons of the Jewish people to conciliate confused minds. And the host nations in whose midst we live would thank us (albeit somewhat later) for this *Jewish* stance rather than for an alleged patriotism.

But this is a ticklish theme, perhaps to be discussed in a better time. However, we have to examine the meaning of Cohen's statements.

He claims that Jews throughout the world owe reverence to Germany, "the motherland of the soul" of all Jews. This establishes the full kinship between Judaism and Germanism. They have a common father in the Judeo-Christian God and a common motherland of the soul. It's an old story. "We have a Father up above,/We have a Mother here,/God is the father of all creatures,/Germany our Mother dear." (Riesser).[31] Cohen, however, declares this "here" as the motherland of *all* Jews. Doesn't he realize that he is thus sanctioning a national-Jewish criterion that would have to lead him *(horribile dictu!)* to Zionism? He sees the French Jew not as a Frenchman, the English Jew not as an Englishman, etc., but as a Jew, who as such has obligations towards Germany, even though—as in this case—they run counter to civic obligations. If that is so, if the French or British citizenship of a Jew is incapable of detaching him from the German "motherland of his soul," then it can detach him all the less from the Jewish "motherland of his soul," from the land of his fathers.

What Cohen says about the Jews of France and England, must obtain for the Jews of Germany as well. If citizenship isn't enough to identify the Jews in France and England as Frenchmen and Englishmen despite centuries of living and successfully assimilating in these countries, and to absolve them of any duties towards Germany—which has a "legal claim on the Jews of all nations"[32]—then German citizenship cannot make the Jews into Germans either, or absolve them of the duty towards the historical Motherland of every Jewish soul. Was Cohen aware of this ultimate consequence? Didn't he notice that by decreeing an obligation of all Jews to Germany, he gave up the criterion of citizenship and took to a national, nay, a Zionist approach?

In the new edition of his book, Cohen makes great concessions to nationalism. He distinguishes between nationality and nation. "State and nationality are not identical. State and nation are identical. It is only the State that fuses the plurality of nationalities into the unity of a nation." It is hard to understand why he makes this distinction between nationality and nation. He probably wants to tone down his great revision of the notion of nation and disguise the contradiction between this concession and his earlier position. Nevertheless, Cohen demands "that it be made an international law for every naturalization that reverence towards one's original state remain a legal obligation and, in its inviolability and perpetuity, be confirmed as the positive law of every state according to international law." This very viewpoint is crucial for the Jewish-national conception of our legal status in adoptive countries.

Elsewhere, Cohen discusses the conflict between an individual's duty towards his original people and his duty towards an adopted Fatherland. He says:

> When a nation has gone under, lost its state, and has become part of another state, a conflict remains between devotion to one's lost state and surviving people, and loyalty and obedience to the new and exclusively authoritative commonwealth. In which direction does the signpost of loyalty point? When an individual or a natural group emigrates and joins another state, how does one divide one's loyalty between the original and, as they say, the adopted Fatherland? Perhaps answering the second question may make it easier to answer the first. In the second case, there can be no doubt that loyalty is due the real and original Fatherland; the new state demands obedience and participation, which we will designate by another virtue to be dealt with presently. Loyalty, however, comes from love; and loyalty to the state and the nation must blossom, ineradicable and unwaning, through all generations, in the hearts of the people who sprung forth from them.[33]

This observation, which, unconsciously perhaps, strikingly characterizes the situation of the Jewish people—a lost state and a surviving peoplehood—would have to lead Cohen to recognize Zionism.

Cohen teaches: The ethical concept of culture is the concept of State. Life in the state is the highest ethical form of existence, and only in the state does the ethical self-awareness of man achieve pure expression. But he also teaches that it is the ethical duty of man to remain faithful to his nation, which has lost its state. Accordingly, the Jews are doomed to live in an eternal conflict between loyalty to their people and the land of their fathers on the one hand, and loyalty to their respective state and their adopted Fatherland on the other. Is there any better resolution to this conflict than the reunification of the old nation with its old homeland? On the one hand: "Absorbing one's ego in the wealth and energy of ethical ways and activities which come together in the unity of the state is what we make a directive for forming the true self-awareness of the ethical personality."[34] And on the other, ineradicable and unwavering loyalty, throughout all generations upon foreign soil, to one's own nation and one's original homeland, that is, to the lost Fatherland. The gap is never bridged, it is merely deepened and widened if one distinguishes between obedience and loyalty. All the more so because Cohen sees civic duty not as a formal, obedient observance of laws, but as a deeply fervent devotion, as an absorption of the ego in the wealth of political tasks, the commitment of the individual's total energy to the good of the community, which is confirmed exclusively in the unity of the state. How shall the Jew divide his thoughts and feelings, his social aspirations and actions, between the duty of "obedient loyalty" to the adopted Fatherland, a loyalty demanding the entire person, and the duty of a "loving faithfulness" to his people and his original Fatherland throughout all generations? He would have to choose one or the other: either the loyalty of obedience would be purely formal, and remain a cold fulfillment of duty, or else the loyalty of love will become illusory. In either case, the individual is guilty (according to Cohen) of an ethical transgression. It is therefore the destiny of the Jewish people to live throughout its many adoptive countries, in an ever-tragic psychological conflict: in divided loyalty, or (if the conflict is resolved) in constant violation of either requirement for loyalty.

There is thus no other solution for, no other salvation from, this duality than the return of the nation to its own country.

Yet not only our enemies but also many Jews deny our people equal rights. The nationalism of others is glorified, while Jewish nationalism is condemned. Cohen lauds the state as the highest ethical form of life, he advocates an army,[35] but he prohibits Jews from having a conception of statehood and praises the prophets of Israel for abandoning their Fatherland in their cosmopolitanism[36] praising providence for our universal dispersion, for the loss of our national "particularism," for the loss of our State. It is terrifying to see what the prophets have to put up with at the hands of the preachers of assimilation. They, the prophets, are made to testify against Zionism. What nation would have tolerated such blasphemy?

Truly, before demanding equal rights for Jews from the various nations, we would have to fight for the recognition by Jews of equal rights for our nation.

I cannot conclude my discussion without saying a personal word. The writing of this article was a personal sorrow for me as an admirer of Hermann Cohen. I understand his good intention, his double intention, the German one and the Jewish one. I understand its contemporary character, which can excuse a great deal. But his work is simply overdetermined, and too much of its smacks of war literature. Last but not least, this tendentious piece of writing achieved the opposite of what it set out to do: the bold attempt to depict Germanism and Judaism as identical or akin could not succeed without belittling the specific nature of the German or the Jewish cultural spirit. Thus Cohen has done violence to, has injured, both Germanism and Judaism. And I would join Vaihinger[37] in saying: if the Master is as hurt by his pupil's criticism as the pupil himself is hurt at not being able to hold his peace, then may the Master forgive him.

6. ZION, THE STATE, AND HUMANITY:
REMARKS ON HERMANN COHEN'S ANSWER

MARTIN BUBER

EDITOR'S INTRODUCTION

MARTIN BUBER (1878–1965), founder and editor of *Der Jude*, was a frequent contributor to its pages. The present essay appeared in Jahrgang I (1916–1917), pp. 425–33.

The controversy was long and quite ferocious. It began with Hermann Cohen's "Religion and Zionism," a pendant essay to his notorious "Germanism and Judaism." Both essays were inspired by his profound and patriotic attachment to German culture and the German state, and were elicited by his concern that the loyalty of German Jews might be questioned, as indeed it had been early in World War I, when Jewish officers were withheld from frontline service in dispute over their loyalty to their fatherland. Hermann Cohen had taken up his intellectual cudgels to describe on the one hand the moral identity of Judaism and Germanism and on the other to protect German Jews from the implied charge of a dual loyalty that involvement in the nascent Zionist movement was felt by him to entail. Martin Buber replied to Cohen in an extended essay in the fifth issue of his newly founded periodical, *Der Jude*, under the title "Notions and Reality" (*Begriffe und Wirklichkeit: Brief an Herrn. Geh. Regierungsrat Prof. Dr. Hermann Cohen*). In this preliminary reply, Buber undertakes to establish the grounds of a denationalization of the Jew, the discrimination of senses in which the Jew is grounded and situated in the state to which he owes the loyalty and support of his natural self while guarding all the while his transforming obligation to be open before the messianic future. Toward that future, the vision of Zion, both terrestrial as communitarian society and transcendent, as Messianic trust, the Jew as Zionist emerges. The natural Jew may be a patriot, son of his adoptive land; the Jew of faith must be Zionist, that is, turned towards an option of expectation. At this time, Buber had not yet turned against the war. During those middle months of 1916, despite the militant opposition of his friend Gustav

Landauer, Buber like Cohen, supported the German cause, arguing from a somewhat more mystical view of German culture than Cohen's that Europe was moving to stifle German civilization. But this stance did not oblige him, as it did Cohen, to subsume the Jew to Germany or Germanism.

Hermann Cohen's answer to Buber's reply revealed the serious malaise of the former's position, its fundamental lack of sympathy for what might be called the warts of Jewish existence, the extent to which Jewish life, in all its immediacy, deprivation, beleaguerments, involved millions of Jews beyond the secure precincts of the German *Reich*. Although Cohen had, as we have noted earlier, protested the demand of many German Jews that the Eastern borders of Germany be closed to the flight of indigent Polish Jews, even there Buber had been obliged to note his demurral from the reasons that Cohen had offered for his views. The system of rational concepts from which Cohen's arguments drew their energy was invariably lofty, humane, universal, ethical; however, it lacked the grit of history, it had neither the rhythm of its grain nor the malignity of its knots. In his historical innocence, which Cohen conceals with his postulation of the ethical humanity to be fulfilled in the Messianic era, Zion remains a particularism of nostalgia whose viability for the Jew—no less than for the ethical non-Jew—is that it signifies universal humanity. "We see the entire historical world as the future abode of our religion" (*Jüdische Schriften*, II, p. 338).

Martin Buber's concluding "remarks on Hermann Cohen's answer," translated here, turns on an essential premise of Buber's conception of the world, a premise later to be elaborated in his essay "What is Man?" in *Between Man and Man*. There are, Buber proposes, two visions of the situation of man, the one describing the composure and accommodation of man to his world, his adaptation to nature and environment, orderly, hierarchical, patterned according to principles of knowledge that secure clear foundations for man's moral and intellectual enterprise; the other, questioning the grounds of security, setting man adrift, contending that there is no certain ground upon which he might stand, placing before man the unnerving contention for truth amid anxiety, faithlessness, and death. The former doctrine, having its roots in classical Greek philosophy and its historical descent through Maimonides and Thomas Aquinas to the great systems of modern German philosophy (Kant and Hegel), includes the Messianic intellectualism of Hermann Cohen. The latter doctrine, emerging from the world-view of the Bible, passes through Augustine, Yehuda Halevi, Pascal, Kierkegaard, and Nietzsche down to the existential thinkers of Buber's day.

The Jew, in his very being, is ill-at-ease amid the contentments and securities defined by others for his world. It cannot be expected that the Jew, given ultimate preoccupations far exceeding the "givens" of the political state, will find his realization by identifying his ethical search with the ethical identity of any political instrument, however pure its origins, humane its purview, or culturally elevated its ambitions might be. *Any* state to which the Jew must be servant is inadequate, since the Jew amid the nations is always "a wanderer," by which Buber means a person discontented with any terrestrial rooting of his interior spirituality.

Buber contends that the Jew, whom Cohen insists upon regarding as coeval with the German and therefore unalienated from his everyday reality, is in fact quite different, but not for that reason alienated. The Jew is different because the arc of his vision exceeds and includes the vision of the nations, seeking to effect reconciliation, the bringing of the nations near to the vision of God (the redeeming reality of Zion). However, ultimate difference does not, for Buber, mean alienation. The Jew of Germany shares with the German "the language that taught us to think, the landscape that taught us to see, the creative depth of a great people," but nonetheless the Jew does not depend upon the German. The vision of the Jew as Jew turns to Zion for the redemption of Jewish interiority, however much Jewish civility requires that the Jew be earnest in his loyalty.

It is not, all things considered, a wholly satisfactory exchange. The frame of the argument between Cohen and Buber retains a kind of elevated abstraction that does not really join the issue. At no point does Buber take on Cohen's innocent confidence in history, his historical unrealism, for precisely the reason that Buber's own doctrine of history, his sense of its dialectical complexity, its uncertainty and chiaroscuro, had not yet reached its later mature sophistication.   [A.A.C.]

ZION, THE STATE AND HUMANITY: REMARKS ON HERMANN COHEN'S ANSWER

1

Hermann Cohen has published a "Reply to Dr. Martin Buber's Open letter to Hermann Cohen" in the K.-C. Blätter.[1] He calls his essay a reply; yet he does not reply, he simply talks past me. Someone is speaking, listening not so much to my words (which he hardly ever tries to contradict) as to an imaginary argument, filled with easily demolishable slogans offered by an imaginary, typical Zionist.

Cohen had accused Zionism of "simply incomprehensible untruthfulness," "cynicism," and "frivolity."

I thereupon pointed out that his reproaches lack any foundation, and I challenged him to be more specific—if he can.

One might assume that a man who regards his mission on earth as fusing Kant's categorical imperative and the ideal of justice of the Jewish prophets could practice the openness of a morally committed person who has made a mistake and make amends for his error by publicly retracting his inaccurate, unsubstantiated charges, thereby repairing the injustice done by his groundless talk. One might assume that he would not only realize, but also declare, that the facts supporting him do not exist, that he would regret his insult, regret it with the candor appropriate to one who has been insulting. Cohen has done nothing of the sort. He says nothing of my statements, he says nothing of my challenge. In a tiny corner of his "Reply," I find a peripheral phrase: "Both parties are fervently concerned about our religious survival. This I will gladly acknowledge."[2] That is all. Even these little sentences, offered in a tone wholly inappropriate to the subject matter, are submerged in new accusations of "frivolity," "absurdity," and "untruthfulness."

2

Cohen not only *talks* past me, he *reads* past me.

My "Letter" stated, "We want Palestine 'not for the Jews,' but for mankind. We want it for the realization of Judaism." Cohen quotes this sentence and then continues: "Thus, the realization of Judaism is exclusively contingent on mankind!" None of this can be found in my text, and no "thus"[3] can be concluded from my words; for anyone reading them dispassionately simply says: In order for Judaism to be realized, it has to gather its strength in Palestine and make it fruitful there. Mankind needs Judaism; but Jews living scattered and apart and precariously cannot give mankind what it needs from Judaism. They must first be regenerated in their own land.

I had also spoken in my letter about the "buried" Judaism within us: the genuine Jewish energy and forms that have been repressed by alien energy and forms. And I had spoken about the "fictional" Judaism outside of us; the pseudo-Judaism, whereby those who call themselves Jews vegetate without living as Jews. And now Cohen actually manages to treat these totally opposed concepts as synonymous. He really feels he is repeating my opinion when he writes: "Only in Palestine, only in the Jewish state, can the 'buried,' the 'fictional' Judaism be overcome and gotten rid of."[4] The buried Judaism, the slumbering potential Judaism within us is to be "gotten rid of"! Is there a single reader, other than Cohen, who misunderstood me so thoroughly?

But these are not the most astounding examples. I had written that some day Judaism might easily, like all nations, be absorbed in Messianic mankind; but in today's mankind, it must tarry, "not, however, as a steadily crumbling fact of nature in union with a religion that is being increasingly reduced to a creed."[5] I don't think it at all difficult to understand what I mean. Cohen acknowledged Jewish nationality, but only as a natural fact. My answer to this is: as a natural fact, Judaism keeps crumbling more and more (through baptism and assimilation), and this process will not stop until a mental and spiritual fact—regeneration through national will—counteracts it. Cohen, furthermore, saw as the only purpose of the "natural fact" the maintenance of the Jewish religion. To which I replied: as a religion, Judaism is becoming more and more of a creed, for the portion of those who profess the Jewish faith without inwardly belonging to it is growing all the time, and this process will not be halted until a renewal of Judaism is achieved. And I linked both my replies by saying that Judaism should continue to tarry among the nations, but not as a crumbling fact of nature in union with a religion become creed. "In union with. . . ." Is Cohen unfamiliar with this perfectly good expression, which means more or less the same thing as "in connection with"? It would appear so, since, unlikely as it may sound, he smells a rat, an allusion to a *Union,* something like the Central Union of German Citizens of the Jewish Faith,[6] or the like. He writes:

> What, however, is my critic thinking of in the sentence where he tries to characterize liberal Judaism compared to the natural fact by means of the 'union with a religion that is becoming more and more of a creed?' Perhaps I do not understand this allusive expression correctly. The way I understand it, however, it contains a grave portent, which I must indignantly reject. Our disagreement has taken on a topical political character."[7]

This is by Hermann Cohen, the author of *Logik der reinen Erkenntnis (The Logic of Pure Knowledge).*[8] Our disagreement has assumed a humorous aspect.

3

Cohen's reading past me and talking past me comes to the fore in his treatment of a chief problem of his polemics: the issue of the relationship of Judaism to the State.

In his first article, Cohen had advanced the thesis: "It is the State that first establishes and founds the one nation with which it identifies itself."[9] I disproved this thesis with a few contemporary examples, reserving a more exact exposition in case Cohen were to argue against my proof. But he does not try to argue against it at all; he is content to repeat "that the nation is constituted only through the State by virtue of an act of political morality."[10] Presumably, then, there was no German nation before 1870! I think it would be superfluous to carry this unhistorical terminology *ad absurdum* through further counterexamples. All the more superfluous, in that what the terminology signifies strikes me as immeasurably overestimated. It doesn't matter whether the Jews are a nation or a nationality; what matters is what we have to do, so that this *Gemeinschaft,* whatever it may be called, can acquire a new independent life, a renewed spontaneity of activity and creativity—whereas today—as for the past two thousand years or so—its life is determined, not by its own will-power, but by the life of the nations on which it depends. It little matters whether the State-*Gemeinschaft* is called a "nation" and its ethnic units are described as "nationalities," or whether the two related terms[11] are left as ethnic units and the State-*Gemeinschaft* is given a name of its own. What matters is that no state be permitted to curtail the vital rights of any of its nations, no matter what they are called, and that no ruling nation that "constitutes" itself as a nation-state should interfere with any of its subject nations in the unfolding and enactment of their particular character. The state must allow them to participate unmolested in the life and work of the whole.

Cohen does not make this demand. His basic motive is not demand but defense. He does write the important sentence: "The States, *in their delusion*[12] say: There shall be no groups among us that lead a statelike, separate existence for any fictive reason."[13] But he does not contrast this "delusion" with the compelling truth about the relationship between State and nation. He merely assures us defensively: "It is our religion that solely and exclusively constitutes the difference between us and our State and, therefore, our nation."[14] He doesn't dare heal his delusion-blinded eyes; he wants only to assist "modern Judaism" to escape the consequences of the delusion.

But this is not true of us. We have never heard Cohen's statement about groups and their special existence from the lips of States, but only from certain State fanatics, who were certainly laboring under a delusion. If required, however, we would point out to these people that national groups within the State do not wish to lead a "State-like" existence, but rather a national one, and that their right to do so is inalienable. For nations are the creative principles in the history of mankind, and states the ordering principles. The ordering principle has always sought to make the dominion of its order more and more exclusive, although it can only rearrange power, not create it. In all times, however, the creative principle has taken a firm stand and has preserved its claim—a claim grounded in the primal law of life itself. And so it shall remain, until his rule, *Malkhut Shamayim* [The Kingdom of God], is established upon earth, until, in the messianic shape of the human world, creation and order, nation and state, fuse in a new union, in the community of salvation.

Cohen makes a statement so self-evident to all fair-minded people, that it scarcely needs the emphasis he gives it (as though he were seeking to invalidate a counterassertion): "No restriction on civil equality can deter us from the absolute thought and sense of duty towards the State to which we belong."[15] No true Jew, whatever his conception of Judaism, will let his relation to the State be determined by the limitation of his civil rights; that would simply degrade his relationship to the *Gemeinschaft* into a matter of huckstering. But on the other hand, I don't consider it suitable for the true Jew to rapturously exclaim: "All our feelings are concentrated in our consciousness of State."[16] Put these words into the mouth of Samuel, Elijah, Amos, or into the mouth of Jeremiah, and it will be obvious how greatly this attitude deviates from that of ancient Judaism. The feelings of those men were concentrated upon their consciousness of God, and not upon the State. If the State fell away from God, then they fought God's cause against the state. Or if we put these words in the mouth of a Jewish teacher of the Law in Babylon, we will understand why Hermann Cohen, albeit a wise and honorable man, is far from deserving the rank of a *Resh Galuta,* a Prince of the Exile, which one of my friends would assign to him. He may have the wisdom, but he lacks the soul, of a *Resh Galuta.* A man cannot be considered a spiritual exilarch if he does not experience this exile, this entire exile with all its misery and all its shame, as the *Galut Shekhina,* the Exile of Divine Glory, if he doesn't raise up this humiliated community above every exalted community, the suffering of the diaspora over the pride of states, and prefer these bitter waters to all the precious wines of the nations. If, although earnestly and rigorously feeling all his duties to his state-community, he doesn't know something higher: the command spoken once to Abraham, to leave the state of the Chaldees and to Moses to leave the state of Egypt—God's command to Israel for the sake of humanity, he can be no *Resh Galuta.*

4

In a profound sense, something else is at stake.

I earnestly and rigorously feel all my duties towards the state-community in which I live, but I have recognized as the highest of these duties one that is the duty of every human being who lives by God: to present the state with the image of true humanity whenever the state transgresses against it. For humanity (to say this, Professor Cohen, is in these times more than ever a duty of a human being who lives by God)—humanity is something greater than the state.[17] Not yesterday's "European" pseudo-humanity, which was incapable of releasing the states from their entanglement in the invisible war of all against all, but that developing humanity that walked through the Red Sea, that awakened humanity, for which a future mankind, gathered around the living God, is preparing itself, and whose organs the nations and whose tools the states shall be. This is not the mendacious and pretentious "humanity" of yesterday, the caricature of a lost ideal, that did not know or wish to know what states are and what they can do, and chattered past them; it is a new, clear-sighted mankind, which has sufficiently experienced these things and does not care to repeat the experience.

Cohen sees in the idea of the state the "quintessence of ethics." For him, "the State achieves the realization of the ethical on earth,"[18] and he is merely adding to this assertion when he says that "we control our religion by our ethics.''[19] I, for myself, reject this world in which religion is "controlled" by ethics and ethics by the state. My ethics are an executive function of my religion: the will to increase God's power on earth and to reduce the power of evil. The state is simply one of the configurations where these ethics prove themselves. One of the configurations: more formal than the family, the community, the nation, which are rooted in life, thus needing much more control than any of these to determine whether it is increasing God's power on earth and reducing the power of evil. These controls, however, can be exercised only by the legitimate authority of the original spirit, to which nations and states are subject: *living* religion. Cohen, who controls religion through ethics, whose quintessence is the idea of the state, wishes, wittingly or not, to bend the spirit to the state, whereas I wish to bend the state to the spirit. Only the evident authority of the spirit could make it possible to build up the League of States, which Cohen talks about, and whose symbol he sees in the state—a deceptive abstraction as long as we fail to say that what is ubiquitously known today as a League of States, the League of States against states, can never lead the way to a true humanity.

5

On one point, however, Cohen does not talk past me: he admits that the conflict between us (not, to be sure, between him and "Zionism," on whose instructions I am not acting, and to whose interpretation I have not been assigned; but between him and me, with myself uttering my personal opinion) goes to the heart of the relationship between the state and religion. I could also say: between the state and the Spirit, or between the state and humanity. For me, religion is not, as it is for him, "one of the concentric specialties within the unity of ethical culture,"[20] and the state is not "the focus of all human culture."[20] Quite the contrary: it is only in religious life that I can see the *unity* of true humanity, whereas in the state I can see only one of its confirmations.

But as soon as he applies this general disagreement to the Jewish problem, he goes wrong. "Our conflict," he says, "doesn't concern the Jewish people so much as the Jewish State. Actually, my opponent recognizes my definition, i.e., that the State is what defines the nation, but he concludes that there has to be a separate State for the Jewish people."[21] What a paradox! My goal as a human being is certainly not the state at all, much less as a Jew the Jewish state. And the "need for power of a viable group,"[22] of which Cohen goes on to speak, is completely alien to me. I have seen and heard too much of the achievements of an empty need for power.

My goal lies elsewhere. It is not the Jewish state, which, were it to come into being today, would again be constructed on the same principles as any modern state. My goal is not one more tiny entity of power in the throng. What I want is a settlement that, independent of the machinery of nations and removed from "external politics," can focus all its energy upon the inner structure and, thereby, the realization of Judaism.

I have said in my letter and I repeat: We want Palestine not "for the Jews": we want it for humanity. We want it for the realization of Judaism. The work of the new humanity we intend cannot do without the specific power of Judaism—the power that once gave mankind the strongest impulse for true life. This power has not perished. It survives amid degeneracy and contains the seeds of salvation for the future. But after that achievement, the power was exiled from Israel's divided life, which ever recreates the great spirit out of the division. And that exile of the power continues in the hearts of individual Jews, separate, unconnected individuals, in every generation. It could no longer be nourished by the nation's vitality, which was obliged to concentrate on a single unrelenting effort: to survive under the most hostile circumstances, where anyone else would have succumbed. The capacity to survive, a natural possession of all nations except in moments of catastrophe, had to be discovered anew from day to day—and with no weapons other than passion of soul and the discriminating strength of the spirit. Cut off from the nation's creative source, individuals reflected and meditated upon what the prophets and teachers had accomplished and were nourished by the resource of those who had scourged the people while remaining deeply attached to its vitality. The ancient Jewish creation of the spirit, even when arising out of contradiction (and it almost always arose out of contradiction), was essentially a creation of the people, the nation; it could survive only latently in individuals. So it came to pass that Judaism could still transmit stimulation and guidance, but was unable to renew its transforming deed for humanity. Even the greatest attempt at alleviating the paralysis of the national spirit, hasidism, that marvelous experiment in spiritual alchemy, that wanted to extract renewal from the undiminished mass of traditional material, failed, and had to fail. When Judaism approached the nations after millenia of isolation, it was only able to take and rework, but not to give, crucial things.

To be sure, a reawakening is now transpiring in individual Jews who have been touched by the spirit. Growing from hour to hour, the creative drive storms through their souls. The seeds of salvation live again. Something ineffable is happening—the faith I once uttered has not deceived me: "In this feverish land, in this shouting hour, the Holy will be born." But it will pass, as all revival in the *Galut* has passed; moreover, since the national unity, hasidism's basis, has vanished, all will remain as thought, speech, and writing, and never assume corporeal life, unless the energy of the people, freed from the unfruitful struggle for bare survival, recovers the consummation of its religiosity. And that is what I mean with regard to Palestine. Not a "state," but this old soil, the promised guarantee of *ultimate* and *sacred* abiding, the hard earth, the only one where the seed of the new unity can sprout. And not out of a "need for power," but only out of a need for self-realization, the need to increase God's power on earth.

6

"The entire history of Judaism," says Cohen, "teaches, in accordance with the sayings of the prophets, that the realization of Judaism is bound up with our dispersion among the nations of the earth."[23]

History, however, has taught us the very opposite: here, in a life of dispersion, deprived of self-definition, Judaism cannot achieve self-realization. We can profess, but we cannot act; we can testify for God with forebearance, but not with creation; we can praise the Jubilee, but we cannot usher it in.

And the sayings of the prophets have taught us the very opposite, too. Not one of them saw dispersion in any other way than that of Jeremiah, whom Cohen cites in particular: "Like chaff blown along by the desert wind,"[24] not one of them saw the gathering in any other way than Jeremiah's: "Then will I cause to cease from the cities of Judah, and from the streets of Jerusalem, the voice of mirth, and the voice of gladness, the voice of the bridegroom, and the voice of the bride: for the land shall be desolate."[25] And truly, the man who in the time of great terror, amid the chaos preceding the captivity of the king and the people in Babylon, and amid the despair, spoke his words of comfort on Judah's earth to the "weary and languishing souls," did not see "this land," toward which he pointed. Not a "symbol," as Cohen would put it in his mouth, but the land toward which his prophet's eyes and the people's eyes turned. Never has anyone so abused the lofty concept of the symbol. But when Cohen misinterprets the words of the prophets that God wants to gather together the remnant of Israel and makes them out to mean that the nations will be streaming with Israel to the light of God, i.e., the teachings of the prophets, then we can in truth find this in the prophetic books only in terms of the proclamation that the nations "on horses and chariots, on litters, on asses and dromedaries" will stream back into the reëstablished Zion, as the "holy mount," the "house of the God of Jacob," "because my house shall be called a house of prayer for all nations."[26]

And this, precisely, is our faith: we believe that Zion restored will be the House of Prayer for all nations and the center of the new earth, the central place of the spiritual fire in which the "bloodied war-cloak shall be burnt" and "they shall beat their swords into plowshares."[27]

The new humanity needs us. Not scattered and striving with each other, but gathered and united; not soiled by false deeds and words, but cleansed and ready; not professing God with our tongues and betraying God with our lives, but serving him faithfully by forming a community of mankind according to his sense. Our obligation towards a new humanity is not to declare and assert that God exists, but to show how God lives within us—how, within us, he lives the true human life: to realize ourselves and God within us.

7

In the light of this view of our mission I see the relationship of Judaism to the nations, to anything assimilated from any portion of the nations. Cohen asserts that "problems and difficulties, much less conflicts of modern cultural life," do not exist "for the narrow confines of this nationalism."[28] I would counter this with statements I made seven years ago in the German and Czech city of Prague to young Jews whose mother-tongue was either German or Czech,[29] and I would neither add to nor subtract from these statements now, but merely emphasize a few words:

> Wherever the natural objective situation of the individual in his relationship to the nation [the untroubled harmony and intimacy of the national feeling] is guaranteed, his life will pass in harmony and secure growth. Where it is not guaranteed, the more self-aware the individual is, the more honest he is, the more resoluteness and clarity he demands of himself, all the more deeply will he enter into conflict, all the more inevitably will he be confronted by a choice between the surrounding world and his inner world, between the world of impressions and the substantial world, between environment and blood, between the memory of his life span and the memory of millennia, between the goals offered him by society and the task of redeeming his own power. A choice: this cannot be seen as aiming to remove, give up, or overcome this or that. It would be senseless to want to free oneself from one's surrounding culture, which, after all, has been processed by our blood's inmost energy and totally assimilated into us. We desire to be aware and must be aware that we, in a more meaningful sense than any other civilized nation, are a mixture. But we want to be the masters, not the slaves, of this mixture. The choice means a decision on the supremacy, on what the dominating and the dominated within us should be. . . . The individual, however, who, in his choice between the surrounding world and his substance, has decided in favor of the latter, must now be a Jew truly from within and *must live as a Jew out of his blood, with the entire contradiction, the entire tragedy and the entire future wealth of this blood.*

In this sense, we are on the way. The statement in my letter, to the effect that every true Zionist is already on the way in the most inward sense, is almost the only thing that Cohen goes into. But he does not fully understand it, for he grasps only the external meaning. His retort goes: "This one word characterizes our whole cultural difference. The Zionist is on the way. We, however, want to be at home everywhere and make ourselves more at home all the time."[30]

Yes, this one word *does* characterize our entire difference. "On the way"—yes, we are on the way, with our old wanderers' hearts and a young will for direction within them. All Jewish souls are still wandering day by day and fail to realize it, and even those who "make themselves at home," are restless pilgrims, and their slogan of being at home is merely like the raven that Noah sent out. We, however, are those who have turned the odyssey of the souls into a wandering towards a goal. And that, precisely, is why we are no longer fugitives and vagabonds on earth, we who are rooted in the goal, we "sons of the Messiah."

The others assure the Germans that they are no *different* from them, in order not to be considered aliens. But we affirm that we *are* different, and we add a truth of our soul, which no one can deny: we are not aliens. The vagabonds plant the stakes of their concepts to have something to lean upon, and when it comes to concepts, Germanism can look like Judaism and Judaism like Germanism.[31] But we, who are on the way and deeply aware of our direction, we see the different but not alien reality and admit that we love it: the language that taught us to think, the landscape that taught us to see, the creative depth of a great people to whom we are grateful for a blissful gift. We do not hang on to the others, but we greet them as only those can greet who are wandering towards the goal: Friends, we are on the way, for our sake, for your sake—for the sake of Salvation.

7. THE HEBREW LANGUAGE AND OUR NATIONAL FUTURE

YEḤEZKEL KAUFMANN

EDITOR'S INTRODUCTION

YEḤEZKEL KAUFMANN (1889–1963) wrote the present essay in Bern during 1917, settled in Palestine in 1920, and became professor of Bible studies at the Hebrew University in 1949. His publications include the magisterial *Toledot ha-'Emunah ha-Yisraelit (A History of Israelite Faith)* and *Golah ve-Nekhar (Exile and Alienage).* "The Hebrew Language and Our National Future" was published in *Der Jude* in Jahrgang I (1916–1917), pp. 407 – 18.

Yehezkel Kaufmann's reasoned polemic against the parity, much less the primacy, of Yiddish as the language of national self-consciousness—in the Diaspora—like so many of the most strenuously argued issues in the pages of *Der Jude,* was dissolved by the Holocaust. One's sense of the *tremendum* is renewed here (as elsewhere in the pages of this anthology), for Kaufmann's investigation of the trilingual complexity of Jewish life in the Diaspora, his reconstruction of the paradigm of normal national existence and the normality of language against which Jewish life is obliged to measure and assess itself, is resolved by the murder of the center of Yiddish language and creation, the masses of East European Jewry. Quite independent of this threnody, however, is the seriousness of his contention regarding the primacy of Hebrew in the psychic life of the Jews and his polemic against Yiddish (the "jargon," as he calls it throughout his discussion).

Kaufmann's interpretation of the emergence and function of the jargon is particularly interesting, precisely because he views language as the vital nexus sustaining the bond of the Jew to the Jewish people—not religion, but language. The Spanish-Arabic Jewries could sustain authentic national self-awareness because their cultural life was conducted in Hebrew, as was that of eleventh-century French Jewry in the time of Rashi. It did not matter that daily transaction was Arabic or old French; what mattered was that the substantive life of the Jews—the modalities of thought and spirit—was elaborated in Hebrew. At that time, unlike later times when Ladino and Yiddish would become third languages of the Jews, Arabic and French represented a gentility, a social civility that Jews employed to effect their transactions with the non-Jewish world. In Kaufmann's analysis, later eras would find that the creative function Hebrew had had in the intellectual and religious life of the people was being traduced by the temptations of both Enlightenment and assimilation; the connection between language and nationhood (ethnicity in exile) was severed, and Jews began their creative work in the foreign tongue, reserving Yiddish for the maintenance of private conversation that could not be overheard by the Gentiles, and Hebrew for sacred address to God.

The critical terms of Kaufmann's moving analysis of the crisis of language—Hebrew, the jargon (which encompasses not alone Yiddish, although Yiddish is principally intended, but for that matter any dialect spoken and culturally transmitted by Jews outside the Land), and the Landessprache, the language of the host people—are placed within the landscape of Exile. The Jewish people and its language constitute an abridgment of the "iron laws of history"—without land, without autonomy, without permission or privilege, the Jewish people endured the millennia of Diaspora and did not pass away. The ground of its endurance was not only that it worshiped eccentrically, or that it obeyed an odd and demanding regimen, or even that—in the period of emancipation and haskalah—it demonstrated its remarkable adaptability to the cultures and polities of the nations among whom it lived, but rather that it preserved a separate speech that, as holy speech, bound it to the horizontal plane of a holy history anchored in the convocation of the people at Sinai and cantilevered to an unknown but promised future. It was rather that speech—Hebrew speech—held it open to a conversation that was holy, that sustained its holiness, that indeed was a principal definer among other definers of its holiness.

Hebrew language was the language not simply of the Book, but of books, that is, it was the language in which the people transmitted and re-created itself. It is not enough to say that Kaufmann's analysis of the dynamics of language has proved wholly accurate, that the jargon of the Jewish people expired as Jews achieved political and economic parity with its host peoples, no longer needing the body warmth of Yiddish or Ladino to express emotion and intimacy amid hostile surroundings. To suggest that the jargon and Hebrew should coexist, that the one is suitable for certain needs, the other for different and exclusionary spiritual occupations, is to render both vulnerable, for languages do not mutually sustain each other (the loan words of Hebrew perhaps supporting Yiddish, but not the other way around). Symbiosis so easily becomes parasitism, deprivation resulting from the inability to separate prey and host, until both waste and die. This, to a certain extent, proved to be the case in Germany where the passing of Yiddish as an enclave language (except among *Ostjuden* who never succumbed to good German and strived longer to preserve traditional Jewish culture) accompanied the efforts of early generations of *Maskilim* to create an artificial Hebraism while encouraging their descendants to master German language and culture, with the result that soon thereafter, as Kaufmann observes, the children could not read the writings of their fathers.

To Yeḥezkel Kaufmann, among the most subtle interpreters of the national life of the Jewish people, a spokesman for the religious homeostasis of our national existence, the challenge of the Hebrew language is more profound, relevant, and immediate than may strike one at first reading. Effect the translation, if you will, of the demand for an invigorated Hebrew language and resultant culture from the dead world of Eastern Europe to the thriving world of the American *galut*. Initially we must contend with the theological anxiety that America, too, is *galut*, that *galut* (not merely a description of the hostile environment of the pogrom and the death camp) is *here*, infesting the American paradise with the claims of alienage. The alienation of the Jew—the inauthenticity that writers such as Hillel Halkin urge against the paradisical *galut* of America—results from the winnowed bonds of culture and language. As Kaufmann argues profoundly, when Jewish spirituality is mediated through a *galut* language—when there is a language other than Hebrew in which Jews address God (as Franz Rosenzweig noted, with embarrassment, concerning his having written *The Star of Redemption* in German, although he thought of it as a profoundly Jewish book and was overjoyed that it was to become *Kokhav Ha-Geulah,* or as I have always thought that my *In the Days of Simon Stern* was quite literally my translation of the Messianic formula, *Bi-yemei Shimon Bar Kokhba* or otherwise "In the Days of the Messiah")—the Jewish people is in degeneration.

If, indeed, peace comes to the Zion of Israel, what will the Jews of the American *galut* undertake to do in order that it shall live? One thing above all: learn Hebrew, conduct the teaching of all things Jewish in Hebrew, create a literature of exile that binds it to Jerusalem. The Jews of Alexandria who thought and wrote in Greek ultimately passed into Hellenism, while the *galut* of Spain and Provence made Hebrew poetry, romance, philosophy, and mysticism the light of the Exile.   [A.A.C.]

THE HEBREW LANGUAGE AND OUR NATIONAL FUTURE

Of all the factors that comprise national existence, language is particularly important because it is through language that a nation takes the shape of a distinctive and unified group. Language is a stamp of history impressed upon the nations, to distinguish them from each other. It is a nation's *principium individuationis*. A language makes a nation a uniform organism occupying a specific place in history. This last statement, however, is not directed against those who seek the essence of the national experience in the "national character" or the "national spirit." Whatever the essence of a nation, its historical development is made possible only through language. Nation is, first of all, *Gemeinschaft*. Language is the means through which the *Gemeinschaft* builds itself. This is as true of daily intercourse of members of the *Gemeinschaft* as it is of higher intellectual creativity. A language is the necessary condition for national unification and for collective participation in an intellectual legacy. Consequently, a nation exists as an historical individual only because of language. Historical events confirm this statement, for the life and death of a nation have always been determined by its language. As soon as a group of people fashion a common language, a nation is born; but the nation as such dies the moment its members lose the common bond of language and adopt alien tongues. It is no coincidence that, in Hebrew, "nation" and "language" are semantically connected (*'umah velashon*).

The special place the Jewish people occupy in world history nevertheless does not constitute an exception to this universal law of language. If we want to name the one feature that gave diaspora Jews the character of a national (not just religious) collectivity (that is, aside from any, probably indeterminable, racial characteristics), that feature would have to be their national language. But no less than in its general historical development, so in its language the Jewish people diverges from all other peoples. Among other nations, linguistic collectivity is generated and maintained by the normal circumstances of existence: the commonly inhabited land creates and preserves the common language. The nations speak their own language because they do not understand any other. If a nation loses its land, it will forget its language and disappear into the new environment that it enters. This is not true of Jews. As early as the time of the Second Temple, the majority of Jews were scattered among other peoples, and came to know their languages. And even in their own land, the great masses probably spoke an Aramaic dialect rather than Hebrew. But although the Hebrew language vanished from the lips of the people, this did not lead to a destruction of the nation, as has been the case with other peoples.

To explain this, we must take into consideration the following: long before the eclipse of the Jewish state, the center of Jewish national life had shifted from a material sphere into a spiritual-cultural, or rather, a religious sphere. After the political unity of the people had dissolved, the unifying bond of a scattered Israel was neither a homeland nor a natural surviving language, but religion. The religion of the Jews became, in consequence, a source of *national* life. It absorbed all the national ideals of the people and made them sacred. It promised the people a future return to the homeland, and, even more important, it remained the custodian of their *language*. The language became a component part of religious culture, and found protection in the shadow of the religion. Yet it was not a language of religion in a narrow sense, especially not of cult. Just as in exile religion became the basis of national life for the Jews, so the language of the religion became the language of their culture. Even after Hebrew vanished from popular speech, it remained as the language of cultural creation among Jews. And thus, the Jewish people constituted a peculiar ethnic type—a nation whose language is not a spoken one but endures and develops as a cultural language alone.[1]

To be sure, the disappearance of the language from popular use was a *factor of assimilation*, but this process was inevitable. Jews everywhere were a minority among foreign peoples, and had no choice other than to adopt their languages for daily use. But when this occurred, the peculiar type of a people in exile came into being: a people that possesses only a cultural but not a daily language.

In accordance with the foregoing, we can distinguish three levels in the Jewish world: a national daily language; a national cultural language; and finally, the common religion. When one speaks simply of the assimilation of Jewry in exile, one generally means the waning of the community as characterized by the second level and the transition to the third. The French Jews at the time of Rashi, for instance, spoke French; but since their cultural language was Hebrew, we do not reckon that period among the assimilationist eras in Jewish history. However, if Hebrew is replaced by neighboring languages in the area of intellectual productivity, then national corruption sets in and the Jewish community is held together solely by the religion (which, to be sure, also includes a few petrified national components). This statement is not meant to pass judgment on the controversial issue of whether Judaism is national in *essence* or merely in *form*. I only want to emphasize the significance of language as a necessary condition of national collectivity, the conveyor of the hypothetical national entity. Without a common national language there cannot be an organic harmony between the individual parts of the *Gemeinschaft*. The national group will consequently dissolve of its own accord, and thus, as already observed, the historical development of the national existence becomes impossible. The fortunes of the Jewish national collectivity are also connected with the fortunes of the national language (in exile, merely a cultural language). From the standpoint of other than cultural conditions, there is barely any difference between Alexandrian and Spanish-Arabic Jewry. Both were deeply influenced by the Greek spirit and both strove for a blending of Judaism and Hellenism. But if we regard the Alexandrian period as one of national assimilation, and the Spanish-Arabic era as a time of national blossoming, then we do so only because the cultural language of the former was Greek and of the latter, Hebrew. This yardstick is by no means an arbitrary one. The fact remains that everything created in Hebrew during the Spanish period has endured as a living force even to this very day, whereas the products of the Alexandrian era have had little or no effect on our people. But this simply means that the Alexandrian era together with its creativity remained outside the sphere of national life.

What holds for individual parts of Jewry, is certainly true with regard to the entire people. Thus, we have to consider the death of Hebrew, as the cultural language of the Jews, as the end of their *ethnic individuality* and as a descent to the third level.

If we consider the present-day situation of the Jewish people from this historical viewpoint, we can clearly understand the nature of the internal crisis it is now experiencing. Throughout its exile, our people has occasionally gone through assimilation periods like the Alexandrian. But these isolated instances never concealed any danger for our nation as a whole. In modern times, however, the whole matter has greatly changed. The emancipation of the Jews in Europe brought with it the danger of assimilation for the whole people; it nurtured in its womb the ruin of the entire nation. Not just in this land or that, not at all, but throughout Western Europe the Jews have been dragged along by the torrent of an alien culture.

Let us now inquire into the exact process of assimilation during the period of emancipation. After all, the number of Jews in Western Europe has actually grown enormously! Is it not the case that Jews occupy a place of honor in art and science, that synagogues function undisturbed, that *Wissenschaft des Judentums* ("Science of Judaism") began to flourish in the age of emancipation, until presently it produces a rich literature? Are not people talking (although with a good many exaggerations) about the "Jewish spirit" asserting itself throughout European culture? No sane person would ever dream of seeing the Jewish acceptance of the surrounding vernacular as assimilatory. The German Jews—who comprise the majority of Western European Jewry—spoke German even before the Emancipation. To be sure, their German was a special dialect. But special dialects are spoken in all parts of Germany. No one would go so far as to claim that their dialect, diverging as it does from the German literary language, could possibly have been the mark of the Jews' national individuality. Then just what is there to the much-discussed denationalization of Western Jews, which exists as an objective *fact,* independent of the *theory* of assimilation, even among peoples in whom national determination has been reawakened.

In point of fact, assimilation involved a process whereby Western European Jews, absorbed through emancipation into the culture of their neighbors, *abandoned Hebrew as their cultural language.* The "liberal" Jew, whose relationship to Judaism is evident only on the Day of Atonement and on the day of his death, is not the only one who no longer participates in a living and organically developing Jewish culture; the Torah-observant Jew of Western Europe is in the same position. He may hold ancient Hebrew literature sacrosanct, but he regards it as a closed matter for ever and ever, and its language as long since dead. He thinks, feels, and creates in the language of the alien culture in whose domain he lives. Although he himself still has the possibility of enjoying the wisdom of the teachers of Judaism in all previous generations, including those of the Exile, he remains ungratefully unsympathetic to the very factor creating that possibility—i.e., the national language. He does not apprehend the monstrosity of the situation—that the abandonment of Hebrew as a cultural language makes such an organic unity impossible; that from now on a universally Jewish activity by, say, a Maimonides, a Karo, and similar great minds in Israel, will be impossible, which even from a purely orthodox viewpoint must be considered tantamount to the decay and ruin of Judaism. Yet it has already come to pass.

The Western European Jew, by renouncing Hebrew as his cultural language, has severed the bond connecting the Jews of Western and Eastern Europe as well as the various Jewries within Western Europe—to be sure, not wholly, for the religious link still survives, but all it connotes is a past, no longer a present or a future. Because of this isolation, Western European Jews have attained, if not national death, then at least a national paralysis verging on death. Western Europe has certainly produced a rich literature in various foreign languages on the "Science of Judaism." (A literature in foreign tongues and with Jewish contents is, incidentally, the true mark of national degeneration in the sense described above, in respect of the Alexandrian era.) But this literature, despite its contents, is not a national creation because it cannot have a fruitful effect upon the general productivity of the nation. For anything that cannot or will not become part of the heritage of the whole nation has no national value. If the entire Jewish people is doomed to the same fate as Western European Jewry, if it loses its language, which until now has sustained it spiritually—then the spiritual and intellectual energy of the people will be dissipated in a plethora of languages, the spiritual bond will dissolve, and the end of our national existence will come at last.

The essence of (though certainly not the reason for) the present crisis can be expressed as follows: Hebrew as the cultural language of the Jews is threatened with extinction. As a result, collective Jewish existence is losing its national character and sinking to the level of a collection of merely synagogal communities. In most Western European countries, this process is already completed. Fortunately for us, this process has only just begun for the majority of our people, that is, for the Jews of Eastern Europe. The future of the Jewish people depends on the solution of the language question in Eastern Europe. If this issue is settled the way it has been in Western Europe, then we shall face the end of the Jewish nation. However, if the Eastern European Jews follow a different path, one leading to a rebirth of Hebrew, then they shall save themselves from a national eclipse and also bring hope and salvation to their Western compatriots. I would like to discuss this latter, positive possibility.

In the life of Eastern European Jewry, three languages hold sway: the tongue of the host country, the Judeo-German "jargon," and Hebrew. Until now, each of these three languages has enjoyed a special domain. The language of the host country was used to communicate with the non-Jewish populace; Judeo-German was the daily language of Jews among themselves. Hebrew, however, was the language of culture and of the spiritual life of the people. To be sure, the jargon was a cultural language, albeit of second rank. Since Jews used the letters of the Hebrew alphabet for writing the jargon, there gradually developed a jargon spelling. In this form, the jargon satisfied subordinate intellectual needs; it was a vernacular and the language of women. But the Jew saw Hebrew as his true cultural language. In Hebrew he brought up his sons; Hebrew was the language of his thoughts and feelings. Not only literary works, but anything that had any sort of permanent significance for the individual Jew was written in Hebrew: e.g., the chronicle-like registries of the community or even the account ledgers of shopkeepers. To be sure, the average Jew's knowledge of Hebrew never went beyond a familiarity with the prayer book and the Torah, but it was the relationship that counted, not the amount of knowledge. Every Jew knew that anyone who didn't understand Hebrew must be an 'am-ha-'areṣ an uneducated Jew,[2] and that the more one studied the "little letters," the greater his prestige as a Jew.

Such a trinity of languages characterizes a period of transition. The Jews have found themselves in a similar situation many times in their wanderings from one exile to another. Buffetted from country to country, the Jews would retain the language of their previous home until it was replaced by a new language. We can recall, say, the Jews of the Rhenish provinces, who after settling there, spoke French for hundreds of years, calling French "our language" in contrast to German, and writing it in Hebrew characters. In the East, too, language had to change, and the language of the country superseded the imported Judeo-German. But the ways the replacement occurred were always different. The surrounding language could only influence colloquial speech. The jargon, as the language of everyday life, made way for the language of the country. Historically speaking, this process would have been unimportant for the ethnic being of the Jews—once Hebrew vanished from the lips of the people, each subsequent change of language is not necessarily to be considered a stage of assimilation. The language of the host country, however, could exert a far greater influence; it could also penetrate the sphere of spiritual creativity. If so, it would annihilate Judeo-German as the language of everyday life and Hebrew as the language of culture with one blow. In the light of the above, the result would be national degeneration. Circumstances have been such that the change of language among Eastern European Jews has started along these latter lines.

The beginning of the Haskalah[3] set this change in motion. The purpose of the Haskalah, of course, was not enlightenment in general but, as a preparation for political emancipation, familiarization with the alien culture prevailing in the state. To be sure, the first consequence of the Haskalah was the renascence of Hebrew writing. A more-or-less rich worldly literature developed. The Hebrew novel, the Hebrew short story were created. Hebrew poetry was revived and journalism inaugurated. But the basic idea animating this entire new literature was "enlightenment"—and in the language of the country. Anyone who wanted to write for the people had to use Hebrew, even those who saw no future for Hebrew (Kovner, et al.).[4] However, there were very few of the latter type. Most of the Maskilim [enlighteners] had a deep love for the "beautiful language." Yet the result was that the generation immediately following the Haskalah abandoned the language. Even the children of authors in neo-Hebrew literature were usually unable to read their fathers' works. After a while, the "celestial" Haskalah removed its lovely clothes and became a mere source of profit. Jewish adolescents left the *Bet-hamidrash* [house of religious study] in droves and descended upon secular schools. Thus, a generation of intellectuals emerged, educated in the spirit of a foreign culture and in a foreign tongue. The language of the country had become the language of both everyday use and culture. Especially culture. Thousands of Jewish intellectuals are still in a position to speak jargon to one another, but the language of their thoughts and feelings is exclusively the language of their country. (This is especially true of Jewish women.) Thus, national assimilation in Eastern Europe began in terms of what has been already expounded. Soon the consistently bad omen of national degeneration appeared: a "Jewish" literature developed in the language of the environment.

Nevertheless, Hebrew culture was strong enough to fight against the damage caused by the Haskalah. The national movement—*Ḥibbat-Zion*[5] and its legacy in Zionism reconstructed what the Haskalah had started to destroy. The Zionists, unfortunately, engaged in a fruitless argument about "material" and "spiritual" work, but they managed to contribute to a rebirth of Hebrew culture. The flowering of Zionism was at the same time a flowering for modern Hebrew writing. The national movement began with the establishment of a new basis for Hebrew culture in Palestine. But meanwhile, a new enemy appeared on the inside—the jargon movement.

The jargon movement is a deformity born of the national movement. Its ideological rationale can be summed up as follows: Jewish national being is an historically indefinite entity. All that exists are people who are called "Jews." The particular features forced upon these "Jews" in particular circumstances make up the characteristics of Jewish national existence. Since the majority of Jews now speak jargon, it is therefore the national language of the people and ought to be the language of its culture. Hebrew has purely historical significance for this jargon-people: however, insofar as it endangers the living vernacular, it must be fought. I have discussed this ideology elsewhere.[6] I merely want to talk about the conditions that have contributed to its propagation.

Aspiring to a secular education, the younger generation of the Haskalah era created a literature that satisfied its aims, that was to become a bridge to literature in the surrounding language. Hebrew, the only language accessible to young intellectual Jews at the time, was used for books on "nature," "telegraphy," etc., in short, on subjects that a Yeshiva boy had to learn to enter *Gymnasium*. Thousands of young men used Hebrew dictionaries to learn the surrounding language. In time, a need for secular culture was aroused in all strata of the people, and now came the era of the second-class cultural language, the jargon: newspapers, folk tales in jargon satisfied the primitive needs of uneducated Jews striving for secular learning, which they could acquire only by means of the jargon. This was really what made the jargon necessary, and for that reason its literature flourished.

Presently, however, the jargon movement bases its democratic "superstructure" on the permanence of those conditions. Its fatal error is its inability to realize the temporal and transitory character of these conditions. It fails to see that the jargon, like Hebrew during the Haskalah era, will form a bridge to the surrounding landscape; it fails to see that this surrounding language is spreading as a cultural language not only among intellectuals but also among the urban masses. The simple Jew, satisfied with a newspaper in jargon, is already making an effort to have his children instructed in the surrounding language. Once the surrounding language becomes the universal property of the masses, the jargon will no longer be *necessary* and will not survive a single day longer—this in contrast with Hebrew, which possesses an historical significance not shared by the jargon. The common people do not venerate and love the jargon and will never struggle for its existence nor waste any energy on maintaining it. Consequently, it is nonsense to build Jewish nationalism on the jargon. The jargon movement will inevitably lead to assimilation, not by intention, but by its nature. Those people who join the movement and give up Hebrew in favor of the jargon will ultimately give up their jargon in favor of the surrounding language. The majority of the people will not rally to jargonism if it becomes extremist. And this factor (its harmlessness) is the positive side of extreme jargonism. On the other hand, moderate jargonism conceals a great danger. This danger—greater because of its sympathizers within the ranks of Zionism—denies the existence of a language struggle. It claims that the struggle is merely being stirred up by people looking for a fight. Hebrew and the jargon are allegedly at peace, "allies" and not "rivals." Hebrew—so they say—can only survive if the everyday jargon helps it along, and for this they offer a conclusive proof: wherever the jargon declined, Hebrew also went under. They conclude therefore that we must defend the jargon for the sake of Hebrew.

This "theory" contains a whole nest of errors and false inferences. Its danger lies in its seeming correctness. As in a number of Western European countries, the jargon in Eastern Europe is being dislodged along with Hebrew. But it would be extremely superficial to see a cause-and-effect relationship in this simultaneous coincidence of two phenomena. First of all, the disappearance of the jargon in Germany and its disappearance in countries outside of Germany have been results of two entirely different processes. In Germany, a special dialect of the prevailing language was abandoned; in other countries, the jargon was supplanted by another language.

This difference leads us to the following question: what factor in the disappearance of the jargon contains the alleged danger with regard to Hebrew? The change of language per se or the nondevelopment (or abandonment) of Jewish dialects? No one would go along with the former. The disappearance of jargon in terms of a change of language has always been a customary occurrence in the *Galut,* without every endangering Hebrew. Thus, for instance, the German Jews, when they first came to Germany, gave up their earlier "jargon" and acquired the language of the country without risking any loss of Hebrew. It was only when they gave up the dialect after the emancipation that Hebrew vanished. Now, if people want to see a cause-and-effect relationship between the eclipse of the jargon and the eclipse of Hebrew, it must be understood as follows: the alleged danger to Hebrew consists not so much in the rejection of the *imported* dialect and in the adoption of surrounding languages, as in the non-development or abandonment of special dialects of the acquired language of the country.

Thus, Dubnow[7] maintains that the rejection of the dialect was one of the *causes* of the assimilation of German Jews. This statement underscores the absurdity of the "theory." It turns history topsy-turvy. In reality, the disappearance of the Jewish dialect in Germany was a *side-effect* of the powerful process of the integration of the German Jews in German culture. The same process had another very powerful effect: the dislodging of the Hebrew language. It was analogous in the Western countries, where the Jews spoke dialects alien to the language of the country at the time of emancipation (e.g., in Holland, etc.). Here two processes coincided: the change of everyday language (eclipse of the jargon) and the change of cultural language (rejection of Hebrew). The complete integration in the surrounding culture dislodged Hebrew, and at the same time did away not only with special everyday languages but also with Jewish dialects. Thus, the decline of Hebrew and the decline of the jargon were *subordinate* processes, independent of one another (albeit contingent on one and the same cause).

The same process is now taking place in Eastern Europe: the language of the country is gaining ground and dislodging both Hebrew and the jargon at the same time. But it is nonsense to believe that an advance in one direction is due to an advance in the other. Jargon and Hebrew are two different spheres. If the surrounding language had been accepted by Eastern European Jews as an everyday language replacing the jargon, then Hebrew (as the cultural language) would not have been harmed at all. This has often happened in the course of our history. But things are happening in such a way in the East that just the Hebrew language is being affected primarily by that surrounding language, which in Eastern Europe normally becomes first the cultural language of the Jews and then their everyday language. In fact, at times, as we have already mentioned, it becomes merely their cultural language. Under such conditions, the maintenance of the jargon cannot help the Hebrew language in any way. And not only that. The conciliatory jargonists forget that the present historical mission of the jargon is a *cultural* one. Yet as a cultural language, the jargon itself is at least as much an enemy of Hebrew as is the surrounding language. If we work for the jargon now, then we are no longer fostering the "language of women and illiterates" but a language that has established itself as a self-proclaimed national language, which even intends to supplant Hebrew.

The basic mistake of the conciliators, which destroys their entire argument, is shared by the extreme jargonists. They fail to realize the part the official language plays in Eastern European countries. Either they completely forget that there is such a thing in those countries and are therefore magnanimously bestowing privileges on both Hebrew and jargon; or else, if they do recall the surrounding language, they believe they can get rid of it through an alliance between jargon and Hebrew. Yet it is all but impossible to gain a proper perspective on the language issue if people refuse to realize once and for all that the surrounding language will force its way through to become the everyday and literary language of the Jew in Eastern Europe. The Jew who leaves or wishes to leave the ghetto must learn the language of the country, and not in a corrupt form as did his ancestors but in its purest and finest form. There is no way of gainsaying this need. The Jews of Eastern Europe must assimilate into the culture and language of their respective countries. It is not in our power to prevent this from happening.

Anyone who fully understands this situation will have little faith in the possibility of a language alliance. In the other areas beyond the sphere of influence of the surrounding languages, especially in the area of our national life, there is room for at most *one* of the two languages. If this is so, one can hardly speak about an alliance. All that is possible is an aggravated, life-and-death struggle between the two languages. An advocate of one must fight the other. Anyone in favor of both simply speaks in ignorance. If a man says we have to retain the jargon as a defense against assimilation and support Hebrew, he is merely saying: since the surrounding language, by becoming a cultural language for Jews, is thereby an enemy of Hebrew, we have to create a second enemy in the jargon, which also aspires to become a cultural language—and this is allegedly the way to save Hebrew, which is doubly threatened. A proper view of the language issue shows that the alliance proposal is nothing but the empty claptrap of faint-hearted pacifists. We will reach our goal, not by spreading ourselves thin over two languages but by focusing our energy on a single language. There is only one possibility: we have to sacrifice one of the languages in favor of the other, no matter how difficult this step may be for anyone involved. The question is merely: which of the two deserves and has prospects of survival?

Hebrew is different from all other languages that the Jews have used in exile in that it can never vanish from their hearts, so long as the Jewish people survive. Every other language vanished completely from the heart of the people as soon as it vanished from the mouth. Only Hebrew is tightly bound up with the people, and it alone has continued as the language of the people's literature for thousands of years after it ceased to be spoken. Hebrew alone the Jew studies with deep love, even though it is not at all "necessary." Even in Western Europe, Hebrew has not died out completely. Here, too, Jews study it—albeit as a religious discipline. The deep roots that Hebrew still has among Western European Jews are revealed by the language struggle in Palestine. (A further argument in favor of Hebrew: it alone is recognized and venerated by Jews in *all* countries.) Our national structure must be founded upon the historical strength of the language. Supported by this strength, we Hebraists do not fear to look the facts in the eye and prepare ourselves with all due austerity for the new situation confronting our people. The cultures and languages of the peoples surrounding us gain influence within our people. Yet we do not despair in the future of our people, but instead maintain faith in its future unity and spiritual power because we believe in the power of our national culture and language. We believe that our culture and language will claim a place alongside those of other nations. The Jews have been studying Hebrew for two millennia—not because a mastery of this language was necessary (like that of the surrounding language), or easy in the given circumstances (like the jargon), but precisely because it was neither "necessary" nor easy. This is the only kind of language that can survive in a nation in exile. A language of books and schools since time immemorial may hope to continue and win the struggle with the languages of other nations. If Hebrew may not cherish this hope, then neither may any other language.

This hope, which fills our hearts, can materialize only after a long and hard labor for the rebirth of Hebrew in exile. The most important thing that this labor can achieve is to gain a place for Hebrew as a vernacular in the diaspora. This is the most important point of my thesis.

Both friend and foe normally believe that any aspiration toward speaking Hebrew in the exile is an empty dream. Yet speaking Hebrew is, at present, the only way to achieve a rebirth of our language. We certainly do not think that Hebrew can become a natural language grounded in normal living conditions so long as we remain in exile. We realize that this is simply impossible, that it is conceivable at the most only for a limited time under certain conditions. (And this is the very reason we do not believe in the future of the jargon.) The spoken Hebrew we strive for, however, should not deprive Hebrew of its main character as a literary language. Instead, it will constantly derive its nourishment from books and schools, the very sources to which it owes its power. We regard the use of spoken Hebrew as merely a necessary expansion of literary influence. Our ancestors had no need to speak Hebrew, since as a cultural language it alone dominated their lives. The entire spiritual and intellectual life of a Jew, from the prayers of the simple man to the ghetto thinker's pilpulistic pursuit of Aristotle moved with the borders of Hebrew. But for the present and for future generations, Hebrew will have to share a place with the language of exile. So, if we do not expand the influence of Hebrew as a vernacular (and thereby undo the harm it has suffered as a cultural language), it will not fasten its roots in daily life, and will not survive. We can observe the necessity of this expansion in the schools. In the old *Ḥeder,* where only Hebrew and its literature were taught, it did not matter what language was used for instruction. But in the modern Jewish school, where a great deal of attention must be paid to foreign cultures and languages, the ensuing damage can be offset by retaining Hebrew as the language of instruction for "Jewish subjects." If any other tongue is used, students will never adequately learn Hebrew. It is peculiar enough that the speaking of Hebrew has not been forwarded as a theory. Instead, the "theoreticians" smiled at the notion or doubtfully shook their heads. It came as a necessary consequence of the love of Hebrew. The young, who inherited from their fathers an ardent love of the language of their people, could only demonstrate that love by speaking Hebrew, because their exclusively literary connection to the language was no longer as close a one as it had been for their fathers. But speaking Hebrew can fulfill a historical mission only if this process is developed into a theory, i.e., if a lucid understanding of its inevitable necessity makes it the foundation of our national work.

The most suitable basis for this national work is Eastern European Jewry. Not only because in Eastern Europe a Jewish social life is far more pronounced, but also because, to this day, Eastern European Jews speak jargon. We arrive thus at what is perhaps the positive aspect of jargon. Eastern European Jews, because they still speak jargon, are now entering a process of *language change:* the surrounding language has still not supplanted the language of an earlier exile. Of course, the earlier exile language has no hope of survival. But Hebrew can profit from the slow process of language change. The national movement must make every effort to see to it that Hebrew plays the part of the surrounding language. We must win a place for Hebrew as the vernacular, especially in the area of national life, where the jargon now prevails, e.g., in the field of national education. This will reinforce the position of Hebrew as a language, surviving alongside the increasingly influential surrounding tongue. The positive aspect of jargon is thus not its *survival* so much as its *waning.* By gradually dying out, it can leave to Hebrew the place it now occupies beside the surrounding language. The task of the national movement in exile is to take advantage of the language change and to create a new synthesis between our national language and the languages of the countries we inhabit—a synthesis that will be adapted to the new conditions facing our people and that will serve as a model for Jews throughout the world.

Will this synthesis come about? There is no way of offering theoretical proof. We have no "iron laws" upon which to rely for support. And besides, the "iron laws" of history were not written for the Jewish people. If our people had ever heeded these laws, we would have long since vanished without a trace. We rely exclusively on the will of our people to maintain its national existence. As long as this will remains alive, it will manifest itself in the relationship of the people to the Hebrew language—its spiritual, its holy language. Those among us (and in other nations alien to the spirit of our people) think they can destroy our hopes by claiming that Hebrew is "only" the "holy" language for our people—as, say, Latin is for members of the Roman Catholic Church.[8] Anyone who knows what Hebrew has been and continues to be for our people throughout history will realize how superficial this comparison is. The Jewish nation calls its language "holy," but is not the entire people in exile a "holiness"? For Jews in exile, "national" and "holy" are synonymous: this is why the only language that the people recognizes as its national language is the language it considers holy. The national movement is founded on the feeling of holiness (of both the land and the language). It strives for the rebirth of the holy land and the holy language. And the rebirth of the language is the more important of the two, it alone can unite the dispersed people with its land and culture. It alone can make the rebirth of the land a rebirth of the people.

8. THE DOGMA OF THE ETERNAL *Galut:*
A CARDINAL ISSUE IN ZIONIST IDEOLOGY

ABRAHAM SCHWADRON

EDITOR'S INTRODUCTION

ABRAHAM SCHWADRON (1883–1957) was born in Zloc-zow, Galicia, and died in Jerusalem. Schwadron translated Bialik's famous poem "Be-'Ir ha-Ḥa-Regah" into German under the title *Nach dem Pogrom* (1919), as well as Bialik's manifesto *Von der Schande eurer Namen: ein Ruf an die Zionistische Jugend* (1920). An infrequent contributor to *Der Jude,* Schwadron wrote this essay in Vienna, and it was published during Jahrgang IV (1919–1920), pp. 103–09.

Abraham Schwadron's essay is noteworthy not only for its passion and intelligence, but—as with many essays in this volume—for its pathos. In 1919, when Schwadron's essay appeared in *Der Jude,* the Balfour Declaration and the deliberations of Versailles were virtually complete, and the acknowledgement by the Great Powers of the legitimacy of Zionist claims to a national home in Palestine were sufficiently well-diffused throughout the Diaspora to give Jews the contingent hope that Zionist fulfillment, unlike the coming of the Messiah, was at hand. Indeed, unspoken and barely mentioned, is the Jewish belief in the coming of the Messiah. It will be noted that the idea of the "eternity" of the *Galut* (Exile) is already implicitly polemical. It was not believed by the religious that the Exile was eternal, for to suggest such a notion would be at variance with both the idea of Exile in historical time and divine deliverance, which would be an incursion marking the end of Exile. No. Quite clearly what Schwadron is opposing are those religious ideologues—no less fierce today—who insist that Zionism usurps the domain of God, and substitutes a salvation wrought by men for a salvation to be realized by God.

Another salient and relevant dimension of Schwadron's exposition—so tragically displaced by events of the second World War—is his talk of the prospective ingathering of sixteen million Jews. Moreover, now, in the face of the calamitous predicaments confronting Israel and Israeli society, one can see that the hope of those early Zionists that the establishment of a State for

Jews would "solve the Jewish question" once and for all was almost insanely abstract and formalist. Last, but not least, readers are directed to the grandeur and misery of Schwadron's concluding strophe: "If the *Galut* is eternal, then Zionism is not holy." That is, if ever there was one, a transvaluation of values, an inversion of immense profundity and ominousness, for among its unargued premises is the unclaimed assumption that the *Galut* was eternal (when in fact all that could be claimed was that the *Galut* would endure until the end of historical time, something rather different than eternity in the view of believers in a Messianic advent), and by implication holy (that is, sanctified by God rather than a symbol of the estrangement of Jews from God and the covenant). These theological ambiguities would be curiosa in a tranquil history, but nothing is a curiosity in the history of the Jews, the least tranquil of human histories.   [A.A.C.]

THE DOGMA OF THE ETERNAL *GALUT*: A CARDINAL ISSUE IN ZIONIST IDEOLOGY

At the birth of Zionism, the most important objection, piercing deep into its foundations was: Palestine cannot accept all the Jews.

The Zionists replied: One cannot say anything definite about the capacity of a country in advance. Its capacity depends on many circumstances other than the productivity of the soil and anything connected with it—not only on what the land offers but also on what its inhabitants need. So many and such incalculable factors determine the extent and kind of needs, or the so-called lack of need, of a population and its satisfaction. People pointed to Belgium, as the most densely populated [European] state, but no one could say that saturation had already been reached. Besides, said the Zionists, if not all Jews migrate to Palestine, then the position of the small number remaining in the *Galut* will be completely different from before, since Palestine will be a center and a home for the Jewish nation.

At first, then, especially in the era of *The Jewish State*,[1] so long as Zionists regarded their task as something easy and soon to be carried out, they never went beyond a gloss of this problem to a discussion of it in depth.

Decades, however, have passed and with them "gracious frivolity" and the belief in quick, easy work. Zionists have now had time to think and to ask themselves questions. And more than one has replied to himself: Palestine cannot really take in all the Jews, and beyond the portion that does migrate, the country can absorb, at most, the annual excess of Jewish births in the diaspora, so that large masses will always have to remain in the *Galut*.[2]

This—rather melancholy—insight was a partly unconscious wish on a deeper psychological level, fathered by the desire to provide a necessary basis for the national-cultural and political *Galut*-demands of Zionism. Since, after all, millions of Jews will remain in the Diaspora, we will have to set up and carry out Diaspora programs.

Now that external political constellations have given us the possibility of hope (to which we actually have no right in terms of our own, direct merit—in the usual state-political sense); indeed, now that we have the obligation (whether or not our hopes come true) to think not only of the necessity, but also of the plan for a major colonization; now that, in pondering this plan and its truly myriad and overpowering difficulties, we have come to a much earlier realization that Palestine is not large enough, etc.—nonetheless I consider it necessary and urgent that we oppose this dogmatic position of Zionist doctrine in principle and in totality.

It will not be by proving the opposite, for the advocates of the eternity of *Galut* are equally unable to prove their point of view, but rather by giving the highest priority to our unswerving determination to totally end the *Galut* and to answer the cogency of opposing arguments with our justified doubts, since no one can know what economic and political forms the Land and its adjacent areas, much less the world, will assume in the next few generations. Herzl posited a maximum technological development for Palestine, and with it an enormous productive capacity, which, it seems to me, can be achieved somewhat more easily than the high social attainments that many people expect our land to realize in the near future. After all, numerous experts had proven to us from their calculations that the land could only absorb a very small number of people, scarcely a few hundred thousand. But along came Ballod and calculated six million for the beginning of the development. He cannot prove this directly and rigorously. It will be proven only when these six million have been brought in. Zionism's ability to settle, say, two million on Palestine's soil will be proven only when they are there. After all, we polemicize daily against countless opponents, against intelligent, practical, informed and competent people who argue against this possibility, too. In any event, for these first two million, the issue of the country's capacity will be insignificant. The other issues, hindrances, insufficiencies, and obstacles, will be so much more serious, so terrifying, that we cannot simply prove the possibility to anyone.

I cannot prove it. I do not know, whether taking the first two or three million to the Land, which has to be cultivated in every way from the ground up, does not make for greater difficulties (according to the opponent: impossibilities) than, subsequently, bringing in the seventh to, shall we way, sixteenth million. I don't even know what the Jews will decide to do once, for instance, Ballod's millions have migrated to Palestine; no matter whether this happens over several generations or just one. I can't say whether or not, once there is absolutely no room in Palestine for the remaining millions, they will not look for a second area of concentration in one of the neighboring countries. Perhaps in an already irrigated Mesopotamia. Perhaps somewhere else. A concentration—I see this most essentially as an antithesis to the *Galut,* to the dispersion. If some Uganda[3] or other was rightfully a danger to the recovery of Palestine, then it will no longer be one as soon as Palestine is made secure by millions of Jews. I just do not know . . .

But one thing I do know: once millions of Jews have gotten a taste of what it is like no longer to live in the *Galut,* then no difficulty in the world will keep the others from exerting all their strength and power to leave the *Galut.*

And this too: the misery and the painful, leaden weight of *Galut* and self-contempt of the *Galut* shall become more and more intolerable to more and more Jews, and, with the progressive freedom of the world, will be felt more and more strongly by them. The sense of a personal, national way of life and its special needs will, along with various supranational strivings, now and for the foreseeable future, grow stronger and stronger among us and others— and along with these an increasing responsiveness to the subtlest goads, precisely because the entire nation is becoming more and more mature. The children of the Helots will scream for liberty. When Confalonieri, Bacchiega, Pellico, and others, during the 1820s, were the first to dream about the national resurrection and liberation of Italy,[4] they were simply the first truly to feel pain at the absence of freedom. Only the Italy that lived in their hearts was unfree. Other Italians, of course, moaned when oppressed, and each in his own way tried to escape the oppression, and to the extent that any one individual succeeded, the shackles on the rest of the Italian nation caused him few sleepless nights, if any. Only gradually did the people become ripe for dissatisfaction, for the sense of suffering over their lack of freedom—until the nation gambled everything and liberated itself. Among us, too, Herzl could ascertain, with more sadness than irony, the customary "individual solution of the Jewish question," and he realized that if a man is healthy and business is good, everything else can be endured. Zionism was meant to disturb this coziness.

I see Zionism in a primary, experiential sense as a rebellion against the *Galut,* against being an eternal minority, against the torment of degradation and the helplessness of dispersion, against the danger of being infected with self-hatred by all the hatred and scorn of the good and the bad people of the world.

Yesterday in a popular café, I was watching a Jewish peddler. He came in, said good evening, offered his wares; I saw the others watching, I heard him say good night and leave. He didn't do anything special, nor did anyone do anything special to him—but I saw in him my entire people of the *Galut,* the way he said good evening and the way people scrutinized him! Zionism, for me, is not so much the great sigh as it arises from time to time; it is the quiet anxiety, seemingly light, seemingly easy to overlook and overcome, yet unremittingly, eternally boring away, fine and still, like the dogged termite, until it reaches despair—until we scream and (if we can) rush out of the *Galut* as though chased by Furies. If Zionism, for you, is merely a world-view, a mission in the world, in mankind's humanity, then any change in its general views can undermine the foundations of your Zionist attitude. These foundations cannot be primitive, not nakedly rootlike enough: the fact that food and drink and light and joy somehow become bitter or stale for Jews in exile—exile, exile, exile!

But perhaps, you say, perhaps the pressure will vanish, the *Galut* will lose its bitterness and, as a consequence of universal, human, truly fervent tolerance and love and justice, will cease being the *Galut*?

Then, of course, Zionism, at least that primitive, direct brand, will become superfluous. For me, virtue does not rise except from a necessity. And likewise, there will be no eternal survivors in the *Galut* once the *Galut* is no longer an exile. Well, perhaps this era will come, even before the migration of the millions posited by the experts. But then you, too, shall be unable to go any further with your limited Zionism, you shall remain caught in the middle. The anti-Zionist believers in evolution or revolution as the sure solution to the Jewish question, all the endorsers of bourgeois progress or the "universal Soviet Republic," etc., all exclaim in unison that Zionism is superfluous since the victory of light over darkness is imminent, and by the time we get the millions across to Palestine, it will be time to bring them back, for the wolf will be living in peace with the lamb. And sometimes I, too, believe somewhere inside myself that some day, some day, all differences between the nations will be lost in a uniform and consistent mankind. Which, incidentally, does not at all strike me as an indubitably lovely prospect. Nor do I know whether in that era there will be just wolves or just sheep in the world, or whether both of them will be wiped out by the disgusting species of the hyenas.

"One day," says the Talmud, "Eretz Israel will spread over the entire earth."

"And it shall be at the end of days and the earth shall be full of reason," proclaims Isaiah.

At the end of days! Let us not make the end of days part of our calculations!

On the very last day before the end of days, the last Jew will escape from the *Galut,* weeping and exultant. On the last day before the end of days, his inner woe will make his blood cry out that he can no longer bear the *Galut.* But the Jew who waits until the evening of this last day is not our concern. He needs no provision for him—at the end of days.[5]

After all, what will other countries do when, according to present calculations, they can no longer hold their populations, two, three, five generations from now? We have been worrying for goodness knows how many generations, though we still have only one-half of one percent of the first generation in the land of hope.

I therefore consider it a negation of the deepest and most essential foundation of Zionism if we spend even one second on the attitude that this movement of ideas and masses does not aim at a total and exhaustive solution of the Jewish question through concentration; if we spend even one second believing that the *Galut* will never end, in the sense that the Jews as masses and yet as unauthoritative minorities, considerable and yet ill-considered, live on in the various countries in any of the present or similar inner and outer frames of mind, i.e., somehow different from other minorities, in peculiar conditions, in "incomparable situations," in which various things "must be taken into account," in which various points are "problems of so unique a nature that they cannot be dealt with in terms of the usual political viewpoint"—in short, if the political, economic, and social Jewish problem remains through all time on a lower level of normality, constitutively or numerically, than, say, the Polish, German, Lettish problem, etc.

At present, however, the dogma of the eternity of this abnormality powerfully dominates our ideology, both explicitly and implicitly, leading it along devious paths, circuitous roads, and return ways, leaving us bewildered and paralyzed and zigzagging. The north star, which is supposed to give our helm a direction and a sure path, is instead wavering and bringing us insecurity, contradiction, irresolution, and a trembling "Yes, but." This is evident in the following argument: If one feels that Zionism does not derive from the determination and the realization of the possibility of totally ridding the world of the problem of the Jewish masses, then one is forced to seek other sources: real and imaginary ones, living sources and broken cisterns. The wavering of the goal affects the starting point, derpriving us of a full, fine, and strong straightness: "Zionism aims at the direct and complete solution of the Jewish question." We have to struggle with assertions about the favorable influence on the situation of those who remain (which may be correct in a certain sense, but can no more be proven than the possibility of leading all the Jews out of the *Galut*). Nor, furthermore, can we simply steer towards totally Hebraizing the entire nation, because, it is alleged, this would be completely impossible in the *Galut* and the *Galut,* after all, will never come to an end.

Finally, we have to pay some attention to the possible influence of this attitude on one of the cardinal issues of our hoped-for future: the question of Palestine's borders. Naturally, I don't know what position our present-day diplomacy (which, incidentally, I consider very intelligent and adroit) has taken and is now taking, in its various negotiations, on the question of Palestine's capacity, including the problems of later developments. It is possible, however, that our dogma of the eternally small capacity of this land has to some degree weakened our proposals. We might have to demand an expansion of borders or the addition of adjacent areas, to enable a gradual absorption of *all* the millions of Jews and their natural increase. I do not consider myself one of those naïve people who feel that our "demands" are decisive, but they do constitute a component and, under favorable circumstances, they may have some effect on the outcome.

Accordingly, the resolute position of the Jewish people on the question of its total salvation through concentration will be of prime importance for the quantity and quality of mass settlement in Palestine. Remember: we have succeeded, i.e., the abnormality of our "situations" (every situation of ours is a defeat) has succeeded in convincing a significant sector of thought and influential leadership of the necessity of terminating this abnormality by establishing a Jewish home in Palestine—thanks, as well, to foreign interests that move in the same direction. Shall this effort therefore not aim, a priori and theoretically, at terminating the abnormality? Shall the Jewish question continue to haunt various countries in some form or other in perpetuity? What necessity for creating this home must we indicate to the world, what compelling alternative? Is this creation not a national luxury for us, if it cannot do away with the pressing fundamental problem, the issue of the Jewish *Galut*, within a reasonable length of time? The Zionist effort has already made the world realize something special and nonanalogous about the Jewish situation,[6] i.e., first, the solution of a national question through the systematic and agreeable resettlement of one of the rivals, and, second, the recognition of the intimate connection between a nation and a land whose distance from one another in time and space runs to thousands of year-miles—to vary a term from physics. Shall we then strive to convince the world of new forms, formulas, and theories for Jewish peculiarities and anomalies? No one can specify how successfully to solve the Jewish question that is left unsolved by concentration. People naturally say that the Jewish masses remaining outside of Palestine should be treated in accordance with minority rights that shall be made effective and valid, in accordance with the principles of national autonomy, etc. I would go along with this and regard the struggle for making these principles come true as an important and useful one (as I have previously stressed). But the complete solution of the problem of our *Galut* remnant through these principles assumes that, first of all, the economic and cultural situation of Jewish minorities is not different from that of other minorities, and that, second, the psychosis of anti-Semitism, which makes the situation of the Jews abnormal even where they live in the same legal constitution as the rest of the population, will no longer exist. These assumptions will simply mean that there will be no more Jewish question. But then the *Galut* will be a thing of the past—and the dogma as well.

Since I deny the eternity of the *Galut,* am I then firmly convinced and confident that all fourteen million Jews, as well as the coming fifteen or sixteen million, shall leave the *Galut?*

No, far from it, nor is it necessary for me to be firmly convinced—but, the fact that we deeply *desire* it, that our entire soul cries for it—makes it an urgent matter!

I cannot say for sure (and I cannot believe those who claim to know one way or another) whether all Jews will want to, or will be able to, emigrate. Nor do I know whether even the first, shall we say, six million will want to, will be able to come. Sometimes I believe it, sometimes not. But what does it matter? It is an incomplete and false opposition to assume that there is nothing in the world but either that which is or that which is hoped for, in whose fulfillment we believe. No, there is a third possibility: that which should be, that which is wanted. The innermost meaning of any ethics is: To establish in the place of what is that which should be, which is good, even if we are uncertain or do not firmly believe or do not firmly hope that it shall be realized. An insight into the *possibility* of realization must suffice for all efforts—my ideal has always been a Zionism without blind trust. No disappointment can shake it.

The future of Zionism can be determined by only two factors: by our, the Zionists', will as the positive force, and the totality of diverse oppositions (minus everything that helps us in the interests of the world) as the negative force. If our will power is a force, then when operating against any other force (here, of resistance), it will be determined by the universal law of the combination of forces: the resultant alone will be influenced by both forces, but neither force will influence the other. Let our resolution go its steeled way—the corrective reality will cause the resultant to automatically diminish itself, and will even diminish the forces opposing us as our will power never could.

If Zionism as an ideology and a goal is not based on the assumption and demand that it will totally and fundamentally solve the Jewish question, no matter when the world lets it begin or allows it to finish, then it cannot invoke two thousand years of Jewish hope and yearning; it would then deserve support by us all, but not the ardent fervor and the meaningless sacrifice of our best people.

If the *Galut* is eternal, then Zionism is not holy.

9. ZIONISM IN MAX NORDAU

LEO STRAUSS

EDITOR'S INTRODUCTION

LEO STRAUSS (1899–1975), philosopher and Hebraist, taught after his emigration from Nazi Germany at the New School for Social Research in New York (1938–1949), and then at the University of Chicago until his death. Among other works, he is the author of *On Tyranny, Hobbes' Political Philosophy, Persecution and the Art of Writing,* and a critical introduction to Shlomo Pine's new translation of Maimonides' *Guide of the Perplexed.* The present essay appeared in *Der Jude,* Jahrgang VII (1922–1923), pp. 657–60.

The clarity and precision with which Leo Strauss, then a young scholar of twenty-three, describes the dialectical complexities of Max Nordau's critique of Herzl's Zionist politics and employment of its difficulties to project the image of his own, reflects an acute and illuminating sense of the underlying issue of *galut* that occupies us to this day.

Galut is at the heart of the matter. *Galut* can be regarded in several ways: as a neutral receptacle, a mere extension of space (the lands and territories outside Ereṣ Yisrael) and a simple synopsis of historical time (the flow of millennia in secular time that contains the personages and episodes of the history of Jews and Jewish institutions in Diaspora); it can as well be conceived of as otherness, the alienated side of Jewish identity, the socioeconomic arena of Jewish assimilation, and hence, phenomenological degeneration; lastly as the necessary condition out of which redemption, Messianic in hope and factuality, is to arise. Whether Max Nordau is criticizing Herzl's innocent pursuit of political power, his effort to create a Jewish homonculus amid real impotence that would be sufficiently weighty to persuade Sultan that Jews would buy off his debts, consolidate support that would relieve the despair of the Jewish masses, mired in poverty and beleaguered by anti-Semitism, and persuade West European Christian princes that the Jews, indeed, were loyal to their suzerainty while at the same time anxious to end their subservience by departing from the historical scene of their discontent, what becomes clear is Nordau's fine ambivalence. Herzl was a publicist with a vision; Nordau came to his cause, already a celebrated author of debunking works that had made him both wealthy and famous.

Max Nordau was born in Budapest in 1849, practiced medicine in Paris from 1880, and while he had been launched as a journalist in the Hungarian press, it was *The Conventional Lies of our Civilization* (1883), a rationalistic assault on the prevailing religious and ethical assumptions of European culture that brought him to prominence. This was followed by other works of criticism, *Paradoxes, The Malady of the Century,* the famous *Degeneration* (dedicated to Cesare Lombroso), plays, and novels. Although Nordau was disengaged from Jewish life and was quite well-situated in the assimilated salons of Paris, the personal authority and undeniable charisma of Herzl brought him to the Zionist movement as one of its earliest adherents. From then until his death in 1923, he contributed to each Zionist Congress he attended a rehearsal of the condition of Jews, country by country, throughout the *galut,* employing this platform as a means of articulating his dialectic of assimilation degenerating into liberal "missionism" and' Messianism consummated in Zionism.

Strauss's inquiry into Nordau's Zionism is developed from the ground of his ambivalence and citations from Herzl's journals reflecting the sense of that ambivalence—Nordau's lofty appeal for a politics of trust, an openness treating both Western Christians and Jews as though both were reasonable, enlightened, charitable societies. Of course, this is what Nordau's polemical essays had urged all along, but in the politics of his Zionism he argues from the assumption of their realization. Remarkably, Nordau's lengthy book *Degeneration* (1895), written after his conversion to Zionism, manages to descry the arrogant egomania of the *fin de siècle* and call for a new era of sanity, responsibility, self-emancipation and moral constraint, without once mentioning the situation of Jews and Judaism. If indeed he would rebuke Herzl for a Machiavellian politics, for assuming the stance of dictator, he could as easily be accused of a rhetoric no less deceptive. Let Europe become enlightened, let it be emancipated, let is rid itself of self-infatuated ideologies and it would be reasonable to assume that the unmentioned Jews would no longer need to be singled out for omission, much less for humiliation. Strauss, well aware of Nordau's duplicitous argument, declares that Nordau's sentimentalization of Herzl makes him a new divinity, but one with clay feet. In fact, Nordau's perspective, in Strauss's view, impedes a true perception of Herzl.

Nordau's affirmative view of Zionism—what distinguishes him (in his own view) as an original thinker from Herzl, whom he regarded as either a politician or a visionary—is that it is grounded in the unfolding of European history: nineteenth-century Europe is normalized and so, therefore, is the Jew; Europe is beyond confessional religion and the sectarian wars it engendered, and so, therefore, is the Jew. The polities of Europe are no longer disorderly, confused, irrational; Jewish nationality and self-identity can now become rational and fulfilled. The Jew may no longer be the bête noire of the nations, but he is still dependent on the model of the nations. In fact, Nordau's contention is that the realization of Zionism follows logically from the French Revolution, the emancipation that followed, the rationalization of the state. It would appear that where Herzl was optimistically visionary in playing out a practical politics, Nordau reads backward into history an almost Hegelian reasonableness that lends credibility to Zionist hope.

Strauss spells out the logic of Nordau's Zionism but inserts into the center of the argument a critique of utmost importance: "the essence of the *galut*" is that "it gives the Jewish people a maximum possibility of existence by means of a minimum normality." This is to say, that the bearing and upholding of *galut* is to concentrate Jewish existence, to internalize it and thereby to withstand assimilation, however in the long run the absence of normality entails debilitation and loss. Persecution erodes not just life but morale. Zionism is thus correctly coupled with Messianism as the counter to assimilation; but where Zionism is terrestrialized and rendered a portion of ordinary politics at variance with the ultimate Messianic dream (itself denatured into Jewish mission), Messianism is surely enfeebled, but Zionism is rendered mundane. It is a powerful critique and as correct and relevant at this hour as it was then.   [A.A.C.]

ZIONISM IN MAX NORDAU

Political Zionism is of the opinion that the distress of Jews can be relieved only by establishing a Jewish state and consolidating the power of Jews into a Jewish national power. Toward this goal, Herzl used the device of playing the power of moneyed Jews (not a Jewish power at all) against the political powers, and the political legitimization of his plan by the great powers (the only ones to decide upon political significance) against the Jews. Herzl had no real control of either factor. However, by playing them against each other, he solidified the politically amorphous power of Jewish individuals into a political will, thereby accruing political significance to the Jewish nation.

While certainly approving of this goal, Nordau rejects Herzl's device as "underhanded." He wants power, but he rejects intrigue as a means of achieving it. He wants power, *but under the condition that we not deploy it at this time.* In this way he passes from political to spiritual Zionism, which makes a principle of the powerlessness of Jews, indeed, of their hostility toward power.

The motive for this defection from Herzl is a spiritual one: "honesty." We know that Herzl's Zionism was basically determined by impulses of decency and loyalty. Yet Herzl knew all too well that in politics there is nothing unambiguous about speaking truth or falsehood. Politics must create realities, and, under certain circumstances, the most effective tactic is to assume the existence of the devices that are the most apt to produce realities, to assume the existence of the presuppositions, especially those of a moral nature—things created by the *strained* and indeterminate efforts of the indolent crowd. By assuming that these conditions have already been fulfilled, one can evoke the necessary effort. If something is untrue today, by pretending it is true one can actually make it come true tomorrow. The celestial blue of Zionist optimism in Herzl was largely dictated by his role as agitator. Nordau himself circulated a legend he did not believe: the fairy tale of a Herzl enthusiastically trusting his nation. Nordau did so in order to make possible, recognizable, a betrayal of the Jewish nation by its leader, that is to say, a political motive. Herzl's accounts in his journals tell us something about Nordau's opinion of Herzl, in a form not dictated by his role as agitator: "Nordau considers me insincere and sneaky in my dealings with rulers and Jews. I believe he will some day make this censure public and embarrass all of us" (III, p. 63). The journals teach us that this "sneakiness" is the essence of Herzl's politics. Nordau recognizes this feature, he condemns it, and demands a politics of trust, instead of the *negotiorum gestio* of the dictator Herzl, the democratic mandating and checking of the leader (*Journals* II, pp. 251f). He not only demands such politics, he activates them to the detriment of Zionism and to the great irritation of Herzl. On the occasion of a speech by Nordau, Herzl[1] remarks: "He made quite unjustified advances to Socialism, exposed all our weaknesses, told about our helplessness, etc." (*Journals* II, p. 258). The sympathy with Socialism and the distaste for secret diplomacy have the same root and tend to dissolve the major issue in Herzl's politics, which have a conservative, "State-preserving" tendency.

In Nordau's statements about Herzl in the *Zionist Writings,* there is no trace of the rebuke that was certainly uttered more than once. On the contrary! "My heart breaks at watching him during his nine years of suffering, when he, enveloped by a fog, as it were, in his fine trust in the Jewish people, felt his way with torn hands through the thorns and nettles of reality" (p. 160). Nordau may have been moved by poetic reasons to write this sentence, which is very typical of his style: flowery, or rather weed-strewn. And those poetic grounds might explain the fatuous expression. Or else he was moved for propagandistic reasons to appeal to the Jewish heart, which is always open to innocent suffering and disillusioned idealism. Otherwise, Nordau's sentence is as incomprehensible as it is absurd. Nor can we say anything else about his claim that Herzl was dominated by the notion that "he was backed by twelve million noble people"; or about Nordau's comment just after Herzl's death that Herzl's "exquisite sentimentality was what made him the author and leader of Zionism." If Herzl now appears to many as a forbearing visionary in Israel (cf. the recent apotheosis by Emil Cohn), then the fault lies with Nordau. From his position as an admirer, Nordau brought Herzl down. By explaining Herzl's greatness to himself and the Jewish people in sentimental categories, Nordau contributed much to stifling Herzl's original impulses. This was all the worse in that Zionist ideology from the very outset fell short of the *niveau* Herzl meant it to attain. And not only ideology. Herzl therefore limited himself quite intentionally to a more accessible and more direct line of argument, while Nordau remained on the slightly lower level, where, in comparison to Herzl, he moved with no less skill and zeal, and with greater subtlety.

"Zionism, like any historical movement, emerged from a strongly felt and clearly recognized need for a normal existence under natural conditions" (p. 178). *For Nordau, Zionism is a product of the newly gained sense of reality, which was lacking in earlier eras of the* galut *and of assimilation.*

The Jewish nation has lived in the *galut* as a *Luftvolk*—as creatures of the air. Literally and figuratively, it lacks ground under its feet. It is totally dependent on the chance behavior of other nations. Life in this condition is sustained by a strong will for existence. All ideas and all forms of Judaism unconsciously serve in preserving the national existence and intensifying the will for that existence. The idea of chosenness and the idea of the Messiah maintain faith in the national future throughout all situations; on the other hand, those ideas prevent faith from being actualized because they aim at something completely miraculous, something beyond human effort. All Jewish customs and habits serve the purpose of separation from other nations and thus help maintain national existence; on the other hand, they prevent normal life by distancing Jews from the terms of the everyday life of nations. The same result comes from the lack of a political center: The Jewish people may not be annihilated at any one point—and on the other hand, for that very reason, any comprehensive political action is impossible. *This is the essence of the* galut: *it gives the Jewish people a maximum possibility for existence by means of a minimum normality.* In the long run, the lack of normalized existence had to ruin our people. Persecution could have such a disastrous effect because the people, lacking any natural mode of existence, lacked the possibility of a true recovery and rise. In the *galut,* Zionism and Messianism coincide in that the return to Palestine is awaited as the miraculous, prayed-for, nonrationally prepared work of the Messiah. This unreal coupling of Zionism and Messianism is abolished by assimilation. Nordau is not grateful: Assimilation has separated the two ideas from one another in order to make possible an easy death for the Jewish people in Europe by the abandonment of Zionism and the enfeebling of Messianism into missionism. *Assimilation has basically no other motive than the egoism of individual Western European Jews.* The illusionism of the *galut* expressed through faith in the "mystical" redemption by the Messiah, deteriorates in assimilation through the secularization of *galut* ideas, which for all their mysticism, possessed a sober purpose in life. Assimilation deprives Jews of the self-assurance of ghetto life and gives them the illusionary surrogate of trust in the humanity of civilization. Assimilation politics is nothing but politics of the *galut,* limited to transitory needs, but expendable. Such politics completely deceives itself about the attitude of the host nations and believes it can wish away the Jewish question simply by closing its eyes. Assimilation is nothing but a "sacrifice to loyalty, to dignity, to historical consciousness."

This was the sacrifice that Western European Jews made to their emancipation. The prerequisite of this emancipation was the doctrinairism of the French revolution, a doctrinairism that deduced syllogistically the necessity of a Jewish emancipation. National conflicts, however, became all the sharper precisely because of the French revolution and its strengthening of civilizing tendencies; this sharpening contradicted the well-intentioned hopes of liberal Jews.

The emancipation came from a change only in the non-Jewish world. This change was toward absolute ideas intelligible to everyone, including Jews (humanity, religiosity without denomination). The secularization of Christian ideas is, for Nordau, self-evident and as rationally necessary as the secularization of Jewish ideas in "missionism" is "foolish and presumptuous"— evidently the idea of chosenness, even in a castrated form, still has essentially less rationality than the idea of universalism in terms of a Christian enlightenment.

Pressured by assimilation, Zionism adheres to the separation between Zionism and Messianism, between the national, worldly goal and the spiritual means. Except that Zionism abandons Messianism. In contrast to the self-destructive will of assimilation, Zionism goes back to the vital will of the *galut*. Nordau deplores the abandonment of Zionism[2] in assimilation, but he refuses to acknowledge that separation prepares for Zionism in a deeper sense. Thus, just as Nordau saw the development of assimilation and emancipation as having been caused by the non-Jewish world, so he must regard Zionism as the product of non-Jewish nationalism and anti-Semitism. Hence he achieves no understanding of internal law, of the Jewish necessity for a Jewish development influenced by, and learning from, European nationalism and anti-Semitism.

There are two things to consider here. First, we see Zionism continuing and intensifying the dejudaizing tendency of assimilation, fighting the illusionism of the *galut* and its unreality, which he rediscovers in the missionism of assimilation. Second, Nordau's critique of emancipation shows something characteristic of prevailing Zionism—how a naïvely enlightening faith in the ideals of 1789 persists alongside a realistic skepticism toward their actual meaning for the Jewish question. In Nordau, as in Herzl, the sober substance of Zionism emerges from the envelopment of the sublime ideas of the French revolution, ideas taken for granted by both assimilation and Zionism.

Zionism is a child of the nineteenth century. In lieu of the "Volcanic" notion orienting Jewish history in its great national catastrophes, Nordau demands the "Neptunian" and less melodramatic notion, which sees the cause of the great upheavals in the many minor facts of politics and economics. Like the distress of Jews, the abolition of that distress loses any semblance of the miraculous: instead of the appearance of the Messiah, "a long, difficult, general struggle" by the Jewish people. Theology must have no say in Zionist issues; Zionism is purely political. The most universal philosophical foundations are offered by a biologically based ethics. There is no question as to the right of applying this standpoint to Jewish issues: This is an unconditional science! Disregarding the matter of the right, it is true that replacing teleology with causalism in considering an organism does permit replacing missionism by the demand for national necessity. Once again we have an example of the universal rule that the change of motives in the spiritual life of German (generally! Western European) Jews is a function of the change of motives in all European spiritual life.

The close relationship to biology characterizes Nordau's Zionism, just as the enthusiasm for technology characterizes Herzl's Zionism. To put it impudently: Herzl has the attitude of the North German engineer: "We'll make it, just with our technological achievements." Nordau has the attitude of the apothecary Homais, who makes his splendid scientific knowledge universally useful for improving cider-making and always emphasizes his virtue.

Assimilation has denied the presence of the Jewish question—Zionism recognizes its presence. One might assume that this recognition is one of the many efforts of the nineteenth century in regard to all the "questions" resulting from the trend to make problems out of self-evident facts of life (the question of capital punishment, schooling, religion, sex, etc.). Nor does Nordau lack this nuance in treating the Jewish question—which comes as no surprise in a disciple of Lombroso and the author of a book entitled *The Conventional Lies of Our Civilization* [*Die konventionellen Lügen der Kulturmenschheit*]. But it does not remain at that level. Nordau has the modern sympathy with the Helots and the corresponding indignation at the Spartans. Yet he takes it for granted that the helotry of assimilation must be replaced by the Spartan spirit of Zionism. This is nothing less than the consequence of substituting more virile causalism for teleologism in regard to ethics and thereby Jewish politics.

10. THE MATURING OF MAN AND THE MATURING OF THE JEW

ERNST SIMON

EDITOR'S INTRODUCTION

ERNST SIMON (1899–   ), teacher, historian, leader of the Zionist youth movement in his native Germany, a member of the circle around Rabbi Nehemia Nobel and Franz Rosenzweig, and in 1923–24 editorial associate of Martin Buber in *Der Jude*. In 1928, Simon went to Palestine, but he returned to Germany in 1934 to help Buber in the work of arousing and strengthening the morale of German Jewry. He returned to Palestine once again in 1936 where he has been Professor of Education at the Hebrew University since 1950, was a founder of the Ichud Movement, and is active in the work of reconciliation between Israel and the Arab world. He was a frequent contributor to *Der Jude;* the present essay, intended as a memorial to Gustav Landauer, appeared during Jahrgang VI (1921–1922), pp. 457–75.

There can be little doubt that in the order of reason, if the Jewish people is not convoked by God and sustained by Him, its claim to the attention of the world and the world's acquiescence to its ambition for peace and security is little different from the requirements of any other people. The Jewish people can claim no privilege by reason of a history of persecution and injustice; such claim of privilege is itself yet another provocation for new injustice. Indeed, if there is no fundamental belief in the reality of Israel as *totaliter aliter*, a "wholly other" existing within the frame of divine-human understanding, the endurance of the Jews is merely an exaggerated example of stubbornness and tenacity that the ceaseless erosions of time will one day undermine.

These reflections are all the more to the point when we come to consider Ernst Simon's admirable evocation of the thought of Gustav Landauer, that remarkable German socialist and Jew who was killed in Munich in 1919 "by the white beast" while serving the revolutionary Bavarian Soviet Republic. To the hour of his death Landauer had conducted himself with luminous consciousness of both the hopelessness of revolutionary action (and its inevitable descent into terror) and its nonetheless indispensable enterprise. He was that remarkable specimen: a critical intellectual who regarded action as both dream and destiny; an analyst of the fallibilities of language, its sources, liturgies, and iconic implication (not different from his contemporaries Franz Rosenzweig and Eugen Rosenstock-Huessy) while requiring that men continue the struggle to speak; an anarchist socialist out of Proudhon (not Marx), who had no choice than to make common cause with doctrinaire socialists and party regulars; a pacifist who recognized that the other side of revolution was the terror; a mystic, like Fritz Mauthner, who did not believe in God; a Jew who did not adhere to Judaism; and a Zionist sympathizer who despised nationalism.

Simon's essay, eloquent and precise, identifies the "Janus-like unity" of Landauer's existence—not simply contradiction, too easily dismissed, but contrariety bound into unity. Landauer did not plaster the contrariety with the thin paste of homogeneity, pretending that all would be reconciled here below, but rather acknowledged in both word and life that however multivalent historical man may be, whatever his confusion or malevolence, these too are a portion of his humanity. Landauer knew man and nonetheless loved him, which Simon takes to be a correct posture for the Hebrew, for whom knowledge and love are spoken with the same word.

"For Gustav Landauer was a Jew."

It is this assertion of Simon's that draws our attention. Early in his life Landauer contended in *Skepsis und Mystik* that "man's blood and his blood-community are his most intimate and most private possession." This blood-community (later to be given a significant function in Rosenzweig's *The Star of Redemption*) is the national unit, but nation is at most a vehicle by which human beings assert their connection with the whole of history and the unique particularity of the self. Nation is a construct, a field of force whose energy is to sustain the universal and the individual. What marks the authenticity of nation, however, is neither place nor boundary, but language and the entrance into language—even the language that appears to be alien to one's blood would make one party to the linguistic nation. Language is an unrestricted passport. It is coherent that Landauer should argue that he has no need "to simplify myself or, through any self-denial, to unify myself. I accept the complex whole that I am and hope to be even more complex than I realize."

Since Landauer was an anarchist socialist (that is, one who repudiated the technocratic state in favor of the small, face-to-face, dialogic community) and a Jew (one who wished the Messianic demand of classic Judaism to assault the enclaves of privilege and overturn them), it is no surprise that his amalgam of the two should resemble the mission liberalism of Reform Judaism. But as Simon warns, the resemblance is superficial, for Landauer's Messianic rhetoric is not as powerful as his critical sense of the frailty of human enterprise. A man is, in Landauer's view, what he can do. The appraisal of ethical possibility is conditioned by where a man finds himself, the injustice at hand, the present situation and the present hour (a conception whose urgency was to play a considerable role in Buber's return from the serene gardens of his prewar mysticism to the existential lists of *I and Thou*). It is upon this foundation that Landauer's criticism of Zionism depends. Zionism is dream and hence delusion; expectation before the future while the abyss is at one's feet.

Simon lovingly scrutinizes Landauer's critique of Zionism and, with the same trenchancy as it was defined, employing virtually the same arguments, destroys it. Landauer's mistake—it is the same everywhere and has not changed—is to effect the unity of the Jewish self and the national community, by denying the particularity of the Jew as though Judaism and Jewish identity were a prosthesis no longer needed now that civic justice and freedom has encouraged the withered limb of pride to be regenerated. Judaism is for the socialist Jew, Zionism for the German Jew (or the American Jew) an artificial limb, which general toleration and accessibility to the national language and culture has rendered narrow and tribal. But as Simon replies "Zionism is the desire for the living order of Jewish people and thus, to the same extent as Socialism—beyond this metaphysical question" (that is, beyond the question of the ultimate solution of human history). Zionism is a response to the real and is thus, no less than socialism, an invitation to both delusion and tragedy.

Indeed, one of the last communications between Gustav Landauer and his close friend Martin Buber occurred on the occasion of Buber's editorial comment on the Russian and German revolutions, both of which occurred toward the end of 1918. In his essay "The Revolution and Us" (*"Die Revolution und Wir,"* Der Jude, Jahrgang III [1918–1919], pp. 345–47), Buber notes that both revolutions are at best beginnings, fulfilling nothing in themselves but starting the process, and that ultimately the ideal will have been reached not by the consummation of the nation, but by its transformation. Buber is led (as Simon is led) to contest the revolution if it occurs without the reformation of society—and the society, envisaged by the utopian Zionist, is one in which the human spirit of community, not merely societal structures, will be revised and renewed. Writing from Krumbach, Gustav Landauer expresses his pleasure with Buber's announcement of his intention to write about "Die Revolution und die Juden." Landauer further inquires whether Buber will describe the role Jews have played in making the revolution. It was an innocent inquiry, but betrayed a portion of the almost unnatural innocence that maked Landauer. A few months later Landauer was to be murdered. (Martin Buber, *Briefwechsel aus sieben Jahrzehnten,* II: 1918–1938 [Heidelberg: Verlag Lambert Schneider, 1973].)

When he wrote this letter to Buber, Landauer had not read Buber's essay, but Landauer might have known that Buber would not be likely to seize the occasion to celebrate the participation of Jews in world revolution—not that Buber would have been embarrassed by the affection of Jews for revolutionary socialism. Not at all. Landauer was expressing an almost jejune enthusiasm for the revolution, which Buber, wholly a Jew, would have regarded with critical distance, subjecting it to a different criterion, that of the Messianic socialism into which Landauer had raised him and upon whose foundations Buber had raised a different structure.   [A.A.C.]

THE MATURING OF MAN AND THE MATURING OF THE JEW

To the enduring memory of Rabbi Dr. N. A. Nobel with reverent gratitude.

I

For danger is the gateway to deep reality, and reality is the highest meed of life and God's eternal birth.—Martin Buber, *Daniel*

Politics, as a life's work and a literary subject, has lost much of the value that it had for people one hundred fifty or even fifty years ago. The experiences of an imperial, a military, and a reformist Germany have collectively created a situation in which a man with higher aspirations, while believing that he can develop his "talent" and more than his talents in the "river of the world," nevertheless feels that, in order to cultivate his "character," he has to choose "privacy." The slogan, typical of our age, about politics' corrupting the character, is the very opposite of the line from Goethe's *Tasso,* to which we have just been alluding. Together with this change in value, however, there is a directly opposite change in practice. A concentration on politics, a relentless devotion to its strictures and loopholes has grown inordinately since the days when politics was so greatly appreciated. The modern-day politician, abandoned to the things of so-called reality, at the same time resignedly watches the decay of his character. He realizes what is happening to him, and cynically admits it, since (he says) he cannot change it. Tacitly or openly, people permit him to use lies as a tool of his profession, just as they permit the poet to use "poetic license," the lawyer to observe his duty of "defending a client no matter what," the businessman to cheat on his income tax, and the burglar to employ a skeleton-key. The opinion about the *individual man,* in those cases and for those people who have come to terms with the above-mentioned professions, is based on what he does and what he is "otherwise," i.e., outside his life's work. Those who can't go along with this have no choice other than to reject this corrupt world and flee into loneliness or a literary café.

But in such times of transition, there always emerge isolated and tragic men whom others regard as utopians. They want to authenticate their "character," their existence and its purpose, in an exposed activeness rather than in remote solitude. They realize that their struggle is ultimately doomed, but they believe in a victory in the world of the true reality that they are helping to build. They engage in politics with the "utopian" device of truth, although (and because) they know as well as the clever know that it won't do. Their call to Socialism, to the true state, to a genuine community, has had various names in the history of mankind, and various consequences. The ranks of these men and their deeds represent a maturing mankind—and, as the most recent member, Gustav Landauer's life and death stand before our world.[1]

II

Whoever is full of himself has no room for God.—Buber, *Baal Shem*

Plato and Jesus, Solon's *Seisakhtheia* and the similar remission of debts during the ancient Jewish jubilee—such is Landauer's ancestry insofar as he is the son of mankind. But he was also the son of his age, and in this respect he had totally different teachers, though always men of rare stature and scope.

His first theoretical work, *Skepsis und Mystik (Skepticism and Mysticism)*[2] attempts to further develop Fritz Mauthner's *Language Criticism*[3] in the birth of which he shared. Here the young and stormily consistent thinker practices a sort of epistemological Bolshevism, struggling through the deepest destruction to find a way towards reconstruction. As in Mauthner, the word is revealed as the omnipotent ruler of our thinking and living and, as such, is flimsy and vain. The solidity of substance and matter is swept into the endlessly flooding and ebbing tide of events and, for that very reason, raised to a new meaning: it becomes the meeting-place and the resolution of counter-currents. Faith in God, the Creator, and in his world is submerged in an atheism that tries to prove that such a concept is *our* concept, i.e., of human origin, an idol—thereby giving the creative ego the possibility of recreating God and the world, or (as Landauer prefers to put it) being itself God and the world. Highest mysticism is thus born out of the deepest skepticism. In this world-view, we recognize traces of Platonic idea-poetry, Meister Eckhart's God-intimacy, the pantheism of Spinoza and Goethe, and Fichte's subjective pride, in a unique and significant new version. The pride of the "I" is tempered by the skeptical knowledge of the exceedingly dubious nature of this word: I, with its God-intimacy unshackled by the fullness of an all-inclusive love for nature and the world—every element is modified, re-fashioned by every other, so that something new and integral emerges.

Landauer's *Weltanschauung* has the closure of a philosophical system, although not in such a way as to stand before us completed, as in Hegel's encyclopedia or in Hermann Cohen's great work. There is a different kind of systematic unity in Landauer's writings and actions: the basic view throbs and breathes in the very midst, at the very core, of all his essays, speeches, critiques. *Aufruf zum Sozialismus (The Call to Socialism)*[4] as well as *Die Revolution (The Revolution)*[5], the older essay collection *Rechenschaft (The Summing-Up)*[6] no less than the new and highly important *Der werdende Mensch (Maturing Man)*[7] always and everywhere show the whole man, always Gustav Landauer. His ego is never full of the swelling sense of its own being. It is always filled with God, the world, and his fellow men of this human earth. This is the point that leads back to another ancestry, characterized by such names as Proudhon, Bakunin, Kropotkin, and Tolstoy. The misleading word "influence" will be avoided when we come to Landauer's relations to these anarchists. Instead, we ought to think physically and actually of the image of these ancestors: each man *discovers* in himself characteristics and impulses of dead forebears, whose direct influence he could not have experienced; this is essentially true of Landauer's fully original thinking. His comment on Walt Whitman applies to himself as well: "Although Whitman was very well read, he by no means read and gathered, he only absorbed what was already in him beforehand." It is in this way that we are to understand the circumstance that we find elements of predecessors in Landauer's social teachings, just as we do in his philosophical views.

There are three basic ideas that Landauer shares with Proudhon, whom, in grateful acknowledgment, he would call the "greatest Socialist": first, a hostility against the State and its mechanizing and murderous principle, which suffocates life and misuses it for purposes alien to life, such as war and exploitation; second, the conception of money, which has been transformed from a useful medium of exchange into a devastating end in itself and which, prolonging itself through a disgusting fission, gave birth to the repulsive monster known as "interest"; and finally, the positive counterproposition, the idea of the cooperative, of free and mutual self-aid, although not confined to the barter-bank, an instrument that was sufficient for Proudhon's time but not for today.

We are reminded of Bakunin's communism when we read about Landauer's concept of *Bodensperre* [land enclosure], to use Franz Oppenheimer's term; we are reminded of Kropotkin's "mutual aid" when we read about Landauer's principles, to which, in both theory and practice, he liked to apply a term that is not worn out for him: "reciprocal effect." And, finally, we are reminded of Tolstoy by Landauer's total rejection of violence, by his protest against the use of unholy means to a holy end, by his religious determination to break through once and for all the vicious circle of cause and effect, utopia and "topia," revolution and restoration, to begin again, to break virgin soil. He becomes the extreme (and sometimes unjust) opponent of all attempts at predetermining through scientific laws the fate of individuals and nations, thereby negating in advance the theoretical possibility of such a renewal. Marx's economic conception of history, Freud's materialistic psychology, and

Hegel's dialectical progression were all equally loathsome to Landauer since each inhibits the free action of the revolutionary individual. Higher development and progress, socialism and world peace need not come, if we human beings do not realize them now, at this very moment, and here, in this very place. The rebirth of the "I" shall lead to the rebirth of the world. Landauer's mystical determination "to find the universe physically within oneself" is also the basis of his social philosophy, which, spreading from the tiniest cell, from the community, in which "love dwells," to greater and greater circles, will build the community of the free nation on a free foundation. "Neither the moral philistine nor the superman is the purpose of the universe"—but, we may conclude, the free citizen. This idea, which is to be found in *Skepsis und Mystik,* reveals the basic roots common to all of Landauer's philosophical and economic teachings.

III

This is the love of human beings, to feel their need and bear their sorrow.
—Rabbi Moshe Leib in Buber's *The Great Maggid*

This, then, is Landauer's main question: how do the Idea and the world find their way to another and jointly create *reality?* Reality is a problem for him. He does not accept it with the naïve realism of the word-believer, nor does he reject it with the naïve idealism of the philosophy professor. He struggles for it in thought and deed. It is not satisfaction, not fatigue, not contentment, and not withdrawal that strikes him as the worthy attitude of the true human being. The will to act and the strength to persist are what he needs. That "which runs in the wide lane between the 'I' and God, between the desiring drive and submission, is called Life." Life—but not suffering—and when, with deep sympathy, he quotes Strindberg's voluntary confession, "I am doomed to suffer," we may say of Gustav Landauer that he was doomed to *live.* He bears his destiny in joy, health, and natural energy. His fine virile head gazes with clear eyes into the world and no illusion dims his view or eases his action. He foresees that this war has to come, he knows and prophesizes that not even the Social Democrats will prevent it; indeed, they will actually support it, and moreover, he knows that the revolution will only be strong in negation and then go to pieces in its stewardship by resorting to the worst means: terror. He fully realizes this, and writes about it relentlessly. Thus, this great man, whom the visionaries considered a compromiser, and the compromisers a visionary, was actually one of the rare men who have lived with seeing eyes. Such men are endowed with the supernatural certainty of a dream, or—as Landauer puts it—of "delusion."

Just as skepticism turned into mysticism, and just as the community is to grow out of the individual "I," the opposites are bound into unity even in this most central area: the knowledge of the world produces the will to delusion.

Delusion is the true mainspring of all activity: God, nation, mankind are simultaneously delusion and reality, just as in Strindberg's *Dream Play*, whose "real fantasy" Landauer admired, dream and instinct *together* form life. In order to fully understand this consistent conception of "delusion" in Landauer, "conscious illusion" in Mauthner, "myth" in Hölderlin, "legend" in Buber, "dream" in Strindberg (and, on a deeper, i.e., pragmatic level, "vital lie" in Ibsen), we should not think of something vague or even contrived, but rather of a reality that is hidden in the midst of life.

Landauer, who calls the reality of "nation" a "genuine delusion," and for whom revolution "has the concentrated tempo of a dream," expresses this concreteness in the statement: "Imagination, the ideal of delusion . . . is life itself; how could we live if we couldn't dream?" Just as, in his linguistic thinking, words, as elements of logic, are merely metaphors, thereby becoming symbols, the ethical will of the "language-critic of practice" creates the realities of dream and delusion for the province of action. Truth, to which we sacrifice ourselves, turns into delusion. But we are meant to sacrifice ourselves and simultaneously realize that this transformation is taking place. Thus he devoted his life to the truth, the delusion, the reality of revolution.

"Preestablished harmony" is the term used by philosophy to describe the condition achieved in its pure state only in the fairy tale: i.e., that all things are connected. Good is always victorious, and evil is always punished. The Sleeping Beauty, after the cursing fairy, finds one last fairy who blesses her, and the beggar-couple in Rabbi Nachman's tale finds seven beggar-friends who once did them good turns and now, one after another, embellish each of the seven wedding days as a "new face." For such is the law: new guests have to be present if all seven blessings are to be spoken. And this tale has the same goal as the law. In life itself, this condition does not exist, any more than the opposite condition, which takes us to the domain of tragedy: preestablished disharmony with everything out of joint. Our life proceeds *between* harmony and disharmony, *between* delusion and the world, *between* fairy tale and tragedy. Times that are meaningful, not necessarily in their production but in their manner, approach the balanced world of the fairy tale; times that are meaningless resemble the earth-heaven dichotomy of tragedy. Philosophers (Aristotle, Leibniz, Hegel) who are content with their own era, pour their system into the static form of preestablished harmony; the discontented opt for utopia, allegory, fairy tales, delusion.

This observation should make two things clear. First of all, the way people of delusion take their behavior so deeply for granted. They go about "with the self-assurance of sleepwalkers" in the most literal sense of the word, and their existence is as balanced, classically formal, and well-rounded as a work of art, until (and this is the second point) they have to activate their "nature" in order to realize their delusion. At this point, they step from the soil of fairy tale to the ground of tragedy. But here too, they maintain within themselves the Apollonian world of their inner assurance, and this is what gives their life that bright holiness and their death that quiet joy. They all *know* the unhappiness of the world, they are aware of it, but they do not *believe* in it. One desire, however, lives within them and incites them unceasingly to the sphere of trial and temptation: the yearning for a world that resembles themselves. Heavy is the burden of their enforced solitude. How heavy, indeed, was Landauer's burden is revealed in his interpretations of Goethe as a politician and Hölderlin as a "Maturing Man." Here, too, he speaks entirely about himself, the more vividly and authentically he tells about these great men.

And *this* is the happiness and the end, the office and the failure of all those people of the fairy tale on the soil of tragedy: they seek the reciprocal effect, the balance, the *unity* between dream and instinct, delusion and world. They do not seek a *compromise,* in which both elements are stripped of their own in order to be capable of alliance; nor do they seek a *synthesis,* in which they are extinguished, neutralized, and then fully fused. What they do seek is a unity of a higher sort, for which even Landauer could offer no better word than "reciprocal effect," and in which both elements are *preserved* as such, fashioning reality in an unending mutual contradiction. Landauer is so dominated by this basic notion of his theory and practice that he even sees Shakespeare fully in this light: the conflict and final compromise between "instinct and spirit," which he constantly discovers in him,[8] signifies, on a poetic level, nothing other than his own politically constructive efforts on the level of life. The last act of the *Merchant of Venice,* in which all antitheses are joined in a profoundly cheerful play, is not so different from the wishful fantasy that prompts Landauer to place his "Socialist Alliance" directly in the midst of the tragic reality of our day.

This passion for unity explains the peculiarity of Landauer's style, his crass juxtaposition of conflicting notions such as "desperately merry" in order to demonstrate their mutually determining, intimate connection. When Landauer says of Whitman that he "like Proudhon, whom he greatly resembles in spirit, combines conservative and revolutionary spirit, idealism and socialism," when he praises ancient Judaism for possessing "rebellion as its constitution" in the year of Jubilee, when he presents Tolstoy and Rousseau as a "unity of rationalism and fervent mysticism," when he cares to attribute true artistic freedom only to the "play of necessity," when he demands "a phlegm filled with action" as the most important feature of revolutionary construction—we sense more and more strongly and keenly, behind all these biographical portrayals and political principles, the great Janus-like unity of his existence. He was a "gentle hero," as Shakespeare says of Brutus—Brutus, in whom Landauer saw more than a model, in whom he saw a replica of his own self, a true brother. But Gustav Landauer was too great and too generous to love only his own kind—he saw the noble and instinctive Cassius, the knowing and great Caesar, even the disgraced and smolderingly eruptive Shylock as human beings and brothers. He was one of those rare individuals *who know mankind and love it all the same.* His love for humanity is not self-deception, his knowledge is not harshness. "Knowledge" and "love" grow together for him, as they once grew together in the spirit of the Hebrew language, which has one and the same word for both of these profound extremes of human apprehension. For Gustav Landauer was a Jew.

IV

They had beset the end, they were consumed in his breath.—Buber in the introduction to *The Great Maggid*

His book *Der werdende Mensch* brings together all the crucial essays of Gustav Landauer. It thus includes that national Jewish and simultaneously German profession, which was written for the Zionist collection *Vom Judentum (About Judaism)* and entitled "Are these Heretical Thoughts?" These *are* heretical thoughts, but their effect is fruitful and liberating. They afford the opportunity of examining, critically and thoroughly, Landauer's position on Judaism within the context of his overall views.

Landauer was aware of his blood very early in life, when he wrote *Skepsis und Mystik*. "Man's blood and his blood-community are his most intimate and most private possession." He was thus a national Jew from the moment of his first self-awareness, when he first tried and tested the foundations of his existence. Yet "nation," no more than any other concept, was never to become an exclusive principle for him. He felt no less attached to the German nation than to the Jewish nation, as much a member of the chosen nation of the "spiritual" as of the nation of "maturing humanity," as akin to the nation of the individual as to the nation of the proletariat. He definition of "nation" is very broad, as this example indicates: "Nation is the specific manner in which a community, belonging together on the basis of a common history, expresses the universally human and the individually unique."[9] The simplest criterion of this community is, in his view, language, which he examines with his linguistically acute sensibility for special ways of expression characterizing the individual nation. He thus sees the possibility of being a Frenchman, if he "can understand a French expression fully and thoroughly without having to translate," and yet he also considers himself as belonging to those who "in various nations belong, as individuals, to Walt Whitman's nation." By which he doesn't mean Americans per se, but specifically Walt Whitman's Americans.

A common language is merely the simplest and most obvious, but not the only, form in which the consistency of reaction can express itself. There is such a form present within different language-groups, and thus Landauer, in this very investigation, explicitly recognizes the Jewish nation, linguistically atomized, as a nation.

We are dealing here with an unusual expansion of the concept of "nation," which, by the laws of logic, would ultimately have to narrow down its substance. Not land, not language, not race but a common form of expression on the basis of common history (which can also be the history of the world proletariat) make up the foundations of a nation. However, such common experiences in the past and the present can link a cultured man with many groups, and for this reason, Landauer accepts the possibility of belonging to many "nations," especially the German and the Jewish nations. "My Germanness and Jewishness do not hinder; they really help one another." He refused to accept the notion of having to choose one or the other, and felt he could choose both—fully in terms of our discussion hitherto—not as an inferior compromise (of assimilation) and not as a cloudy synthesis (of some sort of cultural East-Westness), but as a clear reciprocal effect of two clear components. "I have never felt the need to simplify myself or, through any self-denial, to unify myself. I accept the complex whole that I am, and hope to be even more complex than I realize."

The Jewish component in this complex has, of course, its clearly defined task: it is the "function" of the Jewish people "to abide in exile and dispersion waiting for the Messiah and to be the Messiah of the nations." This theory of a mission borders very precisely on the renowned mission-theory of liberalism and must therefore be very precisely distinguished from it. Gustav Landauer wanted to work for the way of mankind's maturing, not through the abstract propagation of the "ethical postulates of Judaism," but by founding a Socialist alliance, by promoting just human communities in Germany and everywhere in the world—including Palestine. The ethos of his Messianic demand is extremely different from that of liberalism. But—and this must be added—*this extreme difference is merely one of degree.*

From this Jewish viewpoint, Landauer sets about criticizing, with loving care and therefore severity, the Renaissance movement of the Jewish people: Zionism. He showed enormous acumen in recognizing the weak point, which at the time (1913) was not as obvious as it is today: the danger of an idling nationalism, busily turning around itself, like a purring wheel, but lacking the conveyor belt, and therefore a possibility, for moving along something else, outside of itself, the machine, the nation. "Nation is a readiness of disposition that becomes dry and empty and rattling when it appears with no connection to objective reality, goals, and labors, and when it is something other than their origin and coloring."

We may say that the two thousand years of the Diaspora, which were filled with the genesis and continued influence of the Talmud, had a high culture. On the other hand, they had no movement. And we have to admit that Zionism often acts as if it wants to jettison the entire cultural ballast of the past and be nothing but movement, while at the same time representing the entire nation. Culture without movement is *dead,* movement without culture is *empty*—and Gustav Landauer felt that this latter danger was threatening Zionism and thereby the Jewish people. He, withal, wanted to move others, not himself; he wanted to effect and not wait; he wanted a pulsating present, the here and now, and could not content himself with the empty promise of future labor and remote fulfillment. Empty movement, however (that was how he saw Zionism), has no present, it merely has a far-off goal; it has no resistance in the objective world to rub against it, inhibit it, and make it fearsome. All it has is its own propaganda, its self-assertion as a movement. This is why it demands that its followers reject their present and desire nothing more than to be a "bridge for coming generations, a preparation, the seed and the dung." But "no one who feels a mission within himself . . . is able to live in suspension." "Being a nation means having a function"—and fulfilling this function in one's own short human life with one's own energy. Landauer's *now* was Socialism, Landauer's *here* was the German land and the German language—and thus Zion was no reality for him and Hebrew no expression of his Jewish soul.

This viewpoint contains perhaps the most intelligent and in any case the most human conception that ever opposed Zionism. With unfailing respect to Landauer's great mind and even greater life, let us try to refute his thoughts in terms of his own world.

In the province of the fairy tale, of delusion, of preestablished harmony, the choice of the right road occurs only once and then never again—just as in the world of tragedy. Life alone, proceeding *between* the two of them, is the area of *decision,* and of *degree.* Landauer knew this very well and once even explicitly said that in life the decisive things are the differences of degree. But it is beyond human strength to enter the land of tragedy from two sides at once and carry a fairy-tale security into this double jeopardy. Because he sought a developing mankind as a builder and constructed it as a seeker, he failed to realize that contemporary Judaism is not delusion but world, not reality but development. Concentrating on the developing man, he forgot the developing Jew, or failed to see him, and thereby directed a demand for perfection at things and people who were still in a process of development. He thus viewed a distortion of the true Zion-movement; he failed to value sufficiently its utterly physical reality as embodied in the incipient building of the land; he did not see clearly its sweet presentness, which blossomed as the separated sons of *one* nation found themselves and each other; he did not fully understand the very implication of his Socialist Alliance: to rebuild the world from a cell, small and modest, but starting today, and "not to force the end." His decision in favor of a long road and the determination to wait actively were so overwhelmingly present for him in his Socialist action and so absorbed by that action, that he demanded the impossible of Zionism.

Most of all, he was bothered by the *consciousness* of Jewish national feeling, the cramped way of trying to convince others of something that was self-evident. "Seek not, and ye shall find," was more or less what he might have called to the yearning Jew. "Seek not—and ye shall have all that ye seek." This very attitude reveals that he did not see the tragically torn

Judaism—despite Beilis and Shylock! Instead, he made a demand of it, a demand that doubtless obtains for the *ultimate* questions, for God, but not for the *penultimate* questions, which move us mortals if we are Zionists or Socialists.

> Socialism does not stand so high for me—as high as it does stand—that I would tie it to the absolute; or rather, a linguistic utterance for the world-feeling does not stand so high for me that I would make the desire for the living order of man, for Socialism, dependent on an agreement upon these possibilities of expression.

Landauer makes the preceding statement in his essay *"Gott und Sozialismus"* ("God and Socialism"),[10] and we can let his words bear witness against himself. *Zionism is the desire for the living order of Jewish people*—and thus, to the same extent as Socialism—*beyond* this metaphysical question. This does not mean (with regard to either)—nor does Landauer mean—that there is no connection between the last things. Quite to the contrary! The penultimate without the ultimate, the world without God, development without delusion, are not possible—but there are other criteria for action. Decision and choice, consciousness and will, overcoming and strength—not just wonder and nature, self-evident things and gracious play as in God's fairy-tale world. "If Socialism were to depend on an agreement by people as to why man lives, then Socialism would be in a very sorry state. In contrast with these bold questions and incomparably bolder answers, Socialism is a very modest affair." "What is great about socialism is that it leads us away from word constructions to the building of reality. It unites men in a clearly understood necessity as to what is to be done to live up to the moment, men who *are,* and who do not wish to be united in word and delusion."

Let us each time substitute Zionism for Socialism, and Landauer will give us the answer himself. Even the fear of being merely a transition has been removed by this reflection. Landauer himself says that every age was "one of decay and at the same time one of preparation and renewal." What we really cannot endure is the Hegelian thought that one age is *more* of a transition than another and therefore *nothing* but a step toward higher eras. In point of fact, however, every age is both a fertilizer and a blossoming *at once,* just as a man is both a son and a father. And thus we Zionists feel the whole presentness of our being Jews and human beings in this very consciousness: to be both sons of the fathers and fathers of the sons at once, finally after millennia, truly both in one. That was how Landauer felt as a link of developing mankind and as a harbinger and pioneer preparing for all the links that would be coming after him. In the eternally flowing stream of humanity, the individual seeks and finds, not his place of rest, but his place of action—and this precisely, the *mission,* gives him the yearned-for feeling of presentness and the active consciousness of the *now* and the *here.* We can thus apply Landauer's statement about Socialism to ourselves and believe with him: "Those who will live long after us will thank us if we live not for them, but for ourselves, for our souls. For in that way we are actually living for them."

If Gustav Landauer had seen Zionism as it ought to be seen: as an affair of the middle realm that we call life, that is, *populated* but not *dominated* by the figures of fairy tale and tragedy, then his theory of nation would have been clearer and sharper. How could he fail to perceive that a difference of degree exists between the sublime way of "being a Frenchman" through linguistic empathy and the cultural definition that prevailed in his Germanness—that this Germanness has to fit into the historical and biological power of essence that made him a Jew in everything he thought and did? He never *posed* the question about the primacy of what belongs to one's own nation and what to an alien nation, and thus his answer was wrong—namely, in favor of Germanism.

Nor did Landauer ever ask himself about the *primacy of the mission* now existing for the Jewish people. *His mission theory came too early.* Many Zionists hope that some day, in Eretz Israel, they will be able to replace the liberal idea of making the world happy, replace and realize it with national labor for mankind; and every one of our practical steps should receive its meaning and blessing from this ultimate good. But that is the very reason these practical steps have to be *taken* in the first place, just as Landauer, unwilling to wait for the future state, was seeking gradually to turn the "Socialist covenant" into the Kingdom of God. We have to repeat ad nauseam that the principles were the same precisely because Landauer's high image can be readily used by the lukewarm and the lazy, by bourgeois idealists and inactive dreamers, to conceal their own weaknesses. The cheap demand for "everything or nothing" is costly and dangerous for the man who goes all the way with "everything" and dies. The bourgeois, however, regards this demand as a *psychological* safety valve, just as philanthropy and social-security legislation are the *economic* safety valve of the capitalist. He therefore parrots the revolutionary in regard to these things, but he never takes the consequence of "nothing"! And that is why we have to see and regard this cruelest stroke of all, over and over again: Gustav Landauer was murdered in Munich on May 2, 1919, by white beasts.

V

The abyss speaks its ruthless words to the man who dies unvictorious.—Buber in Landauer's Epitaph, *The Holy Way*

"And they murdered him!"

These words, printed under Landauer's picture in the Socialist weekly *Freie Welt*, always express our fresh sorrow when we think of this death. Before we venture to interpret the end in terms of the whole life and work and actually trace it back to a noble error, we shall let the feeling of grief and indignation flare up once again in our hearts.

But then we permit ourselves to pay Gustav Landauer's death the profound respect of objectivity and inquire as to its meaning. He died in an alien nation and on the soil of alien spirit and body. He transferred Jewish fervor and a Jewish tempo of life and change to slower and clumsier people. And this dichotomy destroyed his work.

When Landauer shows us Hölderlin in his deep yearning for harmony with others and his fear of the dreadful loneliness of the misunderstood man, he is depicting presentiments of his own destiny. And thus we may say that Friedrich Hölderlin's madness and Gustav Landauer's death were of the same cloth—that both of them bore the stigmata of a burning passion that could no longer wait and persevere. But the true pain of Landauer's fate, which makes it even more painful than the mental darkening of the brightest of all the German Hellenics, is this: his fate was an error and not a fulfillment, it was not tragic as much as pathetic. We certainly do not mean that he would have found total fulfillment within the Jewish people, but we do believe that he would have attained profound understanding and expansive possibility.

There is something else that makes this death so terrible. Gustav Landauer died precisely because he failed to see Zionism in its living gravity, because he demanded that it be a fairy-tale world and a delusion. For once, he made things too easy for himself—and this error caused his death. The bourgeois, who compromises with or evades "reality" prolongs his life and facilitates his function; the hero, however, the bearer of the divine in this world, falls through such failures. Here his pathetic end is raised into the sphere of tragedy, where at first it did not belong.

Martin Buber, in *The Great Maggid*,[11] tells the following wondrous tale about Rabbi Menachem Mendel of Vitebsk, who was the last to transplant Hasidism to the soil of the Holy Land:

> When Rabbi Menachem was dwelling in the land of Israel, it came to pass that a foolish man climbed up the Mount of Olives unnoticed and blew a shofar from the peak. A tiding raced through the frightened people that this was the sound of the shofar announcing the Redemption. When the rumor reached the ears of Rabbi Menachem, he opened the window, looked out into the world and said: "There is no renewal here."

And that was how Gustav Landauer felt he had to speak to Zionism. But he had the same experience in his own cause before his end.

Gustav Landauer was mistaken. He *had* to be mistaken. But a line from Goethe's *Die Aufgeregten (The Excited)*, which Landauer himself invokes, applies equally well to him: "One can go wrong on the right path and one can go right on the wrong path."

VI

One would always like to bring together the things one loves equally.—Landauer,
Skepsis und Mystik

Martin Buber once summed up the basic feature of his religious demand as
follows: One has to "form the Absolute from the material of the earth, and
carve God's face from the block of the world." These words also describe
Gustav Landauer's faith.

Thus we see these two men, bound throughout their lives by an ardent
friendship, united in the deepest part of their being. Buber, whose systematic
exposition in *Daniel*[12] and whose talks on Judaism were complemented not
randomly but in a highly meaningful way by his historical and anthological
words in the field of Hasidism, also lives as a philosopher in the world of the
Hasidim. And this world makes us comprehend essential traits in Gustav
Landauer's ideology. For he too, though unwittingly, was a Hasid.

The methodical foundation of his philosophy is language criticism, that of
Hasidic thought is the practice of taking the word seriously, of deep responsibility toward the word. It is easy to see that language criticism and letterist
mysticism are opposites only at first glance. In point of fact, they are different
forms of the same instinct: the urge to build the world-ego out of the word-
ego. The freedom towards the word, which language criticism first conveys to
us, is not only and not even primarily freedom *from* the word, but at the same
time and even more so freedom *toward* and *in* the word, freedom of interpretation and freedom of the mysticism that grows out of skepticism. Whether (in
Buber's *Great Maggid*) the Rebbe of Rymanov equates the abuse of the word
with murder, or Landauer seeks to demonstrate the puppetlike frivolity of their
humanity in the affected style of modern writers—both these notions are one
and the same. And likewise in a positive way: a Hasidic tradition justifies its
pantheism (the Spinozistic *deus sive natura*) by calculating the numerical
value of the Hebrew letters in the words ha-ṭeva' (Nature) and 'elohim (God)
to be the same, while Landauer derives the whole of the Middle Ages from the
root *fro*, which at first meant *Lord,* then the Lord's mood *Freude* (joy), but quite
the opposite for his serfs: *Fronarbeit (corvée),* and ultimately, in its final usage
frouwe (lady, mistress), adding the courtly-love service to the signs for church,
feudalism, joy, and labor. We would speculate that this practice of taking
language so seriously is an ancient Jewish impulse (although unrecognized) in
Mauthner's works too, an impulse occurring in Amos's threats and Jeremiah's
visions and then fairly dominating the Kabbalah and Hasidism.

The foregoing example of Landauer's method is from an essay entitled
"Arbeitselig" *("Work Loving")* in *Der werdende Mensch*. The theme of this
study is the fulfillment of the double meaning hidden in the title. *Joy (Freude),*
the blissful pleasure of work and effort, is what Landauer has always tried to
arouse in all his labors in order to bridge the fateful split between vocation and

freedom and to put the whole man organically into each of his activities. We clearly perceive here the similarity to the Hasidic conception of joy as the loftiest duty and the sole possibility of true intimacy with God. With the same enmity and misunderstanding with which Landauer and his *law-abiding* opponents, the Marxists, fought one another, Hasidim and the rabbinically minded *Mitnagdim* feuded with one another. We find the very same human contrast in two different worlds.

In terms of this position, we can understand Landauer's rejection of asceticism and his distrust of any "return to nature." For all his devotion to Rousseau, he did not, like "the great Swiss," see technology and civilization per se as signs and principles of evil—only when they were raised to a self-purpose beyond their mediating function. Thus, in the essay *Die Botschaft der Titanic (The Message of the Titanic)* he actually sings the praises of the newest achievement of the wireless telegraph, which, with its power to connect countries and nations, strikes him as "one of the many signs that mankind is developing." In his essay on Rousseau, he says similar things about the possibility of using the invention of the railroad for the benefit of civilization. This attitude reminds us of the Hasidic tendency not to see the evil urge of man and his earthliness as fit for destruction, but, on the contrary, as worthy of being lifted to the height of the divine.

According to such notions, Abraham is higher than the three angels because, as a human being, he has a possibility lacking for the messengers of God: to transform the animal function of eating into holiness—not through renunciation but through fulfillment. The salvation of man lies within himself and he can achieve it anywhere, at any time—independently of technology, environment, and externality. Everything is useful to the man who uses it and refuses to make himself the slave of the base principle of the world. As a master, he will have a faithful servant even in the evil instinct.

Even the Hasidic idea of transmigration recurs in the very same form in a dialogue entitled *"Bairam and Schlichting,"* (1911) and reprinted in the book *Rechenschaft*. Strongly influenced by Mauthner, it is a "Dialogue of the Dead" in which the advocates of the heavenly Aeropagus, in this case Proudhon and Mazzini, debate the admission of two candidates to the Elysian Fields. Bairam is an Armenian rebel, who was executed because, out of national hatred, he shot and killed Schlichting, a German lieutenant serving the Turks. Proudhon cogently defends Bairam, and Mazzini Schlichting, until the highest judgment finds both men right and wrong. They have to return to earth in a different shape, to keep on with the struggle that they have begun, until they have fought it out. This conception, which Landauer does not merely play with, coincides fully with the Hasidic attitude so clearly articulated in several tales of the *Baal Shem* and *The Great Maggid*. To be sure, the notion that a transmigration must be continued until the stage of final purification is inherent in other religious views as well. But here we also find a specifically Jewish notion, which we already touched upon in discussing the distinction between "ultimate" and "penultimate" things. Only the Creator himself, on the Day of Atonement, can personally forgive sins committed in the "ultimate" area, the area between God and man—the blasphemies of life occurring in the "penultimate" sphere, between man and man, can be forgiven by man alone. And only then, after men have spoken theirs, does the Holy One, may He be praised, speak His redemptive word. Only this interpretation reveals the meaning of Landauer's social mysticism fully, a mysticism for which—as Buber put it—God lets Himself be realized not *in* man, but *between* men.

At this point we wish to remind our readers once again that we are not trying to define Gustav Landauer's unique mind in terms of "models" or "influences," nor are we looking for "predecessors." It would therefore be no contradiction if many of the thoughts we have touched upon were to be found in another mysticism, German and Indian for example, from which they might have affected Landauer. The peculiar connection of every element in his mind, corresponds precisely to the complex of Hasidism, which also has points of contact with many different systems, though not deriving from them. We cannot claim that there is any dependency between Landauer's faith and Jewish mysticism, and it is equally certain that the same mysterious stream of common blood drenched these two manifestations of the divine in the world and brought them to light. We wish to make Gustav Landauer's religious genius a living thing, just as he was unique and whole; and in this aspiration, we find him close to the two central didactic concepts of Jewish mysticism— in the attitude of *Ṣimṣum* and of *Hashpa 'ah,* for which we can credit Buber for his profound clarification in the introduction to *The Great Maggid.*

Ṣimṣum means concentration, gathering, contraction. This concept is close to what German idealistic philosophy (especially Schelling) meant by the negative stance of God, His self-refusal, His self-demarcation against the other, His self-restriction against the world. This is the act of Creation: God releases the world. The world derives from the godly sphere, but no longer lives in it—the world, with the consistency (which Landauer despised) of causal natural law, runs its earthly course, "breaks the vessels" which testify to its divine origin, and thereby experiences the Fall. The divine, even now, is still in the world but the *Shekhina* no longer has any dwelling place—not with the isolated Creator, nor with scattered creatures. And here begins the free deed (which Landauer loved so much) of the individual human being: through *Yikhud,* the act of uniting, which is neither compromise nor synthesis, but a vivifying effect of living men that, at first, streams from the heart of *one* man, the *united* man, the *Ṣaddik.* The just man, who thereby redeems himself, helps towards God's redemption, the unification of the *Shekhina* with the Creator.

Hashpa 'ah, on the other hand, means emanation, radiance, and designates the attitude of a compliant God, who eternally creates and recreates the world anew, showering it with the torrents of his glory. The "divine wave" breaks in the "ultimateness of sensual things," that is to say, again in our own egos—and we find our ways to them and thereby to God himself, when we break through the earthly shells covering the nuclei of ourselves and the world. Thus, Ṣimṣum and Hashpa ʿah are not opposites (as our dear Master Nobel[13] taught), they are the inhalation and exhalation of the divine soul, the systole and diastole of the divine heart: two phases of the same activity.

The God of Ṣimṣum who has created once and the God of Hashpa ʿah who recreates eternally, the transcendent and the immanent God, are united in our souls. Thus we can experience the contraction and emanation as processes of our inner being and selectively maintain them as a stance of our earthly reality. This step takes us right into Landauer's world, and Landauer is characterized by his experiencing the happiness and sorrow of Creation *only* in the ego, but *always* in the ego. For him, "force" and "nature" are the two opposites; "force" is his Ṣimṣum, "nature" his Hashpa ʿah—"reciprocal effect" his Yikhud. In his marvelous lecture on Friedrich Hölderlin, Landauer spoke about the fact that Nietzsche's strength gained the soaring of flight from self-overcoming, whereas Hölderlin's nature is borne along almost by itself, by its own lightness. Landauer loves Hashpa ʿah more than Ṣimṣum; the descent of genius rays upon the astonished world is, for him, a "love life of the self-evident," the contraction, the regathering of the rays, such as the Baal Shem set about prior to a difficult undertaking, has too much of the conscious, of the cramped, the arrogant, so far as Landauer is concerned. But the final unification is prepared here: Hölderlin's *"Der Rhein"* (*"The Rhine"*) comes from the inhibition of fruitful work; and a founder of towns and citizen (albeit no philistine) develops from a man in ferment, a sower of wild oats—and this shows the overarching unity of life, a unity that, from the Ṣimṣum of tragedy and the Hashpa ʿah of fairy tale, shapes the intermediary realm of man.

This dichotomy between "force" and "nature" remains open so long as man lives in a dichotomy. It is bound, in God, to inhaling and exhaling, and likewise, in the central human being, "whose achieved unity" (as Buber so finely put it)[14] "has the purity and the simple strength of elementary unity."

VII

Gustav Landauer is dead. Without the dreadful event of his death, Jewish youth would not be able to look up to him, the eternally developing man, look up to him with such composed hearts, as is possible today. We will refrain from self-chiding and, instead, respectfully, honor the power of the Unseeable, which closes small cracks when it tears open the last and deepest crack.

But a fog is already threatening to falsify his clear image. Gustav Landauer is already being seen as the prototype of the "pure sufferer" by well-wishers—and as the prototype of the "impractical dreamer" by those who fear him.

He was no pure fool, no Dostoevskian idiot, no "idealist." He was a man of peaceful struggle, of a goal-oriented and conscious life, of deeply thoughtful and meaningful deed. Not a saint, but a just man.

It is so necessary to know this because people always like to distance their few great men in a saintly glow in order to avoid having to imitate them, in order to categorize them in a completely different kind of humanity that no one can attain. The saints are the shoddy pretexts of the conscience. The just man is its spur.

The goal of the just man is to erect the holy in the midst of life.

That was Gustav Landauer's doctrine and deed.

That is Judaism's hallowed law.

Let that be the way of our youth!

PART THREE

JEWISH HISTORY AND LITERATURE

11. THE JEWISH CONCEPTION OF REDEMPTION

FRIEDRICH THIEBERGER

EDITOR'S INTRODUCTION

FRIEDRICH THIEBERGER (1888–1958), distinguished scholar of the Czech-Jewish community, was the author of many works, among them *Jüdisches Fest, Jüdischer Brauch: ein Sammelwerk* (1936), *Die Glaubensstufen des Judentums* (1952), *King Solomon* (1946), *The Great Rabbi Loew of Prague* (1954). This essay appeared in *Der Jude, Sonderheft: Judentum und Christentum* (Berlin, 1926), pp. 51–57.

What value to contrast Judaism and Christianity? There is no religious viewpoint that is not bound by the constraints of its presupposition. I cannot imagine, therefore, the comparison of religion, even within the moral neutrality of the discipline of history of religion, which in the characterization of Judaism and Christianity does not find itself speaking of influence, precedence, dependence, leaving one or the other enfeebled by the contrast. This difficulty inheres in Friedrich Thieberger's cameo characterization of the Jewish conception of redemption (*erlösung*). Although he recognizes in his diffident preface that religions cannot be hybrid, that no crossbreeding would allow for the emergence of a more resilient strain of religious sensibility, that Judaism and Christianity—whatever their historical interconnection—cannot be winnowed and refined, each supplying the other with emphases and accentuations until at the end a new religion, bearing the purified vision of both, will emerge. Judaism and Christianity are living communities of faith, not abstractions. Only the religious dabbler, like the gourmet, can enjoy the sweets and sauces of multiplicity. The believer—Jewish and Christian—is existentially engaged and risks everything in the commitment; withholding nothing, the believer lives through the life of the faith-community, joining self to the finitude and imperfection of everything human, anything finite, all things unredeemed.

Thieberger's essay opens with an historical prolegomenon tracing the transformation of the Jewish doctrine of redemption from Messianic politics in which the nation is to be uplifted and restored to the Messiah of mediation, where Jewish suffering and the suffering of humanity are relieved by divine intervention. It is to Hasidism that Thieberger ascribes the overcoming of the political Messiah. Hasidism "grasped hold of the great axis of religious life that Paul saw as the only axis of Christianity: the distress of the individual soul and its need for redemption." Hasidism, however authentic in its Jewish origins, in Thieberger's felicitous phrase "distributed the spiritual Messiah" among all humankind, making of every human being a redeemer of community, animals, nature itself, and "in a sublime, mystical dialectics, the redeemer of God." The mediation of the Ṣaddik is become functionally equivalent to the God-man of Christianity; however, where the latter compromises, in the Jewish view, the mystical unity of divine action and passivity, the Ṣaddik is not one and unique but is replicable in every perfect will.

It is here, in the doctrine of the will, that Thieberger locates the essential difference between Christianity and Judaism. The radicality of Paul, his recasting of the life and death of Jesus into "a total symbol of tragic human existence" arises from Paul's perception of the innate errancy of the human substance, its Adamic taint, and its unlimited vulnerability.

To succumb to the overwhelming evidence of human tragedy required that Paul have a coherent vision of the order of human days, a coherence deriving not from the mythic and aesthetic harmonics of the classic world but from the Hebrew Bible, which developed the doctrine of the uniformity of nature and its divine governance before whose order the despair of man and the transiency of life emerge clearly. Jonah, Job, the Psalms are cited as pivotal indices of the tragic world-view, but Thieberger contends that neither they nor the early rabbinic tradition contemporaneous to Paul could derive a religious ethos capable of facing up to human tragedy. Paul made of the

> life of Jesus both an example of human life and a symbol of the God/Messiah. The weight of this triple congruence—Everyman/Jesus/God—seeks its fulcrum. Each human being at some point stands on Golgotha, in bleak isolation, with the guilt feeling of the sinless man who feels responsible for the suffering in the world and who, with outspread bloody hands, holds the burden of being human against the infinite; yet who can take the infinite guilt upon himself and atone for it? Only the infinite one. Adam on Golgotha is the God suffering from love.

Thieberger asserts generously the Pauline dialectics from which all the odious polarities have derived—law and love, sin and grace, justice and mercy. Shifting the familiarity of reply, Thieberger formulates an interesting variant. Paul's question (wholly Jewish) leads to a reply (wholly un-Jewish): "Paul humanized God." "It is not," Thieberger suggests, "the contrast between Law and Christ, but the contrast between an infinite and a finite God that separates Paul from Judaism." Correctly, Thieberger notes that any antinomy between Law and Christ is a falsification, since the Jewish notion of redemption—redemption for all creation—does not depend upon the Law. The Law is the internal life of the Jew, not the credentials that the nations need present for salvation. Enough that the nations be fully human; no need that they observe the Law. "The Law mirrors the Jewish idea of salvation, but is not identical with it." It is here perhaps that Thieberger retreats from the imaginative construction of his argument, for he offers as the reason for the Jewish refusal to shift "the idea of universal salvation to the visible center of the religious legacy" the aggressive and predominating rise of Christianity and the Christian hegemony. It is a vital historical question that Thieberger has familiarly dodged: why, indeed, from a prosyletizing religion did Judaism become timorous? Rosenzweig offers one explanation in his interpretation of the double covenant that enables Judaism and Christianity to be regarded as congruent, while absolutely independent, ways to God. Thieberger, however, faced with an historical disengagement—theologically supine and pusillanimous—moves from theology to an inquiry into the psychology of guilt.

Salvation is always a release from suffering. It requires, however, a subtlety of self-awareness, a gravity in the engagement of life, to recognize that much of that suffering arises from the simple fact of finitude; we are the flesh of finitude. It is this that Thieberger calls "the suffering of existence." To derive from the isolation of psyche in flesh the absolute character of human aloneness is to miss its counterpart: human entanglement in the life of others, past life and the future, historical connection and interaction, which makes of all human life a web of relations in which each person affects all others. This sense of the enormity of the human universe carries with it, however, the awareness of imperfection. Not guilt before the sin imagined or enacted, but abashedness in the face of finitude affects every human being. Having, however, described a doctrine of congruence in which the suffering servant lifts up and redeems all suffering, finitude no less than sin, imperfection no differently than guilt, Christian salvation can draw no distinction. Metaphysical finitude and human corruption—equal sources of suffering and embarrassment before God—are both relieved by the same salvation. Christianity embraces all suffering without distinction. Buddhism denies all suffering; its sacred egoism identifies neither guilt nor imperfection.

In contrast to these views, addressing the same human complexity, the Jewish response entails a reduction of suffering by the reconstruction of the human community. This is the moral coefficient of theology, the reply Buber's contemporaneous utopianism extracted from the witness of the Hasidic community. Thieberger's answer goes beyond this in an interesting, relevant, and fruitful direction. The suffering of coexistence has one counter: the uniform meaning of the world and of God. The consciousness of suffering, unassuaged by human means, can be relieved only by the rooting of the self to God, the focus that commences in *teshubah* and holds fast in *kavvanah*. "The conception of *kavvanah* focuses a conciliatory light on the suffering that derives from the guilt of coexistence." When the suffering is diminished by adhesion to God, the Messiah is at hand. "This end of days requires us in every moment. We are the mediators of the Messiah."

Thieberger's argument is close to the whole truth, but before he spans the connection that links the transmutation of suffering to that perfecting of self-adhesion, he rushes into the arms of Messiah. Paul is blunted, but not put aside. The argument is harder still.   [A.A.C.]

THE JEWISH CONCEPTION OF REDEMPTION

Every comparison of the religious presupposes that one learn how to disregard the intimate reality with which religion invests the smallest details of the day and lift out and examine only the meaning of human behavior. Religious realities cannot be crossbred and brought to new purity. This is especially true if religious forms of life and their emotional expression, i.e., their affective value and creative impetus, maintain their historical lines of development and the immediacy of chronological continuity. It will never be possible to integrate Corpus Christi into the experience of Jewish religiousness or to reshape the Seder into a living source of Christian religion. Only after a dissolution of both Judaism and Christianity could a new and *single* religious reality arise from uniform religious *ideas* that possessed life-shaping energy.

Notwithstanding that only the creation of religions, never their fusion, is possible, reflection on the abstract meaning of individual religions can mark significant advances in its own right. Even though we may not be able to hold fast intellectually, or even definitively formulate, life-processes such as Judaism and Christianity in a given period of time, it is not to be doubted that there are thoughts and motives that are buried and nurtured in the dark, fertile soil of real existence.

Currently, a peculiar situation has emerged in the Jewish discussion of the meaning of Christianity and in the Christian discussion of the meaning of Judaism: both sides present Christianity as incontestable, as the highest religious value, measuring Judaism by it, and at best interpreting Judaism as being up to the same level. Imagine, however, someone daring to do the reverse and allowing Christianity to nearly measure up to the human idea of Judaism! It has become fashionable even in Jewish circles to regard Jesus as fulfilling prophetic expectations! The spiritual life-reality of Europe, created by Christians, but with Jews in its very midst, has made the absolute value of the Christian idea axiomatic. It is more important for Judaism than for Christianity to permit an unaxiomatic attitude to clear the way for discussion.

Judaism, to be sure, is hardly ready for such a discussion. Martin Buber has supplied the first Jewish answer to human questions discussed by Christianity since St. Paul. Attempts prior to Buber never got beyond the theological.

Subsequently Max Brod and Felix Weltsch brought Christianity and Judaism into sharp confrontation, thereby gaining new insight into Jewish existence. Even the following ideas (an essential one of which was quoted from conversations with Max Brod on the basic viewpoint of his [1921] book *Paganism–Christianity–Judaism* [*Heidentum–Christentum–Judentum*])[1] are simply meant as a contribution to understanding Judaism internally.

It is remarkable that the proximity of Christian ideas to Judaism becomes perceptible during crucial eras in Jewish history. A hundred years after Jesus, while Christian cell-parishes were strengthening everywhere, Rabbi Akiba was obeisant to the Bar Kokhba Messiah. In this he was not, however, playing any political game with the notion and name of the Redeemer. Clearly the great men of earlier times would never have expected the King Messiah to come in their day. They hoped for that marvelous irruption of the infinite into the finite as a remote glow on the horizon. It was most likely in Akiba's century that the prophetic idea of a Redeemer once again became a cardinal goal of Jewish yearning. Its substance could hardly have been restricted to the political liberation of the nation! On the contrary, it included the same religious sensitivity to universal sorrow, an emotion similarly at the basis of Christianity. But after the Palestine era, the influence of the Kabbalah shifted the concept of the Messiah to the divine sphere. The whirlwinds of mystical excitement surrounding [Yiṣḥak] Luria, Sabbatai Ṣevi, and Jacob Frank in the sixteenth, seventeenth, and eighteenth centuries kept putting forth the image of the Son of God as a redeemer through suffering. And it was certainly no simple hypocrisy that the Frankists felt themselves to be cheek-by-jowl with Christianity.

It was Hasidism that first overcame the political Messiah. Ardently, it grasped hold of the great axis of religious life, which Paul saw as the only axis of Christianity: the distress of the individual soul and its need for redemption. However, Hasidism, at an unbridgeable distance from Christianity, distributed the spiritual Messiah virtually among all men, thereby making mankind itself the redeemer of the world (and of animals and nature) and even, in a sublime, mystical dialectics, the redeemer of God. Where Pauline Christianity has the idea of the helping mediator arise from the corruption of the petitioner, Hasidism conducts the *inadequacy of the will* to the idea of the mediating Ṣaddik.

When the rationalist dam of the Enlightenment was burst by the romantic wave, many Jews felt as if the irrationalism of Christianity were carrying them more unrestrainedly than rationalist Judaism—as they understood it—to the mystery of the world. Suffering for universal guilt, the loving sacrifice for universal redemption, was the basic motif of life. Its symbol was Jesus. Never before had so many Jews, in confict with Judaism, been so close to Christianity. As for itself, Judaism tried to compete with Christianity only on an esthetic level.

After the ebbing of the romantic sense of life, a relaxed rationalism swept through Europe's politics and art. Religious concern focused upon the ethical principles of the religions, that is, their historical sedimentation. The actual religious stream appeared to have dried up once and for all. But then new sources were tapped. Dostoevski and Strindberg wrenched man back to the dramatic notion of his being at the center, to the Pauline guilt feeling of existence, to the view that man's actions are inextricably bound up with all that exists. No matter how pure we might keep ourselves, we would still be guiltlessly guilty, we accursed lovers of the good. And art is more disturbing than the theoretical disillusionment of materialism. The heritage of the old religions is passionately rediscovered and once again we witness a trend in Jewish youth toward a religiosity that could be interpreted as Christian.

It does matter from whom we learn to view life! Paul had recast the story of Jesus into a total symbol of tragic human existence, and therefore something of Paul's fire is felt by everyone who, affected by Pauline symbols, begins to gaze at the searing universal tragedy. To suffer from the uncontrollability of instinctual drives around which the knowledge of the good hovers unavailing, the torment of guilt for the suffering that all human action and inaction sooner or later afflicts upon others, the yearning in such suffering, the helplessness in such guilt—that is the true human condition! No one has been more deeply shaken by the latent tragedy of this condition than Paul, and no one has felt the question erupting more torturously within him: how can one exist in such a situation? The question does not belong to any one religion. But, never uttered in antiquity, it became graspable out of the Jewish view of the world. The uniform meaning of the world had first to be discovered before man could despair of it in the helplessness of life. Jonah, Job, the 73rd Psalm are documents of this human struggle of despair with the meaning of the world. They hinted at a solution and slightly covered its tragic presupposition. It is of immense significance that Judaism in the time of Paul did not seem to be able to give him any answer to his renewed universal question.

This may have been because for Paul the life of Jesus was both an example of human life and a symbol of the God/Messiah. The weight of this triple congruence—Everyman/Jesus/God—seeks its fulcrum. Each human being at some point stands on Golgotha, in bleak isolation, with the guilt feeling of the sinless man who feels responsible for suffering in the world and who, with outspread bloody hands, holds the burden of being human against the infinite; yet who can take the infinite guilt upon himself and atone for it? Only the infinite one. Adam on Golgotha is the God suffering from love. All noble Christian attempts at proselytism mean to arouse in the nonbeliever the Pauline notion of the tragic primal condition of man and to convince the nonbeliever by means of the congruence of example and symbol. The dogmatic polarities of original sin and grace are tied to the tragic experience and the yearning for redemption.

It cannot be emphasized sharply enough that Paul's question belongs fully to Judaism, but that his answer, his idea of redemption, leads not away from, but beyond, Judaism: *Paul humanized God.* It is not the contrast between the Law and Christ, but the contrast between an infinite and a finite God that separates Paul from Judaism. The redeemed God himself fights the Lord of Evil for the dominion of the world. Incidentally, the Jewish idea of universal human redemption was never the Law. The Law in its fullness does not address expressly the nations of the world, although Judaism does have humanity in mind. The Law is an internal matter of the Jewish community. It unfolds with the life of the community, develops with it, as evidenced for instance by the cessation of sacrifice. The Law mirrors the Jewish idea of salvation, but is not identical with it.

It is understandable that Judaism, timid before the relentless predominance of those professing Pauline redemption, and without the intention of self-defense or competition, did not shift its idea of universal salvation to the visible center of the religious legacy. Instead, it mixed a political salvation (for the wounds on its physical corpus were still smarting too harshly) with religious salvation. That is why we cannot cite a new historical proclamation; the secret testimony of the Jewish heritage can be sought and detected only in the basic human need for redemption.

Salvation is always simply salvation from suffering. So far as we know human suffering, however, it springs from two quite distinct sources, which, to be sure, often flow together on the surface of our consciousness. The fact that I, a self-experiencing nexus of feeling and motion, am incorporated in a body, totally dependent on its rhythm and delimitation; the fact that I not only painfully bear the shortcomings of this body but am inalienably conscious of being tied to the finite, the enigmatically definite, in all my thoughts and wishes (no matter how self-satisfied they may emerge in me): that is a suffering that even the most abandoned Robinson Crusoe would have to feel, for that suffering is enclosed in the very fact of existence, and for that very reason I would like to call it the *suffering of existence.*

But no one is *only* lonesome. We are all entangled in the great web of present and past existences. The fact that other beings partially determine my life, while I myself can be an unknown, determining being for them, the fact that the most precious people are as suffering and as transitory as I—these recognitions fill me with a suffering that arises from the fate of being a human being among others, that is, the suffering of *coexistence.*

The most significant form of the suffering of coexistence is the feeling of guilt. I have a portion of guilt, of debt, in universal suffering because I am, willy-nilly, one determining part of universal mankind. However, insofar as it is a matter of the suffering of my existence and compassion upon the mere existence of a human being, I cannot speak of guilt feeling, but merely of a suffering-filled feeling of *imperfection.* The Pauline idea of congruence, which I characterized earlier, forced Christianity to regard imperfection as guilt. God redeems because through His suffering he took all guilt upon

Himself; there is no salvation that is not salvation from guilt. If, however, someone suffers from not having any talent as a painter, is this imperfection his own or someone else's fault or guilt? Christianity must answer: it is, perhaps only ultimately, Adam's fault. For after all, every existence is merely a suffering consequence of coexistence, and Christianity does not know any suffering coexistence that is not itself a guilt feeling or permeated by a guilt feeling.

The very opposite is true of Buddha's road to salvation. He negates his participation in the existence with others. In a truly sacred egoism, he breaks all bonds of love and hatred tying him to other people. Levitating in the suffering of existence is the arcanum of Buddha and the revelation of his smile.

It is only in such a contrast that the Jewish idea of salvation can be defined. It has not blurred the two forms of suffering in existence and coexistence; it has not exchanged guilt and imperfection. The notion of guilt has been grasped in a dreadful way. The didactic example of Job, after all, means that the suffering of the individual does not have to be the correlative of personal fault or guilt, but that involvement in life can cause suffering even to the most righteous man because of the guilt of others. Guilt is always connected with the consciousness of action (albeit not necessarily with the knowledge of its consequence). It is for this reason that the "return" (teshubah) of a guiltless life is possible for everyone, because the trial of humanity takes place within consciousness, and consciousness can be falsely directed, but not because man is evil. Hence there is such a thing as responsibility to one's coexisters, not out of practical considerations but out of a basic religious attitude, and the fear of guilt grows with the deepening of such consciousness.

The redemptive path from the suffering of coexistence, to the extent that it is a suffering due to guilt and complicity, can only mean in the Jewish tradition the *reduction of suffering through our manner of living.* We have to take effect here, in this world, not merely as coexisters of a moment, but as guilt-heirs to a past and as codeterminers of a future. It is given to our consciousness as our small portion of freedom to form a community in which the guilt of the suffering of coexistence is constantly diminishing. The Jewish nation should be the first cell for the model formation of such a holy community. Hence the meticulous structure of its Law, which does not—as has often been claimed—quietly and definitively dissolve the contractual relationship between man and God, but merely sharpens the consciousness every moment, to remain responsible for a life with less suffering. It is characteristic that the Day of Atonement does not remove guilt or debt between men, but merely the "guilt" of man as an existence before God. The atonement of this day belongs to a category different from human coexistence.

However, where the suffering of coexistence arises not from guilt but from imperfection, and inheres thereby in all existential suffering, there remains only *one* hope: hope in the uniform meaning of the world, in God. Here there is no self-redemption by man, but merely the stilling of the sense of suffering by means of consciousness. One word can be used to express what Judaism means by its idea of redemption, but it remains inexhaustible in the forms in which it takes place and, like any real life-process, although it cannot be forced, it must still be wanted: *Kavvanah* means to be turned to the uniform meaning of the world. When the high priest on the Day of Atonement undertook the rites of purification in the Holy of Holies, the action, the most sacred known to ancient Judaism, was futile as soon as his *thoughts* stopped focusing exclusively and with tense awareness on the service of God. Not a single one of the seemingly *only* juridical laws of Jewish religious life is valid ("counted," as the old teachers said) if it is not sustained by that focusing on God, that devotion, for which measure and rule are insufficient. Religious movements in Judaism have always been revolutions of *Kavvanah*.

Spinoza aimed at such rational cognition of the world in order to deify it; his doctrine is filled with the Jewish thought of redemption. Spinoza does not distrust this meaning, like the Indian pantheist. Evil is just an unclear direction of thought; the true direction, the one that redeems suffering, is the love of God.

The conception of *Kavvanah* focuses a conciliatory light on the suffering that derives from the guilt of coexistence. *Every guilt has some root in imperfection.* There is an old saying: "No one acts in guilt unless an irrational spirit has struck him." We can lessen the suffering of coexistence but we cannot put an end to it. However, once it is reduced to the last irreducible remnants, we will have the era of the Messiah, who will remove from us all suffering of existence and of imperfect coexistence. This end-of-days requires us in every moment. We are the mediators of the Messiah.

12. DOSTOEVSKI AND THE JEWS

A. S. STEINBERG

EDITOR'S INTRODUCTION

A. S. STEINBERG (1891–   ) is the translator into German of Dubnow's *Geschichte des Chassidismus* (1931) and author of a volume in Dubnow's honor, *Simon Dubnow, l'homme et son oeuvre*, (1963). Steinberg's essay on Dostoevski appeared in *Der Jude, Sonderheft: Judentum und Christentum* (Berlin, 1926), pp. 66–81.

Among the writers of world literature, Dostoevski has a continuous, virtually unbroken appeal to Jewish readers. His fictions seem almost nonfictions, a quality that affords them a curiously paradoxical allure for serious Jewish readers, who often regard the novel as a frivolous medium, suitable for distraction and relief, but not as replacement for philosophy or Talmud Torah. It is not merely a dubiety about the domain of the imagination, but a more serious concern that fiction mocks ideas, avoiding them in favor of an indirect exposition that depends upon detailing character, atmosphere, environment. Very few novelists are allowed that special elevation Jewish readers accord infrequently, sparingly: Dostoevski, Tolstoy, Kafka, Mann, but most assuredly Dostoevski.

The reasons for this special favor are persuasively and subtly documented in A. S. Steinberg's essay. Anti-Semite, most assuredly, vulgar anti-Semite, even, Dostoevski was nonetheless obsessed with Jewish questions, with *the* Jewish question, even addressing a single essay in March 1873 to the consideration of "The Jewish Question." Dostoevski's social observations of the Jew of his day, riddled as they are with odious characterization, ought to make his views repellent to serious Jewish readers. It is hard, is it not, to find oneself vulgarized in literature, to make one's way tentatively through the great literature of the West only to find one's way temporarily barred by an image that bears one's name, that annihilates one's lineage with a stroke of contempt? And yet, as Steinberg is at pains to suggest, even where Dostoevski indicts his *Zhid*, caricaturing his energy, his physical miteness, his usury, there is at the base of his depiction an anxiety and alarm.

The Jew endures. The Jew of Scripture, the Jew out of whose life and times the Messiah of history has come and gone, endures. By rights, by the logic of events, by the sway of power and potency, the Jew should be dead and vanished, off the historical boards, yielding place to the new chosen people, the new Jerusalem, the new salvation out of the East. Dostoevski, Messianist, finds the perduration of the Jew, unlucky Messianist, unfortunate legatee of election, a continuing reminder that Christ Jesus has not returned, that Constantinople, gateway to Jerusalem, is still occuped by the unbeliever, that the Jew continues to say, as he says to Svidrigailov at the moment of his suicide, "This is not the place."   [A.A.C.]

DOSTOEVSKI AND THE JEWS

1

The overwhelming majority of Dostoevski's readers and admirers do not seem to have any difficulty dealing with the question of the great Russian novelist/philosopher's relationship to Judaism and to the destiny of the Jewish people. Is it not obvious at first sight that we find in Dostoevski an unqualified Jew-baiter, an "anti-Semite" of the vulgarest sort, such as we find in the literatures of all nations and countries? Are we not dealing with an individual case of the all-too-well-known dismal rule? This apparently quite plausible reply, which we so often hear from both Jewish and Gentile readers of Dostoevski, was virtually canonized, at least for the Russian public, when the well-known Russian-Jewish critic A. G. Gornfeld gave it literary expression in the Russian *Yevreyskaya Entsiklopediya*: "Dostoevski, Fëdor Mikhailovich, the famous Russian writer," goes Gornfeld's precise definition "is one of the most significant advocates of Russian anti-Semitism. . . . His tirades against Jews," he goes on a few lines further, "contain neither serious evidence nor any kind of original ideas; it is a thoroughly banal anti-Semitism."

If that were so, Gornfeld and the greater public would be right—the author of *The Brothers Karamazov* would really be nothing but a "banal" Judeophobe. We would still be faced however with an extremely difficult enigma: How to explain that this man, so original in every aspect of his being and so hostile to all shallowness, could trip over the "Jewish question" of all things, could prove to be so short-sighted and tasteless on this one point, of all things? However, going any deeper into this enigma would, quite obviously, lead us far away from our topic, so that, rather than attempting a thorough analysis of Dostoevski's relationship to the essence and the historical significance of Judaism, we would be obliged to focus upon, say, the tragic destiny of the Jewish nation, or the borders in which this most comprehensive human genius remains enclosed, and such like. Our special problem, however, as need hardly be underscored, would be fully overshadowed by such general considerations, indeed, it would even totally lose its right to exist.

The very title "Dostoevski and Jews" thus indicates that the problem is far more complicated than people usually tend to assume, and that it cannot be dealt with by using the hackneyed slogan "anti-Semitism." The road to its solution actually leads through a whole maze of "pros and cons" and, particularly, to the ultimate depth of Dostoevski's *Weltanschauung*. The result of analysis cannot be a matter of indifference for a deeper understanding of Dostoevski's creative personality or the modern comprehension of the essence of Judaism.

Before getting down to cases, however, we must first deal with the basis for the widespread impression of Dostoevski's "banal" anti-Semitism and its explanation. After all, the error of the many is always a problem in itself, virtually a cross-section of truth.

2

The chief equipment of a writer is his vocabulary. He is, after all, much more aware than most people that every word has a measure and a weight, and that a word often contains an enormous dynamic energy that can radiate animating or annihilating forces in all directions. Even the word that Russians use for a Jew is riven by such a potential, so that it is certainly not indifferent whether a Russian calls a Jew *Zhid* or *Yevrey* (Hebrew).

The first impression of Dostoevski's anti-Semitism, to the extent that one knows his works in the original, is due to his preference for the word *Zhid* even when he is speaking in his own voice. If his vocabulary, like Gogol's, lacked the second word, which, in contrast to the first, is free of any shade of hatred or scorn, then one could not of course draw any conclusions from his usage. Yet it is easy to prove that Dostoevski is all too good at deploying his entire linguistic power with all its virtuosity when choosing words for the "eternal tribe," as he tends to call the Jewish people. One single example suffices to make this fully clear: In describing the life of old Karamazov, Dostoevski does not fail to emphasize that Fëdor Pavlovich, during his youth, spent a long time in Odessa, where he made the acquaintance of "quite a number of Zhids, Zhid mannikins, little Zhids, tiny Zhids" but also "gained entrance to the homes of Hebrews." Two such lines make clear that the great language artist was quite aware of the weight in this charming word and that he virtually used a precision scale to weigh, with painstaking accuracy, the scorn and repugnance that he meant this verbal material to convey. Countless numbers of such examples can be cited; nevertheless, it would be quite rash to give them a decisive significance in resolving our question.

A second, more crucial reason for stigmatizing Dostoevski as an "anti-Semite" is to be sought not so much in the choice of individual expressions as in the shaping of some of the characters peopling his vast and profound world. To be sure, Jews can be found only infrequently in this world; but when we do encounter them, they emerge as creatures almost without human characteristics, their faces peculiarly distorted. There is, for instance, the renowned Issai Fomitsh, one of the inmates of the *House of the Dead.* What does Dostoevski tell us about his fellow sufferer? "He was," the author reports, "a mixture of naïveté, stupidity, cunning, insolence, sincerity, timidity, boastfulness, and impertinence"; he was ruled by "an unparalleled self-satisfaction, nay, a pleasure in himself." "Naturally," says the writer in another place, "he was also a usurer," so that Dostoevski cannot help being amazed that the other inmates did not constantly torment our poor Isaiah (Issai): "Probably," opines Dostoevski, "because he offered all of them steady entertainment and diversion"; because all in all, he was "as good-natured as a rooster," so that one "could play with him as with a parrot or a lapdog."

How zealously the artist strains to make clear to the reader which features of the portrait are merely individual peculiarities of the original person and which are typical of the entire tribe. Dostoevski ekes out his effigy of the typical Jew with several characteristic traits and nuances, suggesting that the Gentile milieu's relations to Issai Fomitsh are by no means the only possible and natural kind and that even Dostoevski himself saw perhaps more in him than a canine impudence and the good-naturedness of a chicken's heart. However, this merely indicates that here, in Dostoevski, we are dealing with one of those contradictions in evaluating Jews and Judaism, a contradiction that must be examined in greater detail. In this context, we need merely point out that the miserable figure of Issai Fomitsh is by no means a random phenomenon in Dostoevski's world, for the same portrait of a Jew, which we encounter in a work from the 1850s, recurs, nearly unchanged, in *The Devils,* a work from the late 1860s. Once again, the convert Lyamshin is a mixture of cunning and stupidity, impertinence and cowardice, shyness and insolence, and he too, "it goes without saying," lends money at usurious interest. This prototype has unchangeable traits for Dostoevski, or, to put it more bluntly: For a certain kind of human character, for a nature that is both repulsive and interesting, dangerous and yet comical, Dostoevski cannot find a better bearer than the Jew.

That is why even the most radiant of Dostoevski's figures are not immune to the poison of Jew-baiting. It is Alexei Karamazov, God-fearing Alyosha, who offers a telling answer to a question put to him by Liza, who is childlike, pure, averse to all evil. She asks him whether it is really true that the Jews require Christian blood for their repulsive rites, and Alyosha has nothing better to reply than: "I don't know." Doesn't this say everything?

To be sure, excessive conscientiousness could cast doubts on the conclusion by asserting that the artist's personality and the novel's narrator are completely distinct from one another, that, in other words, one must rigorously differentiate between the author of a work of fiction and the narrator within the work itself. To clear away this last doubt, it is worth casting a glance, albeit fleeting, at those works in which Dostoevski speaks about Jews and Judaism not through other people but in his own name and in his very own language.

3

In regard to Jews and Judaism, Dostoevski speaks in his own name and frequently at every possible opportunity, especially in his *Diary of a Writer*. One of the articles in this periodical (March 1973) even bears the title *The Jewish Question* and is inspired by a letter from A. Kovner (all the material on his relationship to Dostoevski is now available in German).[1] This very essay is generally considered Dostoevski's "main anti-Semitic work." We will go more thoroughly into its stance presently, but for the moment we wish to pick out those details that seem to demonstrate and confirm most unequivocally Dostoevski's "banal" anti-Semitism. This task is easily dispatched: Dostoevski accuses the Jews of being wily exploiters; of ruthlessly leeching on the surrounding populace, especially the defenseless and ignorant peasants; of regarding Gentiles as nothing but beasts of burden condemned to slavery; of throning on sacks of gold in Western Europe and, from there, inspiring all politics against Russia, against this land, the only land in which Christianity still represents a living and life-determining power. The politics of Disraeli-Beaconsfield, that *piccola bestia,* as he is named another time, a politics directed against the Slavic nations under Russia's protection, can be understood only if one considers that this "Israel," like all Jews, is intent on destroying the truly Christian Russian realm. If the Jews have been hated and persecuted throughout the world for millennia, there must be some sort of reason: "The universal hatred," he says (verbatim), "must, after all, have some grounds. The little word 'all' cannot be altogether meaningless." And thus he does not fail to emphasize expressly the alleged reason and justification for this eternal hatred: The genuinely Jewish "idea" of "materialism," the "blind animal drive for personal material enrichment," the direct opposite of the "Christian idea of salvation . . . by the closest ethical and fraternal coming-together of all mankind." The practical consequences of this entire reasoning, however, lead to the statement that one can give the Jews full civil rights, but only when they have proven worthy of this benefit. And Dostoevski quickly adds that he himself doubts whether Jews will succeed very soon in offering proof of such a thing.

After all that, it cannot astonish us that Dostoevski eventually goes so far as to exclude the Jewish people from the union of mankind. To be sure, he never expressed this with complete openness, yet it does follow with unmistakable clarity from his Pushkin allocution, which crowned his life's work.[2] This speech, in which he tried to capture the universal Christian spirit of the Russian, introduces a new concept: the "Aryan" race. The universal humanity understood by the Russian national spirit and cherished by it is Aryan humanity, i.e., a humanity from which the non-Aryan, the Semitic Jews, must be excluded. Thus, toward the end of his life, Dostoevski uncritically adopted even the terminology of West European racist anti-Semitism, probably under the influence of Pobednostsev,[3] and it would seem as if our investigation has produced no other conclusion than the obvious one. Is the matter therefore settled with the first impression as the only accurate one?

I reply: Yes and No!

Yes—so far as one believes that the human mind lies spread out before the observing eye like a geometric figure with all its sides and angles clear and simple; no—so far as one realizes that the human heart is an abysmally deep and hidden world, a world in itself, full of arduous mysteries and contradictions. And we owe this teaching, this deeper and more accurate notion of the innermost human essence to many minds, including Dostoevski's creative mind, which knew how to draw its wisdom first and foremost from its own heart. Why then should we wish to recognize him of all men in a superficial reflection, why should we refuse to assume that his relationship to Judaism, along with its particularly obvious elements, also contains hidden and softly vibrating motives and emotions?

4

Dostoevski's "anti-Semitism" is an undeniable fact. But if we search for its underlying rationale it becomes more and more problematic and peculiar.

The most important thing to stress is that Dostoevski's lifelong conception of the Jew is in no way a generalization of his own life experience, a compendium of individual events, as is so often the case with garden-variety anti-Semites; for Dostoevski, the individual phenomenon receives its concrete features to some extent or other from his general *idea* of Jews. One need merely note the word "naturally," with which young Dostoevski begins depicting the parasitical nature of the convict Issai ("Naturally, he was also a usurer"). At this point, mention should be made of the following: in great detail, Dostoevski describes how the unfortunate inmate Issai-Isaiah sanctifies the Sabbath on Friday evening, and the author reports on the sight of the worshipping Jew in the prayer-shawl and "prayer-thongs"(!).[4] This, so far as I can recall, is the only lapse that one can hold against Dostoevski's keen eye. Is it not strange that the writer's eye failed precisely when viewing a Jew? What can be the reason? The answer to this question is supplied by Dostoevski's biography.

Even before Dostoevski entered the thick of life, Judaism (not just a single Jew) had left such a deep and persistent impression on his mind at a very tender age that it haunted him to his very last breath and forced him to see the individual in the light of the *idea* he had formed of the collectivity. This ineradicable impression, decisive for his entire spiritual and intellectual cast, came from—the Bible. At this point I must forego compiling all the citations from memoirs of Dostoevski as well as from his own jottings and letters. Let me merely recall one of the most important passages in *The Brothers Karamazov*.

In the autobiography of the *starets* Zosima, written down by Alyosha Karamazov, Dostoevski's saint tells how he, as an innocent eight-year-old, first heard the "Word of God." He was standing at his mother's side among worshippers in church, and

> lo and behold! Into the middle of the temple came a youth with a huge book, so huge that he could barely carry it, and he placed it on the pulpit and opened it and began to read aloud. . . . "And there was a man in the land of Uz, good, pious, and rich. . . ." Now one day Satan, returning home from his long wanderings, came back to God, and the Lord praised his righteous man Job, who was his pride. Satan protested: "Put him into my hands, and I will show you how your servant Job rebels against you, and even curses your name." And God hands Job over to Satan, and, as though struck by lightning, all the splendor and grandeur of the righteous man vanishes. But what does Job do? He tears the hem of his garment, flings himself upon the ground, and shouts: "Naked did I come from my mother's womb, naked shall I return. The Lord giveth and the Lord taketh away; blessed be the Name of the Lord."—"Fathers and masters," the *starets* calls out, "forgive me my young tears, for my entire childhood arises before me, renewed as it were, and I breathe now as I breathed then with my eight-year-old breast, and I feel the same wonder and confusion and joy as then . . ."

In the chapter entitled "The Holy Scripture in the Life of Father Zosima," the *starets* reflects on how inexhaustible are the treasures that could be conveyed to the entire Russian people from "this Book."

> Let the priest open it and read to the people in all plainness and simplicity, with no arrogance. . . . Never fear! They will understand everything, the Russian heart will grasp everything! Let him read to them about Abraham and Sarah, about Isaac and Rebecca, about how Jacob came to Laban and how he wrestled with God in a dream. . . . Let him read to the little children especially how the brothers sold their own brother, the dear youth Joseph, into slavery.

In this tone of voice, testifying to deepest emotion, the *starets* goes through nearly the whole Bible, to interrupt himself once again with the words: "Fathers and Master, forgive me and do not hold it against me that I babble about all these things like an infant . . . I am talking this way in pure ecstasy . . . that's how much I love this Book!" It is "virtually an image of the universe and of men and of human characters, and in it everything is named by name and marked out."

If up to now we could possibly doubt that we are dealing with a personal avowal of Dostoevski's, our last qualms vanish after the publication of the writer's letter to his wife (June 10, 1875, from Bad Ems):

> I am reading the Book of Job and it transports me into a pathological ecstasy: I
> put the book aside and walk up and down for hours, barely able to hold back my
> tears. . . . This book, Anya, (how peculiar) was one of the first to affect me for the
> rest of my life, I was only a tender child at that time!

Just like the most radiant of his characters, Dostoevski owed the soul of his
soul, the "Word of God" come alive within him, to this Book: the Torah, the
Prophets, the Writings.

And could this heart develop hatred and scorn toward the people who had
brought the divine Book into the world and taken on all sufferings of historical
existence for its sake? We can see: Dostoevski's "vulgar" anti-Semitism
suddenly ceases to be ordinary and simple; it suddenly assumes the character
of obscure bizarreness, if not perversity. The first impression was thus thoroughly misleading, and only now are we confronted with the full complexity
of the problem.

5

In order to fully plumb the gaping contradiction in Dostoevski's
relationship to Judaism, we find it necessary to take a further step and touch
upon the question: How did Dostoevski view other nations, apart from the
Jewish people? His fictional and journalistic writings are quite informative on
this point, especially in regard to the leading nations of modern Europe: the
Germans, the French, and the English, not to mention the Russians. Leaving
aside the Russians for the moment, we can readily say that the other main
pillars of modern culture fare even worse than the compatriots of poor Isaiah.
Thus, according to Dostoevski, the German is doubtlessly good-natured,
upright, and industrious, but as stolid as an unplaned block of wood. The
Frenchman, in contrast, is exceedingly clever and skillful, but inwardly hol-
low, like a sack full of holes. The Briton, on the contrary, is an upright man,
thoroughly reliable, but also a simpleton without the slightest notion of his
boundless narrow-mindedness. Worst of all, however: Every last one of them
has been doomed by History to unavoidable decline. Historical providence
has long since pronounced their death sentence, for there is only one nation in
the world whose existence has not become absurd, to whom the future
belongs, who is chosen for world-dominion and world-salvation: the holy,
God-bearing Russian Messiah-nation.

This *basic Messianic idea* of Dostoevski's has its sharpest and most
penetrating expression when Shatov, the hero of *The Devils,* says:

> If a great nation does not believe that it alone (it alone and exclusively) contains
> the Truth, if it does not believe that it alone is able and predestined to use its
> Truth for arousing all people to new life and bring them salvation, then that
> nation stops being a great nation and turns into ethnographic material. A truly
> great nation can never play a secondary part, it cannot even be content with one

of the primary parts, it can only have the very first part. The man who loses his faith can have no more claim to belonging to the national community.

How odd these words sound to a Jewish ear! Familiar things and long-forgotten things are aroused. Is this anything other than a free translation from ancient Hebrew into modern Russian? And whosoever fails to recognize the Jewish concept of chosenness and the national mission of the Jewish people in these words need merely read the following lines in Dostoevski:

> Every nation is a nation only so long as it possesses its own God and rejects all the other gods in the world uncompromisingly, so long as it believes that with its God it can conquer all other gods and drive them out of the world. This, since time immemorial, has been the faith of all great nations, at least those who excelled in some way, who stood at the head of mankind. One fact cannot be denied. The Jews lived for the sole purpose of taking part in the revelation of the True God and to give the True God to the world.

"A Jew without God is simply inconceivable," says Dostoevski in his own name in the *Journals*.

Now we can understand the origins of Dostoevski's enormous contradiction. He feels he has taken over his chief idea from the Jewish people, from its most powerful creation, the Bible: *his Messianism, his belief in the chosenness of the Russian people,* his religion of the "Russian god" (thus formulated in a letter to Maikov). And all at once he is confronted with the intimidated, drastically funny convict "Isaiah," who, impudent as he is, has the effrontery to exclaim to him: How can that be your heritage? . . . Aren't I still alive? "There is only one Truth," Dostoevski furiously interrupts through Shatov's mouth, "and only one of the nations can call the True God its own." Either we Russians or you Jews; or more precisely: true Judaism is now simply Russianism. The moment the Russian nation gives up the belief that it alone has the right to claim the legacy of the national Jewish, the messianic idea, as perpetuated in the Jewish Scriptures, then it will no longer be historically important, it will sink to the level of "ethnographic material." If, on the other hand, historical Truth, the future, and the fate of the entire human race have been placed in the hands of the Russians, then the still-surviving Jews are nothing but historical dust, nothing but mere human material, then the Jews are simply—"Zhids, Zhid mannikins, little Zhids, tiny Zhids." In an inconspicuous passage in *Crime and Punishment* (Part VI, Chapter 6, toward the end), Dostoevski draws this conclusion, too, with unmistakable clarity.

When Svidrigailov makes his final decision and goes out into the gloomy morning of St. Petersburg to put an end to his life in the presence of an "official witness," his eyes light upon a guard stationed in front of the watchtower of the fire department. "With a sleepy gaze, the guard coolly squinted at Svidrigailov, who was approaching him. The guard's features expressed that everlasting sullen melancholy that, without exception, lends such a sour look to all faces of the members of the Jewish tribe." Svidrigailov reaches for his revolver while the frail Jewish guard with the Achilles helmet on his head keeps stuttering: "This isn't the place." Svidrigailov, however, refuses to be put off, and fires. If we bear in mind that in Dostoevski, especially in the formally most consummate of his works, no scene, no figure, no event is without a deeper meaning, then Svidrigailov's farewell to life poses a riddle, but one that is not hard to solve if we compare Svidrigailov's "idea" with Dostoevski's conception of Judaism. Svidrigailov, in the depths of his soul, rebels against the notion of eternity and immortality as a "wretched infinity," against eternal monotony and the eternal return, and it is the Jew with his everlasting shadowy existence who makes existence for the sake of existence tangible in all its absurdity. Like a tame parrot, all he can do is repeat over and over again: "This isn't the place"—not the place to die, not the place to deny life. Ghosts may dismally put up with this negative assertion of life; the truly living man prefers suicide to this curse of survival. Only the man who is not dragged along by his god, but who prepares the way for him and his anointed savior has the right and the duty to live.

Thus Dostoevski's "anti-Semitism" reveals itself as the other side, the reverse, the true basis of his own "Judaism." The seeming contradiction is in reality nothing but rectilinear, ironclad logic.

6

Nevertheless, this still doesn't exhaust the problem.

If Dostoevski were merely a dry theoretician, obsessed with consistency, his mind could be put at ease by this conceptual construction, and his bizarre, purely logical anti-Semitism would be nothing but the shadow of his "Russian God." But even in his relationship to Judaism, Dostoevski is never untrue to the profound earnestness of his nature; his heart, tormented by problems, the eternal battleground of good and evil, gets its due once again here. *The Jewish Question,* the essay, that we have already gotten to know as a document of explicit hatred of Jews, evinces a whole series of elements that can in nowise be subsumed under the notion of anti-Semitism, and actually quite crassly contradict such a notion. There is, above all, the boundless awe toward the so-called "Jewish Question," a feeling that even the Jewish national hotspurs very rarely possess. "Oh, do not believe," cries Dostoevski right at the start of his essay, "that I intend to broach the Jewish question! . . . A question of this scope . . . goes far beyond my energy. I am not adequate to such a question." And then he continues:

> Disregarding the past forty centuries, we have not yet reached the end of time, and so the final judgment of mankind about this great nation has yet to be passed: the last word still remains for the future. . . . The mightiest civilizations have never been able to reach even half the time of forty centuries and yet they

> lost their political strength and their national stamp. . . . We are thus confronted
> with a world chasm of such depth that mankind for the moment cannot find the
> proper word to describe it. . . . The Jews are a nation without peer anywhere in
> the world.

Has anyone ever heard an anti-Semite speak like that? This is why in the same essay Dostoevski explicitly protests any possibility of being reproached for Jew-baiting. It is the second highly peculiar trait in his personal relationship to Judaism: an anti-Semitism virtually ashamed of itself, a Judeophobia with an inner dichotomy, hating itself and confused by itself. "When and how," exclaims Dostoevski,

> have I shown my hostility towards the Jews as a people? Since I have never
> nurtured such a hatred in my heart, which the Jews who know me and have
> associated with me are quite well aware of [an almost verbatim echo of the
> sentences in the letter to Kovner], I would like, right at the very beginning and
> before even uttering a word, to reject such an accusation, and reject it once and
> for all, so that I need not come back to it.

With what vehemence Dostoevski denies his hatred of Jews in the very same essay in which he utters the basest libels and suspicions against the Jewish people with such forceful conviction!

The attitude confronting us in all these statements no longer betrays a purely theoretical contradiction to be resolved in some logical fashion. Instead, we are afforded a glimpse of the inner struggle in Dostoevski's soul, in the realm of his own conscience. The Jewish question was not simply an abstract issue for him, it was actually one of the most burning problems of his personal religion, of his faith in the ultimate purpose and meaning of his own life and work. Thus, the Russian prophet, Dostoevski, emerges as virtually the counterpart to the Midianite soothsayer in *Bamidbar*. While Balaam wanted to curse the people of Israel and had to bless it against his will, Dostoevski would like to bless it with admiration and gratitude, and yet he has to curse it. He would like to praise Judaism, the way a son praises his spiritual father, but he has to condemn it—for lack of strength to free himself from his one-sided messianism and the idea dominating him, to wit, that the historical blessing can rest on only one single nation. After all, doubt is simultaneously gnawing at his heart; he isn't quite certain that the Jewish nation is merely a shadow of its great past: "The last word still remains for the future." Perhaps—so he would like to say in his heart—his vehement love for his own people has led him astray, perhaps the Russian land and the Russian nation are not at all worthy of giving birth to the savior of the world. The lowliest of "guardian" Jews appeared virtually as chief witness for the opposing party, the hostile party in his own soul.

And so he convulsively clenches his fists and devotes all his strength, despite himself, to proving that the Jewish people really no longer exists; that all its energy and vitality are nothing but humbug, masking a pseudoexistence; that the religious ardor of the Jews, their prayers and lamentations, their sorrows and jubilations, are just wretched play-acting, just learned reflexes. After all, as Dostoevski wrote to his wife toward the end of his life, the Jews do not speak "like human beings, they drone out whole printed pages, whole volumes" (letter from Bad Ems, June 28 and 30, 1879).

To understand the full bitterness of the doubts tormenting Dostoevski, we must bear in mind that he always drew the most practical consequences from his postulates of faith. The flaming enthusiasm with which Dostoeveski advocated Russia's right to possess Constantinople derived ultimately from the fact that the Turkish capital seemed to offer him the key to the "Holy Land," to Palestine. The land in which Christ was born had to become thoroughly Russian, an undetachable part of Russia, so that Russia might some day become the land for the return of the Messiah, who, as Dostoevski confidently hoped, would bring the ultimate salvation to mankind. However, so long as the Jewish people, the "nation of Israel," was still alive, Palestine had to be regarded as the "land of Israel," and Russia's right and her world-historic mission were once again in doubt.

Everywhere and in every way Dostoevski kept bombarding Jews and Judaism: in abstract thought, within his own soul (astir with ardent faith and gnawing skepticism), and in the practical politics of current events. Yet all these were nothing but three rays emanating from a single midpoint, that light source of the absolute Russianism from which he drew comfort and creative energy throughout his life. A figure of truly Biblical grandeur! A figure spontaneously recalling those most ancient Jewish prophets who were incapable of struggling up to the level of universal sentiment evinced by an Isaiah, a Micah, a Jonah.

7

This is not the place in which to examine critically Dostoevski's concept of Judaism. The result we have reached testifies at any rate that a fruitful critique of Dostoevski's relationship to Judaism demands a thoroughly founded viewpoint on the ultimate basis of his *Weltanschauung,* and this realization alone may prevent our analysis from seeming worthless. After all, we hear all too often that the question of Jewish survival is nothing but one of the many national and political issues of the day, that one can show the Jewish nation the right path into the future without any rigmarole about the philosophy of history or metaphysics. The Dostoevski case makes it obvious that for a deeper thinker, even if he is not a Jew, the solution to the "Jewish question" is always tied to the ultimate premises of his faith and the deepest foundations of his will. It is therefore worthwhile to try occasionally to learn something from such "anti-Semites" as Dostoevski. Still, this is merely one side, the formal side. Of much greater significance is the kernel in the substance of Dostoevski's "pros and cons": His discussion once again broaches the eternal question of our fate and future, a question treated here in a sharpened form, albeit in a peculiar twilight. To be precise: Not the question whether the Jewish people "should be" but the much more crucial and indeed preliminary question whether it really "is." Perhaps we only think that we still exist as a nation, whereas in reality we are living corpses? What is the purpose of our existence, what is the goal of our national existence for ourselves and for humanity, or, to speak with Dostoevski and to put it in his words: What is the "idea" of Jewish existence?

This problematic idea of the Jewish people has, during the last few decades, become more and more supplanted and edged out by false and unilateral compromises. Jews live, struggle, even sacrifice themselves, yet they find no leisure to stop for an instant and reflect on what their place is in the world and in world history. Only seldom within "our four cubits" does an urgent question arise from the depths of the spirit; yet dozens of answers are ready on the spot. Is it really true that the Jewish nation is merely a spiritless body, a social organism devoid of an idea, nothing but "ethnographic material"?

This is the question that Dostoevski directs at the Jewish people. It is good for us that the question of our existence and our right to exist is still such a burning issue for the great creative leaders of our neighboring nations. We cannot write them off with the empty and vacuous insult "anti-Semites." For them, too, we must say: "If they didn't exist, we would have to invent them."

13. STRINDBERG'S *HISTORICAL MINIATURES:*
A LECTURE

GUSTAV LANDAUER

EDITOR'S INTRODUCTION

GUSTAV LANDAUER (1870–1919) is discussed at length in Ernst Simon's essay, "The Maturing of Man and the Maturing of the Jew," in the present volume. This essay by Landauer, written in March 1917, appeared in *Der Jude,* Jahrgang II (1917–1918), pp. 97–109.

There is an affinity between Gustav Landauer and August Strindberg. Not an obvious affinity: there is no explicit link between the misogynist, the admirer of *Übermensch,* the paranoid, the Swedenborgian and the Jewish anarchist revolutionary. The connection is more subtle, removing to one side the evident simulacrum—their clear-cut psychopathology—which in the admission is not to demean Strindberg's misery or the nobility of Landauer. Psychopathology need not be criminality; immensity can be wrought from it. In acknowledging psychopathology one does not commend it; the work is honored—the vision, let us say—but we are not required for its sake to go through the same torment.

At the point to which Strindberg had come, only seven years before his death in 1912, the *Historical Miniatures* were a kind of Flaubertian recreation; the opportunity to string together a series of jewels, differently cut and proportioned or, eschewing the precious and semiprecious, taking miniatures at their face value, a traveling case, fitted with the narrative icons of Western history, moving from the origins of Israel in Egypt to the French Revolution twenty small portraits, set pieces describing the themes, continuities, dilemmas, and ultimate paradoxes of human history. And as Landauer notes at the very beginning of his lecture during the winter of 1916 in Berlin, to an audience consisting principally of Jews (most of whom had little interest, one supposes, in Landauer's pacifism, anarchism, or revolutionary élan), the continuous presence in Strindberg's miniatures, "always cropping up in most of the chapters: the Jew, the eternal wandering Jew, always in a new shape."

It is known that Strindberg was obsessed with the absolute, with the hidden and unrevealed divinity, whose obstinacy is sometimes manifest in sheer contrariety and malevolence and at others is collaborative and inspiriting. To Strindberg's view, the same God who made man also made woman—an obvious confusion of intention or, worse yet, a fabrication odious. And beyond woman, the hostile forces of chemistry and electricity, the energies of the universe that threatened sanity. Always Strindberg ascended from the horror of his own situation to lay the responsibility with God. Although he was to be tempted by Catholicism, fascinated by Swedenborg and the Buddha, he was in his earlier days violently against the Christian church. Strindberg's moral ideology, not unlike that of his teacher, Nietzsche, was grounded in a loathing of bourgeois morality—the morality of weakness and resentment. During those earlier years, his hostility to Christianity and his loathing of women seemed to derive from the same source, but during the closing period of his life, eased in his misogyny, he came to a kind of reconciliation. It is from this closing period of his life that Strindberg's ironic, weary, quasimystical reading of Western history derives.

Likewise, Landauer, less than five years before he joined Ernst Toller in the leadership of the Bavarian Soviet Republic and met his death, was to rationalize the universal promise of the self-liberation of the Jew, developing the paradoxical existence of German-speaking Jew, in love with the prospect of Jew leading Germany to a purified human community, while recognizing that in the process the particularity of the Jew would be sacrificed and the revolution would bring with it precisely the violence he abhorred.

Strindberg afforded Landauer a case in point: transcendence to reconciliation, history in the delusion of literature, the Jew tangled in the skirts of Christendom.   [A.A.C.]

STRINDBERG'S *HISTORICAL MINIATURES:*

A LECTURE[1]

Strindberg's book *Historical Miniatures* [*Historiska miniatyrer*], which came out in 1905, bears a title that is both coy and yet too modest: although each section can be read independently, the entire book forms an overall whole, a romance of humanity in selected chapters. Two concerns operate together in the eternally new situations and revelations investigated throughout this work: Man, and the secret, inscrutable guiding of his destiny, visible only in its traces. It is entirely within Strindberg's purpose, if occasionally, instead of showing abstract amazement at this guiding, we, playfully seeking, speak with faith and devotion about the Pilot of mankind and its movements.

And one more person is always around, always cropping up in most of the chapters: the Jew, the eternal, wandering Jew, always in a new shape.

How come? At the end of the book, someone says in regard to the French Revolution, which is only just completed: "You see, now,"—now that mankind is about to become a true reality—"Now the promise made to Abraham: 'In your name, all generations shall be blessed!' is on the way to fulfillment; on the way, I say."

The interlocutor, astonished, asks, as anyone would who hears this unexpectedly: "The promise made to Abraham?" And Strindberg has the first man rejoin: "Through Christ, who stemmed from Judah, we are spiritually descended from Abraham." And he adds: The very faith that mankind is one in this spirit, which comes from Judaism, will redeem mankind.

Anyone unfamiliar with this work might get a rather false picture from this introduction, which links up with the conclusion. This is no dry abstraction; Strindberg is a great writer precisely because, rather than dress up his ideas in figures, he lets his lively, versatile, rich, teeming characters grow out of ideas. Strindberg's secret guiding is at least as secret as it is guiding; and it goes in his world as it goes at the end of his *Queen Christine:* Man follows his instincts, his will, which functions freely in his consciousness, serves selfish and mean ends, and still things can turn out otherwise. He may have dissipated and ruined his personal fortune; but his wildest and perhaps most capricious deeds turn out to have served a cause. Or else: There comes, for him, a moment of crisis, a turning point, a time of reflection and deliberation; he realizes that in his faith, his delusion about the meaning of his own ambition, he has been totally in error. But if now, clear-sighted, he takes up and had—like everything else—sufficient cause, but no purpose. But meanwhile this war has acquired a purpose, and leading, if not apparently responsible minds, have seen the light: A war against war, the final war, a war to renew nations and create their alliance, a war for humanity. Let us call it whatever we will, the Utopia, the ridiculed and scorned idea, that, at least when the war broke out, was particularly overlooked and forgotten, and that forced into its service, and will continue to force, the most horrible lack of ideas the world has ever known.

This work of Strindberg's, consisting of twenty chapters or individual tableaux, which lead us from Israel in Egypt up to the French Revolution and a view beyond our age, shows a characteristic of Strindberg's that makes him a very particular writer and dramatist: the rapidity and sureness with which the images and thoughts associate themselves when he observes an incident. We see the same thing in his *Blue Book:* every bit of reading matter, every notice in the news he neatly turns into a small plot and very often a dialogue, where one thing is dramatically analyzed into its diverse aspects.

In the first piece, *The Egyptian Bondage,* we hear about Abraham's promise in its particular significance for the Hebrews.

Hundreds of years have passed since the land of Canaan was promised to the children of Abraham, and instead, they, the children of Israel, have been in bondage for a long time. Most of them believe nothing any more, especially the educated ones: they are totally assimilated to Egyptian culture. There are still a few left, however, who know they are Jews and use secret signs to remember the promised and expected deliverance.

The Egyptian priests have a secret science pertaining particularly to mathematics and astronomy; there is, however, a despised Jew, a small artisan, an ebony carver and boxmaker, a Levite, as his conversation indicates. He, too, has a profound secret knowledge, going back to Abraham, in these very same areas. And the full initiates know: It is a single God that the two nations, the two cultures, honor: in essence they are one. But thousands and thousands of years of strife and separation will be necessary for the sake of the ways of this One God.

Pharaoh returns from long travels in remote lands and brings back a strange and secret message:

> Wherever I went, I heard whispering and saw movement. The nations have awakened, in the temples they prophesied the return of the gods; for men had been left alone to ply their trades and work their destinies; but they plied them badly and worked them poorly. Justice had become injustice, and truth lies; the whole earth was sighing for salvation.

He knows this, high above, in the sublime; but he doesn't know what to do with this knowledge, he is unable to send this thought out into the world of deeds. This is not human work. This goes along strange ways, and it has a long way to go, as someone says, to designate its ways in a long portion of endless time.

But when Pharaoh returns to the demands of practical, everyday life, to the usual habits of superstition and fanaticism, when he hears that the Nile has refused to flood and that a famine is imminent, when a dream indicates the danger threatening him from the Jews, he acts, without realizing that this might somehow be connected with his loftiest insight. He does something to the Jews, the very worst and thereby the very best, not only for them, but for the entire world: All male babies born to Hebrew women are to be killed. Just through this act, however, the child ascends to Pharaoh's throne, the very child that shall fulfill the promise made to Abraham: "Through your seed, all the peoples on the earth shall be blessed." Moses, hidden in the rushes of the Nile, discovered by the princess, frees his people from bondage, turns it into a nation, and suspends the Tables of God's Law over it.

All this comes out in Strindberg's depiction, not like an imitated, modernized Bible, and not like an ideological construction; it is told in a lively, colorful way, as the experiences of human beings in a certain place, in certain areas and landscapes, mostly in a dramatically dynamic dialogue.

We meet another despised little Jew, again a Levite, in the splendid and thoroughly grandiose second piece, entitled *The Semicircle of Athens*. We are led to Pericles, Socrates, Aspasia, Alcibiades, Euripides, to Greek existence at its height—which means, however, in a mood of decadence.

Cleon, the tanner, representing the immortal mob, wants to call upon the Jew as a witness to a daring dialogue between Socrates' friends; the Jew, however, refuses. In Socrates, he has recognized the man who serves the same one and true God, as he, the Jew does: the Invisible, the Eternal God.

And then, in a conversation between this Jewish cobbler and a Roman citizen who patches buskins in Athens, we hear strange, contradictory things about the ways of History. The Cumaean Sibyl has promised Rome the same thing she promised Israel, that, she, Rome, will possess the earth. And the Roman says: "Perhaps it is the same promise, the same God! Perhaps Israel will conquer through Rome." The Jew in Hellas can only shake his head: the promise was different, Israel shall conquer through the Messiah; and He shall come when Zeus is dead.

Is Zeus coming to an end, the god of pagan life, perjurer and pederast? Orient and Occident mingle in the conversation between the Persian Tissaphernes and Alcibiades, the deserter and traitor. The Persian scorns the corruption of this Hellas, where the Sophists have ascended, the Sophists who recognize nothing as holy or inviolable, who have set the arbitrary rule of the senses above everything else. He speaks to the prototype of Greek decadence about his religion and his prophet Zarathustra:

> If you had known the prophet since your childhood, you would have been able to distinguish between Good and Bad, Light and Darkness, Ormazd and Ahriman. And you would have lived in the hope that the Light would ultimately win out, and that everything would be reconciled through suffering.

A fermentation, something new, foaming out of the Most Ancient, is announced in Greece, too. It recalls the prophecy in the *Prometheus* of Aeschylus, that Zeus will have a son born to him by a virgin; a new God comes from the East, Adonai or Adonis, who bids men to take the road through the gates of death to be resurrected; a goddess comes, Cybele, a virgin and the mother of the Gods.

How strange are men, their grandeur, their nobility, their plans.

Here is Pericles, one of the noblest natures, one of the richest minds. A great plan lives in him: the unification of all Greek states. And here is Alcibiades, the brilliant mind, the man with all the qualities of the unscrupulous politician, from his fascinating imagination to his pandering to the common people. He dreams of the world dominion that shall fall to Hellas. But these are all dreams of decline, a last blaze before death, evening twilight: they dream on a large scale, these civilized men, "but the dreams of the Gods are greater." There is no passage from these thoughts to any reality.

These are basic ideas, worked out and thrust into the foreground, but emerging in literature only episodically in a dazzling picture of the Periclean age, in a whole context of beauty, goodness, and loving kindness.

This shall not be absent when we speak about Strindberg: loving kindness. As bitterly as he keeps aiming at disruption and annihilation, yet he remains (where are there oppositional words, whose reality is mutually exclusive?) one of the friendliest of mortals. One may be reminded of Apollo, the God who, with his arrows, sends the plague among men, and yet is simultaneously the sunny God of gracious Music.

Strindberg is particularly loving in this piece in the way he fashions his relationship to women. He does this in the figure of Aspasia, the mate rather than wife of the great Pericles, and in the conversations pertaining to her.

At Alcibiades' banquet, Euripides' "alleged misogyny" is a topic of discussion. We are given a highly personal confession in an extremely plausible literary form. The words of Protagoras the Sophist in no way clinch the matter, nor should they: "Our friend Euripides has been married three times, and he's had children each time. So how can he be a woman-hater!" But then a higher point is reached. Socrates speaks: Euripides cannot be a misogynist, for he loves (and Pericles is not jealous) Aspasia's spiritual beauty. Physically she is not beautiful, this friend of intellectual men, and Phidias confirms it. Pericles and Socrates together, as in a duet, tell us what Aspasia, the sympathetic woman, means to a creative man:

> Aspasia is a wise woman, for she possesses modesty and tenderness, self-knowledge and intelligence; Aspasia is smart, for she remains silent when wise men speak. But Aspasia can get wise men to speak wisely through the way she listens; she helps them to give birth to ideas. Aspasia (this is spoken by the man of maieutics, the son of the midwife) conceives our impure children and gives them back to us purified. She herself doesn't give anything, but the way she takes gives the giver a chance to give.

That would be the loveliest description of Strindberg-Euripides' attitude towards women. Aspasia herself, however, is not satisfied. She recalls wicked verses that Euripides wrote in his *Hippolytos,* in which the deity is directly petitioned to find some better way of reproduction without women, without sex. And true enough, such verses, like the ones in Euripides' *Phaedra,* were given their strongest and purest utterance in Strindberg's *Dream Play:*

> Why are we created like animals,
> We who are human and stem from Gods?
> Does the spirit need no other garb
> Than this one of blood and filth?

And Euripides-Strindberg replies:

> If I were a Sophist like Protagoras, I would answer "Hippolytos said that, not I."
> But I am a poet and speak through my offspring. I did say it, I did mean it when I

wrote it; I still mean it. And yet I nearly always love a woman and hate her sex. I can't explain it, for I have never been perverse like Alcibiades.

We have all dreamt that strange feeling of being a pupil in a dream-school, standing on the edge of a chasm, and not knowing any more answers, while the split ego has created the dream-teacher, who instructs the ignorant pupil. Likewise, the poet, experiencing dramatically, confesses forthrightly that he is unable to solve the enigma of his own nature, and then lets Socrates find the solution. For Xanthippe's husband, the matter is clear enough: it's quite possible to love and yet hate a woman. Just as the good is bound up with motherliness, the bad is bound up with sexuality. And that is Strindberg's last word on women: that they stand deeper in sex, more solidly rooted in original sin. Strindberg's approach to the battle of the sexes is connected with his yearning for freedom, airy lightness, divinity, with a request addressed to destiny to let him live and love unhampered by a divisive, murderous egotism and a degrading drive, with the question about the meaning and mission of life, with the ultimate thoughts about God and the world, as Strindberg's dying Socrates utters them, grandly and in a lovely and noble resignation.

> I have just enjoyed a nap—I was over there, on the other side of the river; for a moment I saw the primal images of eternal beauty, of which objects are merely dark counterfeits. . . . I saw the future, the destinies of the human race: I spoke to the powerful, the sublime, the pure; I understood the wise order that guides us, and that seems like such a huge chaos; I trembled over the unfathomable secret of the universe, that I dimly comprehended; and I grasped the ineffable scope of my ignorance. Plato, write it down! Teach the sons of man to regard things with measured scorn, to look up respectfully to the invisible, to worship beauty, to cultivate virtue, and to hope for salvation, during labor, in performing one's duties, and through renunciation.

I found it to be a poignant moment when Strindberg, here closely imitating the Platonic-Socratic tradition, expresses the relationship of the idea to reality and at the same time his own personal highest desire and ultimate insight. Goethe (with whom Strindberg is at one in these ultimate words about life and the relationship between daily life and the Eternal) would probably have shaken his head over much in Strindberg and been amazed "at this peculiar sign of the times." But this book, which leads to such high points, he would have loved and—despite everything—recognized as the spirit of his spirit. The calm resignation of this Socrates was his concern; and he would have taken pleasure in the melancholy-cheerful conversations of the men of Athens and then, in a further piece, of the poets of imperial Rome; and he would have accepted the comfort that Horace finds in Strindberg: every age has been a time of decadence and yet a time of preparation and renewal: "Nature, life, and history are always renewed through death."

This is why, in this strange procession of the ages, in which death and life are crisscrossed like beams needing one another's support, there are constant sections that seem to refer to one another, and by complementing one another seem to tangibly produce an integral whole. Just as the idea of humanity, entrusted to Judaism's keeping, once freed itself from Egypt, it now flees back to Egypt. And once again, the two prophecies collide: Rome's dominion over the world, Israel's redemption of the world. Now, the Promised Man, whom the Jews call the Messiah, has come. The Roman, conversing with the Hebrew in Egypt is certain: Augustus Caesar will rule the world and unite all nations under his scepter. The Jew, however, doesn't believe him. "Has he come, as Isaiah prophesied? 'So that his rule shall be great and peace without end?' "—Oh no, the promised KINGDOM is certainly not the Roman imperium. Upon leaving, the Roman, of course, with the eternal sarcasm of the politician, says: "Be glad about redemption through Rome; we know no other salvation." The Hebrew, however, goes back to his wife: "Maria," he says. "Joseph!" she answers. "Quiet. The baby is sleeping."

The child grows up and awakens and lives for the world: Jesus of Nazareth. And again—Strindberg's religion, like Hegel's, is a historical religion. Very much in contrast to the individualist Norwegian, Ibsen, Strindberg is concerned not so much with the salvation of the individual as with the road of mankind and the meaning of history—again the contrast of events in the Roman empire is sharply brought out. The history lesson given by this work is valuable because it provides a meaningful connection between things that are separated in time and space.

We see a man who becomes a god and is worshiped in temples: Emperor Tiberius, who lives like a madman in Capri and is thrashed soundly by his nephew Caligula. And at the same time, the son of Man and of God lives in Palestine, Jesus, the pure lamb, who is also scourged, who does not rule, who is sacrificed and executed. And always, in all these pieces, it is the people who help to persecute their finest men, their saviors, who yell "Crucify! Crucify!"

We keep encountering the contrast between the Roman and the Jew. "You meet the Roman everywhere," a Jew in imperial Rome sums up this relationship in a formula. "He is at home everywhere. You meet the Jew everywhere, too, but he is at home nowhere."

But now Judaism has engendered a spirit: now there are Christians, Roman Christians. They live in the *cloacae*, "like seeds in the earth, ready to sprout," in the underground grottoes, the catacombs, they are "buried with Christ and are waiting for the resurrection."

And ultimately they arise, at first, as God always arises in history, in reality: distorted beyond recognition, disguised. The ways of the Lord are dark; Christianity becomes the state religion of Rome; by reaching the top, it goes downhill; by achieving victory, it decays.

And now comes Julian, a strange mixture of things, an apostate who is more of a Christian than those who style themselves thus. He looked at the three hundred years of Christianity and was horrified: The world has gotten more and more miserable, more and more sordid, the Christians live worse than heathens. And now the individual, whose departure is speedy, and who knows no other world than that of his life, clashes with the spirit of history, which possesses an ineffable amount of time. Julian has no patience whatsoever; he grows furious at the thought of having to wait; and it does no good for pious Eusebius to teach him that impatience is one of the plagues of hell. He, however, is the kind of man under whom the bridge to reality collapses the moment he sets foot upon it. Again, like Pericles, a man of noble spirit, a great planner, who never succeeds in anything, a late-comer, yet ahead of his time, an outsider, no matter: his thoughts are rich and unfruitful. He would fuse all religions, would develop their eternally consistent contents, the meaning of their imagery, would, as a Platonist, combine religion and philosophy in a higher unity, only to fail at everything and come to the bitter realization: "It *is* the Gods, after all, who wage the war; we are merely soldiers."

"Man proposes, God disposes": this old, fine popular saying contains the essence of Strindberg's concept of history. But what sinister, what infernal and demonic, what grotesque devices, this theatrical director and producer employs! The Huns ride out upon the stage of the world. The poet depicts them as hobgoblins in this Attila chapter. Like larvae or lemurs, these yellow devils suddenly creep, as though through cracks and pores of the paint, into the highly polished civilization of the Roman world, which rules everywhere throughout the empire, even among Gauls and Germans. The Huns have nothing of spirit, culture, or soul, not even raw individual energy, and this holds for Attila too. Yet the little fellow is imposing when he appears on the "visible scorn of everything and everyone." Somehow, this seems to be his religion: to grasp himself not as purpose in himself, but to see himself and his people as a demonic device: the scourge of God. And he thrusts forward as a thorn in the flesh of Christianity—ultimately to vanish with his kingdom from History.

But Christianity survives and always keeps submerging deep into its own origin and its true essence. Gregory the Great, the servant of the servants of God, consolidates monasticism, asceticism, a life of humble service. We hear him, while still an abbot of Saint Andrew's in Rome, conversing with a youth who is afflicted with the eternal disease of youth, a lust for life and a despair at life. He is unable to remain in the monastery; the logic of sensuality calls out of him: "The desires can be slaked only by being satisfied." Nothing can be more cogent; and nothing can be more characteristic of Christianity's profoundly *absurd* reversal of the basic concepts of all thinking than the fiery answer of the prior: "You thrall of Satan, don't you understand that the desires can never be satisfied?"

And again comes Strindberg's graceful vanquishing, a pessimism, that leads not only to a flight from the world, but to patient, self-sacrificing labor: "That's how the world is, that's how life is; but if that's how it is, and you realize that that's how it is, then all you can do—is live it; and to consider it a matter of honor to live until death comes and releases us.''

Just as in the scene of Socrates dying, what I find so special and poignant about these words, which no logician could really praise (for what does honor have to do with the question about the meaning of life?), is the fact that this fine gallantry, this blushing bravery towards life, is such pure Strindberg and yet so marvelously expresses the attitude of the pious Christian knight in the Middle Ages of Romanesque churches and fortresses. Blushing bravery toward arduous life. That was Strindberg's ultimate discovery; nor does he conceal how difficult it is. The youth breaks down sobbing, wishes to die on the spot. And the old prior says, in spite of himself: ''Who doesn't wish for the very same, my son! . . . If only you knew . . . if only you knew.'' Yes, he loves death; and for that very reason, he fails to understand how anyone can fear it. When Rome is afflicted by a flood and, in its wake, the plague, he tirelessly, lovingly, even mirthfully takes care of the sick and exclaims: ''Children, what do you fear about death, anyway? Fear life, that is true death.''

He is then elected pope; he refuses, and hides in his Sabine mountains, and has to be dragged by force into the Lateran, where he becomes Gregory the Great, of whom the poet says, summing up: ''His rule was as great as Caesar's, but he had no legions, only a pen and some ink. It was the Kingdom of Christ that was beginning; but it was only a spiritual world dominion, and Gregory was the governor.'' No one need object that this too was not the pure realm of the spirit; Strindberg himself soon sufficiently demonstrates this in powerful colors.

But God has more than one iron in the fire: now, once more, totally unexpected nations, of whom no one has thought, are entering culture. The illegitimate children of Abraham, the sons of Ishmael, come on stage, the Mohammedans. The Moors invade Spain and France. Eleazar, the old Jew, says: ''Nothing comes to an end, it merely changes after it has had its day.'' And immediately, in the next piece, we again see an ill-timed dominion, that came in utter splendor as a vast imperium and quickly crumbles apart because the Idea is going in a different direction: Charlemagne erects his huge European empire, which falls to pieces the moment he closes his eyes. ''How difficult it is to perceive,'' Eginhard writes to Charlemagne's daughter Emma, who was once Eginhard's wife and is now the spiritual sister of the monk in Christ, ''that in history, every powerful thing bears within itself the transitory, and that the heights are always limited by the depth of the fall.''

And then we see mankind at the turn of the year 1000, in an anxious, desperate, and yet almost yearning expectation at a point of crucial concern to the world. Now an Ottonian ruler heads the Roman Empire, one of the Saxons whom Charlemagne was foolish enough to think he could wipe out; that was his deadly sin against the spirit, his desire to convert by force. The author, however, brings someone to the Rome of popes and emperors, the capital city

of guilt-ridden Christendom waiting for the end: a Saracen who says something that sounds like a reflective self-irony, or an exhortation by Strindberg
not to perceive too clearly any intention in the destinies of individuals or
nations. "The Christians," he says, "always have two ways of explaining why
Man suffers. If he is innocent, then he is being tested; and if he is guilty, why
then he has earned his fate."

Christians have been guilty long enough—but this time, when they see
punishment and annihilation as imminent, there is no end of the world and no
Second Coming. And soon thereafter, they look forward to the Crusades as the
great renewal of Christianity. But the Holy Sepulchre is still in the hands of
Islam today; and something that began spiritually and ecstatically came to a
profane and wanton end.

Antiquity rises again, art and beauty, wisdom and science, splendor and
crime come with the Renaissance; and Luther, the young monk, sees all this
Rome and is horrified. And, as in the piece dealing with the Crusades, where a
Jew and his family die a "Christian" martyr's death at the hands of so-called
Christians in the Holy Land, the Jew Elias, who teaches Luther Hebrew, is the
only "Christian" the monk meets in the Rome of Julius II.

With the Renaissance come ages in which historical material acquires more
color, more detail, more psychology. Thus, right at the end of the next piece,
characteristically entitled *The Tool*, the motive thought is very strongly emphasized. The tool is once again a monarchic monster, Louis XI of France. On
the verge of death, he confesses that throughout his life he acted only upon
bad intentions, thought only about himself, used his people, committed
perjury and broke treaties. But then someone steps through the door, a young
priest who takes the admission as a confession: St. Vincent de Paul. He gives
Strindberg's absolution to the man of Absolutism, to the criminal, in the name
of the absolute that has entered into relation and movement, in the name of
the God of History. Louis's intentions were certainly not pure, but unwittingly,
almost unwillingly, he has done something great: a united France now exists.
For a stretch of history, France will become the foremost power in Europe; the
Hundred Years' War with England is finally over, and the impure man has
created a better historical climate than the pure Maid of Orleans, who once
saved France. "Be thankful to God, Sire, that you have been permitted to
serve!" And a man, as bad as the king himself, sarcastically speaks the
epilogue: "Hangmen have their offices too!" Now the time is approaching
when the rod is no longer necessary; the children, the nations, are grown up
and can get along on their own.

The same ironical relationship between the psychic impulses of the individual and the historically heterogeneous outcome is to be found in Henry
VIII's England. What a ticklish relationship between cause and effect! The
king has conscientious qualms about his marriage, and so many scholars and
council assemblies are used to get rid of or justify them. If all these theological
experiences that take place in the upper consciousness are based on erotic

wishes down in the inferior room or even the cellar of our drives and instincts, then world history has a completely different end in view. "Out of all this chaos," says Strindberg, "there emerged a free, independent, and powerful England. When the Germans, in the Thirty Years' War, wanted to free themselves totally and finally from Rome, England was already done with its work."

Strindberg's depiction of the Thirty Years' War shows his determination to refuse the individual any right to happiness, and to permit his right to live if, and so long as, mankind needs his life for its work. The lasting reality of that war is made gruesomely plain in Strindberg's powerful imagery: we see poor wretches who have pulled a corpse down from a gallows and are roasting it as food; sitting in a circle, they are eagerly waiting for their meat to cook. Feeling their terrible sin, they sing a *Miserere*—and yet! "The ultimate freedom from Rome had been attained, and that was something," says Strindberg, the free historical Christian, who assigns different positions to Catholicism and Protestantism, "that couldn't be purchased dearly enough."

The wild and barbarous scenes depicting Peter the Great of Russia lead us in a splendid tempo into a different realm of the antithetical struggle between the individual personality and its historical mission. The figure of the tsar (Strindberg did a thorough job of studying him during his preparatory work on Charles XII of Sweden) stands here solid and sure, like a great dramatic character. This is the barbarian who civilized Russia, the builder of cities, who himself wanted to remain a simple peasant. And with the similing gentleness of a man who needs forgiveness for himself, and in a manner that seems akin to Russian mentality, Strindberg concludes: "Publicly, his life was great, rich, and beneficial; privately, his life was as it could be."

And thus our author, who feels ashamed for himself and for mankind about the badness of our world and yet refuses to stop perceiving God's traces in the earthly and the human, does justice to Voltaire in the final piece. He has the philosopher say and then ask:

> Great men, petty foibles, or rather: great foibles. We, Monsieur, were no angels, but Providence used us for great things. Is Providence indifferent as to whom it takes in its hands? Does it care how we live in the flesh, so long as we keep the Spirit high? *Sursum corda!* Keep the hearts high!

The old pessimist does wish that someday a race of men could come who would see life correctly from the very outset, i.e., as something abject. "Or do we have to properly smear ourselves with mud? Is that part of the therapy?" His body in a mudbath, his eyes turned towards heaven—that is, after all, how Strindberg shows us the poet in his *Dream Play*.

The lines of thought that are plainly brought out in this presentation always grow organically out of the unique situation; and the meaning lives sensually in images that come of themselves. Voltaire, a very old man, on the verge of death, in his Ferney, at the foot of Mont Blanc, speaks melancholy and courageous words: "Good night, Mont Blanc," the old man calls in cheerful resignation, "you have a white head, as I do, and you stand with your feet in cold water, as I do!"

And now for the conclusion, the summit of this epic of humanity: The French Revolution comes alive, but not in a direct depiction. Strindberg loves reflection, a retrospective view that abbreviates and contracts into history, and a setting that symbolically points to past and future. We are led upwards, to one of the towers of Notre Dame. It is the 18th of Brumaire, Napoleon's coup d'état; the revolution is over. The tower room is inhabited by an aristocrat who has been hidden there for the entire period of the revolution, and his former servant, the custodian of the northern tower. The aged but vigorous man has time enough on his hands, and so he does bookbinding on the side. All the engravings about the revolution hang on the wall, bringing back that great and terrible era.

The plebeian is already a hundred years old, and when he steps out on the roof in the roaring storm, he has to hold tight to the demons who live up there in stone. But he has to go out there in order to call out to the bell-ringer of the south tower through a speaking-trumpet: All bells are to be rung, the revolution is over!

Once more, for one last evening, they are brothers, his master and he, once more they sit down to a meal together, then his master returns to life, to nobility; the division, the separation of stations, begins anew. And, at odds as always, they recapitulate what they have seen from their lofty height.

But characteristic of Strindberg in all his periods (despite all his profound changes and his difficult path to maturity, he is always the same)—characteristic is the fact that here as, say, in *Miss Julie,* and for all the playwright's duality, the true word of history is spoken not by the lord, but by the servant. As close as Strindberg's contact might once have been with Nietzsche, he always distinguished between nobility of the emotions and the power of reason and will, found spiritual aristocracy and a tired descent among the old dynasties and privileged people, and a masterful strength to the point of baseness among those who were striving up from below, among the fighters for freedom. When the Count starts talking about the barbarity that accompanied the rise to power of the revolutionaries, the old servant interrupts him and drily retorts:

> Now just wait! Louis XVI had two gentlemen-in-waiting, who received twenty thousand livres a year simply for inspecting his high chamber-stool every morning and carrying it out; even the sans-culottes couldn't have reached a higher level of barbarity.

And thus the guillotining of Louis XVI and Marie-Antoinette is decisively justified; if there is such a thing anywhere in the world, then they were guilty of high treason: "Don't talk about martyrs, or I'll lose my temper! I always lose my temper when I hear a lie."

And the causes of all this? Ah, how far back we have to go, back to the original sin in Paradise. "The revolution was a divine judgment that had to come." And thus they chat on, at variance with one another and yet respectfully intimate, and the old man recalls the greatest thing that the revolution brought him: collective work of all stations and classes in the fraternization festival on the Field of Mars. Are the old things, separation, inequality, and oppression, coming back again? Of course they are, once, twice, and a third time, like a drowning man, but the fourth time, they go down forever. Oh yes, definitely, despite everything, he believes in the good and its realization. "Yes, I believe, I believe like Thomas: when I have seen. And I *have* seen! That time on the Field of Mars, I saw!"

And when the Count asks a reluctant and incredulous question: "How long do we have to wait?" the servant, having reached the age of the seeing and dying Faust, answers with the "final conclusion of wisdom": "We mustn't just sit here and wait, we have to work! Time will then pass."

This faith, which—for all its resignation—is active, will—the servant knows it for sure, he sees it—*will* redeem humanity.

And then they can talk no more: the bells start pealing. He still moves his lips, but not a sound can be heard in the overpowering tolling of bronze: the human lip grows dumb when the Spirit of the ages booms out.

> The tolling seemed to come from the depth of the centuries, ringing out the old century, ringing in the new one, that was to start in just a few weeks, the nineteenth century since the birth of the Savior, who promised to return and who may come back in some way or other.

Patience—time is without end—hope, therefore, and work. With the pealing of the bells, the book fades out.

Afterword: And here, at the end, we hear the words with which I started and which must now be repeated: "Now, the promise made to Abraham is to come true: 'In your name shall all generations be blessed?' *Is* to, I say." Messianic perception, faith, will, is being expressed here. Let no one ask what such a historical epic, which derives from the Jewish spirit and ends in the Jewish spirit, means to a Jew. We Jews do not simply have our mission to mankind; the ways that mankind goes, circuitous, erroneous, arduous, and dangerous; the ways of other nations, taken for our sake too, are also our ways. Not our entire way—they take nothing away from our special task, which is also our way. Our way, too, is the way of Europe, until the 18th of Brumaire; our way, too, what then became March 1848; our way, too, what ensued and continues beyond our times.

14. THE INNER STRUCTURE OF THE YOM KIPPUR LITURGY

DAVID BAUMGARDT

EDITOR'S INTRODUCTION

DAVID BAUMGARDT (1890–1963), a philosopher by train-
ing, taught at the University of Berlin until his emigration in 1932. Subsequently, he was consultant on German philosophical literature at the
Library of Congress in Washington, D.C., until his death. Baumgardt's essay
was published during Jahrgang IV (1919–1920) of *Der Jude*, pp. 274–82.

The liturgy of Israel is among its most astonishing achievements, in its own way as miraculous an endurance as that of the people itself;
subject not less than the people to the depredations of cultural fashion, the
liturgy has been reshaped, excised, cleansed as the sensibilities of those who
do not pray but judge prayer required, but through all historical vicissitudes it
retained its form and continuity. This liturgy—the *Siddur* of the everday and
its culminating Sabbath, the *Maḥzor* of the seasons and its culminating Rosh
Ha-Shanah and Yom Kippur—constitutes the most ancient body of prayers in
continuous use by a single community in the history of mankind. This credits
it, however, with little more than longevity. The appeal to continuity is a
deadly appetite of historical narcissism: what survives the raids of time need
not be its best—witness the useless oddments that the sea discharges after
centuries from the holds of proud galleons or ancient tombs that yield up only
beads and undistinguished bowls of grain. The liturgy is no Jewish artifact,
although the habit of prayer and the poetics of self-scrutiny may well have
become in this age as much to be remarked as the discovery of a nearly extinct
species.

The problem of Jewish liturgy is not the liturgy itself. David Baumgardt's
preliminary study of the structure of the *Maḥzor* for Yom Kippur makes
abundantly clear that its text, grown from foundations in Leviticus (and hence
as ancient as the people), acquired through the course of its employment an

elaboration and texturing that gave each of its principal conceptions a mod-
ulation and emphasis, a shaping and weighting, measure and cadence permitting of no casual entrance and exit. The *Maḥzor* builds upon a structure that
scaffolds the liturgy as a whole, as though its essential anatomy sustained the
whole year and its every day, besides the specific tasks assigned it by the Days
of Penance, which introduce motifs that put to the bones of the ordinary the
flesh of great paradox and contrast. The poets of Jewish literature (incidentally
the great *payṭanim* were as well quite frequently not only rabbis but scholars,
philosophers, and legists), moved by the excesses of their day, addressed the
great issues, containing their historical anguish and offering it up transmog-
rified into new assertion. The liturgy for the Day of Atonement begins with the
prayers of every day—the prayers of creation, the blessings, the *Shema'
Yisra'el,* the Silent Devotion, the *Qedushah*. These are the essentials; however
it is what transforms them from the familiar conversation of man with God into
the language of abashment, pleas, and confession that marks the uniqueness
of the Day. It is here that a millennial imagination, construing in exigency and
emergency, creates the poetry of the Exile that makes of the Day of Atonement
an unparalleled cycle of prayer.

Baumgardt is right to discern the transition and building of the liturgy, its
movement of language from the infinitude of distance between the awesome
God and the humiliated and sinful people to the intimate pleading that asks of
God that the people—here the millions of its single souls—be spared the
judgment, that the inscribing for life and renewal become a sealing for the
new year.

There is, however, a dimension of the drama and passion of the Day of
Atonement Baumgardt could only sense in 1919. He recognizes that the great
poets of the liturgy—Meshullam ben Qalonymus, Rabbenu Tam, and the
author of "Untanneh Toqef"—were poets of the Exile. Whether writing from
Italy or Spain or Germany, whether writing in the midst of expulsion and
murder, they were of the generations that knew the bitterness of the Exile.
We—of this surviving generation—who did not know the bitterness of the Exile
but were no less destroyed, must now learn, in the aftermath of that destruction, what it meant to be in Exile.

"In every generation there are those who rise up against us." That appeal to
the lesson of history, which moves through the Passover liturgy, is absent from
the Day of Atonement. The liturgy there does not command that we remember
the *'Abodah* of the ancient Temple merely to instruct us in the disappearance of
the rite, nor does the text of the "'*Eleh 'Ezkerah*" intend that we rehearse the
martyrs for the sake of the *exemplum* of martyrdom.

The Day of Atonement is for the sake of man's confession and reconciliation to God. It is an instruction, as Baumgardt correctly indicates, to *teshubah,*
to repentance and return. The *'Abodah* describes the ancient penitential rites
of the highest religious personage in Israel—the high priest speaking the
ineffable name while performing the rites of purification and sacrifice. The

high priest makes *teshubah* for himself and on our behalf, but today there is no high priest and no intercession. Each must be his own priest and make his own intercession. Before man is the attention of God and behind him is the brutality of history; before him *'Abodah* and behind him the Ten Martyrs.

Yom Kippur is an elaborate dialectical map of human psychology, built not with orderly system, but in the rhythm of happenstance, taking account of recalcitrance, stupidity, inattention, laziness and surrounding all this murky and ordinary human indifference with the great extremities: the prayers of the *Kohen Ha-Gadol,* the tales of the martyrs, the utter abomination of incest and the arrogance of the prophet who would rather die than preach to the Gentiles of Nineveh. We are surrounded by all this grand and treacherous history. Is it any wonder, then, that on Yom Kippur we should confess our miserable finitude before God and still plead for mercy?   [A.A.C.]

THE INNER STRUCTURE OF THE YOM KIPPUR LITURGY

When addressing the history of ethical humanity, we must particularly emphasize the essential singularity of all that is spiritual. More than for any other aspect, we may say that for the long existence of ethical development, mere repetition of a great spiritual constellation is impossible; every truly spiritual achievement, even if it could be duplicated with qualitative accuracy and equal intensity, would still involve new values imbedded with and alongside its pure repetition. An achievement, which, next to its great predecessors, next to the prophetic books and the psalms, is often underestimated as a work of merely synagogal interest, is, I feel, the *maḥzor*[1] of Yom Kippur.

In purely historical terms, the present-day order of prayer of the festival of Atonement can hardly be isolated from the millennial development of the entire liturgy—the idea of the rite as a religious, ethical, and social institution is already outlined in Leviticus—and the whole spirit of the prayerbook is essentially of the Old Testament. Nevertheless, the depth of the inner construction, of the organic articulation and gradation, the strength of the living concretization that made the sequence of prayers express both a highly individual and a societal desire for purification, the decisive way in which the profundity of its central conception is ubiquitously captured and carried out—these make the Yom Kippur liturgy (even apart from all other synagogal poetry) a creative document allied to the greatest achievements of Jewish ethical struggle.

We hardly require the Kabbalistic quotation: "How can one say that the *shin*[2] [letter] encompasses the entire world? Because it is the crucial letter in *Teshubah* [sudden reversal][2] (from the *Sefer Ha-Bahir).*[2] In Yom Kippur and in its concept of *Teshubah* the "Israelite cult reaches its culmination" (we cannot, therefore, agree with Delitzsch[3] in calling this holiday the "Good Friday of the Old Testament").

Whereas historical analyses in the age of humanism concentrated principally on the intellectual form of doctrine to the extent that they forgot deeper biological and racial differentiation, and whereas the modern age often falsely absolutizes racial concepts, the solution for our more limited task assumes that, while spiritual creation is an expression of race and race is a source of accomplishment, the concept of the living race can never be fixed absolutely. It can only, in accordance with its elements, point out that a uniform picture of the world can never be completed, but must always be constructed with deeper and deeper creativity.

Only when the full scope of the historical premise and of the complex material in all its capaciousness (greatly varying in the numerous rites) has been grasped, can we present a more profound and coherent picture of the conception of Yom Kippur.

The word *Teshubah* does not mean "repentance" at all. It literally and expressly signifies only reversal, return to a point of reference. And this basic fact, on which everything focuses, is, for the Day of Atonement, the idea of the oneness and the singularity of its God. For the Old Testament as opposed to Christianity, Spinozism as opposed to the Higher Criticism (and, say, Fichte as opposed to modern natural science), the deepest division is as follows: on the one side, the idea of the absolute eternal remains the primary impulse, the actual object of research, the driving central concept, while for the other loyalty to the mode, meditation, and ascent from the finite describe the basic fact and the basic approach. Yom Kippur is to be understood as a passionate grasping of the world along the first lines.

Only on this basis can the deeper construction of the liturgy become comprehensible. Only in this way can we grasp the peculiar fact that there is no single prayer either at the beginning or in the middle or at the conclusion of this sequence of prayers that constitutes its gripping and emotional culmination—the *Yiḥud-hashem* [unification of the divine name], the full confession to God that marks entrance into *Teshubah* and avowal to act accordingly on the way to *Teshubah.*

Although the *piyyuṭim* [Hebrew liturgical poems] of the *Yoṣer* [the prayers celebrating God, the creator] and the *Shaḥarit-Qerobah* [the first holiday insertions in the morning liturgy] contain a number of supplications and prayers, a closer analysis reveals that a vast and preeminent space is devoted to completely different chants, especially the twelve to eighteen hymns with the invocation *Uvekhen* [and thus], which are typical for the *Ma'amad* [fundamental structure] of all rites and the *Rehitim,* which follow the *Qedushah* [Prayer of Sanctification] and are attributed to Qalonymus of Lucca.[4] All these songs speak repeatedly and emphatically in the wholeness and free splendor of morning, in Biblical and midrashic imagery, about the power of God, "whose power thrones the clouds," "the One and Only," "the Radiant One," "the Judge," "the Unattainable One, . . . who created Leviathan for his own pleasure," "who casts the light around himself like a garment."

Thus begins Yom Kippur. God's power and uniqueness are constantly depicted in ever-new words and images that almost outdo each other. "He Who sustains the world with his arm," "the Deliverer from the womb," "before Whom the pillars of heaven tremble," "even the seraph covers his countenance," "He Who is hallowed by the multitudes, and feared in light-ning," "Who dwells above the songs of praise and passes through the heavens," "He before Whom creatures of ice, snow, and flame cry: Holy!", "He Who bears the universe over the Void," "He Who heaps up the moun-tains in His strength and gives them to drink from his rich stores."

These dithyrambs to God's power determine the basic tone of the first *Qerobah* [series of prayers interpolated into the blessings of the 'amidah, silent devotion] and the despairing accusation against man is correlative and closely connected to them: man is the void, "dressed in shame, a dry stubble, a dusty shard on the ground." It is only the Creator who makes human devotion possible, "the opening of the mouth," the strength for prayer.

> But how can man be pure before Thee, since even the hosts of Heaven are not pure? . . . He is impure. He is impure by heritage, impure as long as he exists, impure with his death. His days are waste, his nights are void, his self-torment is nothing, like a dream upon awaking.[5]

This contrast between God's vastness and man's nothingness is strongest in the morning prayer, and only upon these basic concepts are the *selihot*, the actual supplicatory prayers, constructed. Yet these "expiatory songs" are also filled with a vehement Mediterranean intoxication with God. Hölderlin's words about the Orient apply here, as well. "Like a splendid despot," the East, "with its power and its brilliance, casts its people upon the ground, and before a man has even learned to walk, he must kneel, and before he has even learned to speak, he must pray." How violently disturbing, how fitting for the worship of God is the accusation that Elia bar Shemayah indites: "The beam out of the timber (of man's house) shall testify (against him), and the stone in the wall, it cries it out" [*Adon beshoftokh*].[6] But the crucial matter for us is the fact that this rift between God and man is accompanied by the road to its healing by means of the embracing concept of *teshubah*. In the two *Shaharit Aqedot*[7] the sacrifice of Isaac exhibits what the true overcoming, the absorp-tion in God's command, requires.

"That morning," it says in the first 'aqedah,' "man reflected no more." Abraham "took the slaughtering knife, and the sacrifice was not to be delayed overnight until the morning."[8] Indeed, "the father was joyous for the son, as at a feast, and the son was jubilant in his sacrifice as in betrothal."[9] Thus, these morning *selihot* indicate the goal of the day, *Teshubah,* the return to God after all "reflection."

Outspoken in its most elementary forms, rendered empirical, the same demand for *teshubah* is to be found in the Isaiah *haftarah* [Isaiah 58:5-8], which follows the Torah portion:

> Is it such a fast that I have chosen? A day for a man to afflict his soul? Is it to bow down his head as a bulrush, and to spread sackcloth and ashes under him? Wilt thou call this a fast, and an acceptable day to the Lord? Is not this the fast that I have chosen? To loose the bands of wickedness, to undo the heavy burdens, and to let the oppressed go free, and that ye break every yoke? Is it not to deal thy bread to the hungry, and that thou bring the poor that are cast out to thy house? When thou seest the naked, that thou cover him; and that thou not hide thyself from thine own flesh? Then shall thy light break forth as the morning, and thy health shall spring forth speedily. . .

The *mussaf* prayer ["addition"; the added prayer read on festivals], which follows the elevation on a return of the Torah and extends into the late afternoon, seems at first to relate only to the *Shaharit* hymns to God's might. Indeed, these great and portentous songs seem even weightier, broader, more meridianal, and more heavily charged. Compare, for instance, the song *'Asher 'eymatekha be' ereley 'omen*[10] with its much shorter counterpart in the *Shaharit* or the *Mussaf Qedusha* of the angels with that of the morning prayer. Until the hymns fade into the thought:

> Thy Holiness is also close to thy farness . . . every heart seeks thee and every essence. . . . The hinges of the world, yes, they hang on thy Word. . . . Those who complete themselves only through thy commands, they call out: the Lord is our God. . . . Those who are pressed upon thy heart like a seal, they reply: The Lord is One. . . . Those whom thou hast saved since the womb, call out: The Lord is our God. . . . Those who cling to thee, they answer: 'The Eternal is One.'

The celebration in the *'Abodah* is then inwardly transformed and reaches a climax. The *'Abodah,* literally the "service," contains nothing less than—in a decidedly wider, epic form—the account of the expiation cult in the days of the Temple in ancient Palestine. This has a twofold significance for the procedure of the great prayer order. First: the yearning for atonement. The supplications for inner renewal, which the morning prayer already transferred from the individual to the race, are here made one with the grappling of all past time. This ardent attempt to bring History into our living moment, the totally Jewish involvement of the past in the present (see the *Passover Haggadah:* "In every generation, let each man look upon himself as if he came forth out of Egypt")[11] is particularly plain in the immediacy with which, even today, the high priest's confession of sin is spoken as our very own. Second, however, the *Yidhud Hashem,* the profession to God, the condition and seed of every *Teshubah* has a new and more intense effect in the *'Abodah.*

Seven days before the Feast of Atonement, according to the *'Abodah* of the German ritual, the High Priest had to begin his preparations for the holy day. He isolated himself, was sprinkled with waters of purification and made sacrifice.

> He was joined by the sages and the elders . . . and they adjured him to change nothing of what he had been instructed. At sundown they gave him little food so that his consecration would not be troubled while he slept. . . . He was seized with fear and wept for being suspected of heresy, and they turned aside and wept for suspecting a man whose deeds are not known, for there might be no heresy in his heart. Then the scout upon the watchtower called out: The morning is dawning! And they spanned a linen canopy to conceal the Priest. He undressed, bathed, donned the golden apparel, and slaughtered the daily morning sacrifice.
>
> But then the sacrificial bullock (for the Day of Atonement) stood between the Temple court and the altar, its face towards the east, its head bent towards the south. And he came to it, put his hand on its head, confessing his sins and not concealing them within him.
>
> And he spake thus: Oh God! I have sinned, erred, transgressed before you, I and my house. Oh, by thy Holy Name, forgive the sins, errors, transgressions through which I have sinned, erred, transgressed before you, I and my house, as it is written in the Laws of Moses, thy servant, out of the mouth of thy Glory: For on this day He will expiate you, to purify you of all your sins before the Lord.
>
> When the priests and the people, who were standing in the Temple court, heard the sublime and glorious Name of God come forth in Holiness and Purity from the mouth of the High Priest, they fell down upon their faces and responded: Blessed be the name of his glorious majesty forever and ever.[12]

Only on the Day of Atonement and only by the high priest was the literal Name of God (for which, otherwise, circumlocutions were used) pronounced; even today it is only these passages of the *'Abodah* and the preceding *'Alenu* [the prayer "It is our duty . . ."] that require the people to kneel. Three times the Tetragrammaton, the Name, was called out in three increasingly sublime confessions of sin, first for the high priest and his house, then for the high priest, his house, and all the sons of Aaron, lastly for the whole house of Israel, and the confessions were interrupted by the solemn, heavily rhythmic libations of the altar, the cover of the Ark of the Covenant, and the Holy Veil. When the high priest emerged, visible, from the Holy of Holies, where he had been concealed from the people, it was according to the words of the *'Abodah,* "as when the sun rises over the earth."

Such individual descriptions of the former temple cult occur until well into the *Mussaf Selihot,* always fused with supplications for forgiveness and salvations for the entire people and for the reconstruction of the ancient seat of Zion for the One God, as in the following supplication before the start of the *selihot:*

> Oh, our God, and God of our fathers, give thy glory once again to the ravaged mountain, appear again, let it shine afar, the reflection of thy Temple, renew the chambers of thy hall, cleanse them of all impurity, solidify their splendor and guide the nations to their light. . . . Oh bring them home, the forgotten tribes. Call, whistle, blow them together . . . . and bring them up again . . . . to thy house. As it is written by the hand of thy prophet: For my house shall be a house of prayer for all nations.

All these exuberances are suddenly cut off with the beginning of the *Minhah* prayer. This is certainly the sharpest, most cutting transition in the liturgy of this holy day: the transition from the expansive, splendor-loving *Musaf* to the terse, almost dramatically concentrated and more subjective afternoon prayer [*Minhah*] and subsequent *ne'ilah* prayer of conclusion.

The *Uvekhen* hymns with their violent, joyous, and radiant soaring, their almost pantheistic brightness, have vanished. They only sound briefly in the *Qedushah*. The Torah portion, with which the *Minhah* begins, speaks about the darkest, most secret individual guilt, incest: "Thou shalt not uncover the nakedness of thy father or thy mother, thy son or thy daughter, thy brother or thy sister."[13] Thus, towards the day's end, the service pierces to the darkest drive of every individual. "You shall not commit any of these abominations . . . so that the land shall not vomit you out because of the abomination with which you defile it."

In the succeeding *Haftorah,* the problem of the ethics of each single human being is presented even more rigorously and more penetratingly. With its characteristic sensitivity, the Talmud has destined the prophetic book of Jonah for the afternoon *Haftarah* on Yom Kippur (see Tractate Megillah, 31 b). The Book of Jonah powerfully portrays the confrontation of a sensual desire for happiness and a supraempirical demand; an individual, egotistical enjoyment of drives and a free entrance into the universal mission of humanity. The prophet Jonah wishes, at first—like the ordinary worshipper on Yom Kippur—to flee from God, for the *Teshubah* within himself and from preaching *Teshubah* to the city of Nineveh. And even after the repentance of Nineveh, Jonah is still in ill humor. He consistently seeks his own death, rather than *Teshubah* and the recrudescence of life. Only sensual things retain the power to win him over to life—for example, the shade of the gourd tree—and they deprive him of fully understanding the world, so that God must ask: "Art thou greatly angry for the gourd?" And, after the withering of the gourd, when he wishes once again for death, God speaks the great words:

> . . . Thou hast pity on the gourd, for which Thou hast not labored, neither didst Thou make it grow, which came up in a night, and perished in a night; and should I not have pity on Nineveh, that great city, wherein are more than six

score, a hundred and twenty thousand persons that cannot discern between their right hand and their left hand, and also much cattle?

This sentence poses the basic question: Shall the unconditionally possible exaltation, purification, and interior ascent of a whole human community fail, because of the fatigue of a single trivial human being? Shall *Teshubah,* as it is necessary for all life at all times, be made impossible by the hindrances of the empirical? This, precisely, is the question asked by *minhah* of Yom Kippur.

However, the martyrologies of the *minha selihot*[14] clearly show how far anything empirical must recede before ethical being and fully merge into it. The enormous number of Jewish martyrs gave away their entire reflective existence, their life, not with laments, but freely, merely to retain the ideal, the profession to the one God. Their torments are reckoned up in detail, and through the strength of their victories and the vastness of their ideals, the power of *Teshubah* is pointed out, and at the same time, like Abraham in the *'Aqedah* of his son Isaac, are seen as propitiating God's severity. "They were crushed like a threshold." "The school children were cast like additional victims for the altar, the disciples and their teachers like an expiatory sacrifice for the people." "But we love our God even unto death," they called. Rabbi Akiba's flesh was torn from his body with combs of iron. "Rabbi Hananya ben Teradyon was thrust upon a pyre of green brushwood and his chest was drenched with water to prolong the agony." Rabbi Ishmael was flayed alive.

> And only when they came to the place where the *tefillin* lie, he screamed bitterly to the Creator of his soul. And the seraphim on high cried out in anguish: 'Is this the teaching and its reward? Thou Who are garbed in light, may the enemy blaspheme Thy great and awesome Name?' And a voice replied from heaven: 'If I hear one more word to the contrary, then I shall pour the universe into water and make the earth into a void again. For such is my decision, and they who study the Law shall abide by it.'

Yes, fathers in full devotion slaughtered their sons and women brought their babies. Despite all this, the overall demand, even in the *minhah* prayer, is never focused on mere asceticism, mere martyrdom, or an expiation turned towards the past; everything urges towards the "day for the cultivating of love and friendship, a day for the end of jealousy and strife."[15]

It is true that during the afternoon and evening prayers, laments, repeated throughout the day, recur: "Oh Lord, let my own blood and substance, which I have lost through fasting, serve thee instead of sacrificial fat and blood." "Oh suppress our sin and sink" (it) "in the maelstroms of the sea, in a place where they will never be thought of and never be mentioned again, and never ascend into all eternity." "Help us, God, for the waters seep into our very soul." "On my back, the ploughman ploughed long furrows." "From sea to sea, we wander like a restless bird and nowhere have we found balm for our wounds." But beyond all lamentation, there hovers the call and urge for a true renewal towards a whole, purer, greater, freer life. "Oh Lord, cut away the yoke-straps from the neck of Thy people." "And you, you tribes, you the still redeemed of Israel, o seize upon purity . . . circumcise the hard hearts, make way, clear every obstruction from out the way, make your crookedness clear and straight . . . and get for yourself a heart of innocence."

In some prayers—notably selihot from the time of the Crusades, the time of the worst persecutions of Jews—the thought of revenge still flares up. "Oh God, do not remain silent to my blood, do not remain silent, do not be still towards my foes, seek, demand it from the hand of my destroyers, let the earth cover it nowhere." But beyond all vengeance, the minhah prayer glows with the strongest human desire for purification, the Messianic idea of the Atonement Day of all nations. It is named again at the conclusion of each Tefillah [a Rabbinic term for the silent devotion, the 'amidah] with Isaiah's words: "For my house shall be a house of prayer for all nations," or in the mussaf: "O lead the nations to the light of your re-established Temple," and just as the same thought finally achieves the most poignant expression in the selihah of Mordecai ben Shabbetai:

> Oh Lord, see on the evening of the day, in the terror of night, see your people raise its eyes and pray before you as . . . Isaac once prayed in the field at eventime. . . . O heal the wounds, sprinkle upon them purifying waters at sunset, wash them and cleanse them in the evening. Be as dew for Israel in the evening that it may blossom like a rose.[16]

> Behold its fasting and the castigation of its soul. Seal it into the book of life! For the day is already turning and the shadows of evening are gathering! . . . Thou Holy One, enthroned above songs of praise, behold, the entire people stands before Thee from morning to evening. In the evening, in the morning, and at noon I supplicate before Thee. . . . O give us a sign soon . . . that the day may come that is known to Thee alone; the day that is not the day nor is night in the evening! (The Day of the Messiah, Zechariah 14:7, 14.)

With these thoughts, everything is now prepared for the final and greatest climax of the day; the prayer between day and night, the ne'ilah. This ne'ilah, which functions as a special concluding prayer for the Day of Atonement alone, is the most simple, terse, and concentrated of all the liturgy. The painful and tortured confession, Al-Het, where each letter of the alphabet is the initial letter of two sins, is absent, although during the Shaharit, the Mussaf, and the Minhah it assumed central importance as the great confession of sin. The Qedushah, the praise of Holy God, had been correspondingly very brief.

Everything now concentrates in one plea, one supplication for exaltation, liberation, salvation towards life, salvation towards God: "O Lord, be mindful of us for life, O King, who wishest that we live, seal us into the book of life, for Thy sake, living God." This is no longer a registration in the book of life, as it had been during the earlier prayers; it is now the sealing of the book itself. Everything becomes deeply ardent and utterly intense.

Nearly every liturgical formulation is spoken twice. Deeply affected by the long fasting and the prolonged prayer, the leader of the service speaks the words slowly, and the worshipers repeat them slowly and clearly. All the angels throng to God's throne. They are to speak "even though no angel is pure before Thee." All pleading shall now be of intense ardor.

> Open for us the gate of prayer, Even at the closing of the gate, Even now that the day has declined. When the day declines into sunset, O let us enter Thy gates. O God, we implore thee, forgive us! Pardon and spare us, grant us mercy; Clear us and suppress iniquity.[17]

> It is not because of our own that we plead before thee, but because of thy great mercy. Lord, hear, Lord, forgive, Lord, heed, act, and do not delay for thy own sake, my God. For thy city and thy people are called by thy name.

> Behold, like the clay in the potter's hand, thus are we in Thy hand. According to his will he stretches it, according to his will he makes it narrow. . . .

> Oh look upon the Covenant and . . . not upon the evil inclination.

> Thou shepherd of Israel,

> Oh bend thine ear,

> Answer us from the heights, Lord, answer us.

> For only upon Thee do we lean.

> Oh let us remain thy possession!

Now, for the eighth time, comes the confession of sins, introduced by the ardent *ki 'anu.* "We are thy children, Thou art our Father; We are thy servants, and thou art our Lord. . . . We are thy vineyard, and thou art our keeper," then, with the deeply passionate, sensual image: "We are your faithful and thou art our Beloved."

"Our God and God of our fathers, may our prayer reach to Thee; do not ignore our plea. For we are neither insolent nor obstinate as to say to thee: Lord our God and God of our fathers, we are just and have not sinned. Indeed, we and our fathers have sinned: *Ashamnu:* we are guilty," *bagadnu:* we were cunning, *gazalnu:* we have stolen . . . , we have lied, we have mocked and been angry . . . we were stubborn . . . we strayed and have led others astray." "But Thou art just in all that has come upon us. Thou hast dealt truthfully, but we have acted wickedly." "What are we? What is our life? What is our goodness?

What is our virtue? What our help? What our strength? What can we say to thee? . . . All the heroes are as nothing in thy sight, men of renown as though they did not exist, and the wise as though without knowledge, the intelligent as though they lacked understanding? Most of their deeds are worthless in thy sight, their entire life is a fleeting breath. Man is not far above the beast, for all is vanity. . . ." "But today, exalt us . . . make us strong. . . ."

Herewith, all pleading is exhausted. No higher appeal is possible.

After the final *'Avinu Malkenu* ["Our Father, Our King"], comes the most obvious, most commanding discontinuity, disclosing the most intimate *pathos* of the entire day: the final words of the long day of pleading and fasting, not a supplication and not a prayer. They once more present, hard and strong, the idea of the "goal," the notion of full ideality, the idea of the One God beyond everything human and beyond all supplications, which have long since passed away beneath him and vanished. All mere meditating, all pleading of the day shall finally be vanquished, the *Teshubah* shall finally be realized. "Hear, Oh Israel, the Lord our God, the Lord is One"—thus the leader calls three times before the closed Ark, and the congregation answers with the same words three times. Then, from the leader and the congregation, we hear three times: "Blessed be the Name of his glorious majesty forever and ever." And, finally, seven times, the call of Mount Carmel with which the people once called out to Elijah: "The Lord (alone), He is God." The *shofar* is blown once and the holy day is completed.

Heightened reflection, looking backward and into the present, also completes the process lived through the *Teshubah*. The same depths of passage, strangely enough, must have been struggled through in Spinoza's *Ethics* or in the *Ḥovot Ḥallevavot (Duties of the Heart)* by Baḥya ibn Pakuda: from the knowledge of God's power and uniqueness, as measured by nature, through all experience, to the *'Ahavat 'adonay,* to the *amor dei intellectualis,* or to the full *Yiḥud-hashem* of Yom Kippur.

And the strength, the unfailing power, which the concept of the absolute radiates through every reality here, as in the Prophets and the Psalms, is crucial for us even today. It shows from where we come and directs us toward our true goal; it shows how far far removed that goal is from the "cultural fertilizer," or the *"Esprit-Judentum,"* the "Jews in spirit," or any such like. We would certainly ill serve the greatness of the idea of Yom Kippur if we only retained its fixed and formal contents. It would be an enormous weakness in an awakening and living Judaism to hold rigidly to even its highest historical creations. We must overcome all overemphasis, mere antithesis, any reactivity of Jewish existence. We cannot stubbornly resist the great modifications that our understanding of the universe has experienced even beyond Spinoza—our last historic achievement. We have to experience Christianity, too, and raise the deep Jewishness in Saint Paul. We must be able to grasp the full continuity of world thought, especially after our eternal exile. But our ultimate and most ardent yearning can only be to purify ourselves into this world thought, to fill it totally with the same fervor, with the same unyielding and deeply moved will to life, that once struggled forth in the idea of our Yom Kippur.

15. JEWISH HISTORICAL WRITING

JOSEF MEISL

EDITOR'S INTRODUCTION

JOSEF MEISL (1883–1958), historian and archivist, was born in Brno and served in Jerusalem as director, until his death, of the General Archives for the History of the Jewish People. His essay on "Graetz and National Judaism" appears elsewhere in this anthology. The present essay appeared in *Der Jude* during Jahrgang VI (1921–1922), pp. 283–96.

Is it incorrect to suggest that all historical writing is a venture of self-interpretation? Indeed, unlike psychoanalytic inquiry, where the mechanism of the aphasic unconscious is near at hand and obdurate, the motives to the writing of history appear less opaque. Historiography is interpretive—the same body of documents, memoirs, archival resources will yield contrary results, depending upon the intent of the historian (note Pieter Geyl's demonstration of this phenomenon in his *Napoleon: For and Against,* and his equally fascinating exploration of the historians of the French Revolution). But having said this, one has really said nothing. Or if something appears to have been said the result is, to philistine intellects, yet another proof of the "relativism" of all things, their lack of weight, value, and truthfulness.

The fact that historical writing is tied—not unlike any other work where the imagination must organize, intuit, and persuade—to self-exegesis does not make it the creation of caprice. The unimaginative are not as aware as they might be that the imagination has a rigorous discipline, a regimen of interior argument, a logic that refuses to be subverted. It is often a question of determining the governance of the imagination to decide whether its logic has been coherently observed, but it is rarely the case that a well-made poem or a great novel or an enduring play is constructed without an obsessional drive, a premise of causality, a notion of how persons and events cohere. The principle may be moral persuasion, the *nature morte* of the real, erotic pleasure, contemplation, aesthetic transformation, but however the general form of the imagination, however its intention may escape us, whatever is written out of the imagination is tied to form. The predisposition to imaginative form is lodged deep in the self, but for all its interiority, it is no less objective and real in its consequences than is water drawn from unseen springs and lava molten in the innards of the earth.

This is all by way of proposing some questions for the once-over-lightly reporting of the historiographic process of modern Jewish history that Josef Meisl has supplied. Clearly the writing of Jewish history had to await the first harvest of the emancipation, which enabled Jews to secure access to historical sources available in libraries other than their own. From the time of Josephus until the beginning of Wissenschaft des Judentums, the writing of history was episodic and narrative, concerned less with the preservation of the record than the preservation of the people. The Kabbalistic scansion of the universe is a mode of historical representation but it is not history; for that matter the transmission of tales, great *exempla* of words and persons, the stuff of chronicles and martyrologies, may all be considered as artifacts for the historian. But it may be wondered whether the *theosofia* of the Kabbalists and their reading of Jewish events as part of a divine imaginative scheme ill-served the preservation of the people.

What I write here is intemperately bold and perhaps ill-advised, for it would appear to attack the enterprise of many whom I admire as being more learned and Jewishly sophisticated than I, but there is something trying, even tedious, in Meisl's critique of Graetz or his foot-dragging about Dubnow, or his half-hearted appraisal of Naḥman Krochmal or the many others to whom he makes passing reference. And beyond them, beyond the time out of which Meisl wrote, who has written Jewish history? There have been no further attempts since Dubnow to write a comprehensive and original history of the Jews. Popularizers many and particularists, not a few of considerable grandeur (Wolfson and Gutmann on Jewish philosophy, Yiṣhak Baer, Zvi Ankori, V. Tcherikover on particular periods and settlements of the Diaspora, Yeḥezkel Kaufmann, Jacob Neusner, among others on Biblical and rabbinic Judaism), but not a single one to describe a millennial filament of the Jewish historical experience.

With the exception of one. Gershom Scholem is the single Jewish historian of the past half-century to have imprinted the whole of Jewish experience with the implication and suggestion of his inquiry. Not a single writer on contemporary Judaism, not poets or novelists claiming Jewish sensibility, nor a single intellectual current of modern Judaism has been uninfluenced by Scholem's recovery and parsing of the sources of Jewish mysticism. It is ironic that the whole of the last century, virtually without exception (the exception being Dubnow) was hostile to the mystic tradition, losing no opportunity—witness Graetz, first and foremost—to traduce and betray the sources, to deny their authenticity, relevance, or instruction. The mystics were fantastical, magical, irrational, uncultured, and worse. That is to say, Graetz and his circle could not present Judaism to the scrutiny of Western Europe, in the tongues of European culture, with the refinements of its Enlightenment, if it had to own up to a legacy that included Abulafia, the Sefer Zohar, Sabbatai Ṣevi, Jacob

Frank, the Hasidim, and had he lived, in our own day, Abraham Kook. But more than the abashment of being obliged to acknowledge the historical presence of the mystic and his perceptions was the fact that the great century of German-Jewish historiography was dominated by a philosophic alter ego that spoke for a messianism of reason and the kingdom of ends (Immanuel Kant) and the absolutism of the Idea, which lent to national religion and internal spiritual edification the dignity of a portion in the universal truth of the rational state (Hegel and Germany).

Scholem has no Kant or Hegel. I make no venture about the philosophic matrix out of which his reading of Jewish mysticism may derive its potency and passion, although I believe the sources are present and evident, but I do suggest that the writing of Jewish history as a mode of self-explication, as a means—one among several—of determining the ultimacy and value of existence as a Jew, is clearly present in every historian of Jewish life, whether he is writing from the perspective of Kant and Hegel, Naḥman Krochmal, or Franz Rosenzweig. The center of the imagination is obscure—few dare, as the rabbis warned, for fear of madness against investigating it too closely, but at the core of every body of historical writing is the enterprise of self-illumination and self-persuasion. Why would someone choose to write a history of a community of faith if not to persuade himself to join it once again?   [A.A.C.]

JEWISH HISTORICAL WRITING

1. The Hegelians

The nineteenth century was a turning-point for Jewish historiography. Quite a number of works have been written about the history of the Jews since the Biblical historians and Josephus; however, even if we except the critical talent of Azariah dei Rossi,[1] what remains was shoddy merchandise, and usually even worse. The Jewish Hegelians, congregating in the early nineteenth century at the Verein für Kultur und Wissenschaft,[2] Eduard Gans, Leopold Zunz, Moses Moser (as well as Heinrich Heine, David Friedlaender et al.) first spurred a proper scientific investigation of Judaism. For the members of the Verein, Jewish research was, by its bylaws, a means of getting to know Judaism; when some of the leaders converted to Christianity, the "Science of Judaism" became the imperishable remnant of that pioneering spirit. The chiefly Hegelian influence on this group of scholars is attributable simply to the time and place of their activity, which has a crucial significance for the structuring of Jewish historiography. Points of contact between Hegelian philosophy and Jewish thought were close enough to prompt, say, Naḥman Krochmal, Samuel Hirsch, or Moses Hess, to base their Jewish ideology on Hegel. Hess sought to present Jewish nationalism as the synthesis that Judaism—as the historical religion par excellence—would have to be very receptive to Hegel's philosophy of history with its constant stress on "sacrifice" and "self-sacrifice," whereas Schopenhauer, Hegel's antipode, appears as the out-and-out advocate of an Aryan ideology (that is to say, worship of nature). Spinoza's influence made for various echoes of the Jewish philosophy of religion in Hegel.

Leopold Zunz was no hard-and-fast Hegelian, but he did pay tribute to that fashionable philosophy and it affected his illumination of Judaism. Starting with abuse of rabbinical literature, *Etwas über die rabbinische Literatur (Something about Rabbinic Literature,* 1818),[3] he demanded its investigation from a more elevated perspective, that is, the treatment of

> the literature of a nation as an approach to overall knowledge of its cultural passage through time: at every moment, its essence forms from the given and the accidental, *i.e.* the internal and the external—destiny, climate, mores, religion, and chance intermesh as friends or foes; and, finally, the present unfolds as a necessary consequence of all past phenomena.

Zunz also demanded the application of a threefold critique: the doctrinal, encompassing ideas; the grammatical, referring to language; and the historical, dealing with the history of ideas. In this manner he thought he would attain a more comprehensive and more impartial assessment of Judaism, which he defined as not simply a religion but as the quintessence "of all relationships, peculiarities, and achievements of Jews in regard to religion, philosophy, history, law, literature, civil life, and all human issues." Zunz employs the concept of the "statistics of the human race," which "comprehends the existence of the human race at the present moment in time," an existence that as "the result of an earlier history" possesses "a character of necessity," *Grundlinien zu einer künftigen Statistik der Juden* [*Outlines of a Future Statistics of the Jews*].[4]

Such a statistics must offer three things: first, "the *elements, i.e.* name, country, origin, language, religion, state"; second, "the *principles,* i.e., the interior, more or less contingent on the elements, such as disposition, custom, way of life, occupation, opinion, cultural level"; third, the *results,* i.e., "the relationships, emerging from external history, to the surrounding people, who either serve, rule, or remain neutral." Jewish history, it would follow, has a threefold mission: First, "the element: origin and religion and everything that has developed through history from the one-time language and abode of the community"; second, "the principle: insufficiently attentive to many problems (e.g., the extremely important question of the relationship between the Jewish and the non-Jewish), but in his later works he left out a great deal of his originally more universal plans because of his Hegelian attitude towards a history of ideas. Jewish history (so he explains in his article on the Hispanic place-names in Hebrew-Jewish writings) is a world of ideas:

in part original, insofar as it came from Jewishness, in part peculiar, insofar as it incorporated outside material, at times visible in the life and work of Jews, at times invisible because of the confusion of men led astray and the disturbing fist of external interference.

In keeping with Hegel's overall idea, Zunz differentiates between the history of ideas, i.e., of Judaism, and Jewish history, which is here virtually identical with the notion of external history. The history of ideas has to register the "blows that Judaism suffered from outside as modifying and motivating facts," but its "real plan must be to present the development of Jews and Judaism as occurring in a necessary context and explaining every activity and situation of the Jews." Only the history of Judaism forms "a single and entire history," which cannot be splintered by the variety of events in the various countries where the Jewish nation was scattered. The historian has the task of "presenting an invisible mother-state, religious and political Judaism, and traveling from there through the familiar spaces of the history of nations to the special colonies of Spanish, Polish, and all other Jews." Since all development is rational, there must be very specific reasons as to "where and when an act took place, where an important man lived and thought, where a book was written, and an activity unfolded between certain neighbors and destinies."

Zunz, who incidentally did not confine himself only to theory but also sought to shed light on the history of Judaism in countless fundamental monographs according to the plan just described, was one of the first to attempt applying general philosophical and historical knowledge to the special area of Jewish history, whereby, with no expressly tendentious interpretation, he envisioned a further goal of working toward a moderate reform of Judaism.

Next to Zunz, Naḥman Krochmal was the most crucial advocate of Hegelian thought. His most significant work, *Moreh Nebukhe ha-Zeman*,[5] depends on Maimonides, Kant, and, above all, Hegel, whose philosophy of history Krochmal tried to apply to Judaism. Krochmal analyzes the process of national culture, particularly the question of how a nation, raising itself from the lowest level of civilization, creates its national God and joins the great "treasury of the absolute spirit." In modest contrast to Hegel, who sees the State as the highest expression of the absolute spirit, Krochmal praised as the special strength of Judaism the fact that it had grown beyond the State and that its national culture is not directly tied to a territory. The historical process develops in three phases: growth, flowering, and decay. The national essence resides in the national soul and the national principle is the source of the historical process and the variety of life. The national deity is the concrete symbol of the nation's characteristic mode of being. The national spirit and the national culture are independent of time and space and can enrich all human civilization even after the physical decline of the nation.

Judaism, embodying the spirit of the universal and the absolute, has thus remained undying and was able after its first flowering was terminated by the Babylonian exile to enter upon a new and succeeding period. This second period went through three phases: after the return from the Babylonian exile until Alexander of Macedonia; next, until the death of Salome, the wife of Alexander Yannai; and finally, up to the Bar Kokhba rebellion. Krochmal sees three phases in the third period: first, until the codification of the Mishnah; second, from the start of the Muslim era to Maimonides; third, from the thirteenth century onwards, the beginning of decay and spiritual stagnation. This certainly arguable scheme was, after all, the first to show a development of Hebrew culture in a grand format. Above all, Krochmal's evolutionary method offered a lucid picture of the uninterrupted development of the oral teachings. The ideal connection between the oral teachings and gnosticism, the doctrines conceived as a product of a four-hundred-year historical process, the customs as the result of a continuous development of religious thought from primitive prejudices and unclear strivings until the loftiest mission of the religion, namely "to fathom absolute truth, the primary cause, and everything having effectiveness and reality with it"—all this was presented by Krochmal with deep historical insight in order to show that ceremonial worship was not merely a means of normalizing and sanctifying life, but the true reflection of the national soul, and that the refinement and development of the concept of God accompanied the refinement and deepening of worship, philosophy of religion being superior in its relation to the pure cult religion.

Like Krochmal's synthesis, S. J. Rapoport's[6] analysis had a seminal influence on Jewish historiography. The Hegelian syndrome is palpable in his writings, especially the biographies, if for no other reason than because Rapoport never wrote any of his major works without first renewing contact with Krochmal. The men whose lives he depicted were, in his eyes, bearers of the ideas of Judaism, i.e., an intellectual world that, even in times of spiritual darkness, refused to deny the principle of development, cultivating and preserving free knowledge. Similarly, S. D. Luzzato,[7] despite his different cast of mind and work, did have one thing in common with Krochmal and Rapoport: a conception of the intimacy between literature and life, the influence of ideas on the historical process permeating all his writings. From this vantage point, Luzzato interpreted the contrast between Hellenism and Judaism and Rapoport showed the 'aggada and the piyyut to the fruits of the national spirit and the national soul in that the 'aggada grew on the soil of prophecy and created the piyyut, both being children of the same spirit, products of a culture in which scholarship and poetry, feeling, and logic go together. It was in the same way that Krochmal traced the great phases in the development of Judaism. The application of the principle of evolution and of a philosophical idealism of a Hegelian stripe created the inner ties between these three great luminaries.

The disciples of Hegel exerted lasting influence on even men like Marcus Jost,[8] whose philosophical knowledge was not deep and who adhered to the factual procession of events with an almost chronic dryness. Of even greater importance, however, is the fact that they paved the way for the influence Leopold von Ranke's philosophy of history exerted on Jewish historians.

2. Ranke's Influence on Jewish Historians

Leopold von Ranke's[9] philosophy of history owed its most essential characteristics to Hegelianism, with which nevertheless it did not always maintain connections. The Hegelian doctrine of ideas, as well as the Hegelian understanding of State and individuals, among other concepts, recur in Ranke. His philosophy of history also stemmed from the concept of religion, the highest motive determining the life of nations and "the spirit of the constitution of a country." The concept of religion is intimately linked with the Hegelian notion of ideas, which Ranke used, however, in a different sense. At times he speaks of innate ideas, which dominate the spiritual life of people and are "driving and regulating factors in human spiritual life"; at other times he speaks of ideas as the result of human creation. At times he speaks of the ideas represented by State and Church; at other times, of cultural communities "as objective ideas carrying within themselves the life of the human race." The very concept of ideas in its manifold meanings would appear to be highly useful for Jewish historiography without need of prior sociological investigation or training, if one thinks in the terms of martyrology and the study of the Law. But other basic notions of Ranke's, such as Church and State as representatives of central ideas, the circumscribed position of the individual, as well as his views on the divine force in history, could easily be reinterpreted for Jewish history, so that, from a certain standpoint, one might imagine that Ranke had distilled some of his notions from the history of the Jewish people. The consequences of such an approach and its one-sided effect on Jewish historiography are attested to, quite strikingly, in Graetz's eleven-volume work, *The History of the Jewish People*.

We have to forego a closer analysis of this specific work of Graetz and restrict ourselves to taking stock of Graetz's *oeuvre*. Over all, we would have to say that Graetz surpassed his forerunners in citing, and partly in working upon, the actual material: he rediscovered many sources, shed new light on old ones, applied his intuitions and premonitions to construct contexts and connections, used non-Jewish writers to compare and explain, grandly utilized the Talmud as history, cast up innumerable problems, and showed new pathways to future scholarship. On the other hand, it must be emphasized that Graetz knew only printed matter and few manuscripts, could not avail himself of many crucial sources, and did not realize the significance of the Responsa literature. In its contents, his work merely presents excerpts from the history of the Jews; events are often listed arbitrarily; facts do not cohere; fleeting quirks sneak in; people and things are dealt with helter-skelter, despite attempts to adhere hard and fast to leading movements and ideas.

But all these things are not the issue; the crux of the matter is that the most essential defect of his work lies in its wrong position. This becomes clear in analyzing the programmatic essay *The Structure of Jewish History* [*Die Konstruktion der Jüdischen Geschichte*] (1846),[10] which preceded the publication of Graetz's *History*. In the conflict between Judaism and paganism or spirit and nature, Judaism was active not only negatively, in combatting paganism, but also positively, in developing the idea of God, which became the idea of the State. Judaism thus actually signifies not a religion but a "State law." Monotheism is not the primary principle of Judaism, but a negation requiring the positive completion of the national substance and the State constitution. Thus religion stands on one side, and Church and State stand on the other. This contrast of religion and politics also leads to a division of history into two halves and three periods, each of which in turn contains three phases. Graetz's scheme is as follows:

First Half:

Bearers of history are political citizens, war heroes, kings "with scant traces of religion."

A. First period from earliest times to the Babylonian Exile, a period of "national naturalness: and "the idea of God struggling towards reality."
   1. First phase: Struggle with paganism, the religious element taking second place to the social and political element.
   2. Second phase: Samuel and the school of prophets, with greater importance accorded the religious element, although the social element continues to predominate.
   3. Third phase: Until the division of the kingdom, there is the total victory of the religious element over the social. Messianic prophetism emerges.

Second Half:

The bearers of the history are pious men, sages, teachers, disciples, sectarians.

B. Second period: Until the destruction of the Second Temple, penetration of the religious element and predominance of the spiritual dimension of Judaism.
   1. First phase: The days of Ezra and the men of the Great Assembly; the consolidation of the religion.
   2. Second phase: The victory over Hellenism gave the religious element a new center and a new missionary function.
   3. Third phase: Party splintering—Pharisees, Sadducees, the Sanhedrin, Jesus of Nazareth—Johanan ben Zakkai.

C. Third period: The Diaspora, theoretical speculation, elaboration of the teachings.
   1. First phase: Recording of the writings, origin of the Talmud and the centers of learning.
   2. Second phase: Creation of the 'aggadic commentary "on the philosophical system." Replacement of ecstatic spontaneity with the pro-

saic interpretation of concepts. The study of the sciences is linked to philosophy, Saadia, Jehuda Halevi, Maimonides.

3. Third phase: Since Mendelssohn, unification of State and religion; Judaism as the revealed Law, which, rather than teaching eternal truths, supplies the guiding principle of action.

This whole development, according to Graetz, culminates in

promoting both the national welfare of the entire Jewish people and the individual welfare of those who profess it. This peculiar legislation has its basis in several metaphysical assumptions and in historical facts that should not be abandoned to the past, but must always remain present in the minds of their custodians, so as to exert the necessary influence. To maintain the uninterrupted memory of eternal truths and historical 'givens,' Judaism has a suitable, practical means: the ceremonial law, which consists of actions. Mnemonic depiction and action circumvent the written record and visual presentation of these truths and facts, which texts and pictures would inevitably become images and idols. On the other hand, the mnemonic depiction and action inspire contemplation and investigation because they transcend language and interpretation, and so point to something different and higher. In Judaism, State and Religion are together or, better, one and the same. The demiurge is both legislator and king, the civic is religious as well as sacred, religion is a civil duty. The civic service is divine service. An offense against religion is not punished by the religion (which has no internal means of criminal law) but by the State. By losing its character of a State, Judaism forfeited the civil prerogatives of discipline and anathema; but the religious laws remain in force until the divine being, who publicly decreed them, rescinds them publicly. . . . What is lacking now is a comprehensive principle of Judaism that embraces and unifies all these aspects, a principle valid in all parts of Jewish life, the dogmatic, religious, political, historical parts, and even its stunted shape.

The mission of "Judaism's idea of God" (thus ends Graetz's overview) seems to be in "organizing a religious State constitution that is cognizant of its activity, its purpose, and its connection with the world as a whole."

In this somewhat jejune attempt to grasp the inner dynamics of Jewish history, the author's treatment of the concepts of State, religion, and nation betrays the influence of Hegel and Ranke, an influence more clearly apparent in later formulations of essential Jewish history. We need merely recall the well-known characterization of the Talmudic era in the fourth volume of Graetz's *History*. He tries to reduce events to a formulaic history of thought and endurance—exploring the wandering, thinking and forbearing, studying and suffering—corresponding to his overall concept of the essence of Judaism. Had Ranke written Jewish history, he would scarcely have expressed his view of history any differently. The central importance of Judaism's religious concepts and ideas, the concentration on Talmud, the entire attitude of the Jew towards the spiritual—all this could be explained, without difficulty or artifice, using what Ranke presents on the position of religion in the life of nations and on "ideas." Furthermore, the Jewish historian could easily derive from the history of his own people the things Ranke told us about human progress, and the cultural survival of those nations deprived of political independence. Then too, Jewish history offered him a characteristic example of the "modification of national existence" by Church and State. Ranke's definition of the nation, at least in its original sense, as a group bound by language, religion, and creed to a common descent, matched Graetz's concept of nation, which he advocated in accordance with Jewish reality. And finally, the religious orientation of the two historians, the devout Christian and the devout Jew, had a point of contact in their tracing all historical events to the guiding power of God.

Ranke's conception of the history of States called for a record of wars and peace treaties, of great deeds and great men: in other words the exceptional, the special phenomena. Likewise, Jewish historiography under Graetz's influence focused only on things out of the ordinary. Here, on one hand, the main roles are played by persecutions, expulsions, and deprivations of rights—in short, martyrdom in its various forms; on the other hand is found spiritual heroism, concentrated in literary production. In Graetz, the sum of the manifold life processes of the Jewish people did not form the essential substance of Jewish history; rather, this substance actually appeared under the pressure of political and social phenomena burdening the life of Jews, appeared as both Jewish passivity and a specific Jewish spirituality and intellectuality.

Since this historiography overlooked or simply did not know the facts of economic life, it could present only excerpts from, but not a complete picture of, Jewish history. Any deviation from his scheme was regarded by Graetz as an unnatural revision of the operative principles of Jewish history. Since Graetz saw rabbinism as the straight and natural line of development, he considered the Pharisees more progressive than the Sadducees, rabbinical Judaism higher than Karaite Judaism or the Kabbalah and mysticism until Hasidism, and he rejected the reform movement as a totally unjustifiable aberration. And since East European Judaism in its historical development had gone along paths that were different from what the ideology of the West European historian accepted as normal, he was quite helpless when faced with the countless problems posed by that chapter of Jewish history. Graetz remained on the surface of things because he could never transcend the common philistine attitude of the German Jew who, in his saturated cultural arrogance, looks down on the "Polacks."

However, life won out against all criticism. Graetz has hitherto created the only textbook and reader of Jewish history to influence Jewish life; and the reasons for this cannot be ignored in a critical study of his achievement. Graetz was the first Jewish historian who presented the history of the Jews as the history of a *people* after the post-Exilic era, who contemplated the development of Judaism, with deeply personal sympathy and empathy. Perhaps often, out of national pride, he saw things as an apologist, but he was no longer influenced, as Jost was, by Christian prejudices. This commitment may not always be compatible with scholarliness and truth, it may embellish or disguise facts, it may measure great men and problems by a small and limited yardstick, and make Graetz's Jewish patriot unpopular to many German Jews as the "prototype of the Palestinian" (Hermann Cohen). But none of these things can change the fact that Graetz's *oeuvre,* despite its dubious inner value, represents one of the most significant, and up to now *the* most significant, chapters in Jewish historiography.

3. Recent Systems of History.
Critique of Historical Idealism

After Graetz, everything was still to be done, both in material and methods. Indeed, intensive efforts commenced to gather, complete, and correct the material. Self-sacrificing detailed work accomplished by individual scholars and scholarly enterprises since Graetz have certainly advanced Jewish historiography. On the other hand, no essential progress has been made in method, theoretically or practically. The Graetz school is still fully accepted in the learned world, although the general science of history has developed far beyond Ranke, particularly in political historiography and cultural history.

Political historiography (Droysen, Sybel, Treitschke, et al.) seeks to demonstrate changeable political ideals as issuing from historical events, and to derive from the development of political thinking, principles that, like laws of nature, shall be valid for all times. Especially in its didacticism, this tendency was a relapse into old methods, and obviously its results were bound to be unilateral. Ranke was already acquainted with the concept of cultural history, insofar as he sought a bridge to the present with its national histories through clarification of the state's primacy.

Another reading regards culture differently, namely as the overall notion, with the State as one component—this characterizes the way Jacob Burckhardt[11] and Karl Lamprecht[12] presented cultural history. Burckhardt, by depicting certain events or characterizing leading personalities, sought universal conclusions about contemporary aspirations, goals and methods of politics, or a prototype of society drastically combining the basic features of his age. (Thus he speaks about a heroic, colonial, agonal, Hellenic, piratical, modern man as representing certain cultural conditions.) On the other hand, Lamprecht points out the way to a universal conception by including all utterances of life "in the stream of time." The State is not, as Ranke taught, the all-embracing structure in the life of nations; actually, like art, literature, or science, it is "one of the manifestations of universal social-psychological life." With the assistance of Wundt's psychology,[13] particularly his distinction between individual and social psychology, Lamprecht arrived at his thesis that within a cultural age certain directions of psychological activity demonstrate specific contents of a psychological nature, which uniformly dominate the life of a nation. This psychological life of interconnected people is to be seen as the real bearer of history; development occurs through the continuous surge of new directions, "new psychological orders of life," or "dominants." Not heroic deeds but conditions are the creative energy of individual eras, the cultural ages, which, for German history, Lamprecht divides into five groups (symbolic, typical, conventional, individualistic, subjectivistic) and claims to detect in the histories of other nations as well.

Without going deeper into the questions and countless issues linked to these theories, and without disallowing some exaggerations, especially in Lamprecht's historiography, we would like to establish that Jewish historiography up to now has in no way profited from the advances of universal historiography. Not even Dubnow[14] can be regarded as an exception, unless one is prepared to view political historiography as progress, which could never be unconditionally the case. Dubnow is the model of a political historian. From his national standpoint, from his conception of the Jewish people as "a spiritual individual" and Jewish history as "spiritualized history," he contemplates historical events in order to influence his readers with his political views. No doubt, such historiography can be uncommonly interesting and informative, for Dubnow is a marvelous narrator. No doubt, we will acknowledge the advantages of his presentation over his predecessors: Jost, so anxious and worried about the odium of an overzealous apologist for the Jews; Graetz, filled with the crassest one-sidedness in his conception and—in his cultural arrogance—misunderstanding myriad issues (East European Jewry, mysticism); Philippson,[15] hypnotized by the idol of emancipation. Along with many admirers of Dubnow, we may have to own that it was high time to present the history of the Jews as a nation and less as a religious dilution. Even so, close examination would have to reveal that, for all his permissible freedom of position on historical events, a historian should understand things in their own terms rather than in terms of whether the emancipation or Napoleon's emergence or the materialistic view of history seems "good" for the Jewish nation. It is not so much a question of that much-misused "objectivity" as it is a question of avoiding mistakes such as those that afflicted Treitschke, and of which Dubnow was not entirely free. And more. Dubnow is still too much oriented toward a history of ideas. He does not appear all that far from grasping the significance of economic factors. But his Jewish history is at bottom merely the resultant of political and spiritual components. People, in his view, merely represent ideas, which naturally inhibits psychological penetration; and similarly, conditions are treated according to their significance in the history of ideas. To be sure, Dubnow's concentration on conditions in politics and intellectual life is a step forward, just as was his gift for systematizing, for grasping processes. The tenaciously consistent articulation of facts in the two published volumes of his *History of the Jews in Russia and Poland,* which cover the period from 1789 to 1881, is a first-class systematic achievement, the equivalent of which could only be found in Dubnow's excellent arrangement of antitheses (Ashkenazim-Sephardim, Orthodox-Reform, Hasidim-Misnagdim). Yet for all their strengths, Dubnow's writings can be considered only a modest stage in the development of Jewish historiography, because he failed to avoid two cardinal errors: first, that of seeing things in terms of the history of ideas; second, that of pragmatism, degenerating into a tendentious distortion, which is basically just a variant of Graetz's approach.

Other trends in the interpretation of history found few advocates on Jewish soil, for instance the theocratic (*Dorot ha-Rishonim* [*History and Literature of Israel*] by Isaak Halevy) or the materialistic (e.g., Kautsky's *Are the Jews a Race?* [*Rasse und Judentum*].).[16] But dealing with these absolutely unsuccessful attempts would take us too far afield. We shall, instead, say something about the one-sidedness of historical idealism found in Graetz and ultimately, to some extent, in Dubnow. According to this view, the only forces to realize "ideas" in history are leading personalities. Heroes, not conditions, are the motors of history; what is crucial in history, is that everything can ultimately be reduced to martyrology or literary history. The upshot was a lack of appreciation of the variety of life. Only fragments of historical development could be presented, the more intimate connection of the historical processes linking isolated adjacencies was lost, one noted only individual events, and the interaction of facts was not understood. No course of development was visible. At best, chronology held together the details. At his point, however, we must indicate one factor. The history of the *galut* [exile] does not possess the same kind of continuity as the history of a nation with closed territorial boundaries. Despite the national bonds between all Jews, despite the common tradition and the practical exercise of doctrine, and even though the hegemonic spiritual and intellectual centers within Jewry constituted a focal point around which all Jewish life in a certain sense revolved, we must nevertheless recognize a particularism in Jewish history and choose the fate of Jews in individual countries as starting points, because historical continuity can best be pursued within the borders of a land. These facts explain the kaleidoscope that Jewish history seems to outsiders.

However, these considerations are really secondary. The primary question is: What does Jewish history have to offer? There can only be one answer: the life of the Jewish nation in all its manifestations. And if that is the serious goal, then one can no longer present history as if it had been "made" by a few people in power on the one side, and by literary personalities on the other side. Without denying and disallowing the importance of the personality, the individual will in history, one must fix one's gaze above all on comprehending conditions, including the everyday events that we otherwise ignore, the street and the behavior of nameless people. For all these things form the basis of understanding the unwonted, the exceptional. With infinitely painstaking, selfless labor, we must try and grasp all areas of the life of the people, economy, family, state, language, knowledge, faith, morality, law, art, in their typical manifestations, in order to draw from them developmental tendencies. This task, requiring deep and difficult preliminary work, lies ahead of us. The way to solve it shall be dealt with in a separate essay on the goals and tasks of a modern Jewish historiography.

PART FOUR

THINKERS AND THEOLOGIANS

16. SECULARIZED RELIGION

MAX WIENER

EDITOR'S INTRODUCTION

MAX WIENER (1882–1950), in later life a professor at the Hebrew Union College in Cincinnati, was the author of the important study *Jüdische Religion im Zeitalter der Emanzipation* (1933), *Abraham Geiger and Liberal Judaism,* which was published in 1962 after his death, and many other works. The present essay—a reply to an essay by O. A. H. Schmitz entitled "Desirable and Undesirable Jews" that had appeared in an earlier issue of *Der Jude*—was published in the journal's special issue on "Judaism and Christianity" (May 1927), pp. 10–16.

The restraint, indeed politeness, with which Max Wiener replied to the pretentious racism of Oskar A. H. Schmitz's 1925 essay, which had appeared in the special issue of *Der Jude* devoted to "Anti-Semitism and Jewish Nationality," tells us something not only about the forbearance of Professor Wiener but also about the editorial generosity of *Der Jude*. I cannot imagine a single Jewish publication in the United States that would have been so tolerant. (And indeed, why should one be? The law is tolerant of unpopular opinion—for that purpose the Bill of Rights has its correct legal advocates—but there is no need to turn open the pages of the Jewish press as a forum for the expression of anti-Semitism or its more subtle incubation, anti-Judaism.) Witness the openness of *Der Jude,* however, the moral candor with which (without bracketing reply or comment, other than that supplied by the concluding essay by Martin Buber, which appears next in the present anthology) Otto Flake's *"Antisemitismus und Zukunft"* and Schmitz's *"Wünschenswerte und nicht wünschenswerte Juden"* were published in its pages.

Schmitz's essay, "Desirable and Undesirable Jews," was delivered with slightly more embarrassment and bravado than at first seems possible. Perhaps the editors believed that he had already condemned himself by his various admissions, but it was already 1925 and the National Socialist Party was not quite insignificant, and the other political parties of German reaction were not without strength, as well. Even so, the essay appeared and Max Wiener, four special issues later, in May 1927, replied.

The first word was to Schmitz. His extended criticism of the dangerous potentiality of secular Jews—Jews of pacifist, socialist, Zionist persuasion—

begins with an epigraph from an earlier book of youthful reminiscences that Schmitz had published shortly before. The epigraph speaks of the Jews as being formed by hoary blood lines—those of all the peoples of the ancient world—now commingled with "another purely Aryan stream." These, Schmitz confesses, coexist within him. With Jewish blood on his mother's side (although he does not admit explicitly to having a Jewish mother and I have no wish to research the matter further), from his father he receives a Rhenish Catholic name; his physical appearance, he acknowledges, shows no trace of Jewish characteristics. Schmitz owns up however, admitting Jewish admixture to his Aryan portion and commends to himself thereby a fuller and more rich entelechy for the accident. (Poor Schmitz. We do not know what became of him under the Nürnberg Laws.) The essay indeed begins by celebrating out of racial mixture the complexity of his intelligence and, with a resentment later to be turned against the Jews, complains charmingly that, alas, its author is trapped between "two stools": not conservative enough for his Aryan readers, too reactionary for the Jews.

This biographical profile, presented with an edge of annoyance and an insufferable arrogance, qualifies (and presumably frees) Schmitz to deliver a series of instructions to the Jews about their betrayal of classic religion, their assimilation to Western secularism, their alienation and *ressentiment,* their envy and jealousy of the Gentile, while, had they the courage of their ancient blood, they would not hanker after Gentile things and would desist from corruption of Aryan cultures. It is the Jewish secularists—born of those same weak citizens who condemned Jesus Christ—who now befoul the nests of Europe.

Max Wiener's reply, *Secularized Religion,* is splendid and moving, but no less absolutely beside the point. And yet, I ask myself again and again, how could he have known to speak correctly, to take the scourge to this miserable ideologue?

The tragic fact is that Wiener's reply, though wholly just, is finally wrong, conceding as it does a posture that can never be granted, which is that Jews should be obedient to the norms set for them by Gentile culture. It is not that Wiener ever says this explicitly, but the form of the argument concedes the premise; that is, he replies to Schmitz without repudiating the ground from which the attack is launched. Schmitz's contention is that the modern Jew, secularized, is cut off from the ancient religious roots that validate his existence. Without religion, the Jew is nothing; by implication, however, he is indeed something—a danger to the Aryan Christian. Wiener's reply is to mystify further the Jewish presence, to contend that the Jew is always, in his depths, ineluctably tied to a moral imperative, to the transformation of the social order, to a prophetic mission. In effect, Wiener's reply is that however apparently secularized (presumably he takes it that the attack is levelled principally against the eroding influence of the Jewish reformers, the scholars of *Wissenschaft,* and the antiorthodox), even the secular Jew is a bearer of religious tradition. It is a hopeless rhetoric with which to respond, for it concedes the relevancy of the attack by granting that all Jews, to be Jews, must be religious. Such a premise is defensible, indeed arguable from the inside, but is wholly without merit when presented as critique from the Gentile world. This is only to say that the Gentile, from whatever religion or culture he comes, cannot but regard Judaism and the Jewish people as a sociological phenomenon, a contingent presence. Only for the Jew is the Jew necessary, and hence the discrimination of the natural historical presence of the Jew (his life among the nations, impinging on their world, obliging conscience, duty, participation in a whole of which he is but a small part) and his supernatural vocation (his eternal life with God, obliging fulfillment of commandments, and holy action on behalf of a whole, which he completely fills) is an internal judgment, completely unavailable and indeed meaningless to the non-Jew. Unfortunately this distinction is not one that Wiener was prepared to make. As a result his reply to Schmitz, while true, misses the mark. It does reveal, however, something about the faulty form of most Jewish-Gentile disputation.

[A.A.C.]

SECULARIZED RELIGION

The efficacy of religion begins with God's revelation to man. It lives in the spirit whose roots in the transcendent, in the divine, are the basis of its terrestrial, worldly existence. It lives there all the more strongly, the more deeply man feels the connection between his piety and the traditional evidence of divine fulfillment in the past, of divine illumination, of the heroic time of religion, when revelation conspicuously poured forth upon holy men and saints. Tradition—the minted form of religious thought and feeling—remains productive so long as it holds together and supports the strength of a person in whom it swells, as in a vessel appropriate to its particular existence.

We who belong to the sphere of faith variously deriving from Judaism are inwardly familiar, emotionally and intuitively intimate, only with a religiosity that, transmitted through the ages to our parents or grandparents as a "positive" tradition, presented religious content in the more-or-less clearly defined form of a creed or concrete doctrine or circumscribed life. For several generations now, we—both Western Christianity and Judaism—have been in the process of loosening or even fully undoing those old ties. No one can tell where or how this process will end. None can tell whether religion will survive religions, whether it will remain comprehensible when the traditional legacy of thoughts, moods, impulses, and youthful memories that have been received as living, effectual things have passed away. It seems to me that the truly religious in religion, that which establishes an enigmatic connection (but one felt to be absolutely real) with a holy foundation of the world and with a providence that gives our personal life a meaning, will ultimately vanish if we no longer find inner contact with the great, now historical, life-worlds of faith. Metaphysical or mystical yearning can scarcely create a new religion. Those historical phenomena had such an enormous impact because, touching the innermost part of individuals, they produced effects upon the community of an unparalleled scope. Yet it is inconceivable that a "free religiosity" or any philosophical or theosophical surrogate could wield such power. Whether the West declines or not, a new religion with even the slightest semblance of what has been called "religion" for a good three thousand years will not come for any foreseeable future.

But not everything in religion is religion itself. One has only to look at the logical process by which religion has always related to the cultural content of the minds subject to its sway. Karl Marx, explaining religion and all ideology of *Weltanschauung* as mere reflections of economic reality, certainly overlooks the independent power and autonomy of religious instinct, the main thing from the viewpoint of its essence. Still, Marx is right on one point: there is no assignable, inherent content in the religious. Such content must be drawn from lived reality to nourish the function that consecrates the experience of highest values by apprehending them as a symbolic expression of incomprehensible, eternally mysterious divine being. All religion claims to reveal something transcendent, but all transcendence manifests itself and finds fulfillment in life experienced on earth. And when God, the Holy, is at the same time the Good, the perfectly Good, that is because goodness, love flowing from man to man, is felt to be the highest value in human relationships. Religious acosmism never actually takes a last step toward unconditional negation and "unselfing" of existence. The significance of mysticism lies not in the silence of the ecstatic; despite painful awakening to the world, it lies precisely in that peculiar waking *in* the world. Religion adds nothing to the cultural substance, however, by taking it over, by not permitting any adiaphorism, religion permeates everything with its omnipresence, becomes a world-view and a world-feeling in one. Reaching beyond these things and encompassing them, it remains the awareness of a dark basis of God, who is never fully known through or by His world.

The discussion began with the Christian antithesis of Christianity (grace) versus Judaism (Law). We can let this stand as an antithesis, although from a Jewish viewpoint the Law was a pure act of divine grace, and countless Jewish blessings thank God because "He made us holy with his commandments." Yet we are not dealing, at least in Schmitz, with Judaism and Christianity as two religions that, operating in their full original vitality, seized hold of two groups of believers, for Schmitz addresses not the devout but the irreligious Jew. Thus, we are comparing Christian belief to Jewish non-belief. Schmitz is judging the irreligious Jew from the standpoint of the devout Christian. If we wish to enter upon this difficult basis for a discussion (and we would like to try), then all we can do, obviously, is test what traces of conceptual, emotional, and voluntary impulses the Jewish religion inculcated in those children of the Jewish tribe who are characterized as "irreligious," and then see to what extent the Jewish religion took lasting possession of those impulses. Thus we wish to examine the Jewish religious spirit in secularized form, as detached as possible from the awareness of revelation, in a pure return to the world. How do Jewish eyes see these Jewish people, whom Schmitz depicts as essentially a product of resentment?

What are the worldly, the intra- and interhuman forces that took hold of the religion in the original, the Old Testament spirit of Judaism, consecrating and elevating it by directing it towards the godly center. The Law, which motivates and dominates from the very outset, from the very beginnings (accessible to us) of Jewish faith in thinking and acting, has as its correlative the faith in a human willpower that is willed by God. It is impossible to overlook the great, even decisive position in the very earliest sources accorded to *ratio*, to discerning cognition. God's thoughts are not man's thoughts and God's ways are not man's ways, but the otherness is certainly meant in a quantitative rather than qualitative sense, and the unattainability of the ideal does not cripple the strength but actually spurs it on to unceasing verification. The Law thus becomes the source of an exertion of the will to the absolute, and the Prophets (whatever their attitude toward the ceremonial and ritual substance of the Torah) become the most passionate men of will, the most fanatic revolutionaries and demagogues in history. This formal character in the religious substance, the ardent will for realization, the completely action-oriented faith in the possibility of change and improvement, the possibility of personal return and strength of obedience of the Law—all these things are the backbone of this religiosity. Its premise, freedom, is the essence of Jewish humanity. All ethical pessimism, with which the Jewish religious writings are also full, is of an empirical and not metaphysical nature. All transcendental belief, which begins, at the end of the Old Testament era, as a reaction of the individual awareness of validation, a reaction to the naïveté of collective thinking, remains an integral component of Jewish piety. Such transcendental belief never uproots the meaning of the earthly, the place of God-given validation of the will, which, in the sense of the German idealist, remains "the perceptible material aspect of our duty" [Kant]. This action is sacred because God commanded it and, by commanding it, consecrated it to mankind. It is the essence of man as God wants him to be. Man's grace (he has no "right" before God) is that he may and shall fulfill the Law.

Law is everything, both ceremonial and love of others. We Jews believe about ourselves that the commandment of realization, of fulfillment, is the supreme Law. We believe that our inwardness is true only when it is real and operative. We do not doubt that those who know themselves to be in the blissful possession of grace, know no higher good, cannot know a higher good. But we have been brought up for three thousand years to see the meaning of our life, and of all human life, in the fulfillment of commandments, in realization with utmost strength. And the average Jew was always more of a Jew (this, too, a fruit of his education by the Law) than the average Christian ever was or is a Christian.

The Jewish religion is not the only religion of the Law. In practical terms, Puritanism, with its essential idea of validation, comes to the same result. Schmitz himself is made aware that for Jews to be accepted into a supposedly class-oriented England they had merely to be *gentlemen*. But when the Jews, after several centuries of expulsion, came back to England, their resettlement was made easier by the fact that, at that time, a predominating Puritanism, with its strong Old Testament orientation, found something in the religious spirit of Judaism that it felt to be akin to its own views. We are able to accept Max Weber's idea that Puritanism was the foremost component in shaping the modern Anglo-Saxon, that the secularization of religion led to the inward-oriented asceticism that, originally for religious reasons, gave rise to an utterly potent worldly and world-interested energy. Religion is here ultimately re-turned to moralism, and its evaluations remain in effect even when its original impulses have dried up or completely died out. That is certainly a sharp contrast to Lutheranism.

The modern, the "irreligious" Jew has dropped the "Law." The *whole* Law? No! Such is a Paulinian effect when St. Paul leveled worship and ethos and turned "thou shalt" into a grace-originating "thou must." The modern Jew (and such strivings are quite earnestly at home in the sphere of Jewish religiosity) has continued only the rationalism within the Law, a rationalism that told prophets and psalmists to reject sacrifice and to found their lives on the passionately apprehended commandments of justice and brotherly love. Why do Jewish socialists and revolutionaries care about the lives of German workers? A sense of justice and law, of human dignity and fraternity! Claptrap? We Jews have passed through a school that for hundreds of generations has taught us that ideas are proven only in deeds and that a man's authenticity and truth are proven only in the will for action. And we Jews believe in all those values, just as we are deeply skeptical of the faith that fails to do all it can to fulfill itself. Here *we* are the naïve ones, the babies, the superficial fools. It certainly is not true that the Jewish search for a better world, for social revolution, for pacifist ends and the reorganization of humanity stems from primarily egotistical motives, be they motives of group solidarity for the sake of improving the lot of our people, or motives of hatred and revenge against a master-caste, or even tendencies of personal ambition, vanity, the lust for self-aggrandizement at any price. A heritage of three millennia has left a naïve faith deep in the Jew, a belief that God's will and work in the world can ultimately be rationally understood and are humanly enforceable.

The Old Testament devised the doctrine that man owes God absolute obedience in following His will as revealed in the Law; the Old Testament has thus become the model of all religious passion. The mold it contained has never been destroyed; it has become the prototype of the Jew. We see it even where it has long been drained of the original substance of the Law: the power of the will of the Biblical God persists as a legacy even in the last apostate descendant of the people of the Bible.

It has been frequently observed that the very Jew who has been estranged from the faith of his fathers finds a substitute for religion by doing works of charity and brotherly love, and the scope and energy of these works and his personal commitment fulfill him totally. Whoever knows such people cannot overlook a very specific dimension of their actions. These actions can be likened neither to an inward sentimental reaction nor to the social effectiveness of voluntary welfare work, nor can they be regarded as deriving from the religious commandment to love thy neighbor. They can only be understood as a surrogate for religion, occurring in this form only among Jews: a strong, hard will to sacrifice, to help others. And this will shapes the Jew alienated from his original religiosity, forming him into that well-known prototype of sobriety and warmheartedness, of theoretical skepticism and unmediated love of humanity and its real cares. Jewish doubt has nothing to do with religion or the lack of it; it is the fruit of the advanced age of a total intellectual formation, which only Jewish history has experienced as stretching across the full breadth of a group.

The very opposite of what Schmitz claims is true: If within the system of a Jew we dismantle the conscious relationship to the religious, then what remains is an ethical one-sideness of astonishing naïveté, a faith—unfathomable to the Lutheran Christian—in the possibility of bettering the world. The genuine tendencies of the European enlightenment have always operated in the religious Jew, and they accompany the Jew who "has lost his faith" as his most powerful component. That is a deeply ineluctable fate. We can desire no other, for inherent within us is desire, the straining of the self to form the world, to shape human community; the "superstition" of freedom springs from our innermost core. A break appears at some point in every "Jewish mechanism." Even Marx—who was, incidentally, a product of Christian upbringing, which shows that childhood baptism does not necessarily lead to success in Schmitz's sense of the word—even Marx, so frequently tongue-lashed, gave self-will a broad place, a decisive function in his theory of society.

The German people had only *one* revolution, Luther's deed, a conservative revolution, a work leading, in its deepest thrust, to quietism. During the past three hundred years, the German people has conceived for the rest of the world the greatest thoughts, but it has never generated enough willpower for fateful decisions. The greatest nation in Europe (Russia cannot be included here) has always been controlled from the outside in all major turning points of its social and political history. The reasons are surely myriad, but was not the most crucial reason the fact that for the German an independent, free action is basically a thing of guilt, that introspection is everything for him? That, too, is destiny. We honor it even though we cannot accept it.

17. PHARISAISM
MARTIN BUBER

EDITOR'S INTRODUCTION

MARTIN BUBER (1878–1965) was, as has been noted else-
where in this volume, the founder of *Der Jude* in 1916 and its editor until
1925. The present essay, as Buber notes in his opening lines, was besought by
the editorial board to comment upon the material that appeared in the first
Sonderheft of 1925 on "Germany and Jewish Nationality," the last issue of
Der Jude as a monthly periodical. It appeared on pp. 123–31.

Buber concedes nothing. There was in him a singular courage,
a precision of tone and clarity that make his polemical apologia of unparalleled accuracy and correctness. His ability to contest with Christian theologians, German nationalists, racists, and anti-Semites, the muddled and half-
baked of any tradition (including his own), stemmed in the greatest measure
from the breadth and charity of his information. He knew not only Hebrew
scripture and commentary, Jewish history and literature, but knew quite as
profoundly the history of Christian argument from the Gospels to his own day.
But it was not only a matter of information. It was the charity of his sensibility
that enabled his polemics to achieve such credible ferocity. It could not be
said of Buber (although it would have pleased certain Jewish readers to say it)
that he despised Jesus of Nazareth or had contempt for Paul of Tarsus. Quite to
the contrary: they were for him also bearers of the Word. It was this capaciousness, a willingness to entertain the contrarieties of Jewish existence (the
dialectic of those who remain within its world as well as those who pierced its
borders and departed) that gave to his replies to the hostile critics of Judaism to
whom *Der Jude* had opened its pages (in its special issue on "Germany and
Jewish Nationality") such power and persuasiveness.

Each of the opponents—Flake, Schmitz, Michel—had in the course of
his respective essay made various references to that Christian bugbear, the
Pharisees. The Pharisees had been for centuries of Christian anti-Judaism, the
emblem of enmity. It could not be expected that Christians would read the
Gospels critically, recognizing differentia between the representation of the
Pharisaic party or the composition of the Sanhedrin or the nature of Jewish-
Roman complicity in the crucifixion, if the Gospels were to be read with a
view to their harmonization rather than as discrete, separate, temporally
distinct reports of the events of the life and death of Jesus. The fact that Mark
was considerably closer to the events and reveals a greater familiarity with
contemporaneous Pharisaic sources—while Matthew and Luke, and most

certainly John, have already incorporated into their narration the animus that elevates history into *mythos*—is ignored in the texts of Flake and Schmitz. Buber corrects, chides, and interprets. The Pharisees who emerge are not merely reconciled to the sentiment of Jesus; such a thing would hardly differ from Montefiore's undertaking of reabsorption, making of Jesus merely an errant son of the Pharisees, acceptable when he is indistinguishable from its teachings and misinformed, misguided, mistaken when he diverges. Enough of such. There is too much at stake to treat these matters as if the only point at issue were the coherence of skin and surface.

The interpretation of the Pharisaic reality makes for observations familiar to any student of rabbinic literature, persuasively clarifying the positions of his opponents. There are several novelties, however, that should be singled out as particularly noteworthy. In his rejoinder to Michel's assertion that the Pharisees had "established themselves and their relationship to God as codex," that is, as something frozen and congealed, Buber incorporates the observation that quite the contrary, it is "present-day orthodoxy" that is fixed into an "altogether neo-Sadducaean structure, except that the Sadducaean sanctuary of the Bible has become a sanctuary encompassing the entire Talmudic *halakhah*." This familiar stricture of Buber against the normative *halakhic* tradition, departing as it does from his conviction that the dialectic tension between the living tradition and the Word of God has disappeared, remains as strenuous an objection now as it was then. This is only to say, modestly, that I agree with it. But it is also an anachronistic criticism since, as Buber recognizes in the same text, there is no possibility of revising Pharisaism—indeed, he acknowledges that it would be pointless to do so. His answer to this question is offered elsewhere, in *I and Thou* and *Between Man and Man*.

The most fascinating attack against Judaism, one hitherto unfamiliar to me, is that devised by Michel, who contends that Judaism is defective to the extent that it is always "struggling impiously against death, in contrast to the 'secret love of death' inherent in the German nature." To this assault—Wagnerian in its complexion—Buber rises with sovereign irony, describing the will to life and endurance in all its nobility and pathos. To be in awe of death, Michel suggests, is to be un-Jewish, and thus any Jew shaken before death is no longer Jewish. "But does he mean," Buber replies, "both things (viz., the people before its extinction and the individual before his death) in regard to Germans? Where and when in history has German peoplehood not struggled against the death of the people? Or, for that matter, any people before its hour has struck? And who would take it upon himself to see the world clock striking that hour for Judaism?"   [A.A.C.]

PHARISAISM

1

Throughout the articles for this issue,[1] which the editorial board of *Der Jude* has made available to me, I found repeatedly the words "Pharisee," "Pharisaic," "Pharisaism." They refer both to a historical category and to one (not *the*, to be sure, but *one*) essential feature of Jews and Judaism. Yet the usages employed reflect so many erroneous and misleading elements that, having been asked by the board to write about any of the topics discussed in the contributions, I have decided upon this, since I regard its clarification as extremely crucial. After all, by using the word in this way, the authors have joined the ranks formed by the evangelists[2] which, in their procession through the ages, are more of an issue to Jews than the whole phalanx of the "anti-Semites." But not merely to Jews. The few indications of truth that I can offer here work for their part toward a historically momentous correction.

2

To begin with, let us establish a few facts.

In one article, written by Oskar A. H. Schmitz,[3] "Pharisaism" is called an obstacle to Jews. The writer adds by way of explanation: "I do not mean this word in today's morally pejorative usage, but in the Old Testament sense." Since the Old and the New Testaments (the latter, after all, established the "morally pejorative usage") cannot be confused, the opinion must be that the word *Pharisee* occurs in the Old Testament. If not, how could it have an Old Testament sense? And indeed, a further claim is made that this "evil demon" exists "in the Old Testament." Since I cannot avoid this humorous situation, it must be established at the outset that the name, first appearing after the Maccabean wars, does not occur in the Old Testament. Neither does the phenomenon.

3

No matter, replies the author, if only we concede that Pharisaism was "always opposed to worldly Sadduceeism."

But this is no more true than the "Old Testament sense," merely more imprecise, and is therefore not to be dealt with by establishing a few facts. We now have to ask "what this really is."

The worldly Sadducees and, therefore, the spiritual Pharisees!

Yet the fact remains that those worldly Sadducees were the party of the priests (whether or not their name is to be interpreted as followers of the "Sons of Zadok," the Solomonic forebears of the priestly dynasty); and that these spiritual Pharisees fought against the Hasmonaean dynasty mainly because they, from their view of the past and the future, had to oppose the priestly monarchy of this dynasty, much as Dante had to oppose the secular power of the Pope.

I cannot understand on what basis the author maintains that they "recommended that Pompey destroy the independent Jewish monarchy of the Hasmonaeans." Josephus, the only chronicler of this incident, tells us only that when the two hostile Hasmonaean brothers defended their claims to the throne before Pompey, "the people," more properly "the nation" *(ethnos),* being discontent with the royal rule, spoke out against both of them.

4

But did not the Pharisees, in contrast to the Sadducees, advocate the viewpoint of the "rigid Law"?

The reverse claim would be closer to the truth.

The Sadducees declared the written Torah to be binding—only the Torah, and that with relentless severity. The Pharisees, however, saw in the written Torah only the kernel of a living tradition, which may have been intended originally as nothing other than the assumption of what was already given by oral tradition; but which, in reality, spoke anew to each new situation in each new generation. And this speaking had to be legitimized by a link with tradition, but expanded, modified, even transformed the existence of that tradition. For the Sadducees, the legal needs of a new situation required priestly regulations that did not have to conform to the law derived from God's word. For the Pharisees, the latter was all that counted, for God's word expressed its meaning in every gathering of those competent to interpret it, expressed it with a force superior to that of celestial voices. Thus, the Sadducees tore the Law dwelling in sacred history and in the sacred Book from the living moment and thereby removed the Law from the path of men. In so doing, they turned against the dominion of the living Spirit, which has, after all, always testified through human mouths. The Pharisees, on the other hand, by daring to "interpret" the Scriptural word, gave it a place in world events. Precisely because their interpretation was ultimately more faithful to changeable and changing life; precisely because they interpreted the rigid letter in the name of God, in order to cope with streaming reality, they served Him, who does not wish to have His manifestation encapsulated, but who, like the work of His creation, "daily renews" His revelation.

5

Yet just what could Otto Flake mean when he says, in another essay in this issue, that "the Pharisee as a human type and the pure man [Jesus], moved by the suffering of the people, clashed in an unforgettable tragedy?"[4]

In what conceivable sense could the Pharisee (naturally not simply any

Pharisee, but one of the leaders) be justifiably characterized as not "pure" or not "moved by the suffering of the people?"

First of all, let us establish a few more facts, not minor or casual facts, but crucial ones.

Flake starts with the usual assumption that Jesus was "killed by the Pharisees." Indeed, he goes so far as to say that if that were not the case "the figure of Christ would lose its idea and its meaning." But, really, only a false idea and a false meaning, thereby gaining a proper idea and a proper meaning! In any event: Jesus was not killed by the Pharisees. Whatever share the Jews may have had in condemning Jesus, one thing is certain: in the highest Jewish authority exercising legal power, the Sanhedrin, the Pharisees of that time were a minority—"*homines novi,* intruders in an area not really their own," for "the actual place of their dominion was the school and life, not the Sanhedrin" (Wellhausen)—and a popular and anti-Roman minority at that, in opposition to the opportunistic aristocracy of priests. And indeed, even the Gospels, when listing those involved in the proceedings against Jesus, name only priests, only Sadducees.

However, the New Testament offers us more than this negative evidence; it also tells how a leading Pharisee behaved in an analogous situation (Acts 5:34 ff.). When, shortly after Jesus's death, "the high priest and all who were with him, the sect of the Sadducees," had the apostles arrested and brought to trial, "then stood there up one in the council, a Pharisee, named Gamaliel" (the grandson of Hillel)

> in reputation among all the people . . . and said unto them: . . . Refrain from these men, and let them alone; for if this counsel or this work be of men, it will come to nought: But if it be of God, ye cannot overthrow it; lest haply ye be found even to fight against God.

This is the same attitude and the same faith evinced by the *Sayings of the Fathers* [*Pirqe 'Abot*] (5:17): "Every factioning that takes place for the sake of God will ultimately endure, and each one that does not take place for the sake of God will ultimately not endure." (Likewise, compare *Pirqe 'Abot* 4:11, as well as *'Abot de Rabbi Natan* 40 and 46, where "factioning" is replaced by "gathering.")[5] This is the genuine Pharisaic attitude and the genuine Pharisaic faith.[6]

How, then, can anyone claim that a man of this attitude and this faith could have been opposed by Jesus as the "pure man moved by the sufferings of the people?" Both were truly of the same breed, and whatever they may have said against one another, they could not ever, in all eternity, be alienated from one another. "Be perfect as your Father in Heaven is perfect," is Jesus' word, combined from two passages in the Old Testament (Leviticus 11:45 and 19:2; Deuteronomy 18:13). And the word of the Pharisees, somewhat closer to the same passage in Leviticus (cf. Sifra on *Leviticus* 11:45): "As I am holy, so shall ye be holy; as I am separated, so shall ye be separated." Separated, *Perushim*, Pharisees. Separated—not divorced from the life of the people, but, precisely in the image of God, whose immaculate glory "dwells amidst their impurities," they are at once devoted and undefiled. Just as when they say that God bears sorrow for His people, enduring all the woe of the nation and all the suffering of the masses in the receptive soul.

What then is the difference between Jesus and the Pharisees?

Three levels must be distinguished:

The uppermost: A reworking of reality by the authors of the Gospels, who are, after all, fighting Pharisaic Jewry for its rejection of the Christian doctrine. A particularly obvious example: the story of the Pharisee who asks Jesus which is the highest commandment. Jesus replies with the words from the Old Testament about loving God (Deuteronomy 6:5) and one's neighbor (Leviticus 19:18). In the unquestionably oldest text, Mark, the Pharisee asks earnestly and receives Jesus' answer earnestly, strengthening it with his own answer, to which Jesus rejoins that he is not far from the Kingdom of God. However, the two other synoptists have the Pharisee speak insidiously in order to "tempt" Jesus, and in the conversation that follows, their replies have been sundered from union in the sign of the divine word.

The second level: Jesus' chiding of the hypocritical Pharisees is admittedly not the consequence of any textual revision. On the contrary, what the Pharisees themselves say in the Talmud (*Yerushalmi Berakhot* 9:5; *Babli Sotah* fol. 22 b), in image-filled irony, about the five hypocritical classes of Pharisees, about the "tinged ones," shows a passion for self-purification no less intense than Jesus' passion for purification. Here, we do not have the pure man standing against the others; instead, the danger threatening the man devoted to the Law from the perversion of motive and abatement of spiritual intention is recognized and characterized in both places. However, the Pharisee carefully distinguishes truth and falsehood, authenticity and disguise, while Jesus, struggling from a more external position, omits such care and seems to include the whole human race in one anathema, as if all were hypocrites.

But then the third, the most inward level: here there is truly an opposition, the sight of which ought to be preserved from any obscuring. We have only to perceive clearly what is at stake.

I have already said: The Pharisees place the Law in the living tradition, which by interpreting it, modifies it, whereas the Sadducees tear open an insuperable chasm between the Law and life. Now what is Jesus' position on the Law?

He rejects the Sadducaean dichotomy between There and Here, between the Revelation at Mount Sinai and the living moment; but he does not, like the Pharisee, in order to find a unification of both, enter the situation of Now. Instead, he wishes to go even further back than the Sadducee. Sinai is not enough for him. He wants to enter the cloud over the mountain, the cloud

from which the voice resounds. He wants to penetrate to the ultimate intention of God, the ultimate absoluteness of the Law, the way it was before its
refraction into the human. He wants to "fulfill" the Law, that is to say, to
invoke its original fullness and make it real. The fact that the people will not be
able to breathe within the original purity any better now than then has as little
effect on him as the sense of how the nations on whom his doctrine will be
imposed will manage to create the semblance of his imitation only by tearing
open a far deeper gap than the Sadducaean gap, a gap between supposed and
actual life, i.e., by sanctioning the contradiction.

This does not hold for the Pharisees. They want reality—not just any reality,
but *the* reality from the Word. They want life—not just any life, but life in the
Presence. They want the People, the People of God, working out of, and living
in terms of, that People. And thus, they have to want the refraction, they have
to content themselves with staying here below, beneath the cloud. The
Pharisees are the people of a holy renunciation.

Jesus says (Mark 2:27): "The Sabbath was made for man, not man for the
Sabbath." With an extracanonical but apparently genuine verse (*Codex
Bezae* to Luke 6:4), which he applies to a man working on the Sabbath, he
says: "Man, if thou knowest what thou dost then thou art blessed; but if thou
knowest not what thou dost, thou art accursed and a violator of the Law." The
Pharisees, mindful that the Sabbath comes from Creation, cannot say it was
made for man; however, they do say (*Yoma* 85b; *Mekhilta* to Exodus 31:14):
"The Sabbath was given to you, not ye to the Sabbath." This they employ to
mean that it is our obligation to enable you to keep God's Sabbath as men.

6

It is therefore incorrect to say, as Wilhelm Michel puts it, that Pharisaic Jews
established themselves and their relationship to God in a codex.[7] Actually,
Rabbinical Judaism became untrue to the Pharisaic form of life to the extent
that it shifted the tradition from the state of continuous corrective discussion,
of continuous opposition with its crystallizationlike transition to that of cooperation, i.e., of an outright post-Prophetic spiritual liveliness not unrelated to
inspiration (and that is the true nature of Talmudic existence). The shift was to
a state of closed validity, unfaithful to the Pharisaic form of life. Present-day
Western orthodoxy is altogether a neo-Sadducaean structure, except that the
Sadducaean sanctuary of the Bible has become a sanctuary encompassing the
entire Talmudic *Halakhah*.

Thus, when Schmitz asserts that the Pharisee actively negates the world,
making sure that as little as possible takes shape, we must counter that this is
not merely an erroneous assertion, but something more remarkable, the exact
opposite of the truth. The Pharisee is the man who makes sure of nothing else
but to have the Word manifest in all things; the man who, not merely with
some, but with all manifestations of his life, actively affirms the world as God's

world. And it was not the predominance but the perishing of Pharisaism that was prejudicial to Judaism. It would, certainly, be senseless to renew Pharisaism (it is no longer relevant and we have other things to reckon with), but denying the former would mean closing ourselves off from the latter.

The most dubious aspect of Schmitz's altogether inadequately substantiated exposition (I would rather not go into frivolous phrases such as the one about "Pharisaic class-hatred") is that he doesn't even shrink from betaking himself to the area of Messianic faith. Here he manages to report that the Pharisee is "to be sure, the bearer of the Messianic hope, but simultaneously the guard who makes sure that no Messiah shall come," for "the Messiah must remain unreal."[8] That, evidently, is why the Talmud interprets every Messianic soothsaying of the Prophets in terms of its very concrete, earthly, "livable," content; that is why it always makes taboo any reaching beyond the Messianic into the eschatological, beyond the salvation of mankind into the transformation of the world. And that, evidently, is why, during the flowering of Pharisaism, the two great Messianic movements, that of the "spiritual" Jesus and that of the "worldly" *Bar Kokhba,* had Pharisees as heralds and recruiters: Paul and Akiba.

7

Wilhelm Michel's comment about "Pharisaic hubris" goes deepest, but in that depth it goes awry. He sees Judaism as having a "primordial and historical failing" that was most clearly manifest in Pharisaism, the defect of "struggling impiously against death," in contrast to the "secret love of death" inherent in the German nature.[9]

Here, I feel, there is no sufficient distinction made between two spheres, that of the people and that of the individual. In Judaism, Michel no doubt means both: the people struggling against the death of the entire people and the individual against individual death; and he does say that the moment he detects a Jew respecting, and in awe of, death, then that man is, for him, no longer a Jew (while Michel's notion of Jewish character is in no way shaken). But does he mean both things in regard to Germans? Where and when in history has German peoplehood not struggled against the death of the people? Or, for that matter, any people before its hour is struck. And who would take it upon himself to see the world clock striking that hour for Judaism?

If, however, we mean those extreme heroic moments in which masses of another nation preferred "death to slavery," very well then, we had our *Masadah* and our *Betar,* when we "were like all nations" in our mortal resoluteness, and more than most knew how to die a mass death as though we wanted to commemorate for all time that we "have no honor" only because it suits us to have none.

Now what about the Jewish "resistance to going under and going across?" Admittedly, all promises say: Life. They are thereby in keeping with the natural foundations of Judaism. But is that really the life of the individual, is it not actually the life of the "seed"? Even when the individual is promised a long life, the meaning turns out to bear upon the linking of the generations. But this linking of generations is never an end in itself; it serves a distant goal that always shines toward us through the promise.

Granted, the individual Jew holds on fractiously to life, but only until that moment when he is summoned by God: then he yields—even more fractiously. No, my dear Herr Michel, he does not need any "action of God." The moment the summoning touches him, he, Abraham, is ready for the sacrifice, which, as you know, is greater than that of his own life. This Jew Jesus and his people are blood-witnesses, my dear Herr Michel, but so are many of these Pharisees. Have you forgotten what happened when one of these many defied the Roman stricture and publicly taught the Torah, and then, wrapped in a Torah scroll, stood at the burning stake? The flame, penetrating the scroll, reached him. "The parchment is burning," he cried, "the letters are flying aloft," and the Roman executioner, seeing the action of the man, leaped with him into the fire.

Love of death, but only for the sake of God, for the will of God, and to God. Love of life, but a love containing a readiness for the other love—I call that piety.

And the people—is its struggle against death not grounded in that promise of life for the "seed," which is used for a distant goal? Does it not wish to live because it is ordered to live? Not just any life but life in the Countenance? The life it misspends and has misspent, but whose promise is still not withdrawn? And can it not and must it not still hope, now and forever, to mature, to purify itself, to break through to that life?

Misspent and misspent! Do you think that the guilt has not yet knocked at the door of Jewish existence? Ever since Moses came down, and at many other moments besides, guilt has been shaking that house without making it collapse, as a storm shakes reeds, and every Jewish heart knows this from birth in its love of life and death. But that is something each of us has to work out alone with God.

And you, dear Christians, learn the word of faith from Gamaliel: "If this counsel or this work be of men, it will come to nought: But if it be of God, ye cannot overthrow it; lest haply ye be found even to fight against God."

18. THE IDEA OF THE HOLY (RUDOLF OTTO)

LEO STRAUSS

EDITOR'S INTRODUCTION

LEO STRAUSS (1899–1975) published his *Der Jude* review of Otto's book in Jahrgang VII, (1922–1923), pp. 240–42.

It is lamentable that Rudolf Otto's *The Idea of the Holy* is not better known to contemporary Jewish thought. It is a book come forth out of the noblest and best in the German intellectual tradition, grounded in idealist thought but transformed by the phenomenological impulse to scrutinize and acknowledge excrescences of the religious reality not easily accommodated by rational inquiry into the nature of God. As Otto himself states in his foreword to the English translation of 1923, it is advisable that one enter upon the consideration of the nonrational aspects of the divine only after he has "devoted assiduous and serious study to the *'Ratio aeterna.'*" This curious admonition gives pause when one recollects that Leo Strauss, reviewer in *Der Jude*, was later in his life the author of *Persecution and the Art of Writing*, which dealt with the cautionary and covert presentation of dangerous doctrine in the history of religious and philosophic thought. In his delivery of admonitory counsel to prospective readers, clearly Otto was not afraid for his own safety. He shows himself no less concerned (whatever the difference in magnitude) than Maimonides was in his preliminary advice concerning the dangers inherent in his speculative *Guide of the Perplexed,* i.e., that the uneducated and vulnerable reader might be spiritually endangered by his inquiry. Otto cautions us, therefore, to be certain about the rational foundations of natural theology before placing ourselves before the *numen ineffabile.*

There is, however, another reason for Otto's admonition. He is explicit in his concern that his exposition of the nonrational might well be seized upon by those whose predilection is the fantastically irrational. "The 'irrational,'" he writes, "is today a favorite theme of all who are too lazy to think or too ready to evade the arduous duty of clarifying their ideas and grounding their convictions on a basis of coherent thought." But, as Leo Strauss correctly indicates, *The Idea of the Holy* is no irrationalist discourse. Written with absolute precision of language, a care for meaning, a lucidity of category, it makes no common cause with those who wish to return religion to necromancy and magic. Rather, as Strauss stresses, the composition of Otto's work is a corrective. In the early centuries of religious history, the fantastical predominated, mankind submitted to an irrational universe—that is to say, a universe run by a capricious divinity, perceived as disorderly, moved by gratuitous impulse, and unpropitiable by other than extraordinary rites of divination and sacrifice.

The age of the irrational gods was succeeded by an equally long and critical retreat to safe distance. God was pursued with the astronomer's lens of category and attribute, man taking shelter within a doctrine of negative theology that protected him from compromising the divine nature or, worse yet, giving it offense. Given the rigor and uncompromising character of philosophical theology, receptivity to the numinal presence of God tended to become the subject matter of mystical thinking, which all too often fell into doctrinal pantheism and theurgic practice. The nineteenth century, barren of both a vital rationalism and mysticism in the discussion of God, was ready for the corrective.

As Strauss makes clear, one portion of the corrective is supplied by *The Idea of the Holy,* which, although not denying the earlier doctrine of divine attributes, encourages them to enter a framework in which other dimensions of the divine consciousness—explicit in the religious literature—are given place. The nonrational dimensions of God—awesomeness, terror, majesty, mysteriousness, are experienced realities. They are not hypothetical. Each, and others as well, is explicit in the Hebrew Bible and Jewish liturgy (from which Otto draws much of his substantiating evidence). These nonrational dimensions are the formal bearer of the familiar attributes; indeed, it may be argued that the doctrine of attributes as we know it (omnipotence, omniscience, atemporality, infinitude) is a rational conclusion from experience of the numinal immensity of God. The predicament to which Otto gave answer in *The Idea of the Holy* is that whereas the argumentation of divine reason and negative theology depends upon the experience of the divine *numen,* that experience has been dropped from consciousness or suppressed. It may well be the case that the role of God as superego in the definition of the rational conscience needs to be elaborated further. God is also ego and aggressiveness, and it is this dimension of the divine nature that is palpable in the *mysterium tremendum* to which Otto's work was devoted.   [A.A.C.]

THE IDEA OF THE HOLY (RUDOLF OTTO)[1]

It often happens in the Zionist youth movement that our young students take philosophical, sociological, and historical theories they have learned at university and apply them, in our periodicals, to our own problems, often without heeding the dubious aspects of such an application. This phenomenon, initially comical, springing as it does from a touching lack of reflection, has a serious background. Ultimately, it mirrors the overall spiritual situation of German Jews. Isn't that what all theologians of German Judaism have done? Haven't they all projected the German milieu, its predominant values and viewpoints, onto judgment and consideration of things Jewish? However legitimate such a projection may be (this legitimacy can be considered the cardinal problem of our spiritual situation), there are two instances where it apparently cannot be questioned by a doubting spirit. In one case, an ideologist of Judaism has taken a creative part in shaping German thought, so that through him Jewish energy, in the form of cultural elements, has entered the German world. Thus, his projection of German attitudes into Jewish things was preceded by his assimilating the minds of both nations. Only the man who has bridged the span himself (and not everyone who availed himself of the bridge) can truly judge the nature of the banks, the width and depth of the chasm, or the difficulty of bridging. The most venerable example of this case is the work of Hermann Cohen.

No less impressive is the second instance, when the German spirit, turning to Jewish tendencies, makes them alive within itself, especially if the tendencies in question are those whose effectiveness is restricted or repressed within the Jewish nation because of its untoward destiny. Such is the Protestant science of the Old Testament, a discipline shedding light on the real background of prophecy. It occurs in Nietzsche's critique of civilization, a critique striking to the pre-"Christian" depths of both the Jewish and the Hellenic-European spirit. And it occurs, last but not least, in Rudolf Otto's theological investigation, to which we shall return shortly.

The importance of Otto's work lies in the viewpoint he suggests for orienting the history of theology (and thereby positioning his own theological enterprise in intellectual history). To what extent can that orientation be applied to the science of Judaism? Earlier theology (whose most essential form for us was the doctrine of attributes during the age of Spanish Jewry) had the task of helping the "rational" elements in religion win out over the primitive and irrational elements. Today, after an all-too-complete performance of that task, theology has the opposite duty. It must leave the realm of the rational and, by means of a conscientious, scientifically irreproachable emphasis on the irrational, proceed to construct a system befitting the matter. Once upon a time, in a world filled with the irrational in religion, theologians had to achieve recognition for the right of *ratio*. Today, however, in a spiritual reality dominated by *ratio,* theology has the function of making "the irrational in the idea of the divine" alive through the medium of theoretical consciousness. Earlier theology speculated in a religiously closed vault—modern theology lives under an open sky and has to exert its own strength to help rebuild the vault. In the past the primary fact was God. Today it is the world, man, religious experience.

Formulating the task this way, we can recognize the question and the results of the doctrine of attributes without having to regard this doctrine as closed. Otto's categories permit the entire doctrine of attributes to enter the greater framework of a new theology. We cannot help thinking that it is not the idea of "attribute" in and of itself, but the hackneyed emptiness of the attributes of omnipotence, universal goodness, etc., that makes for the popular discrediting of the doctrine of attributes. Today, as a rule, people cite the "living fullness of experience," in opposition to the emptiness of the "attributes." Otto's investigation shows that one need not deviate from the straight, linear view of the religious object in order to grasp theoretically the objectiveness of religious life. In the object itself, the rational and the irrational elements are distinguished. The irrational in the religious object is the "bearer," the *substance* of the rational predicates, of the "attributes." The irrationality meant by religion is to be found not in the depth of the subject, but in the depth of the object. Hence we have no need for romantic "religious philosophy." This vouchsafes a connection to the tradition of the Bible and our worship on the one hand, and to the tradition of our theology on the other hand. The latter teaches us the general position of the Jewish theologian and offers us the results of analyzing rational "attributes." The former makes available the most perfect expression that the substance of the religious object could find "in human speech." It is thus no coincidence that Otto derives his substantial categories not least of all from the Old Testament and Jewish liturgy (cf. *Yom Kippur Prayers,* p. 37 f. *Melekh 'Elyon,* translated by Otto, pp. 238 ff.).

Yet at times Otto very keenly stresses the contrast between religion and theology, siding with religion *against* theology. This emphasis is justified in order to establish, from a religious viewpoint, the secondary character of theology. Otherwise, it need not bind us, since Otto, as especially his citations indicate, is strongly influenced here by Lutheran tendencies that cannot be determining for us as Jews, for whom that peculiarly Protestant subjectivism has to be quite remote.

Even so, it is still possible to consider *The Idea of the Holy* as a work of "religious philosophy." But what distinguishes Otto's analysis from the usual kind of religious philosophy is that it turns directly to religious consciousness without undertaking a naturalistic explanation or a transcendental "constitution" of this consciousness.

The great significance of Otto's book is its restriction of the rational element of religion not primarily and not exclusively by citing the irrationality of "experience." Rather, it makes the transcendence of the religious object the self-evident starting-point of the investigation. However justified our skepticism towards the doctrine of attributes, our sympathy may still go out to this type of theology: the very formulation of its task already makes fundamental subjectivism impossible. One would have to *demand* a theology as a doctrine of attributes even if it were simply impracticable—merely in order to have the notion of God's transcendence as a keynote from the very outset. A deeper understanding of the meaning of "transcendence" within a religious context is, if not the intention, then certainly the consequence of Otto's investigation. Transcedence receives a distinction:

(1) as the *experiential* otherworldliness of God, i.e., of God's primacy in regard to religion. If God exists in and of Himself, an entity independent of human experience, and if we know of this being from what is revealed in the Torah and the Prophets, then the theoretical presentation of what we know is basically possible, i.e., theology. Theology is very much the expression of plain, straightforward piety.

(2) as the *living* otherworldliness of God. It is experienced in the "creature feeling" of man, in his "being earth, ashes, and nothing," also and precisely in that of the *nation,* as evidenced in Isaiah 6. It is identical with the completely "nonnatural" character of "God's wrath," and no less with the character of "sacredness" as a "numinous value."

(3) as the *ideal* otherworldliness of God. The final characteristic of the preceding could mislead one to "idealize" God. This danger is abolished by the reference to the character of the "energetic," to the "vitality" of God.

19. SAMSON RAPHAEL HIRSCH (1808–1888)

FRIEDRICH THIEBERGER

EDITOR'S INTRODUCTION

FRIEDRICH THIEBERGER (1888–1958) published this essay in *Der Jude,* Jahrgang III (1918–1919), pp. 33–41.

Friedrich Thieberger's thesis, stated boldly at the outset of his essay on Samson Raphael Hirsch, is that "from Moses Mendelssohn until the period of national awakening—the course of a century—there was only *one* problem for Western Jews: to take Judaism as a complex of teachings and communal customs and raise it to the level of rational truths recognized by non-Jewish Europe, that is, to make it worthy of Europe."

On its face, this is a perfectly unexceptionable formulation, indeed, a commonplace formulation. But for as many years as I have reflected on its significance, I have been unable to shake the conviction that it describes something about the psychological imperatives of alienage rather than the definition of the auspices of Jewish historical thinking or Jewish theology. If, indeed, the line of argument running from Mendelssohn to Hirsch is one in which Jews have tried to define the rational basis for the accommodation of Judaism to secular philosophy and culture, at one extreme describing the connection as merely a treaty between two hospitably contiguous, but differentiated, polities and, at the other, contesting that the revealed principles of the one can be harmonized with the rational foundations of the other, it is no wonder that the issue of the debate would be the lugubrious spectacle of Jews (with the credentials of assimilation) rushing headlong to baptism in preparation for a career in European secularism. In such a reading, Jewish ethnicity becomes either a social disability (corrigible by the engrafting of different identities to the familial stock) or a social eccentricity (emphasizing the intellectual, symbolic, moral value of Jewish religion as a kind of spiritual gymnasium).

In his youth, Hirsch imagined that *The Nineteen Letters* would be the theological prolegomenon (a species of dialectical *Sefer Ha-Mada'*) to *Horeb* (his *Guide of the Perplexed*), which would be followed by *Moriah,* an exposition of Jewish law that would exemplify the principles of his doctrine and their enfleshment in the commandments, in line with his reading of the Mishnah Torah. Hirsch, it appears, had set forth to be Maimonides to his generation. *The Nineteen Letters* proved to be an insufficient first word and *Moriah* was never written. Indeed—and this is most important—Hirsch turned in later life against the theological enterprise, berating it in what has come to be familiar style. Theology in the later Hirsch is little more than a castle of fairy tales, high above the human struggle, shrouded in mists and vapors, reached by precarious paths and drawbridges. Hirsch retired into endless essays, expositions, polemics, and homilies. There was to be no Maimonides redivivus.

The predicament, however, remains in my view one of psychology rather than of philosophy or theology. By the time Hirsch came to the lists of West European thought, Kant, Hegel, and the young Hegelians and disciples had virtually completed their work. The last system of European thought had been produced. It was a system in which the thinker and the thought were virtually one. Such systems entailed the promise of rational clarification, universal applicability, and absolute authority. It was still assumed that the ground beneath the thinker was so solid as to require no special provisions for shifts and faults, and that the heavens, despite Copernicus, could be contemplated with the assurance that the multistoried universe was still in place. The moral provisions of such a philosophic vision were no less neat and limited. Man was well provided by the discernments of reason and the acquiescence of nature and divinity for a life of harmony, intelligence, and productivity.

Unfortunately for this neatness, the Jew was an anomaly. Without a metaphysics, without the habits of the rational tradition, the Jew was the keeper of an ancient code, a remote liturgy, a dead language, a body of ideas and teachings without clear-cut cognates among the nations. Moreover, the Jew was, quite simply, hated. Is it any wonder that the procedures of the reformers of Judaism should become excessively radical, testing the offers of the nations to give Jews their free access by rushing headlong to obliterate anything in Judaism that was not acceptable to free-thinking Christians while neo-Orthodox interpreters, holding fast, nonetheless tried to meet the challenge by devising an exegesis that made everything obscure, arbitrary, and apparently willful in Judaism a manifestation of a hidden motive to ethical conscience and moral instruction.

Both the reformers and the neo-Orthodox, using virtually the same criteria of discrimination (although validating their importance with widely divergent emphasis and enthusiasm), tried to make Judaism a viable reality, a reality acceptable and comprehensible—if not to the outsider then surely to the Jews who were now, for the first time, allowed—indeed, in some cases, encouraged—to make themselves publicly heard and understood.

Of course, theological thinking is not the ideal enterprise for making oneself understood, if one is concerned with making oneself understood by the greatest number of people; when theology demands a constituency for its exposition and confirmation, it is most likely to fail, becoming more a pulse-taking of the psyche than honest thought. Theological thinking can only be making clear to oneself the ground on which it is possible to exist before man and God. If such thinking is framed by Jewish considerations, the presupposition of thought is that the thinker is Jewish, that is, informed by considerations and precedents that are historically accidental, which thought transforms into necessity. There is no way by which hard thought can explain what is given by inheritance. All things inherited by tradition were given either by God or by those who received them on our behalf. We, however, the Jews who survived beyond the emancipation and the modern enterprise of our extermination, have no guide in either the polemics or the homiletics of the past. We have been given nothing that we are not obliged to find all over again, or not at all.

[A.A.C.]

SAMSON RAPHAEL HIRSCH (1808–1888)

I

The tragedy of the uncertain skeptic contains a conciliatory energy precisely because it does not gloss over the human. The tragedy of the self-confident and self-satisfied (tragic for the remote observer) is pathetic and confining because it seems to reveal the full deception of nature against the human. But all human endeavor, and thus all human greatness, lies in the movement between these tragic poles. The intellectual history of Western Jewry from Moses Mendelssohn until the awakening of nationalism follows the peculiar course of an undulant curve—the constantly self-renewing path from agitation to confidence.

Just as before, during the age of Spanish Jewry, this agitation did not originate in the Jewish soul, but was created within it by external enlightenment. And long after the period of *Sturm und Drang,* when a more deeply rooted romanticism had interrupted the progress of the European Enlightenment (it was only the realism of the 1830s that discreetly returned to it), the Jewish soul was still wrestling with the problem of the Enlightenment. In West Europe, the Jewish soul never experienced any *Sturm und Drang* or romanticism, for these movements were based on the feeling of a redemptory national cohesion. The primary issue of the Enlightenment was the rational basis of religion and a religion of reason. We should once and for all cease making the Jewish role in German romanticism the focal point of Jewish intellectual history in the nineteenth century. It was simply scattered Jewish capital invested in a non-Jewish venture. Such participation may be recorded as symptomatic of the Jewish state of mind, but its significance for the development of the Jewish spirit was negligible. It has importance only in a history bent on demonstrating that we are as good as anyone else, and on interpreting the unfortunate situation of self-denying Jews giving of themselves to other nations as a divine mission.

Let me therefore repeat the rough formula: from Moses Mendelssohn until the period of national awakening in the course of a century—there was only *one* problem for Western Jews—to take Judaism as a complex of teachings and communal customs and raise it to the level of rational truths recognized by non-Jewish Europe, that is to say, make it worthy of Europe. Three generations of Enlighteners strove and investigated along these lines. But striving is not growth, investigation is not life. And if we asked what kept drawing those generations to Judaism as an intellectual matter (since Europe did, after all, have more rational systems and more highly developed areas of research), the only possible answer must be: the magic circle of a common life of people who feel physically united. But out of gratitude for civil emancipation (and we should not scorn this gratitude!), the road to a strong community of one's own as a road to salvation had to remain in the shadows; and so it remained until a new shock uncovered it again.

At the same rate that the Jewish community became looser and lighter in consequence of the accretive naturalization of the economic and intellectual life of Europe, those who ventured forth from the vanishing centers of Judaism felt a deep urge to accentuate their Jewish consciousness. *The first generation,* those born by 1790, were the most radical reformers, satisfying their modernism by transforming the service of the synagogue. These Friedländers, Jacobsons, Beers[1] had Judaism within them. Yet their pupils in the coming generation realized that the continuous abandonment of a Jewish heritage might bring one nearer to the Gentile world, but ultimately made possible the kind of fusion that Holdheim,[2] for example, yearned for. Nor did this abandonment take place for the sake of a higher sense of community; it came about at the expense of Judaism and (what even Holdheim's followers defensively anticipated) at the expense of the Jews as a physical nation. Like a block of ice that, floating in the water, retains its form and its own movement for quite a while before it gradually dissolves, Judaism, still isolate, retaining its own shape, was to be liberated gradually from the inhibitions of shape and isolation.

But they reckoned without the miraculous strength of the Jewish soul! The danger of dissolution led *the second generation,* those born between 1790 and 1820, towards new securities: *Wissenschaft des Judentums* [Science of Judaism]. The analogy to Germany's flowering investigation of antiquity inspired and encouraged them along this new road. No slogan was brandished more ostentatiously than the word "scientific." Jews, as full-fledged Europeans, tried to save their Judaism by fleeing into the lucid domain of its literature. There one could discover truths demonstrable and positive. Religion shifted to the study of religious documents; the living word became a matter for philology. This was the generation of Leopold Zunz (1794–1886), Abraham Geiger (1810–1874), Samuel David Luzzatto (1800–1865),

Zacharias Frankel (1801–1875), Ludwig Philippson (1811–1889), Heinrich Graetz (1817–1891), and Moritz Steinschneider (1816–1907), all of whom, despite their different conclusions about ritual, were gripped by the same experience. However, historical explanations can never free a creative national energy. Only the man who discovers the source of the present will open the sluices of the past. Putting down anchors in antiquity could put some hearts at ease, but it meant avoiding the powerful issue of reason, which snared religion at every turn. Gentile investigation evinced a breadth of domains, a courageous examination of the Bible, with which Jews could not compete. Thus the necessity of the times compelled an ethical apologetics of Judaism. But this, too, was a weak dam against the shock waves of the period, so long as Jews merely wanted to demonstrate that Judaism *also* stood on high ethical ground, which it had attained long before the nations of Europe.

The third generation, born between 1820 and 1850, needed an even stronger tie to its Judaism. It had to find a way to rid itself of the residue of its national process and systematize Judaism, not as a catechistic assemblage, but as a philosophical result. This led to Heymann Steinthal's essays *Über Juden und Judentum; Vorträge und Aufsätze,* and Moritz Lazarus' *The Ethics of Judaism* [*Die Ethik des Judentums*].[3] No one shook Judaism more deeply, no one seized upon it more compellingly, however, than Hermann Cohen. He professed Judaism because the process of thought inevitably leads to it, because it is a postulate of reason. Aesthetics would be meaningless without art; likewise, human ethics would collapse without the guarantee taught by the Jewish religion, especially through the Prophets. Cohen's *oeuvre* is the most advanced sentry of the entire period of Enlightenment. As Jews of the West had drawn furthest away from Judaism, there arose the most energetic grappling with the Enlightenment's problem of truth.

The representatives of the first generation were mainly merchants, those of the second were rabbis, those of the third were professors of philosophy. There was, naturally, a dangerous limitation in confining Judaism to a single system. Judaism is more than logical or ethical knowledge, and Jews are not disciples of a specific school of philosophers. The thinking of that period readily welcomed the conviction that we Jews are dispersed throughout the world in order to maintain ubiquitously our special ethics until mankind is ripe for them. This notion of a mission to mankind was the strongest leaven of the Western Jewish community. The earlier generation had already accepted it. But having focused on history, it could only do what its theoretician Samuel Hirsch[4] did, which was to bank on the priority of the monotheistic concept, already a closed issue for Europe. However, the notion of a mission, deeply Jewish in its roots, was reawakened by a movement that ran parallel to the other, like a back-eddy, throughout the century.

Moses Mendelssohn regarded both areas—the Jewish religion and the European doctrine of reason—as noncontradictory (indeed, as equivalent). He could attract both those who wanted to justify the immutability of the reason to their historical conscience and those for whom the sacredness of the religious was the be-all and end-all. This is why the reformers kept claiming that Mendelssohn had been desecrated by his contemporaries and why subsequent orthodoxy, which had always loudly claimed to be the true bearer of an intact Jewish legacy, misinterpreted the desecration of the Orthodox Jew Mendelssohn. The gap between Mendelssohn and, say, Ezekiel Landau[5] was due neither to the fear that Gentile thinking could penetrate destructively into ultimate Jewish thinking nor to the hasty denial of a possible reconciliation between Jewish life and Gentile knowledge. The estrangement was based on something essential: Mendelssohn had profoundly transformed the religious sphere. The two spheres only *appeared* to coexist tolerantly (appeared so only to him). In fact, as stubbornly as Orthodox Jews resisted, even Orthodoxy (I very nearly said: the religion of the Orthodox) was changing, and it remains vital only so long as it keeps changing. I consider this insight a crucial spiritual premise for the future of our nation.

For the Orthodox, the "Law," as the outer garment of established tradition, cannot be changed through any deliberative choice, but it is individual Jews who, from generation to generation, wrap their lives in this garment (which includes articles of faith as well as actions). There must be a continual reestablishment of contacts between the cold mechanism of the garment of the Law and the living center that wears it. The surface form remains consistent, but not the animating energy, not the spiritual motivation. Or, to state it differently: although the Law and its fulfillment may remain immutable, the spiritual relationship of the individual to the Law and to its fulfillment changes. For here lies the intoxicating meaning of development (and all living things take part in it): the incessant reciprocity between things continues to produce new orders, species, and organisms. The Orthodoxy of the Aristotelian Maimonides was different from that of the Enlightener Mendelssohn, and, likewise, different from that of the mystic Baal Shem Tov. The difference was not one of adherence to or deviation from the Law, but one of quality. Since Mendelssohn, the West European Orthodox, like their Reformist brethren, have been grappling with the Enlightenment's dilemma of reason versus religion. And, as happened with the Reformers, the feeling for an inner direction was transformed during the phase of Enlightenment. Mendelssohn siphoned off the last little drop of reason from the religious area in order to give reason a free scope and a clear arena. The outer line of his religious life remained intact; inwardly, everything was subverted. Religion was a legal binding on his activity and had no influence on the search for truth and the discoveries of reason. There was no greater radical among the Orthodox than Mendelssohn.

However, the younger generation was loath to attempt Mendelssohn's logical leap a second time. Kant's ideas on the truth-limits of religion, Schelling's and Schleiermacher's on the religious relationship to the divine in nature and reason, penetrated Orthodox circles and once more agitated the struggle between codified teachings and the considerations of science. This problem of the Enlightenment was a starting-point for Schelling's disciple Isaak Bernays,[6] but his mystic bent led thought in new directions. Bernays descended to the very roots of religious sensibility, where reason and feeling are one and the same—and the distinction between reason and religion struck him as merely historical. He mocked the arrogance of science in trying to get at the meaning of life, but he admitted that religion, too, is involved in this development, and that an ascending line led from Abraham to Moses, and from Moses to the prophets. He felt that no nation's spirit or fate was as valid a vessel for religious creativity as the spirit and fate of the Jews. In this he was seized by the dormant idea of the Jewish nation's mission on behalf of all mankind.

Bernays left the wealth of the Law untouched, regarding it as an inducement to an incomparable, exemplary life. He was thus the only one to break through the trend of the Western Jewish enlightenment. His influence would have been greater had he not refused to reveal himself in some way other than the spoken word. The only work that might have been ascribed to him was *Biblischer Orient (Biblical Orient)*, but he denied its authorship. To be sure, it would have been well-nigh impossible to wrench Orthodoxy out of the Enlightenment trend. His strongest disciple, who joined him at the age of thirteen (Bernays had come to Hamburg as a *Ḥakham* in 1821), developed more and more into a fighter of the age of Enlightenment—Samson Raphael Hirsch.

Bernays had taught Hirsch to pour the fire of religious feeling into tangible rhythms, and the powerfully resurrected idea of the mission of Judaism strenghtened his religious willpower. But the overall basis of his life was still the problem of the coexistence of traditional religious teachings and Western Jewish rationalism. His solution was so energetic and remedial that its very wording became a new religious code for two Orthodox generations. Only the national reversal changed the human premise for this doctrine.

When the Jewish soul had to do its most *thorough* work in order to survive in the face of the Enlightenment, natural forces were released in the threatened soul: now the question as to the objective truth of Jewish teachings was no longer the existential issue of Judaism. The national awakening of Western Jews, anticipated by Moses Hess,[7] is only externally a backlash against assimilation; deep down, it spells a victory over the Enlightenment. Judaism as merely a problem of reason became the problem of the Jewish soul.

2

Samson Raphael Hirsch was a fanatic in regard to certainty. This was the starting point for the entire course of his being and destiny. The certainty with which he established his faith on a solid intellectual basis gave him a superiority that his opponents were unable to counterbalance with any appeal to the emotions. His joy in such certainty makes him a representative of the En-lightenment, as well as of the emancipated Jewish bourgeoisie. His ruthless zeal with regard to the holiness of his faith puts him in the ranks of our great men. But it would be unfair to claim that Hirsch was not fighting for the inner certainty that was both his limitation and his strength. The things on which his disciples lean easily and willingly were based on the Master's deep agitation. Here, too, one can say that the struggle in the individual soul is always a struggle on behalf of all. But understandably, his disciples are reluctant to hear that Hirsch created something new rather than uncovering things that had been buried. They claim the slogan "neo-Orthodoxy" is something coined by the opposition, a misinterpretation subject to further misinterpretation. In truth, Hirsch did not set up any new standards, but by boldly turning the axis, he concentrically aligned the two hostile groups of Jewish religious doctrine and European rationalism. This turning of the axis, new and essential, de-manded a struggle while it was coming into being. When Hirsch, at the age of twenty-eight, published *Nineteen Letters of Ben Uziel* [*Neunzehn Briefe über Judentum*] (1836), with its subtitle alluding to *Horeb,* his magnum opus in preparation, the struggle was already decided.[8] But the decision to join the issue was so recent that Hirsch's reluctance to expose himself led him to hide behind an editor, Ben Uziel, or a fictitious letter writer, Naphtali. *The Nine-teen Letters* alone document that struggle. What he wrote from that time until the end of his eighty years was no longer spoken inwardly, but to the outside world; it was propaganda rather than confession.

Nowhere did the Reform movement of the first generation gain ground so quickly as in Hirsch's native Hamburg. Even those Jews raised in loyalty to the tradition opened themselves to the European spirit. But the Reform movement struck Hirsch's unerring sense of the decisive and the uncompromising. The watchword now, for the first time, was: Do not avoid the issue, face it squarely! He thought the Reform movement through to its ultimate conclu-sion and envisaged the end of Judaism. What a shock! He retraced his steps, scrutinized the methods of the reformation, and realized that they were the same as those Maimonides had used when reconciling religion and reason. Even though Maimonides, calmly and cautiously, had come to a different turning point than the modern, unheeding Reformers, his course was nevertheless a matter of personal logic: the spiritual tendency was the same. This proved even more shocking. Was Judaism thus helplessly lost to rationalism? Was it nothing more than an edifice to be rationalized by philosophy? Did he not feel deep inside himself the undeniable reality of Judaism even when rational reasons spoke against Jewish teachings? But if it *was* a reality, then it would have to be defined by the intellect! Rationalism, the axiomatic doctrine, can test, reveal, and destroy every single sentence of the religion, but it cannot get at religion as a whole. One has simply to locate that spot in consciousness where the two spheres of religious teaching and rationalism appear to interpenetrate and there grasp the axis passing through their centers. From the infinity of existence that courses through me, I experience this One, this Inevitable, this Irrefutable: God. It is not because He is a necessity of my system or because a religious code demands it, but rather because He is an endless reality. It is thus that, positioned for an immense instant beyond these separate spheres, I can look back and behold the brightness of my God streaming towards me out of a wonderful Book, out of every line, out of every plain-seeming word. And the more I look, the deeper I recognize Him alone. A great many things in this Book are still beyond my capacity, but could I therefore deny a trifle without denying the divinity of the entire Book? Could I find in my understanding the standard for distinguishing between the divine and the nondivine in this Book? Since I care about the whole, I remain unfaltering in regard to the least details. And how can my intellectual teachings contradict my divine domain! If it did, that would mean that I had not considered everything on which my intellect relies. But through my rational teachings I see the sacred space of the divine Book, and the more deeply I inquire into the teachings of reason, the clearer and more meaningful its plan becomes. The fog of emotions is clearing more and more. I see the infinite eye resting on me with its demands, on me, the final point of an age-old ancestry. It is not enough for me to believe. My entire life has to be ordered according to this Book, for it is the Book of *my* life-order. How could I ever believe that I was tied to this Book for the sake of my ancestors rather than for my own sake, only because of the past and not because of living reality! Now I am secure, now my entire life is involved in unerring laws, now I can profess God through what I do, now my existence is finally fulfilling its universal destiny: to be exemplary.

None of this is to be read in the *Nineteen Letters,* and yet we feel it in every line of the work. It would, of course, be easy to expose the covered braces of this mental construction and smile at its validity. But the power of thought lies in its human elements and not in its logical demonstrability. The incredible curve from the experience of God to the acceptance of the Sinaitic Law, the conclusion that God exists, ergo, that the Torah is God-given, cannot resist even a child's reasoning. And what a rationalistic impotence to regard the Sinaitic miracle as confirmed because it took place in full view of an entire generation! Maimonides banked on this discovery; Hirsch worked it into his system. It eased his proud and zealous search for inner certainty. This zeal was concentrated in the thought that the texts of the oral and written Law could be only a human account of the Sinaitic Word of God, blasphemy and aberration. If the authentic Word of God were not in our hands, both Judaism and we ourselves would be invalid.

When Zacharias Frankel[9] wrote that the Mishnah encompasses interpretations of the Biblical Law, but that its language testifies to the great age of its authorship, Hirsch lost his temper and safeguarded himself against the arrogance of the "historical school." Hirsch replied that the divine source of the Mishnah was manifestly contained in its assurances. Rapoport,[10] the Conservative, tried to achieve a compromise: the contents of the Laws were, after all, not identical with the form of the Laws and Frankel, he said, had examined only the form. But Rapoport had thereby touched upon the frontier between the Orthodox and the Conservatives: devotion out of conviction or devotion out of love. Only the former guarantees an adherence to the Law. The Law was the crucial point. And whereas Mendelssohn had fettered action but released thinking, clear regulations had to bind all human consciousness. The *Horeb* was intended as a first attempt at this in the form of legal paragraphs. Earlier codifications were merely codifications of "shalts" and "shalt-nots," but Hirsch considered "shalt" and "shalt-not" in terms of divine intention, and so returned them to the substratum of the divine experience. Replying to the Science of Judaism as proclaimed by his contemporaries, he offered his Jewish science with its infinite task of determining the intention of the oral and written Word of God. But the oral and the written Torah do not suffice for grasping the full extent of religious duties. Only seldom and obliquely did Hirsch admit that rabbinical regulations and ordinances could be a third source in the area of the closed sacred tradition (*Gesammelte Schriften*, vol. IV, p. 454).

Hirsch had a peculiar propensity for sound associations. This gave his language a special dynamics, but led him astray into the wildest intellectual leaps. Since he denied the issue of historical strata, he would seek the same kind of explanation for all parts of the tradition. He built artistic bridges from a word of the Law, speculated his way to some great idea about the Universal or about the universal mission of Judaism. And then, the Law was his guarantee of divinity, indeed, an ascent to divine experience itself. Yet, in his exegeses of the Pentateuch, the Psalms, and the Prayer Book, he reveled in linguistic conjectures in the style of Bernays and often appeared to be close to the Kabbalists. The latter, however, had discovered miracles and divine legends beyond the more verbal texture of the Bible, whereas Hirsch frequently noted mysterious discourse that had to be rationally clarified. The eight half-strings of the *ṣiṣit,* which fold up as four whole strings, were, according to Maimonides, to have been *tekhelet* [of sky-blue color], so that the six white half-strings would form three whole white strings.[11] Hirsch, after an extensive investigation, interprets the numerical values as follows:

Sensual physicality, like the rest of the created visible world	=6
Free divine breath, invisibly deriving from the invisible	=7
Jewish calling, as rooted in Israel's historical chosenness	=8

These are the elements of our warp and woof . . . You have Six, but you also have a Seventh and an Eighth—You are an animal, but you are also a human being and a Jew . . .

Hirsch was not embarrassed by the fact that such dialectics connect self-constructed symbols—no matter how bizarre—to a universal ethical idea. None of the objections to his arbitrary approach actually reached him. His reflections merely drew the carefully defined circle of tradition even more intimately into his rationalism, the very opposite of what Maimonides had sought. The certainty of his opponents lay in philological details and historical arguments; Hirsch's certainty was the certainty of vital feeling. His sense of reality tolerated no historicism. Everything was present and real. Every Feast of Joy was for the sake of present joy and every Day of Mourning was for the sake of present mourning. The entire tradition had to be acknowledged and experienced in its topical, that is to say, eternal significance. Such reality-filled belief could not set any store by the assurances of a reward in the afterlife. "The Jewish holy shrine was not erected on graves; death and everything that touches death remained far from its chambers." Jews were to stop associating the concept of rigidity with the concept of Orthodoxy. The only inflexible thing was the formula. But wherever the formula is translated into action, it takes on the variety of life.

Despite all mental suppleness, it would have been impossible to unite an intact Jewish tradition and a universal human rationalism, or as Hirsch liked to put it: *Torah 'im derekh 'ereṣ*,[12] if what he regarded as universal had not been a legacy of the Jewish people; that is, the knowledge of the *One* God, who has put us, his children, between Good and Evil. This is why Hirsch felt that his concept of the universally human was confirmed in Jewish writings, and that was why he rejected, in terms of this concept, any Gentile doctrines that did not fit into Jewish teachings. Azriel Hildesheimer,[13] his spiritual disciple, the head of Berlin Orthodoxy, held this to be a self-delusion; he separated the two areas, which operated by different laws, and never attempted any comparison of what was true about each of them. But he never went so far as to follow Mendelssohn's arrangement; it was enough for him to acknowledge God as the primal power of both areas, the familiar and the alien. Passage to the national idea lay at no great distance from this conception.

Hirsch's universal humanity required the sine qua non of a Jewish national community. This, of course, involved the threat of a dangerous conflict with the efforts of the entire century, with Jewish nationalization. Even though Hirsch recognized equal rights for the Jewish national body only for the sake of the spirit (which he considered the only true justification), it is nevertheless impossible to advocate a national spirit without positing the physical nation. The Reformers had avoided this conflict theoretically. From the perspective of theory, they regarded Judaism as a spiritual or ethical and humanitarian phenomenon, separable from the worldly and civil entity; and, theoretically, they looked forward to a time in which other nations would accept Judaism because of its greater truth while resolutely going their own way, just as someone can, say, make a transition from Newton to Einstein. Orthodoxy was protected from such ideas by the obligations of the Law and by the unique strength of the Jewish tradition, which is indifferent to distinctions between distant and remote domains. The only valid question was: Jewish or Gentile? But anyone translating natural conflicts into thought has an easy time finding intellectual solutions. Since Jewish and non-Jewish teachings could be united without any loss to Jewish tradition (whereby Hirsch ignored any possible distortion by Gentile teachings), it had to be possible to join the Jewish nation to the conditions of the Gentile world with absolutely no loss whatsoever. Hirsch never contemplated this problem in terms of its life consequences. The prospect of the thought itself put him at ease. But this state of ease played its part in Hirsch's struggle for the outer certainty on which his inner certainty was based.

The struggle for this outer certainty increased the courageous joy he took in his work and widened its scope. But his vociferous activity held back the voices of inner ferment and thereby inner growth. His later writings never contain anything like this humble statement from the *Nineteen Letters:* "I am now convinced that none of us who are now alive has grasped Judaism in its purity and truth." Hirsch had to make his Judaism secure in two directions: toward Gentiles and toward Jews. He had to explain himself to Gentiles and defend himself to Jews. Explain himself because it seemed arrogant to claim an ethical chosenness for a people, and defend himself because a properly acknowledged Judaism could not tolerate any varieties. Self-explanation was a safeguard prompted by feelings of deference, necessity, and the spirit of exile; defense was a safeguard prompted by zeal, ruthlessness, and love of the absolute.

The mere thought of Judaism's mission to mankind was a good excuse for a separation from the Gentile world. But Hirsch always became involved in contradictions as soon as he had to explain the goal of the mission. Was Judaism supposed to proclaim the faith in one God and the goodness of man? Such a calling was the pride of other religions and other spiritual movements, including non-Orthodox Jews. And no rhetorical device could persuade anyone that "the seeds of truth, which are planted in the breasts of (all) mortals" will flower so long as only the Jews remain true to "the God-appointed norm." How could the fundamental concept of *Torah ʿim derekh ereṣ* remain standing if not every nation had accepted it? Or does the "God-appointed norm" need additions? After all, Hirsch himself says that European history is a desperate struggle because the proclaimers of the divine teaching (the early Christians) only brought mankind a new faith, while, "in their weakness, remaining silent on the new Law, and yet it is only the Law that brings salvation." The linear consequence of his thought is that the universally necessary "Law" is universally binding, yet it is precisely this consequence that he skirts. "Jewish wisdom waits for the light to fill all hearts on earth; the Jewish Law knows this only for Abraham's sons and daughters." This makes the human mission of Judaism a national mission. Being a "Man of Israel" means ascending beyond the universally human to the calling of Israel. He used such monstrous artificial constructions, hoping thereby to assimilate anything of value that had come into being outside of Judaism at a universally human preliminary stage.

And yet, for all his latent nationalism, Hirsch had little sympathy for Moses Hess, who, lonesome and far ahead of his time, recognized the Jewish problem as one of a national soul rather than one of truth. Hess personally sent Hirsch a copy of *Rome and Jerusalem* [*Rom und Jerusalem*], but Hirsch, uninterested, put it aside. After all, the Orthodox propaganda that Kalischer[14] had inaugurated for settling Palestine had rubbed Hirsch the wrong way, despite the acquiescence of important Orthodox Jews such as his old Talmud teacher, Jacob Ettlinger.[15] The true cause of these contradictions did not go very deep. Hirsch did not want to change the overt political situation of the Jews; an indifferent condition of full civil rights would be the most lasting security: there was to be no outward distinction from Gentiles (thus, Hirsch welcomed his sabbath guests in a tuxedo). Were a Jew attacked in the area of civil rights, he could retreat victoriously to the concept of universal humanity; were a Jewish right threatened, one could wave the banner of religion. Of course, after some hesitation, he was safeguarded from this by his national instinct for regarding the human mission of the Jews as confirmed in their Diaspora. Because the "Law" had been ignored, God fled into Exile with those who remained loyal to him. But our calling could only be fulfilled in our homeland. And in thinking about our homeland, his soul went beyond all nebulous considerations:

> The future will find Israel, not dispersed over the face of the earth, but gathered about the peak of the Sanctuary of the Law, in Palestine. There the nations seek it, yet it has not returned there to establish its own state and practice the ways of culture and political life that it has learned from the nations in the Diaspora; no, it has gathered there again to fully realize the morals of man and the ways of the citizen as taught by God, and it will thus, by knowing and fulfilling the Law and the Word of God, make itself the priestly nation of mankind. Israel will not bring European culture to Palestine; it will bring the culture of mankind through God's Law and Word from Palestine (cf. Hirsch's essay on *Isaiah*).

This Messianic era will certainly not come about through a mere settlement of the country. Hirsch, however, refused to recognize that it might be safer for the Jewish nation to await the Messiah in Palestine than in Frankfurt, Germany.

His energy concentrated on making the full scope of development a certainty, and giving it a concluding present-day relevance. That was why he became uncritical despite his rigor, and self-satisfied despite his humility; that was why, despite his great sensitivity to language, he did not scorn the gloriole of conventional, sentimental adjectives. But it was only in the struggle against non-Orthodox Judaism that his joy in certainty streamed forth unrestrained. Even back in the time when he had been a rabbi, first in Oldenburg and then in

Emden, the Reformers had recognized him as an opponent who could cause them a good deal of trouble. In Nikolsburg, Moravia, where he had come to succeed Mordecai Benet,[16] an old-Orthodox, people were taken aback by the modern touch in his outer conduct. It was only the call in 1851 to the new Orthodox community in Frankfurt am Main that situated him properly. There, he found a powerful support in Rothschild.[17] Hirsch made Frankfurt the metropolis of central European Orthodoxy. He set up schools to guarantee the future of his community; he founded the magazine *Jeschurun* (1854)[18] as an organ of propaganda against the times and the muddled heads of his day. He never fought against anyone who openly denied the divinity of the Jewish religion. He only wanted to expose the people who, while seemingly acknowledging its divinity, violated the *Shulḥan 'Arukh*.[19] Moreover, he refused to recognize degrees of apostasy. On the other hand, Hirsch ignored the fact that he himself went against the attitude of the *Shulḥan 'Arukh,* which proscribed any study of non-Jewish knowledge, especially in a non-Hebrew language. So long as the limits of religious action did not shift! And it wasn't enough for him to recognize for himself the faith—true Judaism—he wanted it confirmed in the eyes of the whole world—objectively, as it were. Relentlessly and ruthlessly, he put Judaism as high above the Jews as the Divine above the Earthly. His spirit was behind the Lasker Bill, which was passed as the Law on Leaving a Religion (1876).[20] The warnings of Orthodox friends did not frighten Hirsch. The possibility of leaving the community and forming a new alliance without dissenting from Judaism itself, struck him as a salvation for the Orthodox minorities, i.e., for the purity of true Judaism, i.e., for the ethical strength of mankind. And he dared to take the step. So long as Judaism was a problem of reason, such ethical consistency overtowered even the pure will of the Reformer.

There are two kinds of religious shock among Jews, and those who absorb them can become both martyrs and saints: the groping, the despairing, the denouncers of God, who even while cleaving to the world remain alone; and the secure, the knowing, the upright, who want to sweep the entire world along in their flaming faith. Such a man was Samson Raphael Hirsch.

20. HERMANN COHEN
JACOB KLATZKIN

EDITOR'S INTRODUCTION

JACOB KLATZKIN (1882–1948) published the present essay in *Der Jude* during Jahrgang III (1918–1919), pp. 33–41.

Who are our philosophers? We know only too well that we have few if any theologians. But philosophers? None. Ours is, as it was during the early nineteenth century, an age of historians. This is curious. Jews are again engaged in recovering the scored rocks and scarred riverbeds of the past, examining them as fossils of modern history, seeking to describe the immense torrent that swept away the millennial societies of the European Jewish world, collecting remains, founding archives and institutes to conserve and codify them. Our historians are busier than ever before, moved not only by the immensities of recent generations to document the events of the past half-century, but moved by these same events to reconstruct earlier skeins of interpretation.

Old Jewish historiography, the collection of manuscripts, the identification of the genera and species of Jewish production—the lepidoptery of Zunz and Steinschneider, for instance—has given way to interpretation of the whole structure and underpinning of Jewish social, economic, cultural, and religious history. The work is remarkable not alone for its richness and scale, but also for the fact that increasingly these Jewish historians find less and less need to establish (as had the earlier century of Jewish historiography) the canon of historical relevance by reference to the criteria of non-Jewish history, European culture, and Christian religion. The Holocaust put an end not only to European Jewry, but to Jewish apologetic ideology.

But this trend (about which much much more could be said than I have said here—all the paradoxes and conundrums of Jewish historical sensibility and consciousness) was curiously anticipated by Jacob Klatzkin's remarkable eulogistic essay on the death of Hermann Cohen in 1918. For Klatzkin, an era came to an end with the passing of Cohen, "the greatest son of the Jewish enlightenment in the West." In Klatzkin's reading, Cohen the philosopher, relentlessly committed to the cause of rational intelligence, supremely and uncompromisingly abstract, had joined the lists of the Jewish struggle for emancipation and culture within the context of the German nation. He did so not to vindicate Jewish particularity but to offer it as the principal witness to universality. But is this not an unexceptionable course for the philosophic intelligence? Build the system, renovate its historical origins, describe the extent of its application and relevance, and then, by the patient order of descent, return to the everyday, the commonplace, and allow the universal idea to find its exemplification.

The son of the cantor of Coswig returned to Judaism by entering into combat with Heinrich von Treitschke's attempt to establish anti-Semitism on historical grounds. Cohen's essay, *"Ein Bekenntnis in der Judenfrage"* (1880), his reply to Treitschke, was marked by Cohen himself as his return to Judaism. But was it? It seems that this "Confession on the Jewish Question" was less the essay of a *baàl teshubah* than an expression of the anguish of a thinker who regarded Treitschke's challenge as an assault on the implicit direction of the philosophic idea. The system was built by 1880, the various expositions of Kant *renovatus* were done, and all that remained before Cohen was to demonstrate that the purity of the idea, the unity of mankind, and the ethical ground of the social system and the national state were already implicit in German idealism, German humanism, German religion. What was implicit all along—how many hundreds of times had this pious son of the cantor read *The Sayings of the Fathers* on Sabbath afternoons or studied the prophetic books before he became a professor of philosophy—was that the ethical nobility of the German people was grounded upon Jewish sources. Treitschke had not betrayed the Jew; he had betrayed Germany, betrayed reason, betrayed the foundations of ethical humanity!

Hermann Cohen was the last son of the Enlightenment, last in the sequence, but quintessential in its ideology: his exposition of Judaism was profoundly and unavoidably assimilationist. Cohen supplied to German Jewry an argument from historical reason not alone for its assimilation but for simultaneous apotheosis. Cohen would have angrily repudiated the charge that he was an assimilationist whose doctrine would result ultimately in the vanishing of the Jewish people, but he would acknowledge and indeed vigorously defend the idea that the Jewish people reflects the finest and best ambitions of the German nation, since it constellates within its origins, history, and literature the moral excellence of Germany. By assimilation the German is converted, not the other way round.

It is pointless to criticize Cohen. His argument was transparently naïve and, with the hindsight of history, false. Klatzkin's demolition amid praise, his irony amid celebration, does all that needs to be done.

What is undone is our reply to the very first question. Who are our philosophers? The essential difference between the great age of Jewish philosophy that stretched from Saadia Gaon to Levi ben Gerson and the century of Jewish apologetics from Moses Mendelssohn to Hermann Cohen is that, whereas for the former there was no social reward for the pursuit of truth, the modern age has conferred immense benefit for the sacrifice of particularism. It was not imagined by any Jewish thinker of the medieval tradition that the exposition of metaphysics, or the incorporation of Biblical models into the system of cosmology, or the description of the institution of the Biblical polity as the analogue of the theocratic state would secure for Judaism or the Jewish people any benefit in the form of toleration and charity. The philosophic inquiry was collateral to observance of the Law, an instrumentality by which the *praxis* of revelation was afforded a *theoria*. Jews were careful to make certain that, however much they may have learned from classical philosophers and Muslim scholars, they did not fall into paganism or heresy. Christianity supplied at the most a social penumbra to Jewish thinking, and though Jewish thinkers had an influence upon Christian philosophers, it is much more difficult to document the reverse. (This has much to do with the sociology of conversion, for many Jewish converts brought Jewish texts into the mainstream of Christian life. Moreover, the intellectual sponsorship of many conversions laid upon Christian scholastic texts an incubus of suspicion that was inexpungable.) The isolation of Jewish thought has diminished during the past century, the benefit accruing to philosophers who are Jews being that the subject matter of thought need not have specifically Jewish content. The problems of philosophy have changed since the medieval tradition; it is no longer necessary for Jewish philosophers to be Jews in order to philosophize. I am not at all certain that it would be possible or even desirable to reverse this trend.

It is of course completely different when one speaks of theology. The philosopher of the medieval tradition was as much a theologian as philosopher. Philosophy was king, but theology was its crown. Presently, with the restoration of Jewish internality and particularism, the repudiation of dependency, even interest in the currents of Christian thought and doctrine and the renaissance of the Jewish nation, its language and history, philosophy is become an historical discipline and theology merely the annotation of ideology.   [A.A.C.]

HERMANN COHEN

He was seventy-six years old—but this doesn't comfort me at all. . . . I find it hard to free myself of the painful realization that Hermann Cohen has been carried off suddenly and prematurely. Until his very last day, he remained youthful, creative, and cheerfully militant. His end came virtually in the midst of his life, his young soul passed on in the midst of his work. We knew that he had reached old age, the time in which Death gleefully toys with human beings and teases them until it has fulfilled its mission. But this knowledge never really took root in us; it faded and vanished under the impression of strength and youthfulness that informed all of Cohen's final creations, the late progeny of the great thinker—as though the usual course of events had been reversed, as though the promise of youth had overtaken him in old age. Other people tend to start on a small scale and conclude on a large one, but Cohen until his seventieth year never found time to write articles and never contributed to philosophical reviews; he, the teacher, never even participated in the periodical literature that had emerged from his school[1] and was created by his pupils. His own productivity began with large works, which in their time were consequential and revolutionary; he gave the world gigantic books, heavy with thought and instruction for generations to come. It was only a few years ago that he began to bother himself with the mundane, as it were, the issues of everyday living, and became in a certain sense a publicist, a journalist—which is no disparagement. At seventy, he descended from the heights of the eternal truths to conquer a place for himself in the realm of magazines, pamphlets, and the ephemeral literature. It looked as though the old man was worried about the fruits that had fallen from his tree, the crumbs that had dropped beneath his table, so that he—a successor to himself—repeated his teachings in the most diverse forms, gathering gleanings after gleanings, discovering new relations and connections in order to cover up their age. But this is not true. A new manner and a new style are revealed in his journalistic works. Something of a new beginning, a new soaring comes forth in the powerful rhetoric and the brilliance of his speech.

No sooner had be begun to unburden his inmost self, no sooner had he opened a gate to the stormy life that he had previously repressed by the hard work of cool thinking, no sooner had he begun teaching with a hand extended to battle, to attack and defend, upbraiding, warning, making suggestions, and demanding improvements—than suddenly, the mighty flow of words that flashed fire under the cloak of careful logic broke off. The words broke off and will never be continued.

With the death of Hermann Cohen, the greatest son of the Jewish enlightenment in the West has left us. The last among the great men of that era, the last in time, the first in significance. He took his generation's indecisive notions about Judaism, thought of assimilation in the name of Judaism and for Judaism, and elevated it to a system of amazing lucidity and consistency. His doctrine of Jewish ethics, permeated with national pride, is a justification as it is, of that quasi-assimilation. Sometimes we feel a qualm: if such a great thinker as Hermann Cohen could surrender to the idea of this assimilation and commit himself to it with such tremendous zeal, with the strength of an unshakable certitude, with the stubbornness of an indomitable faith, and fight for it until his last breath, how can we nationalists deny it any right to exist and look upon it with contempt?

Yes, at times the courage of the national Jew falters in the face of this peculiar phenomenon: an acute thinker, who descends into the very abyss of thought, who perambulates the lofty heights of his heaven like a native citizen, who knows all its paths and all the twists and turns of its trails; a thinker who proclaims the doctrine of unity and wholeness and who has stigmatized the doctrine of duality and antithesis, of spiritual contradictions and fissures as the root of all sin—is it possible that he failed to notice the infirmities of the idea of assimilation, this most crippled of all the products of halfness and duality, twisting in the convulsions of an injured, broken, isolated, sin-stained soul?

Here lies the tragedy of this brilliant thinker. He had received a legacy from his generation, a legacy that became a stumbling block for him. He remained true to his era and that was his punishment. For what have the fathers of the enlightenment left for us? A fissure in our hearts, a duality in life, a spirit that has forfeited its forms, colorless thoughts whose wellspring had gone dry, dogmas of a rational faith whose sap had run out, torn-off branches without any soil to take root in, fragments of the tablets of an empty Judaism, bankruptcy—that was the legacy of the fathers of Jewish enlightenment in West Europe. Cohen did, of course, come to save our goods, but he never touched the foundations of the decay that led to our degeneration, he never undermined them, he actually strove to strengthen them—and so he went forth and constructed an imposing edifice of spiritual Judaism on the ground of the one that had been torn down. It is particularly ironic that Cohen was destined to cover up the bankruptcy of his age, to elevate the negation, the insolvency of a Judaism torn away from reality, into a positive thing, to a progress in the development of the Jewish spirit. Only the acumen of a mind that is capable of anything, that was a master of all the tools of rationalistic architecture, could assume such a hard task.

It is therefore no surprise that this great thinker could not emerge with even an apparent victory from his disputations with the nationalists and Zionists. He was nearly always defeated. His faculties never weakened, they never deserted him for a moment; on the contrary, during the last few years, they were brilliantly confirmed in his polemics. It was not the weakness of his personality, or an incapacity of his logic. It was the insufficiency of an archaic position that, based on an inner contradiction, was developed into a system and connected variously with sublime thoughts about mankind and Messianism. It was sometimes painful to witness the defeat of this giant when even a dwarf from the camp of the Zionists and nationalists could stand up to him and instantly disprove his ideas. . . . And the rebuttal was correct! But it wasn't Cohen's fault. It brought no shame upon him. It was the fault of a generation, the shame of an era, which Cohen defended as well as he could. Thus he stood like a mighty rock in his splendid isolation, never bending to any worldly storm, faithfully keeping watch over the errors of the fathers, a cerebral giant guarding the legacy of an indigent generation.

The giant has fallen. Gone is the last of the great sons of an era that was weighted with responsibility. He was the last in time, but the first in importance. Gathering at the bier of Hermann Cohen the Jew, we stand at the coffin of an entire epoch.

Hermann Cohen reached the age of seventy-six, but he did not live to see his teachings disseminated among the general public. Even his colleagues have failed to pay him his full due. The textbooks on philosophical history tend either to ignore him or to dispose of him with a few words of recognition or disparagement, saying little that is appropriate. Even the representatives of the neo-Kantian school, which absorbed most of Cohen's doctrines, fail to cite their teacher's name.

There is reason to believe that Cohen's upright Judaism, which was not merely a defense but was also a struggle against Christianity and its dominion, prevented his receiving full recognition. There is an inadvertent admission in the words of Kuno Fischer, who writes off Cohen's teachings with the words: More race than philosophy.

Kuno Fischer uttered a true statement without sensing the deeper meaning of his words. Cohen's philosophy entails many elements of the Jewish spirit. His ethical system supports, and is supported by, the ethics of Judaism.

Many Jewish thinkers, intent upon establishing peace between science and Judaism had long been seeking a satisfactory compromise between them. They barely managed to assimilate an impoverished philosophy into a powerful Judaism, giving it a subordinate and submissive position to set their hearts at ease. Cohen, however, never sought any legitimization for alien thought or connections with the teachings of Israel. He was fully devoted to the doctrine of Hellas. But his observation of the world, his promotion of an ethics on the basis of the Idea and the Absolute led him to the teachings of Judaism, which he scaffolded into a system in order to make it presentable to philosophy. Thus he paved a new way. Before him, Israel's teachings had managed to survive only through self-confinement and national self-limitation; only a distortion could reach the various nations and national splinters, who twisted Israel's words, adulterating her rallying-cry and denying her merits. It is only now that this doctrine, having passed through the breadth and depth of philosophy, can become a world-view. If Cohen's teachings are accorded their due, they will elicit in the forum of science recognition for the full scope of Jewish ethics. Humanistic studies, their literature, and their universities will then have to leave room for Jewish ethics as a special way of thinking, a special approach. Cohen is the source of a philosophical school of Jewish ethics. Spinoza stood outside the pale of Jewish thought, and wherever he touched it he attacked it. No wonder that even the best non-Jewish thinkers felt alien to Cohen and consciously or unconsciously ignored him and his goal of Judaizing ethics.

A contributing factor to this situation was the peculiar terseness of Cohen's delivery and the hardness of his style. His works are inaccessible to the average reader. His ideas require concentration; they demand explanations and commentaries, and no philosophical writer has as yet taken on the task of popularizing Cohen's ideas.

Forty years ago, Cohen published his great works on Kant.[2] He wanted to clarify his teacher's doctrine and to present its true substance; he discerned a new dimension in it and found it necessary to fight against many interpretations that had been read into Kant. Cohen's works provoked an uproar and dismay in the Kantian school. Kant's most renowned disciples started a violent feud with Cohen. Ultimately, there was a schism, Cohen and his followers separated from the others and founded a new school, the school of epistemological and practical idealism, of the doctrine of "purity" in thought and will—the Marburg School, named after the place where this young destroyer-creator taught after the death of Friedrich Albert Lange.[3] Cohen was nicknamed: Interpreter of Kant.

This sobriquet is derogatory. It underestimates him. Cohen's significance is by no means limited to his commentaries on Kant. They are merely the starting-point, not the full extent of the road he traveled, or the limits of his gigantic strides. He grew beyond these commentaries. The interpreter became a revolutionary. Even as a commentator, he had renovated his teacher's system, thereby making it his own. Cohen's strength, his vital nerve, was as a renovator. A creative tremor runs through all the channels of his youthful thoughts. Meanwhile, he demolished numerous axioms of Kantian doctrine, raising a new system on the ruins, a system encompassing the full scope and depth of all areas of philosophy. Cohen's final works certainly release him from the modest title, "Interpreter of Kant."

Perhaps no name fits Cohen better than that of architect. Thought has two recognized paths for its expression. The logician tends to rise gradually, moving up a ladder from reasons to directions, from premises to conclusions, from the particular to the universal, thereby achieving the thesis. We are witnesses of his cautious road to his resting place. He lets us participate in the growth of his ideas from the ramified roots to the foliage of the treetop. There is, however, a different approach, one that frees thought from the forced labor of logical form, that robs it of its focus and its enchantment. This is the road of soaring freedom. We are not permitted to see the embryo of the thought, its components and elements, its development and composition. It does not lay itself bare to us, does not reveal the secret of its texture, the construction of its parts; it stands before us as an organic whole, covering its face with the veil of creation, without towing along a bundle of reasons.

Cohen chose neither of these roads, and yet his way possesses characteristics of both: the precision of logic and the chastity of the artist. He never surprises us with the brilliance of his theses, never frightens us with the weight of his detailed motives. He covers up his thesis, conceals his motives behind the plan he specifically created. His words grow almost spontaneously, out of sight, under piles of thoughts and thought fragments. We do not notice their growth. We recognize it only at its maturation—but we have given in to his teachings, which have gradually conquered our mind without our realizing it. We watched their genesis but did not recognize it as such, and thus we joined it, unresisting, on its long road, without noticing the twists and turns—and now we are caught.

To all appearances, Cohen is merely presenting and explaining other people's opinions, but in doing so he permits few deviations and leads opinion in a specific direction. To all appearances, he is merely connecting them with his topic, but in the course of his treatment, he secretly introduces the elements of his doctrine, his explanations, and his special nuance, which join together into a system. He forms analogies, reveals differences, establishes one relationship after another between the concepts, secretly ties in the fibers of his creation, weaving them into a finely woven, variegated texture. To all appearances, everything is fully exposed; try, however, to find the opening and the concluding knot, or to examine the run of each thread and its concatenations.

Cohen is an architect of ideas, his greatness lies in the way he links his concepts together. By putting them in order, he constructs them. Do bricks and mortar belong to the architect? Construction consists in ordering.

Cohen is a rationalist. Ordering and systematizing, the dominion of method—this is one of the chief characteristics of rationalistic apperception and construction.

This appreciation of Cohen almost contains a censure. A plan submissive to form, a form that prepares its own material, an order pointing in a specific direction—do not these imply preconceived thinking? The point of a secret purpose [Tendenz]—sometimes visible, sometimes hidden—is concealed in the order of elements, slowly skewering them, impaling them. Doesn't this dent any notion of the simplicity of thought?

But we cannot censure Cohen for these things, unless we wish as well to censure the style of the Jewish spirit, which is marked by knowledge based on will and goal. The Jewish spirit takes a road and is tied to its direction, being fulfilled only at its very end. It takes no pleasure in mere observation; its sole enjoyment is in study and application. Can you censure the Jewish spirit for wanting to construct the world for man's sake according to a preordained plan? Can you censure it for announcing its truths with the pride of a pioneer and demanding their acceptance with the pedantry of a teacher? The high rhetoric of morality and its severe voice accompany Cohen's thought so that he never feels the humility of ideas and never heeds the rebuke of their peaceable innocence.

We have already indicated that Hermann Cohen follows the ways of Greek philosophy and that his teachings are nourished on the natural sciences and mathematics, which, however, merely serve as premises for the teachings of Israel. He brings Plato over to the Prophets. His assertions in logic serve him as premises in ethics. A torrent of the will surges through Cohen's thinking, even where it is enclosed in the rigid husk of a cold mathematics. It is this that explains the emphatic tone and the hair-splitting, the passionate and biting polemics.

Cohen's approach and delivery exhibit additional characteristics, most of which are typical of the Jewish spirit.

Wherever he reveals his profundity, he also manifests his extremely subtle, barely comprehensible acumen; the cautious scholar is also capable of "tearing out mountains and hanging them on a hair." His terse precision is found alongside the breadth of a commentator. He inserts his most personal reflections into world ideas and subjects his opinions to the critique of others; he interprets them in order to absorb them into his system. He was in the habit of quoting Kant's dictum about Plato: if you think out an author's ideas to their ultimate conclusion, it is proper to probe even deeper in order to discover things that he was unable to find. This is what Cohen did with Kant. Cohen remained, in this way, an interpreter, an expounder, even after creating his own great system.

Architectonic power is shown in Cohen's style as well. Every word has its carefully measured limit, every expression its dominion. The least phrase has its definite location, the least movement is indicated through stroke and color. No letter, no dot could be changed without shaking the entire structure. A thick beam is often supported by a crooked post, concatenated rings run, concealed, through the entire edifice, from the deepest foundation stones to the highest cupola. The huge cupola is sustained by forces calculated to support one another: the vertical corresponds to the horizontal, the rise to the fall. The calculation has to be dead right. The slightest deviation, the least subtraction or addition would disturb the equilibrium. Calculation—Cohen should not be censured for this, although it might seem to detract from naive creation. There can be no construction without a blueprint, no blueprint without calculation.

Some readers complain about Cohen's difficult style, overlooking its charm and attraction. The difficulty lies in the synthesis. His style is made up of the deepest and loftiest things in the language, coherent with the depth of his thought and the soaring of his abstraction. The difficulty lies no less in Cohen's personality, which refuses to draw upon what is already accomplished and insists upon doing its own seeking in order to find, straining itself with even the most pedestrian expression and reanimating finished language. Cohen takes nothing that is banal or commonplace from language; he does not acquire anything that has already been picked and happens to be lying in the road, he climbs into the secret shaft of language, tests every word to make sure it meets his purposes, picks over words until he finds the proper expression. He virtually lifts if from the ground and hews it aright, thereby stamping his thoughts upon his style. Since he doesn't take his diction from an available storeroom, since language adjusts to his thoughts only after struggles and compromises, every word, even the most worn, shows the aches and pains of the mating struggle between thought and language.

And there is something else. Philosophy is Cohen's methodology, the crown of the sciences, and not a special science in itself. When he teaches logic, ethics, or aesthetics, he always touches upon natural science, mathematics, physiology and psychology, fine arts, music, and architecture in such detail as to reveal the expert and specialist. Thus, his style has to struggle through many disciplines, through all kinds of twists and turns and contacts, before mounting to a synthesis.

It is worth spending some time on the great phenomenon of Hermann Cohen as a Jew.

At first glance, he was highly problematic. For him, the spirit of Judaism is, pure and simple, the spirit of mankind. He acknowledges progress in the world only to the extent that the nations grow culturally closer to the ethics of Judaism. He says: "The monotheism of Judaism is the unshakable bulwark for the entire future of ethical culture." And elsewhere: "Along with the concept of man and mankind, the concept of the one God is the central problem of the development of the spirit of culture." He taught: Anyone constructing an ethics without the concept of the God of Israel, has raised an altar to the idol of materialism or pinned his ethics on a nonentity, a mystical superstition, something unreal. Such a doctrine does not bear the seal of truth. And again: "The destiny of God rests on the shoulders of Israel." And then too: Judaism is a primal source and is therefore indestructible. "Such a primal force is irreplaceable."[4]

But the same Cohen, who proudly fought for Israel's teachings and conquered a place for them in the world of thought, struggled simultaneously and with the same strength against the idea of our national rebirth. Does this not require an explanation?

Let us look upon that era, which Cohen so marvelously represents.

When Western Jews were about to be found worthy of "humanity," they bowed their heads and exposed the degeneracy of Judaism: it is dead and decayed, they announced, and all that we can do is bury it. They never tired of offering proof after proof that Judaism had already breathed its last. It was then that a generous "mankind" acknowledged them: Your assertions are believable; henceforth, you can be regarded as human beings. And the apostles of freedom were overjoyed at having disposed in such a kindly way of a burdensome nation, who with its prophets and merchants had made the other nations uneasy and brought upon them the shames of the Inquisition and anti-Semitism. Now, there would be no further impediments to equality and fraternity. The adepts of a naïve enlightenment were happy that they had succeeded in reconciling "mankind" and acquiring emancipation as their reward.

That is how that generation appears to us at first glance. However, the leaders of that generation were in fact satisfied that, in reality, the teachings of Israel had not been conquered by, but had conquered, the culture of the nations, from whom the force of evil had receded, touched as the nations had been by a breath of *our* spirit, a breath of the spirit of liberty, equality, and fraternity, for which our Prophets and merchants had ubiquitously and tirelessly served as guides and agents. At one and the same time, Western Jews proclaimed the death of the Jewish nation and sang praises to the eternal spirit of Israel.

In that hour, when peace between Israel and the nations (mankind, so-called) was declared, our national instinct went astray. The great wall, religion, which had faithfully protected us in the galut, was torn down. Judaism shed its outer coverings and exposed its essence, and behold, it was the essence of a universal mankind and its thoughts were "universal thoughts." The children of that time, seeing Judaism in spiritual nakedness and beholding mankind building on the foundations of its spirit, were faced with the question: Why do we stay separate from "mankind"? This question could arise only after the drive for self-preservation had collapsed and abstract thought could pierce it with the thorn of its investigation and its aspirations.

The clever drive for self-preservation found a narrow escape hatch, a cunning solution, easy for the time being, however difficult for the future. The universal human foundation of the spirit of Judaism was seen as its right to exist, its destiny, the mission of justice, bettering the world, illuminating the nations. Those who thought in such terms did not sense that the national drive to self-preservation was obscuring their perceptions and leading them to national hubris. In justifying the spirit of Judaism, they were forced to denigrate the spirit of the nations: for apologetic reasons, they had to present us as a guide for the nations of the world.

This was the greatest irony of the dissolution of Judaism: one half, submissiveness and surrender to the culture of the nations, the other half, national hubris in the self-awareness of being the chosen people.

Within the dissolution, the national purpose still writhes and battles death so long as a Jewish spark still flames. It seeks compromises, even between Judaism and assimilation. The assimilationists removed from Judaism everything that had a national and political stamp and read a false meaning into it; they went so far as to demand assimilation and, falsely invoking the names of God and the Prophets, urged an abandonment of Judaism in the name of the spirit of Judaism itself. They failed to realize that their striving to justify the dissolution in the name of the ethical spirit of Judaism was inspired by the national drive for self-preservation which, in its agony, is still struggling against death and asserting its right to live.

The worthiest advocate of this complex doctrine was Hermann Cohen. He fashioned it into a great system and became the savior of its honor. In this way he shows himself in his full stature as an interpreter. After all, Judaism, like loosened soil, is perfect for absorbing all possible interpretations and explanations, an arena for pettifogging, a public domain, like its unfortunate people, for anyone wishing to bless it with teachings and missions.

Only an important philosopher like Hermann Cohen could take that thought, the thought of a generation, a thought that arose in dichotomy and lived in dichotomy—only Hermann Cohen could raise it to a grandiose system.

Great is the tragedy of this brilliant Jew, greater its irony, the irony of our destiny among the nations.

21. APOLOGETIC THINKING
FRANZ ROSENZWEIG

EDITOR'S INTRODUCTION

FRANZ ROSENZWEIG (1886–1929), philosopher, educator, and author of the twentieth century's most important work of Jewish theology, *The Star of Redemption,* was not only a thinking, but a living, Jew, that is, one who studied the Law and observed the Commandments. This essay appeared in *Der Jude,* Jahrgang VII (1923), pp. 457–64.

It is a continual temptation when dealing with Rosenzweig to italicize the man, allowing his life to replace his thought, a convenience rendered all the more popular by the conventional wisdom that regards his life as exemplary and his thought as obscure. And yet it was to guard against precisely this misemphasis that Rosenzweig required that *The Star of Redemption* be published without introduction, without descriptive allurements or short-hand exegeses. It was not that Rosenzweig wished to maintain the impenetrability of his text (any more than Walter Benjamin—according to Scholem's report, "an avid reader" of Rosenzweig's *Star*—wished to prevent the reading of his *The Origin of German Tragic Drama* by introducing it with an immensely imbricated epistemological essay), but rather, I believe, that he wished to serve notice to the reader that the issues at stake were of the highest importance, easy neither to grasp nor to state.

The conviction that theology was the single discipline of knowledge preceding the right conduct of life, that no other knowledge mattered so much as grasping the intersection of God, world, and man, made Rosenzweig not only a thinker intolerant of pretense, but utterly tolerant of serious, if mistaken, enterprise. He could not bear the collection of sermons by Rabbi Emil Cohen of Bonn, whose style of preaching he demolishes, unabashedly and with immense wit ("Ein Rabbinerbuch," *Der Jude,* Jahrgang VII [1923], pp. 237–40), focusing his complaint on the absence of the clear spiritual center and the consequent misregistration of voice; while in the essay "Apologetic Thinking" he sets out two important works of his generation—Max Brod's *Paganism–Christianity–Judaism* and Leo Baeck's *The Essence of Judaism*—and submits them to intellectual scrutiny, a bath of acid, in which the question is not one of love, respect, or collegiality, but truth.

It is this criterion of truth that is consistently absent from lesser examples of apologetic thinking than Brod's and Baeck's. The opposite of truth is not necessarily falsehood, but the method of falsification, from which falsehood, quite as unpredictably as truth, can result. The difficulty is that the method of falsification (which leaves argument open, indifferently, to error or truth) cannot be correctly judged. Since the intent of apologetics is defense, the interest of self-protection is overriding. Of course, the aggrieved and injured, the vulnerable (in a word), have every right to defense, and vulnerability excuses all defense as legitimate in the interest of the beleaguered. Rosenzweig is sensitive to this justifiable *caveat,* yet by the time of this essay (the early summer of 1923) he had already made the center of Judaism his home, and his anxiety lest Judaism be distorted by misrepresentation was vastly less than that of Max Brod—who wrote out of confession—or Leo Baeck, who was a liberal rabbi. For Brod, Judaism was magnified by ideality and the otherness of Christianity could be faulted in its real particularity: in such an apposition, historical Christianity would always lose to ideal Judaism. No less, Baeck could extrapolate commandment from mystery, without having to contend with the obduracy of the Law.

Apologetics—the historical form of self-interpretation before theological enmity—has been, in Rosenzweig's view, the traditional mode of Jewish theology. Apologetics is contrasted with dogmatics.

Dogmatics enforces the systematic exposition of dogma from within the circle of faith, while apologetics—never relying upon an inheritance of received and generalized dogma—is conditioned by the occasion that evokes it. Even Maimonides' *Guide of the Perplexed,* never an adequate system (and hence an inadequate dogmatics), is regarded by Rosenzweig as apologetic, continually contesting the opposition raised by the *Kalam* to Jewish rational theology, defending Judaism against the charge of anthropomorphism, examining issues not according to their interior coherence and requirement but according to the demands of the occasion. Apologetics is occasional thinking, that is, thought generated by the challenge of opposition. Systematic theology is thought within a community of received tradition of credal adherence. Christianity could develop scholastic theology and later systematic theology as interreferential domains precisely because the Christian councils had established the explicit dogmas of Christianity, leaving to theology the interpretation of their meaning within the scheme of alternative metaphysics and "science." The issues of nominalism and realism could agitate centuries of Christian thought as internal argument, modalities of exegesis being alternatively validated or denounced according as conciliar opinion regarded them as confirming or undermining the true dogmas of faith.

"Judaism has dogmas, but no dogmatics." And the most profound and binding of Jewish dogmas is nowhere expressed as dogma, being in fact, as Rosenzweig suggests, taken for granted. This is the dogma of the chosenness of Israel. It is precisely at a juncture such as this that the whole difficulty of

Jewish theological thinking becomes apparent. The belief in the chosenness of Israel is so quintessential an article of faith—supporting all others, all miracles of history, all penultimate salvations and benefices of God—that to express it and give it the form of yet another article of faith would be redundant. The liturgic formula of the Haggadah's *dayenu* is precisely this: it would have been sufficient, any of God's grace would have been sufficient, because to have received that grace at all—in any of its particularities—is an excess, a going beyond the election of Israel. The election of Israel is the ground on which the Law and the commandments rest. And yet, observe that precisely because the election of Israel is the ground of Judaism, the merest earthquake of history is enough to shake that foundation and shift its soil from self-evident truth to cosmic fault. In our time, the denial of that election (commonplace among the radical reformers and reconstructors of Judaism) is consummated with such assurance and complacency that what is so self-evident as to be unmentioned as dogma is the first item to be dismissed as ethnocentric pride, egoism, doctrinal prosthesis.

Rosenzweig concludes his stunning essay with an example of philosophic dithyramb that would elude a reader not intimately familiar with the argument of *The Star of Redemption*. Apologetics, Rosenzweig avers, collapses finally because the apologetic thinker is led by the pressure of self-defense to identify the essence of his thought with the depths of the self, ratifying argument by the witness of confession, validating dialectic discrimination by the appeal to the authenticating metaphysical ego. The difficulty of such procedure is that the more the argument seeks to move outward to self-proclamation and clarification the more it must first proceed inward to the core of the self. As Rosenzweig shrewdly notes, the deeper a man delves the self, the more that self merges in the order of abstraction with the self of every man: hence particularity and discrimination—which is the triumph of apologetics—is lost in the generality of every man. To reverse the procedure and vindicate the self by engaging the particularities of outward limits, the external history of the self abroad in the world of others, is to lose the argument from the other side: the individual is merged with history. This is the dilemma of apologetics: it always falls into one or another extreme, the purely inward or the purely historical. The truth, however, which transcends the occasionalism of historical provocation or authentication by resort to interior essence, requires a different method of theological interpretation. Naturally, that method is the method of *The Star of Redemption*, which crosses the boundary line of the objective and the subjective, the self and history, by describing a universe before life is lived. To stand outside the universe, which permits thought to think not in opposition or in contrast to life but as a modality of life, is the Archimedean fulcrum about which Rosenzweig speaks in the earliest pages of *The Star*.   [A.A.C.]

APOLOGETIC THINKING

1

Often it has been said and even more often repeated that Judaism has no dogmas. As incorrect as this statement may be (a superficial review of Jewish history or a glance into the Jewish prayerbook teaches the opposite), it nevertheless has something correct about it. Judaism has dogmas, but no dogmatics. Even the point at which the Talmudic literature enters the discussion (to which later attempts at establishing Jewish dogmas had to revert) is rather peculiar in this respect: in connection with the regulations governing criminal procedure and criminal law, we encounter the problem of punishment in the hereafter [M. Sanhedrin, 10]. Items of belief are listed that, were a Jew to deny them, would deprive him of his "portion in the world to come." It was here that Maimonides and others were able to find a point of departure. Within a legal context, therefore, problems of religious metaphysics appear. This is surely remarkable even if we recall the often-cited and, for the moment, surely firmly entrenched metaphysical inclination of our people.

Moreover, the matter becomes even more remarkable when we observe the substance of these dogmas. The discussion concerns God, the revealed Law, the Messianic redemption, and related ideas. It ignores the conception that wholly permeates Judaism, which alone makes the Law comprehensible, which alone can explain the preservation of the Jewish people: the chosenness of Israel. This truly cardinal concept of Judaism, which a Christian scholar, coming from Christology, might expect to find in first place or at least immediately after the doctrine of God in a Jewish system of dogma, is totally absent from Maimonides' *Thirteen Articles of Faith,* as well as from his philosophical work that was intended to be a guide for anyone perplexed about the basic truths of Judaism. The chosenness of Israel is here, as everywhere else, a prerequisite for thought and life, but it is never articulated. It is taken for granted. Prayer and poetry never tire of giving it a new verbal garb. The exegetic legends [*midrashim*] mirror it with myriad facets. Mysticism sinks deep into it, to the point of mythological hypostasis. It becomes word, meaning, form, but never a dogmatic formula, never (with the great exception of Jehuda Halevi's *Kuzari,* which, however, was deeply influenced by all these other allied authorities) an item of philosophic credo.[1] Existence is filled with it and borne by it, all immediate expression of existence is moved by it—however, when consciousness seeks to soar beyond mere existence, it denies this chosenness.

The reasons are deep and the consequences far-reaching. A spiritual community withdraws its inmost being from spiritual illumination. This means that the community does not wish merely to be a spiritual community but also seeks to be something that it actually *is* in contrast to other communities organized solely by the spirit: a natural community, a nation. The immense reality of Jewish being has created for itself a self-protection. What operates here to protect and to preserve reality, that is, the removal of consciousness from the secret wellspring of life, would have had a paralyzing effect on life in a purely spiritual community, as, for example, the Christian church. In the church, the continually renewed awareness of the basis of existence, in this case the constant reformulating of Christological dogma, becomes the inner condition for the external duration of the community. Inaccessible mystery as opposed to inexhaustible mystery, substantiality as opposed to spirituality.

This polarity has an effect on the direction and scope of scientific thought in general. Not only has Jewish patristics never produced an Augustine, a thinker whose vision defined the setting for the history of the coming millennium (although Judaism did bring forth powerful swimmers through the "sea of Talmud"), but Jewish scholasticism never brought forth a Thomas Aquinas. His *Summa,* that mighty system of a total Christian science (whose grand, truly systematic intention could not overcome the congenital defect of Scholasticism's apologetic and dialectic method and therefore could not realize itself), has a Jewish equivalent in Maimonides' work, not in his philosophical *Guide of the Perplexed* but in his *Great Ḥibbur,*[2] as he himself designated his gigantic *halakhic* opus, which, like Thomas's *Summa,* captures the entire universe, but in the sieve of Jewish law. Here, in a different way, we find the same immediate totality that St. Thomas intended, the same determination to make the heart of the author's own religious life the center of a spiritual cosmos. Scholars have been correct in interpreting "my great *Ḥibbur*" as meaning "my *Summa*" (although their approach was based on different reasons). *The Guide of the Perplexed,* however, would be a disappointment to anyone coming to it in search of a system. Beginning with a lengthy discourse that unfolds all the material relevant to the problem of Biblical anthropomorphism, it unravels the same apologetic thread throughout all the individual discourses that make up the work. The defense is directed against the attacks of philosophy, but not, or only peripherally, against other religions, by which they could only partially be taken over. The basic apologetic position gives the work a totally unpedantic air that still refreshes the reader today and never strikes one as the least bit "scholastic." Its thought possesses something that systematic thinking tends to lack: the charm—and truthfulness—of occasional ideas. But it loses, thereby, the restraints that only systematic thinking can impose: precisely the restraints of occasion. Only systematic thought determines the sphere of its subject matter. Apologetic thought remains dependent upon the provocation of opposition.

And in this sense, Jewish thinking remains apologetic thinking. Characteristically, it never reaches the state that independent thinking in a culture regularly attains: the struggle of schools within a common tradition of thought. The conflict between nominalism and realism has its Jewish counterpart in the conflict over Maimonides, with its labor pains and after pains, and with its two phases, separated by a century. This is not a struggle *within* thought; it is a cultural struggle over thought per se, the struggle between those who heeded the call of occasion and those who refused to do so. Nor was it any different in the nineteenth century, when, after a four-hundred-year interval (in the Germany of the 1820s), a new Jewish philosophy emerged, whose accomplishments have still not been given their due. Despite all reservations about apologetics, the legitimate method of thinking itself remained apologetic. No one became a Jewish thinker within the private domain of Judaism. Thinking was not thinking about Judaism (which was simply taken for granted, and was more of an existence than an "ism"); it was thinking within Judaism, learning—ultimately ornamental, rather than fundamental, thinking. Anyone who was to think about Judaism, somehow had to be drawn to the border of Judaism, if not psychologically then intellectually. His thinking was thus determined by the power that had brought him to the border and the horizon of his gaze was defined by the degree to which he had been carried to, near, or across it.

Apologetics is the legitimate strength of this thinking, but also an inherent danger. Two important modern works will now be considered from this double viewpoint.

2

Gustav Landauer (in this magazine)[3] reacted to the publication of the germ-cell of Brod's confessional book with a retort that was spurred by an injured sense of justice. He saw it as an attempt to seize one's own domain in its ideality while grasping the alien domain in the full scope of its historical and historically tainted reality. I would think that this is the sort of danger that can be easily avoided precisely because it is so obvious. On the other hand, the danger of all apologetics strikes me as residing in the process of taking one's own domain (which, after all, one does know) in the full scope and depth of its reality while taking the alien domain (of which one has "taken cognizance," mainly from books) merely as ideal. Every real observer of human nature knows that one must exert a great deal of caution in using personal statements as source material, not because, for reasons of natural bias, they create an excessively favorable impression, but because, on the contrary, they tend to be too theoretical, too absolute, too dry and bony, lacking the revision of theory by practice, the flesh covering the skeleton. The well-known utterance by a man who ought to know: "Give me two written words by anyone and I'll bring him to the gallows" holds for intellectual movements as well. We all know what a tragicomic distortion of Judaism results when, with seeming objectivity, we string a series of quotations together. Nor does it much matter whether Jews or anti-Semites do the assembling; on the contrary, the things that Eisenmenger[4] and his predecessors offer as "fiery Satanic bullets" from the arsenal of the Talmud could truly draw one to the Talmud more readily than some recent collections of carefully filtered "rays of light." All this is certainly related to what I discussed in the first part of these observations: the peculiar lack of self-consciousness in Judaism. It is genuinely impossible to make any Talmudic passage comprehensible to someone who doesn't already understand it. Each time, one would have to open virtually a whole illustrated atlas of Jewish history, Jewish faces, Jewish life, which is, of course, impossible. But, even though Christianity is based on (and aims much more at) self-consciousness, one could do it no greater injustice than to present it in terms of its own catechism. The primary duty of theoretical neighborly love (which is no less important to creatures committed to mutual observation and judgment than to the more practical brand—for being perceived wrongly is no less painful than being treated wrongly) is always to ask ourselves in regard to any opinion we form about another person: can this other person, if he is really as I depict him here, still be able to live? For that is what he wishes and ought to do, after all—"like myself." Those legalistic machines, devoid of soul and sense of humor, whom the Christian loves to imagine in the "Pharisees," would be incapable of living no less certainly than those pale lilies whom the Jew—basing his opinion on a reading of the Sermon on the Mount—would recognize as the only "true Christians." If one wants to understand a spirit, one cannot abstract it from its adhering body. A body is not a degenerate manifestation of the spirit; likewise, one cannot write off as degenerate or corrupted those things that, in a historical picture of a community, do not comport with its classical documents. For all we know, those very things could well be a necessary and, in a certain sense, originally "intended" correction of origins. An adult can spend all his life yearning for the purity of childhood, but that does not make his adulthood a degenerate version of the child. On the contrary, perhaps we recognize the full meaning of the traits of the child only when they are plumbed in the familiar lineaments of the adult.

And this pinpoints the weakness of Brod's book. A real weakness because it is unnecessary, not a weakness that shadows a strength. The fact that he unduly schematizes "paganism" matters far less. Paganism, despite the three-part title and the three-part basic schema, has no portion of this book's bloodstream, which otherwise pulses with experience. But the depiction of Christianity, precisely through its proximity to the heart of the book, suffers greatly from the method of "unfair idealizing," whereby the author lends credence to schoolmasters and theology professors rather than to saints and knights. Typically, two living Christians who do not spring from the catechism—Dante and Kierkegaard—are admitted into the book because the author was too close to them to leave them outside. But, as comical as it may sound, he treats them, not as Christians, but as Jews who have been isolated within Christianity. If only he had gone here by experience—even if his own—rather than by theory.

His fidelity to his own experience in the essential part of the book is its strength. It is exactly what its subtitle says it is—in a good sense of the word—"a confession." But it does not burden the reader with the private affairs of the author, as one might have feared. Instead, it narrates the life of an understanding, and because that life embodied that of a generation, the ultimate goal has a more than private significance. Brod, in his own manner, worked his way through the fog of theories to the reality of historical Judaism. He succeeded because he ignored the theoretical question of true Judaism, urged on by the practical question of a true life. This book answers the question of the essence of war with the essence of Judaism. It became a good theological book because (oh strangest, easiest, and most difficult of sciences!) it is not a theological book. By origin and dynamics, it is a war book. And it became a bad theological book as soon as it tried to be, and to the extent that it wanted to be, a theological book.

With splendid élan, the book works its way from the concepts of "noble" and "ignoble misfortune," which were discovered personally and unscholastically during the war (and probably the prewar era) through the elevated vantage points of the "incompatability of things that belong together" and "earthly miracle," and goes right into the 'aggadah. The nineteenth-century concepts that Sunday school teachers dragged down to their own level remain unused. It is obvious why: after all, the internal apologetics of the book takes to task those very concepts, which, foolishly trying to make Judaism "more relevant," simply mummified it. This book's novelty resides in the intensity with which it thoroughly investigates the 'aggadic. Brod deals with very few Talmudic passages, but these he probes with a methodical earnestness that a Talmudist of the old school, confronted by the "merely 'aggadic" would find alien, even unintelligible. Brod, the 'am ha-'ares, modestly initiates a new method in the ancient field of Talmudic studies. Issues that hitherto only the preacher (and in modern times perhaps the historian) considered worthy of detailed attention are now taken seriously, even one might say, halakhically. The eyes of a generation returning home with a new attitude towards the old Book behold not simply the old Book, but something new and youthful.

Here we see how the strength of apologetic thinking can achieve results inaccessible to naïve thinking. But there is a danger. When Brod discovers in Judaism things that help him surmount his pressing intellectual crises, he all-too-readily discovers the "specifically Jewish" in them. He never asks himself whether the remedy he has discovered for his human crisis is not as human as the crisis itself, and whether Judaism participates in it precisely because of its participation in the human. Would not the restriction of the human (both of the particular and of the species), necessary and elevated as it is in its effect upon the individual, result rather in an equally necessary and equally elevated concentration of color from that dazzling whole light that has continuously shone upon the human race? In Christianity, Brod himself clearly sees where the point of this restriction is located: the unlimited possibility that divine grace has of finding its way to mankind is confined to the one dogmatically correct point of the experience of Christ. This is certainly true. Judaism's greatest strength lies in not knowing and not being permitted to know such an attachment to divine grace—not even, as is true of the Christian, to its own greatest deed. Here Judaism must preserve for its children the heavenly wine that it prepared unadulterated in its primal fire. But Brod failed to notice something that he could easily have recognized in his story about Simeon ben Yohai and his peculiar "institution": there is a point where Judaism, too, draws the line. In faith, we must be absolute. God does not prescribe the way of miracles for Judaism, but He does prescribe the way of man's action. In this Judaism is not absolute, only restricted to the one condition of the Law. That the circumference of this condition is so enormous that it never intersects any conceivable circumference of the world and its action makes no difference: it restricts as surely as the Christian experience of Christ, which potentially touches all human experience, is yet a restriction of faith. As a result, although Brod is kindly disposed and open toward the Law, measured by the general antiliberal atmosphere of today's intellectual genera-tion, everything he says about the Law remains on the nationalistically ruffled surface of the problem. And so when his book descends into the depths, it touches a pulse that the title question, complete with contradictions, cannot follow, and where the words he speaks in the name of his—and our—Judaism, are ultimately, but not penultimately, true.

3

In one passage of his book, Brod, with one of those broad gestures that enhance his confessional work, sweeps "the humane mediocrities of a Baeck or a Lazarus" from his table. We sense that in the rush of his personal thinking he never had the leisure to read things that were thought out before him. Thus Lazarus does not merit the harsh judgment, or—may I speak for once for our generation, both mine and Brod's—prejudice. Lazarus's book, attacked by Hermann Cohen in the prime of his Kantianism, is better than its reputation, which Brod is prolonging here. Goethe's aphorism, which wholly applies to Baeck, I wish to extend to Brod (and in memory of earlier prejudices, to myself): *"Pereant, qui ante nos nostra dixerunt"* ["Let those perish who have said our things before us"]. For, in both outer and inner form, one could hardly imagine a greater contrast than that between Brod's confessional book and Beack's *The Essence of Judaism*.[5] Brod constantly shows the road that led to his goal, and not the least charm of his book is the way it obliges the reader to accompany him on this road. In Baeck's work, however, the scaffolding had been almost totally dismantled. All we can see is the completed structure. So much for the form. With regard to content, however, the two books are as similar as two books of such dissimilar form can be. Baeck's book, too, is apologetically occasioned. The part that Christian words and deeds played in Brod's social milieu was taken over, for Baeck, by a literary event: Adolf von Harnack's *What is Christianity? [Das Wesen des Christentums]*.[6] This book, in its typical scholarly innocence, depicts a Judaism whose only possible viable purpose is as dark background to Christian light, one that, deprived of this function, would be so untenable as to crumble to pieces. It prompted Baeck (not contra Harnack, but for himself and for us) to depict Judaism as something in its own right, in its own rounded fullness, not merely as a foil for something else. Baeck portrays, not with the passion of the discoverer and confessor, but (especially in the second edition [1921], in which the book has grown to its full inner and outer weight) with the deep calm love of a servant completely at home in and familiar with the entire mansion of Judaism, even those things that agitated Brod, namely, the emergence of freedom from grace, or in Baeck's terms, commandment from mystery, the earthly miracle, or, again in Baeck's language, the great paradox. Brod depicts them in the powerful and spare dramatics of his confession and life story; Baeck depicts them in the tireless and never tiresome dialectics of his book of essence and knowledge, which compresses a variety of material into a narrow compass. It is a matter of individual taste whether one prefers substance in the authentically ecstatic form of one author or the authentically classical form of the other—and it may even be a matter of one's personal maturity of understanding. After all, in the life of knowledge, the time of blossoming is no less valid than the time of fruit.

As in what they offer, the two books are strangely similar in their weaknesses. What has been said above about Brod's treatment of Christianity could be repeated almost verbatim for Baeck. It may not be so clear in the peripheral treatment of Christianity in *The Essence of Judaism,* but it is all the more obvious in the more recent publication *Romantische Religion* [*Romantic Religion*],[7] tempered at best by a certain methodical awareness, deliberately posing the problem with a degree of abstraction. This, however, in no way lessens the danger for the reader.

Likewise, the kindred fundamental constellation of both books leads to their failing with the problem of the Law. Again, Baeck strikes me as having a keener awareness of the problem. But Baeck realizes as little as Brod does, that the critical point lies here: that what he recognizes as the essence of Judaism is more the *essence* of Judaism than the essence of *Judaism*. And (as is the case with Brod), it may happen here with the action derived from faith, that the Christian reader will follow him quite unhesitatingly, while the Jewish reader will falter. We should, however, take note that Baeck, peripherally and with no center of gravity, says very fine things about the Law, just as the liberal rabbi, especially in the second edition, says things about the Jewish people and Jewish history that are so profound as to far outstrip what any Zionist writer has to say about them. The Jewish present may possibly have no more hopeful sign than this exchange of roles.

4

Why has the word *apologetics* acquired such a bad reputation? The same seems to be true of the apologetic profession par excellence, that of the lawyer. A general bias against him sees his legitimate task, as it were, as lying.

Perhaps a certain professional routine appears to justify this prejudice. Nevertheless, defense can be one of the noblest of human occupations—to wit, when it goes to the very bottom of issues and souls, and ignoring the petty device of lies, ex-culpates[8] itself with the truth, the whole truth. In this broad sense, literary apologetics also can defend. In so doing it would not embellish anything, much less evade a vulnerable point. Instead, it would make the basis of defense the points of greatest jeopardy. In a word: it would defend the whole, not this or that particular. It would not be a defense in the usual sense, but an open presentation—not of some random thing but of one's own province. To what extent the two books under review approach this high concept of apologetics may be gathered from the above.

Both are answers to attacks. Their theme has been determined by attack. The theme is the authors' own essence. One could imagine that the result might have reached the highest consciousness. But the very nature of such thinking, its apologetics, prevents this. The thinker, by looking deep into his inmost essence, indeed, sees this essence, but is far from seeing himself. The thinker is not alone his inmost essence; he is also his outermost as well, and most particularly the link binding both the road on which the inner and the outer must associate with each other. He, however, with no further circumspection, equates his inmost with his self, and fails to realize that his inmost, the more inward it becomes, becomes the inmost of every human being. Thus, although meaning himself, he speaks about man, about all men. And thus his own self, the binding of the elements of mankind into something that he is himself, remains a mystery to himself. This barrier is never crossed by apologetic thinking. It is denied the ultimate strength of knowledge and spared the ultimate suffering of knowledge. Ultimate knowledge no longer defends; ultimate knowledge judges.

22. FRANZ ROSENZWEIG'S THE STAR OF REDEMPTION
(A REVIEW)
MARGARETE SUSMAN

EDITOR'S INTRODUCTION

MARGARETE SUSMAN (BENDEMANN-SUSMAN) (1872–1966), poet and philosophic and literary essayist, lived in Zurich from 1933 until her death. She contributed frequently on philosophic subjects to *Der Jude*. The present essay appeared during Jahrgang VII (1923), pp. 457–64.

It was Margarete Susman who first referred to "the exodus from philosophy" in the German-speaking world just after World War I. Scholem, who remarks upon her observation, has taken this to mean that the study of philosophy had passed from its preoccupation with the nuance and doctrine of idealism to existentialism and finally theology. Susman alludes to precisely this point in her opening comment on Rosenzweig's theologico-mystical work, *The Star of Redemption*. This book comes forth, Susman affirms, "at a great turning point, a time of decay, of the degeneration of the philosophy of pure thought that has dominated the Western world from Parmenides to Hegel." Susman continues, echoing the opening passages of *The Star* (passages, Nahum Glatzer informs us, that Rosenzweig placed at the beginning of the work after he had completed the rest of it): "At this moment, when life and death enter the center of consciousness with their final, decisive questions, we can see that the philosophy of pure thought has no strength left to resolve life and redeem us from death."

Readers of *The Star of Redemption* at least understand its introduction. In its opening paragraphs on death they are able to recognize the beginning of an argument that seems interesting, obliging, existentially relevant. The hopeful expectation conferred by that inaugural contemplation of death is further extended by Rosenzweig's exemplification of the implicit pretentiousness of philosophies that would encompass the All, chipping away at them with the hammers of Schopenhauer, Nietzsche, Kierkegaard, until it becomes clear that what had been attempted within traditional philosophy had illuminated everything except the thinker who raised the question in the first place. From that point, however, hardly a few pages into the work, it has been customary to find readers dropping away, taxed beyond endurance by the complex involution of the argument, put off not alone by the inventive, frequently neologistic, English translation of William Hallo, but by the German original as well.

What are the difficulties of Rosenzweig's *The Star of Redemption?* Why the exasperation of readers? Moreover, why Rosenzweig's own recognition of the work's density, which constrained him to recommend to some that they bypass Parts I and II and proceed directly to the configurational intermeshing of the elements and their path that constitutes the more-accessible final section of the work? Why, even, did Rosenzweig undertake to write a gloss on the entire work, *Das Büchlein vom gesunden und kranken Menschenverstand,* which when completed was withdrawn by him from German publication? (Decades later, I published *Das Büchlein* as *Understanding the Sick and the Healthy,* translated by Thomas Luckman and edited by Nahum N. Glatzer [New York: The Noonday Press, 1953].) The last question, especially, is pertinent and exceptionally difficult to answer, but it seems worth attempting.

Let us examine for a moment, the procedures of the *Six Theosophic Points* and the *Mysterium Magnum* by the German Protestant mystic Jacob Boehme (1575–1624). Boehme develops every phase of his gnostic meditation (and I intend gnostic here, not as a mode of heretic ambition, but rather, as Nicholas Berdyaev writing of Boehme has explained, only "to indicate a wisdom grounded in revelation and employing myths and symbols rather than concepts—a wisdom much more contemplative than discursive") on the narrative of Genesis *(Mysterium Magnum)* and the sophiological tree of life by discriminating between natural reason, wherein the evidence of the senses, the operation of normal reason, the argument from consciousness describes a familiar world of nature, man, and the principles governing their conduct, and ecstatic consciousness, in which the reason of man is elevated and transformed by revelation. Clearly, no ordinary sensibility, school-trained and culturally indoctrinated, will willingly submit to such an outrageous elevation of our faculties. Nonetheless, bearing with Boehme on his journey, one comes at a certain moment to a crossroad of intelligence where the traveller is obliged by the gradually enlarging domination of the way by signs followed and directions taken, to a forsaking of conventional reliances and the introduction of a different means of continuing the journey. Whether he has conducted the argument (as Boehme does in the *Mysterium Magnum*) by beginning the exposition of Genesis with familiar categories of Christian exegesis only to oblige the reader, in turn, to recognize that the hidden language of scripture is now revealed as ordinary wisdom, unknown theretofore not because it is obscure but because it is so obvious as to be overlooked by reason; or as in the discourse of the *Six Theosophic Points,* to employ the familiar moral dilemmas of theodicy to press a vision of divine potency and the unexplored fires of divine freedom, Boehme is always insisting that his truths are obvious and commonplace. The mystic doctrine is mystic, not because it exceeds reason, but rather because it lies at its base. Indeed, the gnostic wisdom of Boehme illuminates less because of its fantasticality, irrationality, implausibility, than because it probes a dynamism in the divine that bridges dualities, reconciles historical opposites, and restores a harmony broken by the great dispute of Plato and Aristotle in Western Christian philosophy.

The reading implicit in Margarete Susman's interpretation of *The Star of Redemption* (and, I might add, my own) is compatible with a view that accords Rosenzweig's text the status of the most original work of mystical gnosis in modern Judaism. On the face of it both factors would repel Jewish readers, and yet neither should prove repellent, reflecting as they do traditions with distinguished precedents in Jewish thought. The argument of *The Star of Redemption* presses not merely the exegesis of a metaphor—the points of the Star's emplaced triangles, the path of the angles of the Star, and the fire that burns at its center and its nodes. Were this *only* metaphor, adopted as a device of exposition, we should have nothing here but a more sophisticated literary example of precisely the apologetic thinking that Rosenzweig criticized. Clearly, the metaphor is no device of art, but a metaphysical gift, a divine *donatus,* a form given as a unit to Rosenzweig's "intuition" (or imagination) and employed by him as the means of texturing and layering the argument. The resort to a quasi-mystical language is necessitated by the breakdown of rational philosophy, by the inability of philosophy to encompass both the *objectivum* of the world and the perilous standpoint of the thinker. In the place of the philosopher (confident of being capable of possessing the All) is the individual thinker (certain only of the coming of his own death). In order for such a thinker to restore himself, to reclaim the energy that life demands to be lived in the face of death, the breakdown of "common sense" must be healed. (This, it should be noted, is the image that Rosenzweig introduces, without irony, into his popular exposition of the early portions of *The Star* in *Understanding the Sick and the Healthy.*)

It is common sense that has been made sick by the arrogant pretensions of philosophy, and common sense can be restored only by recognizing that God is a reality before world and man, that the world is a potency energized by God and man, and that man is a creature formed by God and set in motion upon the passive stage of the world. The relations of the elements of the cosmos and the course of their renewal and consummation reflect a wisdom acquired, in a certain way, outside the conscious self, beyond the canon of familiar rational inquiry. Outside and beyond, but never against reason, never against what is the ordinary portion of human life, and hence, in its way, common-sensical. Common-sensical because to stand on the side of life and health and sanity is an enterprise of ordinary wisdom. It is what Scripture bids us to become—alive, that we may live in Torah, and not die in it. Another way of suggesting the grandeur of Rosenzweig's undertaking is that he entered into the circle of faith and not only never sought again to step outside it, but once discovering himself within that forest (having long since dropped the thread that might have led him outside again, back to the familiar despair and the humdrum misery of the world), he never even entertained the return as a possibility. The absurdity of the paradox was no longer absurd, the existential pathos ceased to be pathetic, the risk of faith had long since disappeared as risk and what was won was a whole language of conceptualization that is utterly clear and lucid—if one has the key. The key is there in the life, but it is also there in the book. Finding the key and recognizing that it is in one's grasp—as evident as common sense—is another matter, one to which I feel personally bound to return.   [A.A.C.]

FRANZ ROSENZWEIG: THE STAR OF REDEMPTION (A REVIEW)[1]

A name is not sound and smoke, it is word and fire. The name must be named and professed: I believe in it.—Franz Rosenzweig

This book comes, self-consciously, at a great turning point, a time of decay, of the degeneration of the philosophy of pure thought that has dominated the Western world from Parmenides to Hegel. At this moment, when life and death enter the center of consciousness with their final, decisive questions, we can see that the philosophy of pure thought has no strength left to resolve life and redeem us from death.

In Hegel's system, philosophy's culmination—the unity and universality of knowledge enclosing everything, even God—the philosophy of pure thought found its end. "If from this peak we are to take another step without plunging into the abyss, we must first shift the foundations and bring forth a new concept of philosophy."

And it was brought forth. The moment a thinker first shifted the problem of his own person, his personal self, to the center of comprehension, something uncomprehended, incomprehensible, unthinkable outside of the thinkable became visible. The moment Schopenhauer first asked the question about the worth or worthlessness of a man's life, for his own person, rather than about the essence of the world, like all prior thinkers; the moment Kierkegaard introduced the deep consciousness of personal sin and personal redemption, a consciousness seeking its personal solution far from the essence of the world; the moment Nietzsche, last but not least, presented the now ineradicable "fearful and demanding image of the unconditional allegiance of the soul to the mind"—at that world-historic moment, when, at the midpoint of living and thinking, the human individual became a visible, self-centered, fully alone, otherworldly human individuality, living out of its own responsibility, dying for itself alone—at that moment, the sphere of the all-embracing one and conceivable universe was burst. "An enclosed unity had rebelled and, by sheer obstinacy, obtained its withdrawal."

And it was only now, with the entrance of this ungraspable, unthinkable into the innermost sphere of human problems, that life and death were suddenly here in their full, shattering reality, demanding their solution. Life in all its depth, solitarily rooted in the abyss of the self; death in all its horrific factuality—not as death per se, such as previous philosophy had known it, but as the countless deaths of innumerable individuals, dying by and for themselves. It is now a matter of embracing this life, isolated and boundless in its plurality—it is a matter of overcoming the real and true death of the individual. For death had always been the deeply frightening enigma driving against all philosophy, and yet no philosophy had ever been able to overcome it, precisely because each philosophy understood it only as an abstract death, which it snuffed out in its one existing universe. "For indeed, a universe could not die and nothing would die in the universe, only the particular can die, and all dying is lonesome."[2]

The one-dimensional form of the system, a form that was scientific only on the assumption of an objective world and a single and general thinking, crumbled before the wealth of overflowing individual life. But the first consequence of that plurality of thinker-individualities, growing aware of themselves, more lonesome, living out of themselves, was a tremendous peril for all philosophy: there *was* henceforth to be no more philosophy—merely philosophies, ideologies, self-contained, isolated standpoints: a complete relativism of knowledge. Every thinker, every cognizant individual now carried about his own space, time, and truth.

But just as the full, burning desire for overcoming death was first kindled by a fully experienced, lonesome, real death (a victory different from anything that the philosophy of pure thinking had ever known), so too this utmost, perfect relativism, this immensely isolating subjectivity of knowledge, kindled the full, the innermost desire for overcoming death in a real, collective truth, which is also an experienced and a lived collectivity of existence, in which all separated selves find and redeem themselves.

This will, this yearning of present-day time, gave birth to Franz Rosenzweig's book *The Star of Redemption*—the will to grasp life and death in their living, concrete plurality, as it emerges only from post-Hegelian philosophy, and to overcome life and death in their true shape by means of a spreading, universal truth. In this will to grasp all life in its full breadth, height, and depth, the book declares war to the blood against the one-dimensional idealism of all ages, that mortal foe of all living wholeness and from that yearning, the book embraces all powers of life as forces of immediate revelation. And from the yearning as well for redemption in a universal truth, the book shifts its demand in accordance with its overall foundations, urging towards a fully changed form of cognition: to knowledge out of the revelations of life itself. Thus life and truth roar for it into a vast chord; it is not a matter of grasping the truth of thinking, after all—but of unveiling the countenance of *living* truth out of life and death and overcoming both by means of an everlasting brilliance.

This is the only possible way of understanding this book: as the will to climb down to the origins and there draw immediate life for the still unshaped elements of being; as the will to see and to speak clearly the outlines of all living things in the full, burning light of day; and as the will to ascend to the stars and expose pure eternity in its place again—and thus exhibit all the deepest and highest things of life in their steady places below and above man—so that the clearly viewed order will make directly visible to man his eternal meaning and, thereby, the redemption through truth itself.

The one thinkable universe does not surround us immediately: this certitude comes first. Before knowing and thinking, we find realities in and around us. Hence, that one universe is not the prerequisite for our cognition—these realities are the prerequisite. Just as the one universe is not the prerequisite to our thinking, so too, the lack of a prerequisite for our thinking is not the mere void. Instead, countless disparate, separate "voids," one for each problem, precede our cognition. Every particular knowledge begins with the void of the as-yet-unthought reality underlying it, preceding it as a dark, struggling life-will to cognition. The void is grasped as the place where this special problem dawns, as "the visual place of the beginning of our knowledge."

For everything, after all, became different for cognition when the one thinkable universe was no longer the all-embracing whole. Not only was the universe smashed into many particular subjects of cognition, but the subject of the thinker, having forced its retreat from thinkableness, necessarily finds itself confronted by a different world from the thinkable one that heretofore included the thinker. With that retreat, the universe was also abandoned by that which hitherto, as the point of utmost unity of subject and object, inwardness and world, held the universe together: God. Thus the thinker no longer faces that thinkable universe but rather a trinity of independent realities, into which the universe has crumbled, and each of which confronts him as a perfectly unthinkable, self-enclosed, and sealed whole, the trinity of God, world, and man. None of these three realities has previously been known, no, or even seen in this self-dependence, this inmost isolation that mocks any common precondition. Each of these three must first be sought out in its own "void," must be pulled into the light of cognition and utterance from the darkness of all preconditional life. For that is one and the same: the Word, discourse, is also revelation. The fact that the mute, primal words, which precede all speech, are spoken is the same as the process by which reality becomes visible. And, from the mute night of their voids, the three last great primal beings slowly ascend. In a deep, wondrous view of their being, they unravel more and more clearly from the mystery of their voids, and the sought-for "everlastingness, not needful of thought in order to exist," is disclosed to us. Still directionless, still mute, still fully self-enclosed, they arise from the hush of preconscious life, exist for themselves in towering loneliness: the metaphysical God, the metalogical world, the metaethical man. Disconnected, unrelated to one another, they are pure in their being, unfolded from their innermost ardent core, pure products of the seeing spirit. Each sets itself up monistically as the whole. "We have the parts in hand, we have truly smashed the universe." What can be done so that they shall not remain parts, mere disintegrating elements of life? How shall the mutually alienated elements combine anew, become reality again, the reality we know them to be—the truly existing All?

There are many ways in which they could move in order to come together again, just as there have been many interpretations of God, the world, man, and their mutual relationship—and yet, in this orgiastic chaos of possibilities, this veritable *Walpurgisnacht* of confusedly whirling shapes, only one can be the true, the real. Only movement out of themselves towards one another can combine the elements into the meaningful togetherness that constitutes our reality. What is that one path, the only one matching their inmost being, which, in and out of itself, overcomes the elementary internal mangling of reality?

The answer to this question exposes the full depth of the abyss separating this philosophy from previous modes of cognition. No thinking can achieve the eternally valid fusion. Only reality itself achieved it and continues to achieve it. From the night of preconscious being, in which we found each element by itself, within the realm of wellsprings, which is their realm, we are carried upward in the full light of day by the only river in which we find the elements in their unique and eternally valid fusion: History. History, considered not in its mere, extant factuality, but history as a specific meaningful structure, a unique development, "the one river of world-time, which . . . from world-morning through world-noon to world-evening brings together what was flung apart into the darkness of the Something: the elements of the All, in the one world-day of the Lord."

"In the one world-day of the Lord"—such language is no longer that of philosophy. And together with the question of the new fusion of the elements of the All, which had been flung apart in the breath of the full reality of life, we once again hear that first question: Given the collapse of philosophy into countless subjective viewpoints, how can truth be possible? Is not the loss in richness of life that the objective systems of idealism suffered in reality more than made up for by the greater objectivity of cognition of truth? Must not this lack—in regard to subjectivity of standpoints—be replaced by an even greater one, that of renouncing any possibility of objective truth?

Rosenzweig sees the full scope of the danger. But in seeing it, he has already found the path to overcoming it—a path none other than the one that leads the rigid, disintegrated elements back to the living reality. The same path leads to both reality and truth. Most likely, this turn, despite total rethinking, will still appear strange and surprising—but only to him who does not reexperience the deeply felt ascendancy of the living person to grasp meaning over the power of pure thought.

Alongside the abyss to which philosophy of knowledge had led, another abyss opened, and another failure became clear: the failure of theology, which likewise had come to the end of its road. Just as philosophy threatened to fall apart into individual, disconnected standpoints and just as it thereby seemed compelled to forego objective truth, so theology also was threatened with having the foundation of truth erode beneath it when it deprived itself of its hitherto most solid pillar, the understanding of revelation as a miracle, and had replaced once-and-for-all established truth more and more completely with mere experience. Rosenzweig realized that the one specific for both philosophy and theology was for each to help the other since each possesses what the other lacks. After all, both philosophy and theology have the same content: life from its most modest foundations to redemption—except that for theology revelation *is*, while philosophy must prove the merest precondition of revelation, that is, its cognitive basis. Philosophy, as the theologian understands it, becomes the prophecy of revelation, the Old Testament of theology. By supplying the grounds for revelation (and thereby precisely what theology has lost) philosophy becomes the new *auctoritas* of theology, restoring to revelation its lost miraculousness by prophesying revelation and thereby disclosing its superhistorical truth. Philosophy is intended to bring subjective cognition to theology and theology the great objective truth to philosophy, the objective truth that it lacked and that will henceforth be justified by philosophy itself. For the bridge from "deaf and blind selfness to the most radiant objectivity of reason" is built only by the theological concept of revelation. From now on every philosopher must be a theologian, i.e., must have faith, and every theologian must be a philosopher, i.e., must seek cognition; they must join forces to achieve the interpretation of Being, the one true, living, and whole interpretation. And just as their union overcomes the subjectivity of the philosophy of viewpoints, so, too, their certitude overcomes the particularization of the elements of the All—for now they enter, have entered into the great torrent of the historical process of salvation and are united into the All in a world-day of the Lord.

Their path is also thereby unequivocally determined. The way of brightness lights up in the dark heaven of eternity, the way described by the star of redemption, which is heaven itself. In a rigorous triple form, in the shape of the double three-pointed star, the new All emerges before us from the motion of the primal elements towards one another from the innermost essence of the star shape—and the new All that results is a tremendous interpretation of the meaning of the world, of the soul, of God in a living relationship: creation, revelation, redemption. These are the three great eternal pathways, at whose final points, God, the world, and man achieve living contact. Only the concept of creation can achieve what had demolished the great universal concept of idealism: the interpretation of the phenomenon of constantly renewed life, of the living, torrential abundance of forms, of the spiritual permanence of the wholly extraspiritual, thoroughly unthinkable Being; and at the same time, the interpretation of the essence of God, which arises over the darkness of the everlasting world of old as an eternally renewing creative will, developing that old world into a flowering world of light, the world of formed creation. Likewise, revelation alone can determine how man comes into the world, how he is freed from the deaf and blind soul into the soul beloved by God, a soul that carries the love it received back to creation and thereby returns creation back to God. Freed only by God's love, it can betake itself to the last of the three great pathways, which leads from man by way of creation back to God.

Redemption is thereby put into the hands of man. Just as the world completes itself in creation, so too, man, the self, is completed in the sacred, in the servant of God. Yet the final word of redemption is spoken by God. For what shall come is the Kingdom: redemption, the self-perfection of God. "God becomes in redemption that which the frivolity of human thought has always and everywhere sought, everywhere claimed and yet nowhere found, because it could not be found anywhere, for it did not yet exist: All and One."

Here the All, the one and All, becomes visible—but only visible. It has not yet been found. It has yet to exist. For it is not the thinkable All, but the All given to us as a total reality, the All for which living fulfillment is to be achieved by our redemptive love, which comes from God. The rashness of human thought is opposed by the unattainable as the eternally indissoluble living shape. The shape is not thought, not evoked; it reveals itself.

And so, next to living revelation, all other religions sink back into religions of knowledge and the pagan-mythological religions, which knew living forms, are placed higher than the profoundly mystical and shapeless cognitive religions of the great Buddha. Form and life—these two burn in the heart of this redemption book, from which the mystic is spurned for elevating the I on its road to form.

All redemption is to become a formed whole. Our free deed of love, coming over the living, growing world of creation, forms pure, blind Being into a living superworld of the formed whole and matures growing life toward the Kingdom of God. The deed of love works, not like the artist, who only forms images of life, but as a living soul shaping real life towards its innermost meaning and thereby towards redemption. And the life of creation comes towards our love, turns toward redemption. The space and time of redemption are determined by that life, by the creation in which space and time are at home. Hence the moment is unequivocally, immovably established within the historical process. Each time has its special form of redemption. And the great historical forms of redemption demonstrate the position of the world-clock. Thus, for us too, our era's great position of knowledge and experience must be traversed in a living way if we are to recognize—and profess—our present-day truth. It was only from that excess of enlivenment and affirmation of all life and personal destiny in all its heights and depths, it was only from that thoroughly alive relationship to reality, which only Goethe succeeded in achieving and which could only be attained at that moment—it was only from that superhuman isolation of later minds, that gigantic upward swelling toward individualism and relativism, that the tremendous will for truth could break forth, a will that can find repose again solely in God. It was only for us that the *"donec requiescat in te"* ["until He comes to rest in you"] could again become authentic life. Hence, pure faith is not enough—only he "who summons God with the two-fold prayer of the devout and the undevout will not be unheeded by Him."

It is clearly only in history, in which redemption takes place uniquely, that redemption becomes visible as the entrance of the eternal into time—which redemption transforms from the amorphous torrent of mere flow into a meaningful, eternity-touched shape of the hour. For the hour no longer belongs to the world of creation; "bells begin to strike the hour only in the kingdom of redemption." All redemption, as we know it from history, is a redemption from time to the shape of time; redemption to the hour and the day, the week and the year, in which life ripens toward the time of eternity, the Kingdom.

It is for the reasons just given that redemption presents itself in the cycle of the spiritual year, as it takes shape from the miracle of revelation. Judaism as the bearer of eternal life goes first. Within it, eternity has already returned to immediate life, caught in the seed of original existence. The Jew is born as a Jew. His birth makes him part of the holy nation and gives him a part in eternity, in redemption. For "there is only one community . . . that cannot pronounce the 'we' of its unity without hearing deep within the complementary 'are eternal.' "[3] All other nations are mortal in that they are tied to a specific land, a specific earthly home, for which the blood of their sons flows. "We alone trusted the blood and left the land . . . and were alone of all the nations on earth in redeeming our life from any fellowship with death."[4] The land belongs "to the Jew in the deepest sense as only the land of his yearning, as—the Holy Land."[5] The blood-fellowship alone makes the Jew a Jew, whereas every Christian, by reason of adhering to his earthly homeland, is pagan by birth, reaching Christianity only through an inner conversion, through the conversion in the sign of the cross. So Judaism has paganism outside of itself, the paganism that the Christian bears within himself and must overcome only throughout history, and can never fully overcome. That is why the Christian always lives in time and in the world, whereas the Jew is refused any participation in the temporal life of the surrounding world, for the sake of the eternal life that is his share. Land, language, custom, and law, in whose living development the Christian nations live, have, for the Jew, long since left the circle of the living. He has no part in those forms that shape Christianity into life: church and state. For, whereas the eternal lives in the Jew merely in his continual procreation, the Christian is always on the way. Christianity does not continue by means of procreation, but through its constant expansion in the sphere of historical life: through the mission.

Both Judaism and Christianity have drawn eternity down into time by the great division of all life according to its inherent eternal meaning: Judaism in the form of the pervasive immortality of its life; Christianity in the form of simultaneity, which is the principle of space and time and the fraternity that outsoars all human distinctions.

Neither Judaism nor Christianity has the entire truth, each has its share, and each thereby, in order to experience eternity, divides in its own way the even flow of time in the spiritual year. And thus the year itself becomes an image of the circle of redemption.

Separated, therefore, under various signs, in various circles of redemption, the Jew and the Christian, the bearers of the revelation, come before the face of God. Neither is whole unto itself. A final individual element remains in the relationship to the Eternal. No human structure, however ripe, is itself the truth. God alone is truth.

In this jubilant certainty, the book [*The Star of Redemption*] comes to an end: God is truth—not truth God, but God is truth. We—and here the subjectivity of individual standpoints is resolved—we are those who have eternally only a portion in truth. Not as the whole that it is and shall become, but only as a part allotted to us. And our task is to prove ourselves with this share: to say *verily* to truth.

In this way alone is death overcome: the cognitive viewpoint of the self, which has a knowledge that is individual, definite, and transitory, because it is always attached to a portion of individualized, doomed reality, claims however a share in the encroaching divine truth. Death is overcome when the eternal is professed and dying individuality is abandoned. Only the individual dies.

By stepping before the countenance of the divine truth that radiates everywhere, each of us in his place and in his time, speaking *verily* to our share in the truth, the share that the truth bestows, overcomes death and isolation in the fellowship of the living.

Truth lies not at the beginning, not in our having, but at the end, in our proving ourselves. The final thing demanded of us is trust, but trust is grand proclamation. "It is the very simplest thing in the world and for that very reason the most difficult thing."[6]

It is known to him who has written this book, which is so full of ardor and brightness, promise and eternity—but only for the man who trusts, the man who wants to believe and can believe. It is the enormous attempt at drawing faith, simple, immediate faith in God, into the life of cognition. There is no other way of saving our present point in time. Only faith can save us, the faith in the unity of truth, which all systems were incapable of proving, and which, in our time, was definitively swept away by the tempest of life. But faith is not just demanded here, not just preached: faith is believed. The book is full of the light of revelation that it proclaims. At its peaks, the language itself becomes revelation. It finds words of love as no other book in our day; for here alone, as the path from God to man and from man through other men back to God, love has once again become the love that never ceases. All the eternal, age-old names regain their original life, become word and fire by the profession of those names.

And for this faith, this profession, the star of redemption finally flares up as the face of God itself. The eternal superworld of the formed whole sends to man as the last image the miracle of the countenance, not its own face, but the miracle of the divine countenance. For "truth cannot be uttered otherwise. It is only when we behold the star as the countenance that we have fully come beyond all possibility of possibilities and simply behold."[7]

The image of Saïs[8] is unveiled—but the dreadfully shattering image of the self, which is shown to the knower, becomes the unveiled countenance of God in the eternal superworld of the formed whole. And that removes from the unveiler the curse of the image of truth: He no longer sees himself in utter intensity and distortion as soon as he seeks truth in faith rather than knowledge. He beholds God.

It would be impossible and meaningless here to practice a "criticism" that does not spring from the inherent presumptions of this book, which has borrowed language from the elements of the world of old as well as the light of the superworld. As Rosenzweig says at one point, the concept of creation, with which he opens the innermost Being of the phenomenal world and its relationship to the divine and the human, cannot be taken as a scholarly or scientific hypothesis to be accepted or rejected according to proofs and counterproofs. Likewise, the entire rich, torrential, wide-branching book can only be accepted, beyond any demonstration, as a disclosure, illumination, and beholding of ultimate, eternal connections of Being. It may still seem too early to open our eyes to full truth after the immeasurable, dreadful separation from it; it may still be too early to behold God, who concealed Himself from us for so long in heavy fogs, clouds, and shrouds, in strident lightning and thunder; the entrance of theology into philosophy may at first remind us all too intimately of the support that the lame man offers the blind man; the bubbling fullness of life, which only just burst forth to us, may seem pressed and violated under an excess of construction, under the all too rigorous lines of truth and eternity—each of these protests is countered by this book with a radiant, overwhelming *"And yet."* It means to make visible, to give shape to, what is as ineffable in its origin as in its end. The pathways of the radiant double triangle, which lead from the origin to the end, must cut sharp and solid through moving life, and must therefore, albeit living pathways, cut only life to shreds. And if we catch the utterance, that today only the devout man may philosophize, it strikes us, despite everything, as a veritable solution and redemption from the distress of this our age. For it is, after all, the living truth and not the thinking truth that Rosenzweig drives to a new revelation—and where would living truth ever be found for man if not in faith? Whatever one may feel about this book, written in the face of death and with its gaze upon God, it unveils in its depths the mortally wounded truth of our time, which nonetheless powerfully struggles for the truth's healing.

NOTES

N.B.: All notes are by Arthur A. Cohen except those initialed by the author of the article, the translator (J.N.), or the general editor of the Judaic Studies Series (L.J.W.), or otherwise identified.

Introduction: Arthur A. Cohen

1. Cf. Hans Kohn, *Martin Buber* (Hellerau: Verlag von Jakob Hegner, Hellerau, 1930), p. 20. In note 1, Kohn points the reader to a fuller discussion of Weininger as an example of pathological *Selbsthass* in his essay in *Der Jude,* Jahrgang V: "*Das kulturelle Problem des modernen Westjuden,*" pp. 281–97.

2. Kohn, op. cit., p. 24.

3. Martin Buber, *Briefwechsel* (Erster Band: 1897–1918), (Heidelberg: Verlag Lambert Schneider, 1972), p. 179f.

4. Martin Buber, *Briefwechsel* (Erster Band: 1897–1918), op. cit., pp. 32–34, "*Anfänge des Zionismus.*"

5. Martin Buber, *Briefwechsel* (Erster Band: 1897–1918), op. cit., p. 213.

6. Cf. Martin Buber's editorial note on the publication of Ahad Haam's *Ost und West* (East and West), which opened a virtually exclusively Ahad Haam issue of *Der Jude,* Jahrgang I, Heft 6, pp. 354f.

7. Paul Robert Flohr, *From Kulturpolitik to Dialogue: An Inquiry into the Formation of Martin Buber's Philosophy of I and Thou* (doctoral dissertation), (Ann Arbor: University Microfilms, 1974), pp. 109–20. For a list of contributors to *Die Gesellschaft* and those Buber had contemplated inviting, ibid., pp. 114–16.

8. Hans Kohn, *Martin Buber,* pp. 28f. Also the summation essay of Ruth Link-Salinger, "Friends in Utopia: Martin Buber and Gustav Landauer," *Midstream* (January 1978), pp. 67–71.

9. Hans Kohn, *Martin Buber,* p. 29; Link-Salinger, op. cit., p. 67.

10. Cited by Flohr, who discovered the letter in the Jerusalem Martin Buber Archive, 376/I. Correspondence of Buber to Hans Kohn, September 30, 1914. Flohr, op. cit., p. 136, footnote 2, p. 306. As well see Flohr's excellent discussion of Buber's rationalization of German aggression against Belgium in his controversy with the Dutch pacifist and poet Frederik van Eeden. Op. cit., p. 137f.

11. Martin Buber, *Daniel. Dialogues on Realization,* translated with an Introduction by Maurice Friedman (New York: Holt, Rinehart, & Winston, 1964), p. 115f (with minor editorial modifications).

12. Martin Buber, "*Die Losung,*" *Der Jude,* Jahrgang I, Heft 1 (April 1916), p. 2.

13. Martin Buber, *Briefwechsel* (Erster Band: 1897–1918), op. cit., Letter #306, pp. 433–38. Cf. as well Flohr's excellent summation of the controversy, op. cit., pp. 143–49.

14. Flohr, op. cit.

15. Paul Flohr, op. cit., pp. 150–60, particularly pp. 150–53.

16. Martin Buber, "*Die Losung,*" *Der Jude,* op. cit., p. 3.

17. Martin Buber, ibid., p. 3.

18. This text appeared on the contents page of every issue of *Der Jude*. The cover of the periodical contained only the identification of the periodical, the year *(Jahrgang)*, issue number, issue date and the name of the publisher, which was R. Löwit Verlag of Berlin and Vienna from 1916 until the fifth year, when publication was taken over by Buber's Jüdischer Verlag in Berlin. Thereafter, as long as the periodical appeared, through 1923 as a monthly, although Buber had ceded editorial place to Siegmund Kaznelson and Ernst Simon, Buber retained his name on the masthead as founder of the periodical while the names of the new editors did not appear. There were, from April 1916 through March 1924 continuous appearances, although many issues were double-month numbers in leaner periods. After March 1924 a series of special numbers, confusingly dated, appeared under the name *Der Jude*. These *Sonderhefte* (special issues) were: *Antisemitismus und jüdisches Volkstum* (Antisemitism and Jewish Nationality), the last issue called "a monthly," although it is copyrighted in 1925. The second special issue on *Erziehung* (Education) already identifies the periodical as *"Eine Vierteljahresschrift"* (a quarterly) and is dated 1926. *Judentum und Deutschtum* (Jewishness and Germanism), the third special issue, appeared in 1926 and the fourth, *Judentum und Christentum* (Judaism and Christianity), was released in May, 1927. Fittingly the last of the special numbers, with which *Der Jude* ceased publication, was dedicated to *Martin Bubers fünfzigstem Geburtstag* (Martin Buber's Fiftieth Birthday). It appeared in 1928, roughly a half-century before the present anthology.

19. The stories appeared in *Der Jude*, October and November, 1917. Tracking this particular connection entails following the letters of Brod to Buber and presumably from Buber to Kafka, alluded to in Kafka's appreciative reply to Buber's invitation to contribute. Cf. Martin Buber, *Briefwechsel* (Erster Band: 1897–1918), op. cit., #284, p. 409 and note 1 on p. 409. Also see Franz Kafka, *Letters to Friends, Family, and Editors* (New York: Schocken Books, 1977), in which the translators, Richard and Clara Winston, supply a number of useful letters relative to Kafka's interest and involvement with *Der Jude*, namely, pp. 131–33, 135, 148, regarding Löwy's essay on Yiddish theater published in *Der Jude;* and p. 349 on Kafka as a possible editorial successor to Buber, in which Kafka comments to Brod, "it is only in joke or in a semicomatose moment that my name should come up in connection with the vacant editorship at *Der Jude*. How could I think of such a thing, with my boundless ignorance of affairs, my complete lack of connection with people, the absence of any firm Jewish ground under my feet? No, no."

20. Martin Buber, *Briefwechsel (Erster Band:* 1897–1918), op. cit., #303, p. 429, in which Brod writes from Prague on 2/5/1916 after seeing the inaugural issue of *Der Jude.*

21. See the editor's A Note About Selection in which these lengthy (and hence unexcerptable) essays are reviewed briefly.

22. Hans Kohn, "On the Arab Question," *Der Jude*, Jahrgang IV, Heft 12, p. 567; also Fritz Sternberg, "The Significance of the Arab Question for Zionism," *Der Jude*, Jahrgang III, Heft 4, pp. 148–63; Arthur Ruppin, "The Relation of Jews to the Arabs," *Der Jude*, ibid., pp. 453f. There were others, but the above offers a sample of the concern.

23. Rosenzweig's translations from Jehuda Halevi appeared as filler in *Der Jude*, Jahrgang VII, pp. 44, 97, 376, 551; his translation of a Sabbath hymn of Israel Nagara was published in *Der Jude*, Jahrgang VI, p. 692.

24. Arthur Ruppin, "Counting the Jews," *Der Jude*, Jahrgang II, pp. 139–44.

1. Nationalism: Hans Kohn

1. Georg Simmel (1858–1918), German philosopher and professor at Berlin and Strasbourg, died shortly before the end of World War I; he was, however, published extensively after his death and Kohn is undoubtedly citing a posthumous work.

2. Gustav Landauer (1870–1919), German social philosopher and critic, long associated with Martin Buber, on whose social thinking he exercised a profound influence. See the Introduction to the present anthology and Buber's essay on "Landauer" in *Paths in Utopia* (Boston: Beacon Press, 1958).

3. Friedrich Meinecke, *Cosmopolitanism and the National State (Weltbürgertum und Nationalistaat)* (Princeton: Princeton University Press, 1970). Kohn cites p. 3ff. of the fourth edition of the German original.

4. "Should we not bring back some of the Enlightenment ideals that we have given up?" Wilhelm Dilthey, *Das Erlebnis und die Dichtung [Experience and Poetry]* (Leipzig, 1912), p. 174. "Today, in many respects, we are in a position to wage a new battle for the Enlightenment's gains in clarity and freedom of spiritual life, and perhaps a harder battle than the Enlightenment won." Wilhelm Windelband: *Die Philosophie im deutschen Geistesleben des XIX. Jahrhunderts [Philosophy in 19th-Century German Spiritual Life]* (Tübingen, 1909), p. 94. [H.K.]

5. Johann Gottlieb Fichte (1762–1814) wrote his famous *Addresses to the German Nation* in 1796; their influence on the brothers Schlegel and the educational theorist Wilhelm von Humboldt was enormous, as Kohn indicates.

6. Friedrich Schlegel, *Lyceum Fragments* [38 *Lyzeumsfragment*]. Both Schlegel essays referred to by Kohn are found in one volume in English: *Lucinde and the Fragments*.

7. Johann Gottlieb Fichte, *Nachgelassene Werke [Posthumous Works]*, II, p. 512. [H.K.]

8. See my foreword to the collection *Vom Judentum [Concerning Judaism]*, which reflects these trends in the Judaism of the younger generation. *Von Judentum: Ein Sammelbuch,* edited by Verein Jüdischer Hochschuler Bar Kochba (Leipzig: Kurt Wolff Verlag, 1913). [H.K.]

9. Gaston Riou, *Aux Ecoutes de la France qui vient* (Paris, 1913), p. 21. [H.K.]

2. Yiddish: Moses Calvary

1. Undoubtedly Calvary refers to Martin P. Philippson (1846–1916), historian and son of Ludwig P. Philippson, who was chairman of the Deutsch-Israelitischer Gemeindebund from 1896–1912 and was founder of the Verband der Deutschen Juden.

2. The Yiddish gutturals actually derive from medieval German. [J.N.]

3. Klaus Groth (1819–1899), a poet of the *Holsteiner Plattdeutsch,* worked on an orthography of Holstein dialect and published many treatises on dialect (*Briefe über Hochdeutsch und Plattdeutsch,* 1858, and *Über Mundarten und mundartige Dichtung,* 1876).

4. An unidentified poem in *Plattdeutsch,* which Theodor Storm (1817–1888) wrote, presumably early in his career, since his poetry, unlike that of his countryman, Groth, was not involved with Holstein dialect. The English version of Storm's poem is by the translator.

5. Fritz Reuter (1810–1874), a Mecklenburger, distinguished by his humor and the

employment of *Plattdeutsch,* which he raised to a literary level, notably in his novels. The translation of this example of Reuter's light verse was amiably pieced together by Professor Robert Rosen of Baruch College.

6. *Ut mine Stromtid* (From My Farming Days), a trilogy by Fritz Reuter was written between 1862–1864.

7. I. L. Peretz, the great Yiddish story teller, translated the poem of the Russian Jewish poet, Shimon Shmuel Frug (1860–1916), who, influenced by Michel Gordon and Yehuda Leib Gordon, drew his themes from the Biblical prophets and Talmudic legends. Peretz's Yiddish version of Frug's Russian text is translated into English by Laurance Wieder.

8. Isaac Leib Peretz (Yiṣhaq Leibush Peretz) was born in 1852 and died in 1915. His first long ballad, which aroused immense interest, *Monisch,* was published in Sholem Aleichem's Yiddish anthology, *Folksbibliotek* (1888). The two Yiddish stanzas are translated by Laurance Wieder.

9. Both popular folk songs cited by Calvary are translated into English by Laurance Wieder.

10. These two ditties, known in English as a song about ten little Indians, were translated by Professor Robert Rosen of Baruch College.

11. Morris Rosenfeld (1862–1923), Yiddish poet, who after leaving Russia in 1882 settled in America in 1886. While laboring in sweatshops he wrote and recited his labor lyrics, among which his *Song Book* (1897) was most famous. One of these is translated into Yiddish by Calvary and the German version is presumably by Berthold Feiwel (1875–1937), a colleague of Buber's in the Jüdischer Verlag. Both English translations are by Professor Robert Rosen.

3. Graetz and National Judaism: Josef Meisl

1. Details concerning Graetz's *History* and his relation to questions of contemporary Jewish life are contained in my forthcoming book, *Heinrich Graetz. Eine Würdigung des Historikers und Juden zu seinem 100. Geburtstage 31. Oktober 1917 (21. Cheschwan).* (Heinrich Graetz. An Appreciation of the Historian and Jew [i.e., of Graetz] on his 100th Birthday. October 31, 1917 [21st of Ḥeshvan].) Meisl's essay was published by Louis Lamm in Berlin during 1917.) [Buber's note]

2. Heinrich Graetz's *Geschichte der Juden* was published from 1853 to 1870, commencing with the fourth volume, working forward and then backward, concluding with the eleventh volume, which saw the history of the Jews brought to the fateful year 1848. Graetz had no interest in dealing with personages still alive.

3. Isaak Markus Jost (1793–1860) was, as Salo Baron has called Jost's *History of the Israelites* (nine volumes of which appeared from 1820–1828), "the beginning of modern Jewish historiography." Jost added a tenth volume in 1846 to bring the narrative up to his own time. Cf. Baron's essay, "I. M. Jost as Historian," *History and Jewish Historians* (Philadelphia, 1964), pp. 240–62.

4. Baron refers, however, to Graetz's youthful religious crisis, which was contained by his reading of Samson Raphael Hirsch's *Neunzehn Briefe über das Judentum* (Altona, 1863) and subsequently by his religious apprenticeship to Hirsch, with whom he lived from 1837–1840. Cf. Baron, op. cit., p. 263. See as well Bloch's essay, "*Heinrich Graetz. Ein Lebensbild,*" first published in *Monatsschrift für Geschichte und Wissenschaft des Judentums* (1904) and subsequently included as the introduction to

the second edition of the first volume of Graetz's *Geschichte der Juden;* also Israel Abraham, "Heinrich Graetz the Jewish Historian," *Jewish Quarterly Review,* 1892; Rippner, *"Zum 70. Geburtstag des Professor Heinrich Graetz,"* Brülls *Populär-wissenschaftliche Monatsblätter,* 1887.

5. Ben Uziel was the name adopted by Hirsch for the protagonist of his *Neunzehn Briefe über das Judentum,* translated into English (The Nineteen Letters of Ben Uziel) by Bernard Drachman (New York, 1899) and into Hebrew, under the title *Iggerot Ẓafon* by M. S. Aronson (Vilna, 1892). Meisl cites Bloch's essay, idem, pp. 90–91, which includes passages from Graetz's journal confirming this point.

6. Reference to the shattering controversy between the partisans of the reformer Abraham Geiger and those of Solomon A. Tiktin, who had occupied the chief rabbinic post of the community of Breslau from 1821 until 1839, when Geiger was elected to the second post in the community. The polemics, both personal and theological, to which Meisl alludes, found Graetz strongly in support of Tiktin. Cf. W. Gunther Plaut, *The Rise of Reform Judaism* (New York, 1963), pp. 63–70.

7. The *"Neue Agende"* Graetz opposed in his essay in *Orient* in 1843 (pp. 391–92) refers to the agenda of the Reformers at the rabbinical conference convened by Abraham Geiger at Wiesbaden in 1837, and the *Kasualfrage* (derived from the Church formulation of *casualia*) raised the question: to whom should fees for ritual services (circumcision, redemption of the first born, marriage, funerals, etc.) be paid, the rabbi directly or the community? This issue Graetz addressed in his 1844 essay in *Orient,* pp. 171–73, 179–81, 203, 232–34, 257, 283, 356.

8. Graetz both admired and was supported by the conservative Rabbi Zacharias Frankel of Dresden, whom he congratulated upon his demonstrative departure from the Frankfort Rabbinical Assembly in protest against growing sympathy with the Reform movement. Later Graetz collaborated with Frankel's *Zeitschrift für die religiösen Interessen des Judentums* and in 1853 became, at Frankel's invitation, *Dozent* in Jewish history at the recently founded Jewish Theological Seminary in Breslau. Cf. Baron, op. cit., p. 264–64.

9. Reference to Moses Mendelssohn (1729–1786) whose achievement as translator and expositor of traditional Judaism had enabled him to bridge the gap between the world of Christian enlighteners who regarded Judaism as an incommensurable polity and Jewish traditionalists who considered accommodation to non-Jewish society to be coeval with conversion. The polemics of Mendelssohn's supporters and opponents marked the first great internal struggle of the Western European haskalah. Cf. Alexander Altmann's magisterial *Moses Mendelssohn* (University: The University of Alabama Press, 1973); also Arthur A. Cohen, *The Natural and the Supernatural Jew* (New York: Pantheon, 1962), passim.

10. Joseph von Wertheimer (1800–1887), Austrian-born Jewish educator and author.

11. *Allgemeine Zeitung des Judentums, Israelit, Neuzeit, Jeschurun,* 1863-64. Also cf. Theodor Zlocisti in *Brünner Jüdischer Volkskalender,* 1903-04, pp. 115–24. [J.M.]

12. Heinrich Graetz: "The Significance of Judaism for the Present and Future" in *Jewish Quarterly Review,* 1889–90. [J.M.]

13. From Heinrich Graetz's anonymously published work *Briefwechsel einer englischen Dame über Judentum und Semitismus* [*Correspondence of an English Lady on Judaism and Semitism*], (Stuttgart, 1883). There is more about this very interesting work in my book. [J.M.]

14. Heinrich Graetz, "The Construction of Jewish History" in Frankel's *Zeitschrift für die religiösen Interessen des Judentums* (1846), pp. 88–89. [J.M.]

15. Heinrich Graetz, *History,* Vol. X, pp. 59, 297, Vol. XI, p. 41; letter to Dr. Skomorowsky in Kiev in *Hamagid*, 1885, no. 5. This was why Graetz refused to let his *History* be translated into Yiddish. "I must definitely protest against translating my *Popular History of the Jews* into the Jewish jargon," he wrote. "A jargon is a great shame for a class of people. . . . If I may quote Rabbi Jehuda Hanassi "Be 'ereṣ Yisra 'el Lashon Sursi Lamah? 'Elah 'ee Lashon Haqodesh 'ee Lashon Yevanit." ("Why speak Syrian? In the Holy Land either Hebrew or Greek! Please, dear Mr. Skomorowsky, prevent such a profanation of my *History*.") [J.M.]

16. Letter to Dr. Skomorowsky, ibid. [J.M.]

17. Cf. M. L.'s critique of Vol. XI of the *History* in *Literarisches Zentralblatt,* (1879), pp. 29–31; Heinrich von Treitschke in *Preussische Jahrbücher,* (1879), p. 572ff. and p. 666ff. ("*Herr Graetz und sein Judentum*"). [J.M.]

18. *Erwiderungen an Herrn von Treitschke,* Schlesische Presse, 1879, no. 859, and "*Mein letztes Wort an Professor von Treitschke,*" ibid., no. 907. [J.M.]

19. Heinrich Graetz, *Die Verjüngung des jüdischen Stammes (The Rejuvenation of the Jewish Race),* op. cit. [J.M.]

20. "Historic Parallels in Jewish History," translated by J. Jacobs, Publications of the Anglo-Jewish Historical Exhibition, 1887 (Lectures held at the opening of the Exhibition in London on July 16, 1887). [J.M.]

21. Moses Hess (1812–1875), German-born social philosopher and in his later years author of *Rome and Jerusalem* (1872), a work that proved of importance as a Zionist precursor.

22. According to various unpublished papers, as well as information from Professor Dr. Bloch in Posen, and cf. Graetz's *Briefwechsel* [*Correspondence*], etc., pp. 77–78, as well as Moses Hess: *Jüdische Schriften* [*Jewish Writings*], ed. by Theodor Zlocisti (Berlin, 1905). [J.M.]

23. Hermann Cohen, *Ein Bekenntnis in der Judenfrage* [*A Confession on the Jewish Question*], (1880), p. 16ff. [J.M.]

24. *The Memorandum on the Conditions of the Jewish Communities in Palestine and Particularly in Jerusalem* (Berlin, 1872, 6 pp. in quarto) appeared as a printed manuscript and was sent to all Palestine associations, but it did reach the public anyway. [J.M.]

25. *Israelit* (1872), no. 27, (1873), no. 9. *Allgemeine Zeitung des Judentums* (1872), no. 28, (1873), no. 21. *Neuzeit* (1872), no. 28, 33. *Israelitische Wochenschrift,* nos. 27, 33, 1873, no. 23, 1875, no. 12. Various letters in Ḥabaṣelet, 'Ibri 'Anokhi, Hameliṣ, Haṣefirah, Hammaggid, from 1872–73, and unpublished material, as well as information from Professor Dr. Bloch. [J.M.]

4. The Polish Jew: Hermann Cohen

1. Dov Berush Meisels (1798–1870), rabbi and author of a commentary on Maimonides *Sefer ha-Miṣvot,* maintained contacts with the Polish nobility that enabled him to occupy an important position in Jewish life during the Cracow Republic (1815–1846). Meisels participated in the Jewish Council to the government, and during 1848 was a member of the delegation that petitioned the emperor for a special

status for Galicia. In 1856 he was elected rabbi in Warsaw and took part in the rebellion of 1863.

2. Count Vyacheslav Konstantinovich von Plehve (1846–1904), a leader of Russian reactionary circles during the time of Alexander III and Nicholas II. In June 1903 Count Plehve called for strict measures against the Zionist movement. Herzl met with Plehve and subsequently with Finance Minister Witte, to plead for an independent Jewish state to absorb Russian Jews whom Count Plehve wished to force out of Russia. Plehve was assassinated on July 15, 1904.

3. An allusion to Rabbi Joḥanan ben Zakkai (circa first century CE) who, according to tradition, left the besieged Jerusalem in a coffin, made his way to Yavneh, and established there a center of Jewish studies and the seat of the Sanhedrin after the fall of Jerusalem.

5. Germanism and Judaism: Jacob Klatzkin

1. Hermann Cohen's essay, originally published in two parts, the first being revised and expanded in a second edition under the title *Deutschtum und Judentum. Mit grundlegenden Betrachtungen über Staat und Internationalismus* (Giessen, 1915) "Von deutscher Zukunft. 1. Stück." ("Concerning the German Future. Part 1"). The second edition, published in 1916, carried the additional information: "Durchgesehen, ergänzt und mit einem kritischen Nachwort als Vorwort." ("Reviewed and supplemented, with a critical afterword as foreword.") The second portion of the essay, carrying the same generic title, was subtitled "Vom inneren Frieden des deutschen Volks" (Concerning the inner peace of Germanic people) (Leipzig, 1916). Both portions of the essay, published in volume three of Hermann Cohen's *Jüdische Schriften,* edited by Bruno Strauss, with an Introduction by Franz Rosenzweig (Berlin: C. A. Schwetschke & Sohn, 1924), are the subject of Klatzkin's extended rebuttal. All citations within are to the Strauss edition.

2. "Deutschtum und Judentum" (Germanism and Judaism), ed. by Bruno Strauss, *Jüdische Schriften,* Vol. III, p. 237.

3. Cohen, Hermann, *Ethik des reinen Willens* (Ethic of Pure Will), (Berlin: Bruno Cassirer, 1904), p. 200; *Der Begriff der Religion im System der Philosophie* (The Idea of Religion within the Philosophic System). (Giessen: Verlag von Alfred Töpelmann, 1915), p. 13. In both passages, as Klatzkin notes, Philo the Jew of Alexandria (First century CE) is treated by Cohen as mediate to Moses and Plato, that is to revelation (theology) and philosophy.

4. Cohen, Hermann, *Religion und Sittlichkeit. Eine Betrachtung zur Grundlegung der Religionsphilosophie* ("Religion and Morals. Reflections about the foundation of a philosophy of religion.") (Berlin: Verlag von M. Poppelauer, 1907), p. 39.

5. *Der Begriff der Religion,* p. 13.

6. Klatzkin refers to the well-known fact that Maimonides' *Mishneh Torah,* whose opening section, the *Sefer HaMadda* (The Book of Knowledge), offered a limited conspectus of philosophic teaching as it is appropriate to the consideration of God, the revealer of the Law to the exposition of which the *Mishneh Torah* is devoted. Klatzkin's formulation is somewhat ambiguous. What he implies, however, is that Maimonides was better diffused in the Jewish world through his magisterial commentary on the halakhah than through his metaphysical *Moreh Nebukhim (Guide of the Perplexed),* which has remained a glorious arcanum to the generality of Jews.

7. *Der Begriff der Religion,* p. 27–28.

8. In the struggle against the metaphysical incoherencies of anthropomorphism, the pre-Socrates posited *nous* (intelligence, intellect, mind) as a motive principle in the universe external to the sensible world. Klatzkin's selective reference to Anaxagoras is appropriate because it was to him that we ascribe the effort to purge the idea of God of accident and contingency, although Empedocles (who strove to reconcile Heraclitean and Pythagorean emphases) might have served more efficiently, because Empedocles provides a more efficient response to Xenophanes's pantheism, against which both Hermann Cohen and Klatzkin press their opposition. (Cf. Peters, F. E., *Greek Philosophical Terms: A Historical Lexicon,* New York, 1957, p. 132–39.) Klatzkin follows in his text with numerous proof-texts from Cohen's writings and his own regarding the scandal of pantheism and the prophetic, nonphilosophic origins of the idea of God as transcendent to all. Cf. *Ethik des reinen Willens,* pp. 52, 203, 380–83, 407–08, 439; *Religion und Sittlichkeit,* pp. 30, 32, 40–43, 48; *Der Begriff der Religion,* pp. 27, 33, 45–46.

9. Cohen, Hermann, "Innere Beziehungen der Kantischen Philosophie zum Judentum" ("Inner Relations of Kantian Philosophy to Judaism"), *Jüdische Schriften,* Vol. I, pp. 284–305; "Spinoza über Staat und Religion, Judentum und Christentum" ("Spinoza on State and Religion, Judaism and Christianity"), idem, Vol. III, pp. 290–372.

10. First published in 1912, in a different version in *HaShiloah,* the great Zionist Hebrew periodical of the Diaspora, Klatzkin later revised this material and it was published in a number of issues of *Der Jude* under the title, "Grundlagen des Nationaljudentums" ("Principles of National Judaism"), *Der Jude* (November 1916), pp. 534–644, et al. Among the "Irrwege des nationalen Instinkts"—the wrong ways of national instinct—which Klatzkin discusses in this essay and in the present text, is Christianity.

11. The specific source of this quotation, not noted by Klatzkin, could not be identified in Cohen, but that is not surprising, because its import is everywhere.

12. *Ethik des reinen Willens,* p. 314.

13. Ibid., p. 239.

14. *Religion und Sittlichkeit,* p. 16.

15. Friedrich Karl von Savigny (1779–1861), Prussian jurist and statesman, a principal founder of the historical school of German jurisprudence. He was the author of, among other works, *Geschichte des Römischen Rechts im Mittelalter* (6 vols., 1815–1831).

16. *Ethik des reinen Willens,* op. cit., p. 238.

17. Ibid., p. 280.

18. Ibid., p. 436.

19. Ibid. Chapter 8 is called "Das Ideal" ("The Ideal") and Chapter 9 is called "Die Idee Gottes" ("The Idea of God").

20. Cohen, Hermann, *Die Religiösen Bewegungen der Gegenwart. Ein Vortrag* ("Contemporary Religious Movements. A Lecture"), (Leipzig: Buchhandlung Gustav Fock, 1914), p. 20. Cf. also *Jüdische Schriften,* Vol. I, pp. 36–65.

21. *Jüdische Schriften,* p. 264.

22. *Jüdische Schriften,* p. 304.

23. Ibid., pp. 299–300.

24. *Die religiösen Bewegungen der Gegenwart,* p. 17. Klatzkin continues in the

text, although it is properly a scholarly addendum: "Cf. also Cohen's discussion of the Christian concept of eternal damnation (Religion und Sittlichkeit, op. cit., p. 52) and his discussion of the Jewish belief in man's ability to purify himself of sin (Der Begriff der Religion, op. cit., p. 104)."

25. Der Begriff der Religion, p. 66.

26. Ethik des reinen Willens, pp. 44 and 46.

27. Ibid., p. 51.

28. Die religiösen Bewegungen der Gegenwart, p. 20.

29. One must assume that as fierce a polemicist as Klatzkin cites Treitschke as much to embarrass Hermann Cohen as to illuminate the argument. It should be recalled that Cohen dated his own return to Judaism to his essay of 1880, "A Confession on the Jewish Question" (Ein Bekenntnis in der Judenfrage, Jüdische Schriften, Vol. II, pp. 73–94), in which he replies to the anti-Semitic attacks of the nationalist historian Heinrich von Treitschke (1834–1896).

30. Deutschtum und Judentum, p. 256. Klatzkin's observation about the proprieties of Cohen's polemic against Henri Bergson (1859–1941) are certainly well-taken in the light of Bergson's pained recollections "of his father" in the closing year of his life when "Germany's ideas" proved less than noble and benign. It will be recalled that although Bergson had expressed the wish to join himself to the Catholic Church, he refused to do so, regarding such an action to be a betrayal of the Jewish people from whom he came. Instead, it is reported, he registered with the German authorities as a Jew and wore the Yellow Star.

31. A famous couplet by Gabriel Riesser, a Jewish publicist for the emancipation of the Jews. [J.K.]

32. Deutschtum und Judentum, p. 277. This remarkable phrase of Cohen's, describing the debt of the Jewish people to German culture, is "Rechtsanspruch auf die Juden aller Völker." The citations from the revised text of the essay Klatzkin employs in what follows solidify this conception but unfortunately could not be located in the Strauss edition of the essay.

33. Ethik des reinen Willens, p. 557.

34. Ethik des reinen Willens, p. 410.

35. Deutschtum und Judentum, p. 286

36. Ethik des reinen Willens, p. 204.

37. Reference to an unidentified passage in the writings of Hans Vaihinger (1852–1933), founder of the Kant Society (1904) and author of the influential philosophic work Die Philosophie des Als-Ob (The Philosophy of As If) in 1911.

6. Zion, the State, and Humanity: Martin Buber

1. Hermann Cohen's controversial essay, "Religion und Zionismus" (Religion and Zionism) was published in K.-C.-Blätter, 11 (May/June, 1916), pp. 643–46 and was later published as the title essay of a collection (Crefeld: Verlag der K.-C.-Blätter, 1916). Martin Buber replied in his essay Begriffe und Wirklichkeit (Notions and Reality), Der Jude, 5 (August 1916), pp. 281–89, and Cohen responded to Buber, Antwort auf das offene Schreiben des Herrn Dr. Martin Buber an Hermann Cohen (Answer to the Open Letter of Dr. Martin Buber to Hermann Cohen), K.-C.-Blätter, 12 (July/August, 1916), pp. 683–88. Buber's second reply to Hermann Cohen, translated here, bore the title "Zion, State and Humanity," although Strauss cites the title only as

"State and Humanity," *Jüdische Schriften*, Vol. II, p. 479. Cf. *Jüdische Schriften*, Vol. II., pp. 319–41 for the text of Cohen's original essay and his reply to Buber as well as Bruno Strauss' notes on the controversy, pp. 477–79.

2. Cohen, Hermann, *Antwort auf das offene Schreiben des Herrn Dr. Martin Buber an Hermann Cohen* (Answer to the Open Letter of Dr. Martin Buber to Hermann Cohen), p. 336.

3. Buber, Martin, "Begriffe und Wirklichkeit," (Notions and Reality), p. 287; Cohen, Hermann, ibid., p. 339. Buber's reference to "no 'thus' " is not an accusation of misquotation, but of misunderstanding.

4. Cohen, Hermann, loc. cit., p. 333.

5. Buber, Martin, loc. cit., p. 287.

6. *Zentralverein Deutscher Staatsbürger Jüdischen Glaubens* was organized in 1893 in Berlin. By 1926 it numbered sixty thousand members in 555 *Ortsgruppen* (professional groups, literally: local groups) and 21 regional confederations (Landesverbänden).

7. Cohen, Hermann, loc. cit., p. 337.

8. A reference to Hermann Cohen's systematic logical treatise—part of his reformation of Kantianism, published in 1902 (Bruno Cassirer, Berlin).

9. Cohen, Hermann, "Religion und Zionismus," loc. cit., p. 322.

10. Cohen, Hermann, *Antwort auf das offene Schreiben des Herrn Dr. Martin Buber an Hermann Cohen*, p. 330.

11. Reference to the subtle distinction Cohen draws between *Nation* and *Nationalität*, relying upon a philosophic technical terminology derived from Kant and even more, although less explicitly, from Hegel.

12. "In ihrer Verblendung," in Cohen's phrase, is cited by Buber with his own italics since he makes use of the delusionary assumptions of Statists who deny national existence as a means of rebuking Cohen.

13. Cohen, Hermann, *Antwort auf das offene Schreiben des Herrn Dr. Martin Buber an Hermann Cohen*," p. 332.

14. Ibid., p. 333.

15. Ibid., p. 334.

16. Ibid., p. 331.

17. Something of a reversal from the conservative, aggressive views Buber had espoused from the beginning of World War I until early 1916.

18. Ibid., p. 332.

19. Ibid., p. 334.

20. Ibid., p. 331.

21. Idem.

22. Idem.

23. Ibid., p. 339

24. Micah's parable about the dew (5:6), to which Cohen refers, should be read in its entirety, and not just as a fragment out of context. Micah says quite plainly: "As dew and rain depend upon God alone and not on the doings of man, so is Israel among the surrounding nations." And he continues (5:8): "And the remnant of Jacob shall be among the Gentiles in the midst of many people as a lion among the beasts of the forest. . . ." Cohen, however, interprets as follows: "It is our proud awareness to live on as a divine dew amid the nations, and to remain fruitful among them and for them." The proof that Micah's utterance does not refer to dispersion can be deduced from the

fact that he has just been talking about delivering Israel from the Assyrian "when he cometh into our land." (Micah 5:5). [M.B.]

25. Jeremiah 7:34.

26. Isaiah 2:2.

27. Isaiah 2:4.

28. Cohen, Hermann, *Antwort auf das offene Schreiben des Herrn Dr. Martin Buber an Hermann Cohen,* loc. cit., p. 333–34.

29. Buber, Martin, *Drei Reden über das Judentum* (Frankfurt a. Main: Rütten u. Loening, 1911), pp. 25ff; "Die Juden und das Judentum," *Reden über Judentum* (Berlin: Schocken Verlag, 1932), pp. 13–14. Buber added the bracketed phrase in the quotation for its use in the present essay only.

30. Cohen, Hermann, loc. cit., p. 337–38.

31. An unmistakable reference to Hermann Cohen's essay, *Deutschtum und Judentum* (cf. infra, Jacob Klatzkin's reply), to which Cohen had himself referred in his *Antwort* (loc. cit., p. 329). Clearly, Buber's reply to Cohen's *Religion und Zionismus* was coupled with his critique of Cohen's interpretation of the nexus of Germanism and Judaism.

7. The Hebrew Language and Our National Future: Yeḥezkel Kaufmann

1. Ahad Haam is in error when he tries to erase the difference between the relationship that other nations have to their languages and the relationship that the Jewish people has to its own language (especially in exile). [Y.K.]

2. With all ferocity, Kaufmann elaborates the meaning of ʿam ha-ʾareṣ as "*minderwertiger Jude,*" "inferior Jew," which in fact may have been the social and cultural implication of ʿam ha-ʾareṣ even in its original rabbinic usage, since one who is unlearned in the Law is without culture and consequently socially inferior. It should be added that this notation can be examined for its ontological sexism, as well. Women were not called ʿamei ha-ʾareṣ since it was a fact of their ontological constitution that they knew and obeyed only the portion of the law appropriate to them and their obligations. When a woman, such as Beruryah, the wife of Rabbi Meir (circa second century CE), became learned, it was noted to her credit, but for the most part women were not thought to have the time, the responsibility, or the aptitude for *talmud torah.* Only men are singled out to be called ʿamei ha-ʾareṣ, that is, ignorant by virtue of being unlearned (and by implication willfully delinquent) and hence inferior, however much they may have been pious and observant. The consequences of this term and its meanings are far-reaching and deserve exploration.

3. The word *Haskalah* means "enlightenment." As Shalom Spiegel defines the Haskalah (*Hebrew Reborn,* New York, 1930), it was "aimed to enlighten the Jews, to bring them closer to general culture, to secularize, and to Europeanize" and, ultimately, to acculturate them by the subtle process of employing Hebrew language and literature as a means of diffusing European values through the Jewish world.

4. Abraham Uri Kovner (1842–1909) in his booklet *Ḥeqer Davar* criticized Haskalah literature and its dubious value and contended even more strongly in *Ṣeror Peraḥim* that Hebrew was a dead language.

5. Ḥibbat-Ṣion (Love of Zion) movement began in Russia in 1882 in response to the

pogroms of 1881. Its slogan "To Palestine" prompted societies all over the *Pale* to engage in the purchase of land in Israel.

6. *Hashiloaḥ* (October, 1914). [Y.K.]

7. Simon Dubnow (1860–1941), born in White Russia, is remembered principally for his *History of the Jews* which, contrary to Graetz's historiography, emphasized the unique social organization developed by the Jews in Diaspora and distinguished periods of Jewish history according to the diversity of their cultural and social centers.

8. Professor Hermann Strack in the *Vossische Zeitung* (May 14, 1917). [Y.K.]

8. The Eternal *Galut:* A Cardinal Issue of Zionist Ideology: Abraham Schwadron

1. Reference to Theodor Herzl's pamphlet, *Der Judenstaat,* published in 1896.

2. The author has a footnote here, which is unnecessary for an English translation, to wit: "I am using *Galut* in the feminine, as in Hebrew." [J.N.]

3. Reference to the early twentieth-century effort by certain French and German Jews to establish a Jewish settlement in the African territory of Uganda.

4. Count Federico Confalonieri of Milan (1785–1846), and Silvio Pellico (1789–1854), poet and author of *Francesca da Rimini,* were involved in the movement of Italian liberation.

5. But if a man disbelieves in the eternity of the *Galut,* he need not oppose satisfying the needs of the *Galut,* oppose the politics of the *Galut,* oppose the present-day work. All this is important, extremely important, even if it turns out to be useful for only a few generations, if it serves not only to maintain a human reservoir for Palestine or for some other concentration, but also to make it more resistant, more capable, better prepared. [A.S.]

6. Cf. my article *Etwas zum Thema: Der Pazifismus und die nationalen Fragen* in *Dokumente des Fortschritts,* April, 1916. [A.S.]

9. Zionism in Max Nordau: Leo Strauss

1. To document the accuracy of Herzl's opinion, we can cite particularly Nordau's address at the Eighth Zionist Congress (pp. 174–87) and his talk in Amsterdam (pp. 288–311). *Zionistische Schriften* (Cologne, 1909). [L.S.]

2. Nordau uses *Zionism* to mean two different things, with no possibility of confusion. [L.S.]

10. The Maturing of Man and The Maturing of the Jew: Ernst Simon

1. Gustav Landauer (1870–1919), German-Jewish social philosopher and critic whose staunch belief in socialism, anarchistic opposition to the nation-state, and pacifism proved particularly inflammatory during the First World War. In addition to these activities, he was a distinguished literary critic and a principal influence on the social philosophy of Martin Buber, who edited his correspondence for publication in 1938. Landauer was killed by anti-revolutionary troops in Munich while serving the Bavarian Soviet Republic as "Kommissar für Volksaufklärung." See within Landauer's essay "Strindberg's Historical Miniatures."

2. Gustav Landauer, *Skepsis und Mystik: Versuche im Anschluss an Mauthners Sprachkritik* (Berlin: E. Fleischel, 1903). [E.S.]

3. Fritz Mauthner (1849–1923), philosopher and essayist, was the author of a history of atheism and a philosophic critique of language to which Simon refers. His *Die Sprache* appeared in Buber's series *Die Gesellschaft* in 1907.

4. Gustav Landauer, *Aufruf zum Sozialismus. Ein Vortrag* (Berlin: Verlag des Sozialistischen Bundes, 1911).

5. Gustav Landauer, *Die Revolution*, Band XIII. *Die Gesellschaft* (series ed. by Martin Buber) (Frankfurt am Main: Rütten & Loening, 1907). [E.S.]

6. Gustav Landauer, *Der werdende Mensch. Aufsätze über Leben und Schriften* (Potsdam: Gustav Kiepenheuer, 1921). [E.S.]

7. Published in accordance with Landauer's last wishes by Martin Buber at Verlag Gustav Kiepenheuer, Potsdam, 1921. [E.S.]

8. In his work on *Shakespeare* (2 vols.), which Martin Buber published in *Literarische Anstalt* (Frankfurt am Main: Rütten & Loening, 1920). [E.S.]

9. From the essay "Zum Problem der Nation" ("The Problem of the Nation"), *Der werdende Mensch*. [E.S.]

10. Cited by Simon without source.

11. Martin Buber, *Der grosse Maggid und seine Nachfolge,* Literarische Anstalt (Frankfurt am Main: Rütten & Loening, 1922). [E.S.]

12. Martin Buber, *Daniel* (Leipzig: Insel-Verlag, 1913). English translation by Maurice Friedman (New York: Holt, Rinehart & Winston, 1964).

13. Master Nobel to whom Ernst Simon refers is the same Rabbi Nehemia Anton Nobel (1871–1922) to whom he dedicates this essay. Rabbi Nobel of the Gemeinde-Synagoge am Börneplatz in Frankfurt am Main was the author principally of sermon collections and was honored by Simon, Rosenzweig, and Buber as a preacher and teacher of astonishing power and truth.

14. In the introduction to *Reden und Gleichnisse des Tschuang-Tse (Speeches and Parables of Chuang-Tze)* (Leipzig: Insel-Verlag, 1914). [E.S.]

11. The Jewish Idea of Redemption: Friedrich Thieberger

1. Max Brod, *Paganism–Christianity–Judaism,* translated from the German by William Wolf (University: The University of Alabama Press, 1970).

12. Dostoevski and the Jews: A. S. Steinberg

1. *Beichte eines Juden (Confession of a Jew)* by L. Grossmann. German edition published by René Fülöp-Miller and R. Eckstein (Munich: Piper & Co., 1927). [A.S.S.]

2. Dostoevski's famous allocution at the unveiling of a monument to Pushkin, originally scheduled for May 26, 1800, was postponed and delivered on June 8 at a session of the Society of Lovers of Russian Literature in the hall of the Noblemen's Assembly.

3. Konstantin Petrovich Pobednostsev (1827–1907) was procurator of the Holy Synod and tutor in the Russian royal family. It was he who advocated a policy that would solve the "Jewish problem" by starving a third, murdering a third, and exiling the rest.

4. A reference to *tefillin* (phylacteries), which are never worn in the evening.

13. Strindberg's *Historical Miniatures:* Gustav Landauer

1. One of a series of eight lectures that I delivered in Berlin this past winter [1917] to an audience consisting mostly of Jews but responding to a general invitation. If I now set store by publishing it in *Der Jude,* I do so because it presents a writer's view of history that concerns us Jews. I present his view, not measuring it by my own, or criticizing it. I am simply—to vary a term of Strindberg's—experimentally employing his perspective. My goal is to grasp a literary work in its full context; I am using my eyes to see Strindberg as he was. If I then see the world through his eyes, my eyes are doing the very service that I ask of them. [G.L.]

14. The Inner Structure of the *Yom Kippur* Liturgy: David Baumgardt

1. Maḥzor (Hebrew, "cycle") is the prayerbook for the festivals of the Jewish liturgy as distinct from the order of prayers for the ordinary days of the week and the Sabbath *(Siddur).* It is customary among the Ashkenazim of North America to maintain a *Maḥzor* exclusively for the New Year and the Day of Atonement, with the order of prayer for the other major festivals presented as a festival prayer book.

2. The *Sefer Bahir,* according to Scholem, was edited in Provence during the twelfth century. It contained "compilations and editions of much older texts which, together with other writings of the Merkabah school, had made their way to Europe from the East." (Cf. Scholem, *Major Trends in Jewish Mysticism* [New York, 1941], p. 74f.). *Shin,* the twenty-second letter of the Hebrew alphabet, is the critical letter in the Hebrew word for penitential return, since by replacing it by any of several other letters, different words would be formed.

3. Franz D. Delitzsch (1813–1890), German philologist and Hebrew scholar, active in missionary work to the Jews, translated the gospels into Hebrew and was the author of the first scientific appraisal of Hebrew poetry *(Zur Geschichte der jüdischen Poesie,* 1836).

4. Leopold Zunz: *Literaturgeschichte der synagogalen Poesie* (Berlin, 1865), p. 108, although Zunz's ascription does not appear in current prayerbook annotation. [A.A.C.] For the text see *Maḥzor for the Day of Atonement,* D. Goldschmidt ed. (New York: Leo Baeck Institute, 1970), p. 182. [L.J.W.]

5. From part three of the above *Qerobah* by Meshullam ben Qalonymus of Lucca (tenth century). See D. Goldschmidt, op. cit., pp. 117–19. [L.J.W.]

6. Cf. Zunz, op. cit., pp. 244–46, where this *selihah* is ascribed. [A.A.C.] See the text in D. Goldschmidt, op. cit., pp. 212–13. [L.J.W.]

7. The first *Mefalti 'eli* by Mordecai ben Shabbetai of Kastoria is listed in I. Davidson, *Thesaurus of Mediaeval Hebrew Poetry* (New York, 1924–1933), Mem 2096 and is to be found in *Mibḥar Hashirah Ha'ibrit,* Brody and Wiener eds. (Leipzig, 1922). The second *'Emunim benai ma'aminim* was composed by Benjamin ben Jeraḥ and is listed in Davidson, op. cit., 'Alef 5627. For the text, see D. Goldschmidt, op. cit., pp. 228ff. [L.J.W.]

8. From the *'Aqedah* of Mordecai b. Shabbetai. See Brody and Wiener, op. cit., p. 256, lines 25–28. [L.J.W.]

9. From the *'Aqedah* by Benjamin b. Zeraḥ, see Goldschmidt, op. cit., p. 228, line 8. [L.J.W.]

10. "Though thou art revered by the faithful and mighty angels," attributed to

Yannai, the fourth-century Palestinian poet. See Goldschmidt, ibid., p. 374. [L.J.W.]

11. Cf. *The Passover Haggadah*, ed. by Nahum N. Glatzer, translated by Jacob Sloan (New York, 1953), pp. 48–49.

12. This entire passage is to be found with variants in the Birnbaum *Maḥzor*, op. cit., pp. 570–76.

13. A paraphrastic condensation of the principal theme of Leviticus 18, read as the Torah portion for *Minḥah* on the Day of Atonement.

14. Cf. the *seliḥa* by the poet Yehuda beginning with the words *'Eleh 'Ezkerah* based on *midrashim*, from various periods, on the Ten Martyrs. Cf. Goldschmidt, ibid., pp. 568–73 for the text of the *seliḥa*. [L.J.W.]

15. This is a rendering of the *Mussaf* prayer concluding the *'Abodah*, *" 'Abal 'avonot"* (However the iniquities of our fathers . . .). Birnbaum, op. cit., p. 597.

16. Cf. Zunz, op. cit., pp. 336–38. The citation is from his *seliḥa Me'itkha tehilati*. See Goldschmidt, ibid., pp. 643–45. [L.J.W.]

17. Birnbaum, op. cit., p. 376.

15. Jewish Historical Writing: Josef Meisl

1. Azariah dei Rossi (c. 1511–1578), Italian scholar who lived in Bologna, Ferrara, and Mantua. Influenced by Renaissance humanism and the author of poems in Italian, Hebrew, and Aramaic, Rossi is particularly important as the author of *Me'or 'Enayim* (1574), in which he employed contemporary records as means of illuminating classic Jewish history and literature; and for translating the Letter of Aristeas (second century BCE) from Greek into Hebrew.

2. The Verein für Kultur und Wissenschaft der Juden was founded on November 17, 1819, with the intention of bringing Jews "into harmonious relations with the age and the nations in which they live."

3. *The Jewish Encyclopedia* states that this essay was published by Zunz in December, 1817 (Berlin: *Gesammelte Schriften*, 1875.) Vol. 1. 1–31.

4. Zunz's *Grundlinien* was published in the *Zeitschrift für die Wissenschaft des Judentums*, which commenced publication in 1822 and ceased after one volume had appeared.

5. Naḥman Krochmal (1785–1840). *Moreh Nebukhe ha-Zeman (Guide to the Perplexed of the Time)* was edited by Leopold Zunz and published in 1851 after his death.

6. Solomon Judah Rapoport (1790–1867), friend of Krochmal and Luzzato, was born in Galicia. His monographs on the Jewish scholars of the Gaonic Period and the first portion of his Talmudic encyclopedia were particularly noteworthy.

7. Samuel David Luzzato (1800–1865) of Padua occupied a central role in nineteenth-century Judaism. In addition to his polemical works he was a pioneer student of medieval Hebrew poetry, editing the poetry of Jehudah Halevi, and writing verse in Hebrew in the style of the Italian Renaissance.

8. Isaac Marcus Jost (1793–1860) wrote a history of the Jews from the Maccabean Period to his own day (nine volumes, 1820–1847), translated the Mishnah into German, and later wrote a history of Judaism and its sects, with particular emphasis on the Karaites (three volumes, 1857–1859).

9. Leopold von Ranke (1795–1886), considered the "father as well as the master of modern historical scholarship" (Fritz Stern), was author of *The History of the Popes*

(1834–1836), *German History in the Time of the Reformation* (1839–1843), and other works.

10. Heinrich Graetz's *Die Konstruktion der Jüdischen Geschichte. Eine Skizze* (1846) was published in a critical edition by Schocken Books (Berlin, 1936), with an essay by Ludwig Feuchtwanger.

11. Jacob Burckhardt (1818–1897), German-Swiss cultural historian, native of Basel and author, among other works, of *The Civilization of the Renaissance in Italy, Der Cicerone* (1853), and *The Age of Constantine the Great* (1852).

12. Karl Lamprecht (1856–1915), a prolific German historian who challenged the established political historiography on behalf of a method that would emphasize economic and sociological factors.

13. Wilhelm Wundt (1832–1920), philosopher and psychologist, and author of numerous multivolumed works. Among those to which Meisl appears to refer is Wundt's *Völkerpsychologie* (2 volumes, 1904; 10 volumes, 1911–1920) and his *Grundriss der Psychologie* (1896).

14. Simon Dubnow (1860–1941), historian born in White Russia, whose history of the Jewish people in ten volumes—in opposition to Graetz—stressed the role of East European Jewry and the importance of social factors in the formation of Jewish history. He was the principal proponent of spiritual autonomism within the Diaspora.

15. It is presumed that Ludwig P. Philippson (1811–1889) is intended, since he was an active supporter of both nascent liberalism in religion and Jewish emancipation. Philippson was author of *Die Entwicklung der Religion im Judentum, Christentum und Islam*.

16. Isaac Halevy (1847–1914), Talmudist and historian, whose principal, uncompleted work, *Doret ha-Rishonim,* covered the period from the Hasmoneans to the close of the Gaonic era. Karl Kautsky (1854–1938), revolutionary theorist and author of *Rasse und Judentum* (1914).

17. Pharisaism: Martin Buber

1. Buber's essay concluded the first *Sonderheft* of *Der Jude,* its last as a monthly periodical. This special issue dealt with "Antisemitismus und jüdisches Volkstum" and contained contributions by numerous Jewish and non-Jewish writers.

2. Buber employs *Evangelisten* in the sense of proselytizers.

3. Buber discusses the essay in this *Sonderheft:* "Desirable and Undesirable Jews" by Oskar A. H. Schmitz, which was the subject of the preceding essay by Max Wiener. The passages Buber appraises appear in Schmitz's essay on pp. 22, 31, 32.

4. Otto Flake's essay, *Antisemitismus und Zukunft (Antisemitism and the Future),* appeared in the same *Sonderheft,* pp. 10–17. Buber quotes from p. 11. The Pharisee is indeed described as "ein menschlicher Typus" to whom is contrasted "der reine, vom Leiden des Volkes bewegte Mensch."

5. *'Abot de Rabbi Natan* is one of the extracanonical minor tractates of the Talmud. It is "a commentary and amplification" of the Mishnaic tractate, called *Pirqe 'Abot (Chapters of the Fathers).* Cf. Goldin, *The Fathers According to Rabbi Nathan* (New Haven, 1955), p. *xvii.*

6. Cf. the account of the Pharisaic position on the accusation against St. Paul (Acts 25). [M.B.]

7. Wilhelm Michel, "*Deutsche und Juden,*" *Sonderheft: Deutschtum und jüdisches Volkstum,* op. cit., pp. 52–58. Cf. for Buber's reference, p. 54.

8. Oskar A. H. Schmitz, op. cit., p. 31.

9. Wilhelm Michel, op. cit., p. 55–56.

18. The Idea of the Holy (Rudolf Otto): Leo Strauss

1. Rudolf Otto's *Das Heilige: Über das Irrationale in der Idee des Göttlichen und sein Verhältnis zum Rationalen* was first published in 1917. It was translated into English by John W. Harvey and published in 1923 as *The Idea of the Holy: An Inquiry into the Non-rational Factor in the Idea of the Divine and Its Relation to the Rational.*

19. Samson Raphael Hirsch (1808–1888): Friedrich Thieberger

1. David Friedländer, Israel Jacobson, and Jacob Beer were among the principal figures of the first generation of German-Jewish religious reformers.

2. Samuel Holdheim (1806–1860), traditionally educated, became a leader of German reform Judaism and from 1847 until his death led the Berlin Reform Community.

3. Heymann Steinthal's (1823–1899) collection of essays *Über Juden und Judentum (On Jews and Judaism)* was published posthumously under the editorship oᶠ Gustav Karpeles in 1906. His brother-in-law Moritz Lazarus (1824–1903) published his famous *Die Ethik des Judentums (The Ethics of Judaism)* in 1898.

4. Samuel Hirsch (1815–1889), radical reformer who left Germany in 1866 to assume the pulpit of David Einhorn in Philadelphia. His most important book, alluded to here, is his *Religionsphilosophie,* in which he sought to establish in Hegelian terms the character of Judaism as an "absolute religion," a dignity Hegel had denied it.

5. Ezekiel ben Judah Landau (1713–1793), Talmudist and rabbi of Prague, opponent of both Sabbatai Ṣevi and Hasidism, as well as of Mendelssohn's German translation of the Bible.

6. Isaac B. Bernays (1792–1849) became chief rabbi of Hamburg in 1821 and was the first orthodox rabbi in Germany to preach in German, introducing it as well as the language of instruction in the Talmud Torah, while maintaining stout opposition to religious reform and prayerbook revision. Bernays, for reasons still obscure, chose the Sephardic title Ḥakham instead of the familiar Ashkenazic designation of rabbi.

7. Moses Hess (1812–1875) was the author of a principal Zionist precursory work, *Rome and Jerusalem* (1862), which, after years of neglect, was acknowledged as a major influence on the thought of Pinsker, Ahad Haam, and Herzl. Cf. Arthur A. Cohen, *The Natural and the Supernatural Jew* (New York, 1962), pp. 54–62.

8. Thieberger's reference here is not quite clear. The *'Igrot Ṣafon: Neunzehn Briefe über Judentum von Ben Usiel* (Altona, 1836; trans. into English by Bernard Drachman as *The Nineteen Letters of Ben Uziel: Being a Spiritual Presentation of the Principles of Judaism)* was, however, undoubtedly preparatory to *Horeb: Versuche über Jissroels Pflichten in der Zerstreuung zunächst für Jissroels denkende Jünglinge und Jungfrauen* (Altona, 1837), and the relation between the two works and Hirsch's undoubted wish to become the Maimonides of his generation are described in Noah H. Rosenbloom's *Tradition in an Age of Reform: The Religious Philosophy of Samson Raphael Hirsch* (Philadelphia, 1976).

9. Zacharias Frankel (1801–1875), founder and leader of the so-called "historical school" of Jewish opinion, which steered a course between the reformers and traditionalists. He was editor of the *Zeitschrift für die religiösen Interesses des Judentums,* which was succeeded by the *Monatsschrift für Geschichte und Wissenschaft des Judentums,* and he in 1854 founded the Breslau Jüdisches theologisches Seminar. The work referred to here is Frankel's *Darkhei ha-Mishnah ha-Tosefta, Mekhilta Sifra va-Sifri* (1859).

10. Solomon Judah Rapoport (1790–1867), a pioneer of the Wissenschaft des Judentums, born in Galicia and rabbi in Tarnopol and Prague, combined scientific critical techniques with broad rabbinic scholarship. His monographs on Gaonic Judaism are noteworthy, and he was a friend and correspondent of Naḥman Krochmal and S. D. Luzzatto.

11. The ṣiṣit, attached to one's garment or worn as a special undergarment, according to Biblical commandment, was interpreted as a spiritual instruction by Hirsch, *Horeb* 277f.

12. Torah, here, in the broadest sense is the implicit to the law of the nations (the custom of the nations being *derekh 'ereṣ*) and hence where Gentile doctrines teach something other than that affirmed by Torah, they may be disregarded.

13. Israel Hildesheimer (called Azriel, 1820–1899), orthodox rabbinical scholar and rabbi in Berlin until his death, founded and led the Berlin Rabbinical Seminary (1873).

14. Ṣvi Hirsch Kalischer (1795–1874), pupil of Akiva Eger, was rabbi in Thorn, Prussia. His book *Derishat Ṣion* (1862) advocating the up-building of Palestine influenced Moses Hess and the formation of *Ḥibbat Ṣion.*

15. Jacob Ettlinger (1798–1871), the rabbi in Mannheim to whom Hirsch came in 1828 to prepare for the rabbinate and to study Talmud. Author of a famous collection of responsa, *Arukh la-Ner,* Ettlinger was a strict traditionalist, but he was also interested in the modernization of traditional education. Ettlinger founded *Zionswächter* in 1845, which had a Hebrew supplement. Rosenbloom, op. cit., pp. 58–63.

16. Mordecai Benet (1753–1829), Hirsch's unalterably orthodox and pietist rabbinic predecessor in Nikolsburg, Moravia. Hirsch apparently scandalized the Jewry there by being seen in public with his wife and permitting a bride's mother to attend her at marriage. Cf. Rosenbloom, ibid., pp. 8, 63.

17. Reference presumably to Wilhelm Rothschild (1828–1901), and to Mayer Karl Rothschild (1820–1886), who succeeded Amschel as head of the Frankfurt Rothschilds.

18. *Jeschurun* was edited by Hirsch for about sixteen years, until 1870. It was notable for publishing articles dealing not only with obvious subjects but with education, law, current events, even literary subjects. Cf. Rosenbloom, ibid., p. 105.

19. *Shulḥan 'Arukh (The Prepared Table),* compiled and elaborated by Joseph Caro (1488–1575), is the abbreviation of Jacob Ben Asher's *Arbaah Turim* and the principal referent for any Jewish householder to the interpretation and definition of specific *halakhot.* [F.T.]

20. In July 1876 the German parliament ruled (in response to a protest from Edward Lasker, a liberal Jew, and his supporters) that the *Austrittsgesetz,* which was designed to facilitate Catholics' leaving their state-supported religion, applied to Jews as well. Hirsch supported Lasker in this undertaking, even though it meant that assimilation was now legally facilitated. Cf. Rosenbloom, ibid., pp. 112f.

20. Hermann Cohen: Jacob Klatzkin

1. Reference to the neo-Kantian school of philosophy founded by Hermann Cohen at the University of Marburg, the Marburg school *(Marburgschule).*

2. Cohen, Hermann, *Kants Theorie der Erfahrung* [*Kant's Theory of Experience*], (Berlin, 1871); *Systematische Begriffe in Kants vorkritischen Schriften nach ihrem Verhältnis zum kritischen Idealismus* [*Systematic Concepts in Kant's Precritical Writings in their Relation to Critical Idealism*], (Marburg, 1873); *Kants Begründung der Ethik* [*The Foundation of Kant's Ethics*], (Berlin, 1877); *Kants Begründung der Ästhetik* [*The Foundation of Kant's Aesthetic*], (Berlin, 1889), among other works dealing with the reformation of Kantian doctrine.

3. Friedrich Albert Lange (1828–1875), Cohen's predecessor at Marburg, was a neo-Kantian philosopher, sociologist, and economist, who introduced Darwinian thinking into German academic philosophy.

4. The sources of these quotations have not been discovered, but they are echoed by many passages in Cohen's Jewish writings and in his *Religion der Vernunft aus den Quellen des Judentums* [*Religion of Reason from the Sources of Judaism*], (Berlin, 1919).

21. Apologetic Thinking: Franz Rosenzweig

1. Rosenzweig uses the Greek *philosopheme,* unitalicized, which is translated as "an item of philosophic credo" or "a philosophic formulation."

2. An allusion to Maimonides's, *Mishnah Torah,* the compendium of the entire *halakhah,* which Maimonides called his "great Ḥibbur," viz., literary composition.

3. Rosenzweig refers to the note Gustav Landauer wrote in response to Max Brod's "Franz Werfels 'Christliche Sendung' " (*Der Jude,* Jahrgang I, Heft 11, pp. 717–24), which appeared under the title: "Christlich und christlich, jüdisch und jüdisch (*Der Jude, Jahrgang* I, Heft 12, pp. 851–52.

4. Johann Andreas Eisenmenger (1654–1704) developed his compendium of sources inimical to Jews and Judaism in large part from the rabbinic literature, wrenching context and freely misinterpreting. Despite efforts to have the work suppressed, *Entdecktes Judentum (Judaism Revealed)* was published in 1711 in Berlin (although the title page read Königsberg) and to this day has been a principal source of anti-Jewish literature.

5. Leo Baeck's *Das Wesen des Judentums* was originally published in 1905; however the considerably expanded and enfleshed second edition, to which Rosenzweig refers, appeared in Berlin in 1921.

6. "During 1899 and 1900 Adolf von Harnack, the influential interpreter of early Christianity and historian of the development of Christian dogma, delivered a series of sixteen lectures at the University of Berlin. These lectures were transcribed and published under the title *Das Wesen des Christentums.* They were translated and published in English under the disguising title *What is Christianity?* (1901). Baeck first reviewed the Harnack book and then subsequently wrote *Das Wesen des Judentums* without mentioning Harnack's original work. Cf. Arthur A. Cohen, *The Natural and the Supernatural Jew,* loc. cit., pp. 105–09.

7. Leo Baeck's *Romantische Religion (Romantic Religion)* was first published in the *Festschrift* for the fiftieth anniversary of the *Hochschule für die Wissenschaft des*

Judentums (1922). It is this text that Rosenzweig discusses, although the revised text of this essay was published in *Aus drei Jahrtausenden* and it is this latter text that Walter Kaufmann has translated and edited for Leo Baeck's collection of essays *Judaism and Christianity* (Philadelphia, 1958), pp. 189–292.

8. *Ent-schuldigt* is hyphenated by Rosenzweig to indicate a subtlety of sense that is carried in this translation by "ex-culpate."

22. Franz Rosenzweig's *The Star of Redemption* (A Review): Margarete Susman

1. *Der Stern der Erlösung* was first published in 1921. The second edition, enlarged at Rosenzweig's request by the introduction of a register of Jewish sources, as well as a name index prepared by Nahum N. Glatzer, was published in 1930. Verlag Lambert Schneider of Heidelberg published a third edition in 1954 and a Hebrew translation by Yehoshua Amir appeared in 1970. An English translation by William A. Hallo was published in 1971. *Der Stern* was reissued in 1976 as the first publication of a projected *Gesammelte Schriften Rosenzweigs* by Martinus Nijhoff.

2. Rosenzweig, *Der Stern der Erlösung*, op. cit., p. 8, translated by William Hallo as follows: "For indeed, an All would not die and nothing would die in the All. Only the singular can die and everything mortal is solitary." Wherever possible the *variora* of the Hallo translation will be supplied.

3. Hallo translation: "There is only one community . . . which cannot utter the 'we' of its unity without hearing deep within a voice that adds: 'are eternal' " (p. 298).

4. Hallo translation: "We were the only ones who trusted in blood and abandoned the land . . . we were the only ones who separated what lived within us from all community with what is dead" (p. 299).

5. Hallo translation: "This people has a land of its own only in that it has a land it yearns for—a holy land" (p. 300).

6. Hallo translation: "It is the very simplest and just for that the most difficult" (p. 424).

7. Further explicated infra Rosenzweig, op. cit., p. 418.

8. Saïs, an ancient Egyptian town, important during the twenty-sixth Dynasty, was a seat of priestly wisdom. The legend of the veiled image of Saïs is, however, of later Greek origin. (For this piece of information as for many others I am indebted to Professor Nahum N. Glatzer, always so generous with what he knows.)